International Per: Early Childhood Education and Care

MW01088238

The first volume in this Early Childhood Education in the 21st Century: International Teaching, Family and Policy Perspectives miniseries provides a snapshot of early childhood education and care from 19 different countries around the world. The intention is to provide a description for the policy and provision for young children and their families in each of the unique contemporary contexts. The selection of countries includes every continent in the world to provide variety across cultures, socio-economic status, location, population and other unique factors. Some chapters also share the development and history of early childhood in their country, including economic and political transitions that lead to changes in early childhood provision and policy. The book provides essential takeaways for early childhood educators, researchers, early childhood organisations, policy makers and those interested to know more about early childhood education within an international perspective.

Susanne Garvis is Professor of Child and Youth Studies at the University of Gothenburg, Sweden. She is the leader of the funded Nordic Early Childhood Research Group (NECA) and currently works on national and international research grants around early childhood education and care.

Sivanes Phillipson is Professor of Education and Associate Dean International at the Faculty of Health, Arts and Design, Swinburne University of Technology, Australia. She is also the Routledge Series Editor for Evolving Families, and is currently working on a number of national and international grants on families and children's education.

Heidi Harju-Luukkainen is an Adjunct Professor at the University of Helsinki (Finland), Associate Professor at the University of Gothenburg (Sweden), and a senior analyst at the University of California, Los Angeles (USA). She has conducted more than 20 different research projects around Europe, the United States and Saudi Arabia.

Evolving Families
Series Editor: Sivanes Phillipson

This series focuses on issues, challenges and empirical best practices surrounding evolving families that impact upon their survival, development and outcomes. The aim of this series is twofold: (1) to showcase the diversity of evolving families and the multiple factors that make up the function of families and their evolution across time, systems and cultures; (2) to build on preventative, interventionist, engagement and recovery methods for the promotion of healthy and successful evolving families across generations, social and political contexts and cultures.

International Perspectives on Early Childhood Education and Care

Early Childhood Education
in the 21st Century Vol I

Edited by
**Susanne Garvis, Sivanes Phillipson
and Heidi Harju-Luukkainen**

Routledge
Taylor & Francis Group

LONDON AND NEW YORK

First published 2018 by Routledge

2 Park Square, Milton Park, Abingdon, Oxfordshire OX14 4RN

52 Vanderbilt Avenue, New York, NY 10017

Routledge is an imprint of the Taylor & Francis Group, an informa business

First issued in paperback 2019

British Library Cataloguing-in-Publication Data
A catalogue record for this book is available from the British Library

Library of Congress Cataloging-in-Publication Data
A catalog record for this book has been requested

ISBN: 978-1-138-30393-5 (hbk)
ISBN: 978-0-367-37582-9 (pbk)

Typeset in Galliard
by Apex CoVantage, LLC

Contents

Figure

Tables

Contributors

Karyn Aspden is a Lecturer at the Institute of Education, Massey University, New Zealand. She began her career as a teacher and leader in a range of early childhood services before moving into initial teacher education. Her teaching and research interests include practicum, professional practice, effective teaching practice, early intervention and infant/toddler pedagogy.

Maria Birbili is Assistant Professor in Early Childhood Education at Aristotle University of Thessaloniki, Greece. She has taught at different levels and in a variety of contexts in Greece and England. Her current research and teaching interests include children's interests and funds of knowledge, teacher and student questioning, assessment for learning in early childhood education and concept-based teaching.

Tijana Bogovac is a preschool pedagogue from Serbia. She works in a preschool institution in Belgrade as an expert associate. She studied an International Master programme in early childhood education and care. Tijana is interested in the issues of teachers' professionalism, preschool education in international perspective and innovative practice.

Şenil Ünlü Çetin graduated from the department of Early Childhood Education at METU, Turkey. She earned her master's and doctoral degrees in the same department at METU. She is now working at Kırıkkale University, Turkey, as an assistant professor. Parent involvement – particularly father involvement – is her area of specialisation, along with music in early years, outdoor education and infant-toddler education.

Sue Cherington is the Associate Dean (Academic) in Victoria University of Wellington's Faculty of Education, New Zealand. Sue has extensive experience as a kindergarten teacher and in teacher education. Sue's research focuses predominantly on EC professional and pedagogical practices, including teacher thinking and reflection; professional learning and development; and ethical and professional practices.

Ifigenia Christodoulou is a kindergarten teacher with 26 years of classroom experience. She has a master's degree in Planning Teaching and Learning in the Early Years from Aristotle University of Thessaloniki, Greece. Ifigenia has extensive experience in the mentoring of student teachers and teacher professional development. Her current research interests include values in education, mathematics, assessment for learning and teacher parent collaboration in the early years.

Kristín Dýrfjörð is an Associate Professor at University of Akureyri, Iceland, School of Humanities and Social Sciences, Faculty of Education. She has long-term experience as a pre-school principal, working for the teachers union and has taken part in the development of the national curriculum at the Ministry of Education. Her research interests are early childhood studies, democracy, policy studies and neoliberalism.

Susanne Garvis is Professor of Child and Youth Studies at the University of Gothenburg, Sweden. She is the leader of the funded Nordic Early Childhood Research Group (NECA) and currently works on national and international research grants around early childhood education and care.

Heidi Harju-Luukkainen is Adjunct Professor at the University of Helsinki (Finland), Associate Professor at the University of Gothenburg (Sweden), and a senior analyst at the University of California, Los Angeles (USA). She has conducted more than 20 different research projects around Europe, the United States and Saudi Arabia.

Pernille Juhl (PhD) is an Assistant Professor in the research programme, Social Psychology of Everyday Life, Department of People & Technology, Roskilde University, Denmark. Her main research interest is children's everyday lives across families and daycare (0–6 years). Another research interest is marginalised children and families and social interventions.

Eugenia Koh is a polytechnic lecturer in Singapore with a deep passion for inclusion and playwork. She is currently pursuing her postgraduate studies in Inclusive and Special Education with Monash University, Australia. She is also a junk collector and enjoys transforming community spaces into junkyard playgrounds to promote inclusive play.

Rachel Langford is an Associate Professor in the School of Early Childhood Studies at Ryerson University, Canada. Her research and scholarly work focuses on childcare advocacy and policy development, workforce professionalisation, and conceptualisations of care and care work. She is a co-editor of a 2017 UBC Press edited volume, *Caring for Children: Social Movements and Public Policy in Canada*.

Lasse Lipponen is Professor of Education with special reference to early childhood education at the Faculty of Educational Sciences, University of Helsinki, Finland. His research work is directed to cultures of compassion, children's agency, pedagogical leadership and play.

Yvonne Yu-Feng Liu is from Taipei, Taiwan, and holds a BA and MA in Early Childhood Education and a PhD in International & Comparative Education.

She has been employed by Minghsin University of Science and Technology in Hsinchu county in Taiwan as an assistant professor of the Center of Teacher Education since 2014.

Claire McLachlan is Professor and Head of School, Te Hononga, School of Curriculum and Pedagogy at University of Waikato, New Zealand. Her primary field of research is early childhood curriculum, with a particular focus on early literacy and physical activity. Claire is widely published in the fields of curriculum, pedagogy, assessment and evaluation.

Tara McLaughlin is a Senior Lecturer in the Institute of Education at Massey University, New Zealand. She has worked with young children and children with disabilities and their families in inclusive learning settings in the United States and in New Zealand for over 15 years.

Elisabeth Mellgren is a Senior Lecturer at the University of Gothenburg, Sweden. Her research focuses on early literacy and transition between pre-school, preschool-class and primary school and quality issues in early childhood education. She is collaborating with the Swedish National Literacy network and the Nordic Early Literacy network.

Sharmini Mohamed Sharif has been an early childhood practitioner since the year 2000. She is an Education Development Specialist with Professional Practices Development-HQ, run by an Anchor Operator in Singapore. She visits childcare centres to support and discuss good practices.

Elin Eriksen Ødegaard is Professor in Early Childhood Pedagogy at Western Norway University of Applied Science and a visiting professor at UiT – the Arctic University of Norway. Her research perspectives embrace narrative research, self-reflexive designs, cultural historical perspectives, children, institution and families.

Tiia Õun is an Associate Professor of Early Childhood Education at the School of Educational Sciences, Tallinn University, Estonia. She specialises in early childhood education and the main areas of her research are quality and leadership of early childhood education, curriculum development and different learning and teaching methods in early childhood.

Tiina Peterson is a Chief Expert of the General Education Department at the Estonian Ministry of Education and Research. Her main professional tasks are management of preschool educational and early childhood intervention policy in Estonia and advising heads and teachers of preschool institutions. She is currently a PhD student in education sciences at Tallinn University and her research interests are preschool quality, leadership development and preschool teacher professionalism.

Joanna Phillips has experience in both the New Zealand and Australian Early Childhood sectors. She is completing her PhD while working as a teaching associate and research assistant at Monash University, Australia.

Her research areas include family-preschool partnerships, teacher professional development, early intervention and children's social and emotional development.

Sivanes Phillipson is Professor of Education and Associate Dean International at the Faculty of Health, Arts and Design, Swinburne University of Technology, Australia. She is also the Routledge Series Editor for Evolving Families, and is currently working on a number of national and international grants on families and children's education.

Antti Rajala is a postdoctoral researcher at the Faculty of Educational Sciences, University of Helsinki, Finland. His research has addressed dialogic pedagogy, educational change, and agency in education. He is currently working on the project Constituting Cultures of Compassion in Early Childhood Education (funded by Academy of Finland, 2016–2020).

Gerarda Richards is a doctoral student with Swinburne University of Technology, Australia, with postgraduate qualifications. Her research areas of interest include early childhood education, family studies and teacher education. She is currently a research assistant within an Australian Research Council Linkage Project and a teaching associate at Monash University.

Brooke Richardson has recently completed her Social Science and Humanities Research Council-funded PhD in Policy Studies, Social Policy stream at Ryerson University, Canada. She has been actively teaching in Ryerson's School of Early Childhood Studies since 2012, working primarily to develop and teach early childhood education and care policy courses. Her research interests include the discursive representation of childcare in social policy debates, the critical examination of the pan-Canadian childcare movement and care as political practice.

Alicja R. Sadownik is an Associate Professor at the Department of Kindergarten Pedagogy at Western Norway University of Applied Sciences. She researches on kindergartens as arenas for trust within multicultural environments.

Sojung Seo is a Professor in the Department of Child & Family Studies at Kyung Hee University in Korea. Her main research areas span a range of issues related to quality of early childhood education and care (ECEC). She is currently doing research on teachers' teaching efficacy and its impacts on teachers and young children in ECEC settings in Korea.

Sonja Sheridan is Professor in Education, University of Gothenburg, Sweden. She specialises in research on quality issues related to preschool quality, the preschool profession and conditions for children's wellbeing and learning in preschool. She is the leader and member of several research projects and is published worldwide.

Igor Shiyan is a PhD in Psychology, Chairperson of the Laboratory of Child Development, and Deputy Director of the Institute of System Projects of

Moscow City University, Russia. His main interests are cognitive development of children and adults and preschool education quality.

Olga Shiyan is a PhD in education and is Leading Scientific Researcher of the Laboratory of Child Development of the Institute of System Projects of Moscow City University, Russia. Her main interests are preschool education quality and cognitive development of children.

Macarena Silva is a psychologist, MSc in Educational Psychology (Pontificia Universidad Católica de Chile), and a PhD in Psychology (Lancaster University). Her research areas are reading comprehension development and early childhood education. Currently, she is a research associate in the Center for Advanced Research in Education at the University of Chile.

Pauline Slot is a researcher at Utrecht University, the Netherlands. She is involved in national and international research projects into curriculum, structural and process quality in ECEC provisions and relations with child development. Her main interests concern professional development in view of enhancing quality and promoting diversity and inclusiveness in ECEC.

Salwa Sujuddin is a trainee principal from an international preschool in Singapore. She has a bachelor's degree in Early Childhood Studies and is currently completing a Master of Education in Educational Leadership and Policy from Monash University. To stay current in ECE, Salwa attends professional conferences locally and overseas, such as the ISSA Conference.

Gaye Tyler-Merrick holds an adjunct position with the School of Health Sciences, University of Canterbury, New Zealand. Her teaching and research interests are in the areas of children's socio-emotional competence and learning, behaviour screening, functional behaviour assessment and evidence-based interventions for families and teachers.

Claudia M. Ueffing is a Professor at Munich University of Applied Sciences, Germany. Her foci are on intercultural education, diversity, professionalisation, management in ECEC and comparative studies on ECEC in Europe. She was leader of several EU research projects and is currently study program director of the transdisciplinary MA 'Social Change and Participation'.

Aino Ugaste is a Professor at the Institute of Educational Sciences at Tallinn University, Estonia. Her field of research has been connected with the study of early childhood education, teachers' professional development and children's play. More recently she has investigated intercultural education in early childhood.

Alexander Veraksa is Doctor of Psychology, Corresponding Member of the Russian Academy of Education, and Head of the Department of Psychology of Education and Pedagogy at Faculty of Psychology, Lomonosov Moscow State University, Russia. He is Vice-President of the Russian Psychological Society. His main interests focus on preschool cognitive development and educational process.

Nikolay Veraksa is Doctor of Psychology, Professor, Head Scientific Researcher at Moscow City University (Russia), Professor at Moscow State Pedagogical University and Leading Researcher at the Russian Academy of Education. For more than 40 years, he has been involved in theoretical and empirical research in child psychology and education.

Pia Williams is Professor in Child and Youth Studies at the University of Gothenburg, Sweden. Her research is focused on conditions for children's learning and development, education and care. She has authored a wide range of books and articles in Early Childhood Education.

Preface

Early childhood education and care is a complex field and leads to much discussion in research communities. This book was conceptualised at an early childhood education and care network workshop at the 2016 Nordic Educational Research Association. After a morning of early childhood education and care presentations from different countries, it became clear to the group that we did not really have a clear understanding of early childhood education and care beyond our own contexts. While we tried to guess what it might be like in other countries, we could neither confirm nor deny the actual situation.

We began to talk further about the literature surrounding the early childhood education and care field. Within the field of early childhood education and care, many books are published based on content and research from a specific country or region. Few books have provided an international perspective that offers readers insights into all continents of the world. This book draws together a diverse range of countries to show the complexity of early childhood within a contemporary world. It is important that as early childhood moves into a discipline of being "international", people are also aware of similarities and differences across contexts. While a uniform term of 'early childhood' might be used, across the world the actual practice is diverse and varied, based on economic situations, positioning of early childhood within education, universal access, human rights, access to resources as well as teacher education, professionalism and involvement with family.

From this discussion came the idea for this book series on early childhood education and care and the first volume to explore different countries around the world. Together we mapped the different countries that we thought would be important to know about. We found that different country authors were ready to contribute a chapter from their own experiences. It was from here that the idea became a reality with strong commitment from many early childhood academics and researchers across the world.

We would like to thank the many people involved in the production of this book. Firstly, we would like to thank all of the authors who have been able to contribute and share information about their own country's early childhood education and care system. Without the authors, the book would not be possible.

We would also like to thank external reviewers from all of the countries in this book that acted as peer reviewers. The reviewers generously contributed their time in providing constructive reviews and feedback for all the chapters in this book. The reviewers' comments and suggestion on their own context and culture are extremely useful and important in making this volume of high quality and international standard. Our appreciation for this invaluable contribution goes to Wendy Goff, Sharryn Clarke, Ivana Bankovic, Ebru Ersay, Jennifer Cartmel, Georgina Barton, Prasanna Srinivasan, Arniika Kuusisto, I-Fang Lee, Ali Black, Traci Flynn, Deborah Moore, Liz Chesworth, Kristiina Kumpunlainen, Karin Lager, Gillian Busch, María José Opazo and Hilary Monk.

Finally, we would like to thank the editorial assistants involved in this project. A big thank you to Gerarda Richards for helping with all aspects of the book and assisting with the organisation and administration. Also thank you to Sarika Kewalramani for helping with the copy editing process. Both of you have done an amazing job in making the process towards publication a smooth one.

As you read this book, we hope you will develop a stronger understanding of early childhood education and care from around the world. By learning from each other's contexts and cultures, we can develop a shared understanding about ourselves and ways to support constructive development of early childhood education and care in our communities. Through this shared understanding, we can start to realise the many similarities and differences we have in supporting the development of children's learning and wellbeing.

1 An introduction to early childhood education and care in the 21st century

An international perspective

Susanne Garvis, Sivanes Phillipson and Heidi Harju-Luukkainen

Introduction

Early childhood education and care are current interests in many countries following international studies, which have shown the importance of children starting their early years within a high quality education and caring environment. A number of longitudinal research projects in the United States, Australia and the United Kingdom support the notion that high-quality (compared with low-quality) preschool is more likely to support the optimal social, emotional and cognitive development of children, promote growth experiences (including nurturing and attachment), and facilitate positive interaction among teachers and children (Gordon & Browne, 2014; Sylva, Melhuish, Sammons, Siraj-Blatchford, & Taggart, 2010). These positive developmental and social experiences, as well as a supportive and nurturing environment in the preschool are commonly translated into improved school readiness and subsequent successful academic achievement in areas such as reading and mathematics (Ramey & Ramey, 2004). This suggests that if policy makers are interested in supporting children's academic achievement, they must start with providing quality early childhood education and care environments that support children's learning and social wellbeing.

While the benefits of early childhood education and care are acknowledged in the literature as universal, is the research actually true for all countries? This type of reflective questioning also brings us to other questions, such as what early childhood education and care in the 21st century actually look like. Does early childhood education and care look different in different regions? Is early childhood teacher education the same? Are curriculum and learning frameworks the same? What are cultural constraints to early childhood education and care across different countries? This book draws together leading early childhood education and care academics from across the world to explore contemporary early childhood education around teaching, family and policy. The book is able to draw on authors from across the globe to show similarities and differences within the early childhood education and care landscape. This book shows the complexity of policy and provision around early childhood education and care across 19 countries, highlighting shared enablers and barriers across the world. Given that we live in a globalised world, it is important that we understand the context of other countries and similarities and differences for young children, their families and early childhood teachers.

The countries represented have low, medium and high economic statuses with a variety of government systems and cultures. Some countries have had well-established early childhood education and care systems, while others have only recently implemented early childhood education and care systems. Some countries have aligned early childhood education and care with formal schooling systems, while other countries have placed early childhood education and care within family and social services. Given this diversity, readers will be able to learn about other contexts and cultures as well as reflect on their own. Such a consolidated approach of understanding the movements of early childhood education and care internationally provides new opportunities for cross-fertilisation of ideas in early childhood education and care and for developing an international perspective.

This first book in a series of three is based on three major themes to allow the reader to develop a better understanding of country differences within the field of early childhood education and care. The three themes are:

1 Quality goals and regulations in the country's early childhood education and care.
2 Design and implementation of curriculum and standards in the country specific to early childhood education and care.
3 Cultural constraints and gains surrounding early childhood education and care.

The first theme is designed to highlight each country's priorities and how they have regulated early childhood education and care. This could include past and recent decisions surrounding quality, access, teacher qualification and many other important topics. The second theme explores the implementation of curriculum and standards in the different countries. For some countries the introduction of a learning curriculum or framework have been relatively new. Some sectors in some countries may also still lack an official curriculum for children. The third theme gives insights into the cultural context of each country and asks the authors to share important information about the context.

Outline of the book

Authors were asked to share their understanding of these three themes based on their own knowledge about their country and culture. The intention was to allow authors to explore each of these themes from their own perspective, while at the same time sharing their knowledge with people from other contexts and cultures. As editors, we did not want to impose too many boundaries on the authors, recognising that each context and culture is different.

The diverse list of countries begins to provide an 'international' understanding of early childhood education and care. What emerges is that, while we may talk about early childhood education and care, there are many differences in what ECEC actually means across the country contexts. Some countries have aligned early childhood services, while other countries have very fragmented provisions for early childhood services. Quality of staff and their qualifications appear as a major issue in all countries, regardless of economic background.

The countries visited are diverse in regards to early childhood education and care. The countries and content include:

- In the second chapter, Gerarda Richards, Susanne Garvis and Sivanes Phillipson and share details about recent changes in Australian early childhood education and care, including the national quality standards implemented to enhance quality.
- Brooke Richardson and Rachel Langford provide details about Canadian early childhood education and care in the third chapter. We learn that Canada is entrenched in neoliberal ideals, creating fragmented services across the providences.
- The fourth chapter outlines information about Chile. Macarena Silva writes that Chile has an early childhood and preschool education spanning 153 years.
- Pernille Juhl explores the notion of child participation in the Danish context in chapter 5. She highlights the current narrow political understanding of child learning.
- In the sixth chapter we learn about Estonia. Tiia Õun, Aino Ugaste and Tiina Peterson describe the success of an immersion programme, as well as the general strong access across the early childhood sector.
- The seventh chapter describes the context of Finland. Antti Rajala and Lasse Lipponen share current understandings about narratives of compassion in Finnish early childhood education and care.
- In the eighth chapter, we learn about Germany from Claudia M. Ueffing. Germany appears focused on quality improvement and has implemented a number of professional learning programmes for teachers.
- Chapter 9 is about Greece. Maria Birbili and Ifigenia Christodoulou write about the professional up-skilling of educators that is occurring to improve quality.
- In chapter 10, Iceland is presented. Kristín Dýrfjörð writes that, while Iceland shares many characteristics with its Nordic neighbours, the importance it bestows on the social welfare system is different. The concept of playschool is also explored.
- Sojung Seo describes Korea in chapter 11. Korea has made significant investments in early childhood education and care to try to tackle low birth rates, increase women's participation in the workforce and provide children from disadvantaged backgrounds a better start in life.
- Gaye Tyler-Merrick, Joanna Phillips, Claire McLachlan, Tara McLaughlin, Karyn Aspden and Sue Cherington present New Zealand in chapter 12. The chapter provides a current critique of the main shifts in policy direction

around early childhood education and care and shares implications for the future development of early childhood policy.

- Chapter 13 shares the context of Norway from Alicja R. Sadownik and Elin Eriksen Ødegaard. Norway's democratic roots and national governance support a holistic approach in Norwegian early childhood education and care.
- Chapter 14 is about Russia. Igor Shiyan, Olga Shiyan, Alexander Veraksa and Nikolay Veraksa explain the influence of Vygotsky and the zone of proximal development. Preschool education is for children aged 3–7 years and consists of a full-day programme, three hot meals and an obligatory daytime nap.
- Tijana Bogovac shares the context of Serbia in chapter 15. We learn about the history as well as recent initiatives to enhance the early childhood sector, including the up-skilling of early childhood staff.
- Sivanes Phillipson, Eugenia Koh, Salwa Sujuddin and Sharmini Mohamed Sharif describe the context of Singapore in chapter 16 and showcase recent changes implemented by the Ministry of Education.
- Chapter 17 explores Sweden with Pia Williams, Sonja Sheridan, Susanne Garvis and Elisabeth Mellgren. We learn about the strong focus on children's wellbeing as well as the strong provision for access to early childhood education and care.
- In chapter 18, we learn about Taiwan from Yvonne Yu-Feng Liu. Many reforms have taken place in Taiwan to enhance quality and attendance.
- Pauline Slot shares the context of the Netherlands in chapter 19. Currently, more than 80% of two and three year olds participate in early childhood education and care services in the Netherlands.
- Chapter 20 is about Turkey. Şenil Ünlü Çetin describes the importance of parental involvement in the Turkish early childhood system.
- The final chapter, chapter 21, provides an overview of the key variables of ECEC in the 19 countries covered within this book. These key variables are, namely, terminology, governance of ECEC, qualifications and wages of ECEC practitioners and universal access or children's rights to education.

Conclusion

This book is designed to share with the reader the diversity of early childhood education and care around the world. The 19 countries are all located in different regions – Asia Pacific, Europe, North America and South America – and are based on different ideologies and systems of governance. The chapters provide information about the history and development of early childhood education and care, as well as the contemporary contexts and current concerns. Current concerns include but are not limited to teacher qualifications, access, quality, working with diversity and reduction of fragmentation across regions in the same country. It is hoped that, as readers engage with each chapter, they will learn a little about the contexts and concerns of other countries that are less well-published. Readers can then visualise the similarities and differences in relation to their own context. Hopefully, the concept of early childhood education and care will also be recognised as a complex term that cannot be reduced to a simple understanding. Rather, the term early childhood education and care is dependent on the culture and context in which it is understood, evidently moving away from prescribing to dominant ways and practices as espoused by well-researched and published ECEC players like the United Kingdom and United States. We need to continue to have discussions about what these terms mean to increase our own understanding and learning, while at the same time reducing the assumptions and misunderstandings we may have.

References

Gordon, A., & Browne, K. (Eds.). (2014). *Beginnings & beyond: Foundations in early childhood education*. New York: Cengage Learning.

Ramey, C. T., & Ramey, S. L. (2004). Early learning and school readiness: Can early intervention make a difference? *Merrill-Palmer Quarterly, 50*(4), 471–491. doi:10.1353/mpq.2004.0034

Sylva, K., Melhuish, E., Sammons, P., Siraj-Blatchford, I., & Taggart, B. (2010). *Early childhood matters. Evidence from the effective pre-school and primary education project*. London: Routledge.

2 Early childhood education and care in Australia

A historical and current perspective for a way forward

Gerarda Richards, Susanne Garvis and Sivanes Phillipson

Introduction

Globalisation can be understood as an international sharing of ideas, products and other elements (Grieshaber, 2017). In recent years, the Organisation for Economic Co-operation and Development (OECD) has been viewed as a major influence on policy production, particularly in the Early Childhood and Education (ECEC) sector. The OECD has produced significant reports about ECEC, which have been used as blueprints for governments to support educational reforms and funding decisions (Grieshaber, 2017). The OECD 2006 report suggested gaps in the provisions for ECEC services, highlighting the lack of quality and access for young children from low-income and second-language groups. The review that was directed to the report examined the influence that policies, services, families and communities have on young children's learning and development. This information led to the rapid growth in early childhood education and care provision in many countries. As a result of research showing how increased spending in the years before formal school sector reduced short and long-term costs to society and promoted the development of better education, health and socio-economic stability, governments paid closer attention to investment in the early years before compulsory schooling (Heckman, 2006). This observation is further supported by Dornan and Woodhead (2015), who suggested that supporting children's developmental growth through early intervention is the best strategy to prevent later disadvantage. However, the quality of early interventions in particular, in ECEC plays a major role in the lasting effects on the educational outcomes of the child (OECD, 2012).

Over the past decade, Australia has implemented a number of policy reforms to improve quality and access to early childhood education with an overall goal of becoming one of the world's leaders in the area. Australia is known as a Commonwealth country, which consists of a Federation of six states and two territories. At the time this chapter was written, the population was estimated at 24, 498, 964 million (Australian Bureau of Statistics [ABS], 2017a). The Australian indigenous population was estimated to be 3% of the total population (ABS, 2011) and approximately 28.5% being born overseas, therefore representing the

migrant population (ABS, 2017b). Australia is one of the most culturally and lin-
guistically diverse countries in the world (Australian Early Development Census,
2015). In 2014, out of the 3.8 million children aged 0–12 years, approximately
48% of children attended childcare (ABS, 2015). It is important to note that
in Australia, ECEC is defined as ages 0–5 years or 0–8 years in Victoria (which
includes primary school levels of foundation, grade 1 and grade 2).

It was in 2008 when the new Australian government implemented the largest
and most significant 'Early Childhood Reform Agenda', This consisted of the
'National Quality Standards', which have several components that are discussed
later in the chapter (Sims, Mulhearn, Grieshaber, & Sumsion, 2015). The 'Early
Childhood Reform Agenda' in Australia was prompted by the international
research and by the OECD. The evidence from such research highlighted the
importance of children's social and emotional development in the early years of
life and the economic impact this has on individuals and, in turn, society (Sims
et al., 2015). The reform agenda was also prompted by the inconsistencies across
jurisdictions, and the separate provisions for the varying types of ECEC services,
making it difficult for parents to return to work after having children. Through
the reform agenda, the Australian government has tried to make a higher-level
commitment to improve the quality and provision of ECEC services for all
children. Another contributing factor, was when in 2001, a private for-profit
organisation became the first publically listed childcare corporation in Australia
(Adamson & Brennan, 2014). It was the collapse of this large private organisation in 2008, which had over 1,200 centres in Australia, that led to increased
government intervention. At the time of the collapse, the private provider had
25% of long day-care services in Australia with 120,000 children and 16,000
staff (Ellis, 2009). Fifty-five centres closed after the collapse. Profits were created
from low staff wages and cost cutting, leading to low quality provision (Jokovich,
2002). The Australian government injected 24 million Australian dollars to keep
the remaining centres open.

In the last decade, government regulation has been implemented around a
National strategy, learning framework and quality assurance standards. The
intention has been to provide greater control over the early childhood sector.
This chapter outlines a historical perspective of ECEC in Australia to provide a
detailed understanding about the Australian context. This historical perspective
is followed by an overview of current policy provisions with regards to strategies,
frameworks and intervention in the early childhood sector. The chapter concludes with suggestions on the way forward for Australian ECEC, especially in
relation to tackling challenges arising from meeting the needs for children from
socio-economically disadvantaged backgrounds.

Historical overview of ECEC in Australia

In Australia, the federal government first recognised the importance of quality
care for the early years and passed 'The Childcare Act' in 1972 (Sims et al., 2015;
Logan, Press & Sumsion, 2016). The main reason for the new legislation was to

provide funding to establish and operate childcare centres for working families, due to the increase of women in workforce participation (Raban & Kilderry, 2017). During the 1980s, strong beliefs about mothering influenced the long day sector. A deep-seated belief existed in the community that mothers were the best to care for children, forcing the long day-care industry to be privatised, rather than being a community responsibility (Elliot, 2006). Changes in community perceptions and values towards women's rights and workforce participation resulted in exploring the importance of regulating ECEC in Australia. As a result of these shifting perceptions, government funding was also extended to long day-care places by providing more hours of care to allow women more time to participate in the workplace (Elliot, 2006).

In the 1990s, the Australian government prioritised a drive for the expansion of childcare services to provide accessible, affordable, quality ECEC settings (Raban & Kilderry, 2017). However, during this time it is important to note that in order to build or apply to run a childcare, there had to be evidence of the need for one in that area, which is vastly different to the current climate. The Prime Minister of Australia at the time, as part of his Labour government campaign, signalled two major policy shifts within the early childhood sector; (1) establishing a mixed market for childcare; and (2) the concept of regulating quality of ECEC (Logan, Press & Sumsion, 2016). In 1993, the government introduced a quality assurance system, known as the Quality Improvement and Accreditation System (QIAS), to regulate all long day-care centres (Tayler, Ishimine, Cloney, Cleveland, & Thorpe, 2013). The idea behind this system was to provide quality assurance for working families across the nation (Harrison, 2008). This led to a series of varying regulations and government initiatives implemented within the early childhood sector.

In the year 2000, the Australian government launched the 'Stronger Families and Community Strategy', which focused on emphasising the role of families and communities to provide stronger social support. This strategy was created to focus particularly on the needs of families with young children, to strengthen relationships and to enhance the balance between work and family (Press & Hayes, 2000). Shortly after this initiative, the 'OECD Thematic Review of Early Childhood Education and Care Policy – Australian Background Report' was released. This report highlighted the importance of parent participation in the workforce, as well as providing respite for parents or children and supporting the disadvantaged. The report acknowledged the need for a national framework, which encompassed all relevant jurisdictions. At this point of time, each state and territory in Australia had its own policies and framework for ECEC.

In December 2008, the 'Melbourne Declaration on Educational Goals for Young Australians' was agreed on and created by all Australian Education Ministers. The declaration brought to light the importance education played in creating an equitable, democratic and just society. The overarching goals of the declaration stated that "Australian schooling promote equity and excellence; and all Australians become successful learners, confident and creative individuals as well as active and informed citizens" (Barr et al., 2008, p. 7). The declaration also highlighted the importance of ECEC and partnerships with families to offer support for the wellbeing of young people. To establish the role of families in a child's future, the government began to focus on policy that encouraged building stronger relationships between family and education.

This initiative by the government was further strengthened through the development of the 'National Early Childhood Development Strategy, Investing in the Early Years', a move to create an equal opportunity platform for all children. The Strategy document was a collaborative pact between the Commonwealth of Australia and the state and territory governments, "to ensure that by 2020 all children have the best start in life to create a better future for them and for the nation" (Council of Australian Governments [COAG], 2009, p. 4). Most importantly, the COAG indicated the importance of providing early childhood programmes to improve cognition and social development of children, to facilitate easier transitions to school and improve the overall rates of access to schooling and school completion.

Furthermore, the National Early Childhood Strategy aimed to strengthen the economy through investing in human and social capital. This was particularly evident in COAG's use of research in the strategy, with references to Human Capital theorists Carneiro, Heckman and Masterov (2005). The Strategy's main vision was that "all children have the best start in life to create a better future for themselves and the nation". The focus being to "collectively as a nation improve children's outcomes and to contribute to social cohesion, health, wellbeing and productivity of Australia" (Sims et al., 2015, p. 19). The outcomes of this vision were to provide support for vulnerable children, engage parents and communities, strengthen maternal child health services, strengthen family support and support the development of skills for the ECEC workforce.

Originating from the National Early Childhood Strategy was the National Quality Framework (NQF). The NQF was introduced nationally in Australia on the 1 January 2012, by the Labour government. The NQF replaced the previous Licensing Standards and QIAS, processes and service coverage that governed preschools, which was managed differently between jurisdictions. The new NQF consisted of National Quality Standards (NQS), National Laws and Regulations and a learning framework (Australian Children's Education and Care Quality Authority [ACECQA], 2017a). A national governing body known as 'Australian Children's Education and Care Quality Authority' (ACECQA) was set up, given the diversity of ECEC settings within Australia, and still operates today. ACECQA is an independent authority, which aims to ensure consistency of quality of ECEC settings across Australia (Raban & Kilderry, 2017). As part of ACECQA's role is to ensure quality, they assess and rate services according to the NQS, this is discussed in detail later in the chapter. Furthermore, ACECQA assess the teaching and learning that occurs in ECEC settings using the learning framework, which is discussed next.

Moreover, the learning framework, called the Early Years Learning Framework (EYLF), is Australia's first ECEC national learning framework. This document provides a framework for ECEC settings to guide educators' pedagogical practice in developing learning for young children across Australia. This document also had a political element, in that it was part of the government's reform agenda to raise industry standards through policy and practice (Knaus, 2015). Its aim is to "extend and enrich children's learning from birth to five years and through to the transition to school" (Department of Education, Employment and Workplace Relations [DEEWR], 2009, p. 5). The framework views children's lives through belonging, being and becoming. Each element is translated to children as individuals. *Belonging* focuses on knowing where and whom we belong with, this includes family, culture and the wider community (DEEWR, 2009). The next element is *Being*, where the child has an opportunity to seek and make meaning of the world around them, including being present, understanding relationships and challenges of the everyday. Finally, *Becoming* focuses on the child's identity, knowledge, skills and understandings. The interplay of the three elements reflects "the process of change that occurs in the early years as young children grow and learn, emphasising learning to participate fully and actively in society" (DEEWR, 2009, p. 7). The EYLF focuses on these elements through five detailed learning outcomes. The outcomes are (1) Children have a strong sense of identity; (2) Children are connected with, and contribute to, their world; (3) Children have a strong sense of wellbeing; (4) Children are confident and involved learners; and (5) Children are effective communicators. The outcomes are further supported by contemporary theories and research evidence that make up the 'principles' of the framework. The principles underpin the pedagogical 'practice' for educators. The practice, in turn, articulates the approaches to learning and teaching that educators are to draw upon during the early years. The EYLF also highlights the importance of working in partnerships with families in order to engage children actively in their own learning. In summary, this document guides educators to "ensure all Australian children have the best start to life to create a better future for themselves and for the nation" (DEEWR, 2009, p. 5).

The Framework (EYLF), along with National Early Childhood Strategy, including the NQF, NQS, laws and regulations, is still in place in the current ECEC context. To further illuminate the current state of Australia's ECEC, the next section begins by exploring the types of ECEC settings, the challenges families face in accessing those settings and the curriculum practices associated to the settings.

Current state of ECEC in Australia

The Australian ECEC is considered a complex federation, in which the states have had jurisdiction over the varying aspects of ECEC. This often leads to variations in the regulatory environments (Nyland & Ng, 2016). To add to the complexity, Australia has had varying ECEC provisions, in terms of the type of settings offered to families. The labyrinth of ECEC services is attributed to the historical underpinnings of early 'education and care', national and state policy, community beliefs and legislation (Elliot, 2006). The Australian ECEC settings consist of Community Kindergarten/Preschool, Long day-care/Childcare, early learning centres within independent schools, family day-care and 'out of hours school care' (OHSC). These are explained in more detail in the following section.

Community preschools (the year before formal schooling) are owned by each jurisdiction's education department. The management, however, differs greatly between jurisdictions as the State's provide different levels of funding. For example, in South Australia, most community kindergartens are operated by the state's education department, and, in Victoria, Early Years Management (EYM), formerly known as Clusters, operates preschools, but they are often non-governmental organisations (NGO). Also, there are still many preschools operated by a Committee of Management, and these services are run by a committee of parents. Preschools offer programmes only for children aged 3 to 5. These services operate on sessional bases offering 15 hours a week, usually over a three-day period. The sessions are determined by the setting and can range from a few hours each day, to up to 7.5 hours to cater for working families. For example, there are many kindergartens that offer 2 x 6 hours and 1 x 3 hour sessions across the week. In South Australia, some kindergartens are offered 2 days one week and 3 days the following week to equal 30 hours per fortnight. This same model has been operating in Queensland for well over 10 years. However, the issue with preschools is that they do not operate during school holidays, therefore making it difficult for working families. Currently, kindergartens are funded by state government to offer all four-year-old children education and preparation for primary school for 10 hours, whilst the federal government provides funding for an additional 5 hours until December 2018. This cut to funding leaves Australia falling behind on the world scale of economic investment in young children. In comparison, for example, Sweden funds up to 50 hours a week of ECEC, including capped fees and subsidies (Municipal Association of Victoria [MAV], 2017).

Nevertheless, some Australian kindergartens also offer 3 to 5 hours a week for three-year-olds. In some states, kindergartens operate within a school setting, such as independent private schools. These types of kindergartens run within normal school hours for 30 hours a week, offering 3 to 5 year olds early education prior to formal schooling, however in a formal manner. Most kindergartens have tertiary (Bachelor of Early Childhood Education) qualified teachers (with most centres having vocational certificate III to diploma qualified educators) and run programmes in accordance with the EYLF and the Australian National Quality Framework (Raban & Kilderry, 2017).

Another predominant type of ECEC setting in Australia is long day-care centres, also referred to as childcare, crèche or nursery. These facilities were established originally to allow women to increase their workforce participation. However, with the international evidence of the importance of the early years, along with the NQF, education is also an important element (Raban & Kilderry, 2017). Long day cares are operated in a centre-based form which offers full-time (up to 11 hours per day) or part-time care for children from the age of 6 weeks old to approximately 5 years old. A preschool programme is included in most long day cares. However, funding depends on jurisdiction. Currently, 49% of ECEC settings are private, for-profit long day-care centres (ACECQA, 2017a).

In the current Australian ECEC climate, 1,250,270 children attend ECEC settings. The number of children attending ECEC settings has increased by 2.1% from the previous year (DET, 2017a). Another ECEC service available is family day care, which involves one carer, typically based in their own home, offering care for other people's children (Sims et al., 2015). This setting offers care for children from birth to 5 years and school age children. Family day care is also legislated and required to meet state and federal regulations. Another option for school age children is known as 'out of hours school care' (OHSC), which provides care for children in the morning before they attend schools and after school up to 6.30pm in some places, allowing families to participate in full working days. OHSC is also mandated by the same legislation as ECEC settings (Sims et al., 2015). For families to receive any government subsidy for childcare, the child must attend an approved or registered provider that meets the required legislation and regulations. This is obtained through ACECQA's assessment and rating process. This is discussed in the following section.

For an ECEC setting to become an approved provider, it must meet requirements in seven quality areas from the National Quality Standards which sit in line with the 'Education and Care National Law' in their jurisdiction (ACECQA, 2017b). The ratings are one of either excellent rating, exceeding NQS, meeting NQS, working towards NQS or significant improvement required. The services must display their rating at all times and the ratings are published on national registers and other government websites. The assessment and rating process is designed to involve services and the regulatory authority in a collaborative manner to enhance the outcomes for children. These ratings also allow transparency and accountability and offer the parents an opportunity to access quality education and care for their children (ACECQA, 2017b). To be a registered service, the educator must be registered through ACECQA, which involves an accreditation process meeting the jurisdictions requirements.

One important consideration is that in Australia, participation in ECEC is not compulsory. The Australian Government funds preschool/ kindergarten programmes for young Australians the year before school. The Universal Access scheme ensures a quality preschool programme is available to all Australian children, as research shows quality preschool can increase positive educational outcomes down the track (DET, 2017c). However, families need to choose whether to firstly send their children to ECEC, and secondly, the kind of ECEC setting. These decisions are often influenced by availability and location, the option of workforce participation and the affordance of care. Furthermore, the availability of high quality ECEC is less accessible in low income and disadvantaged areas (Cloney, Tayler, Hattie, Cleveland, & Adams, 2016).

The Australian government subsidies for working parents are subjected to various family elements. The Childcare Benefit (CCB) is income tested and offers families a per day percentage payment made either directly to the registered Childcare or OHSC, or refunded to the family at the end of the financial quarter. The second subsidy offered to families in Australia is the Childcare Rebate (CCR), which provides a 50% return on Childcare of OSHC without being means tested. However, it is capped at $7,500 per year, per child (DET, 2017a). Families are currently given a choice as to how their CCB and CCR is currently paid, with one of them being to the childcare supplier (approved provider). Therefore, the difference will be that only the childcare supplier can claim the benefit for eligible families and then issue the gap fee. CCB and CCR is a very complex issue as it relates to approved and registered providers of ECEC (explained earlier). Families with children attending kindergartens can access CCR if one of the educators is registered as a childcare provider. Families accessing preschool with a health care card also can receive preschool for their child for free, but this is different in different jurisdictions.

The change in the way families can access ECEC came with the Australian government's request to the Australian Productivity Commission for an inquiry into the ECEC. The goal of the inquiry was to report and make recommendations on the access to affordable, high-quality ECEC and to evaluate the current and future needs for ECEC, which includes families in rural, regional and remote areas, families with shift work arrangements, and families with vulnerable or at risk children (Productivity Commission, 2016). The broad findings of the inquiry suggested that most children had some exposure to ECEC prior to formal school. There was also support for the NQF within the ECEC sector. The inquiry took into consideration feedback from families, ECEC settings, businesses and the community (DET, 2017b). The findings of the inquiry have led to the most recent suggested reforms for the ECEC sector through the implementation of the 'Jobs for Families Childcare package' initiative, which aims to reduce the complexity of funding and make ECEC more accessible, flexible and available to those who need it (DET, 2017b).

The Australian Government intends to invest 37 billion into the ECEC system over the next four years, starting in July 2018 (DET, 2017b). This includes a childcare subsidy similar to the CCB and CCR mentioned earlier. However, the childcare subsidy would be paid to the childcare supplier and to eligible families who are income tested. It is not available to families earning over $350,000 per annum, as in the past the CCR was available to all families. This initiative also includes additional funding to families through a 'Childcare Safety Net', which aims to target families with children with additional needs and support parents and family members returning to work. The term 'additional needs' includes children with a disability; indigenous children; children who have culturally and linguistically diverse backgrounds; refugee or humanitarian backgrounds; serious medical conditions; children with language and speech delays and children presenting disruptive behaviour (DET, 2017d). This fund also includes extra support for children suffering neglect or abuse, and for families experiencing temporary financial strains or grandparents as the main carers. Furthermore, this package initiative includes a 'Community Childcare Fund (CCCF)', which aims to strengthen communities of large disadvantage through providing a grants programme. The programme's objective is to reduce barriers to access of quality childcare, provide sustainability for vulnerable childcare services and to increase the supply of services in areas of high demand (DET, 2017b). As part of the CCCF, the 'Connected Beginnings' syllabus has been put in place to support indigenous communities, through the integration of childcare with maternal child and health, along with family support services. These further educational reforms in the ECEC sector in Australia are concrete steps towards ensuring all children, particularly at risk children and families, are better supported and to encourage parents to enter or return to work (DET, 2017b).

The most significant difference between CCB/CCR and childcare subsidy is that the new childcare subsidy will be means tested and will also replace family tax benefit. This means that, even if families choose not to use childcare, they will be worse off financially because their family tax benefit will be taken from them and instead used as the childcare subsidy for families who do use childcare. The other significant difference will be that families who are not working or studying will have access only to 12 hours of care per week under the new subsidy rather than the current 24. This is very problematic for disadvantaged families who will now not be able to access the extra 12 hours, especially as research suggests that children experiencing disadvantage should have more access to high-quality early childhood settings rather than less. Whilst these children may be in disadvantaged communities, only children at risk of abuse or neglect (known to child protection) may potentially access the additional funding (but not necessarily hours). In addition, services will not be restricted as to how many hours they have to operate per week. At this stage, the new suggested funding for families is still undefined and still under development.

Despite all these steps, the Australian ECEC landscape continues to be problematic for children at risk from socio-economically disadvantaged backgrounds. While the government has been able to provide some evidence of improvement, they have also highlighted further problems within Australian ECEC. These problems include (as cited in McKenzie, Glover & Ross, 2014, p. 5):

- 32% of children living in the most socio-economically disadvantaged Australian communities are developmentally vulnerable on one or more of the Australian early development census domains (Centre for Community Child Health and Telethon Institute for Child Health Research, 2009).
- 17.5% of these children are developmentally vulnerable on two or more of the Australian early development census domains (Centre for Community Child Health and Telethon Institute for Child Health Research, 2009).
- The proportion of children enrolled in preschool in the year before full-time school is lower for children from low socio-economic backgrounds.
- The National Quality Standards have revealed that low socio-economic status and remote students have a lower quality of care in early childhood than their counterparts (ACECQA, 2017).

This data shows that supporting disadvantaged children needs to be a national priority and current Australian ECEC policy does reflect this, to a certain extent. Nevertheless, policy reform needs to provide high-quality care for all children, regardless of background. Actionable provisions are also needed for children's participation in preschool, especially for children from socio-economic disadvantaged backgrounds or with additional needs. This provision can begin with a review of the cost and availability of preschool services. If preschools are too expensive, parents are not willing to send their children. Therefore, it is paramount that ECEC is affordable to all families and perhaps this is a way forward for Australia.

The way forward for Australian ECEC

In the past 10 years, Australian ECEC has been viewed as a place to develop an innovative workforce to fulfil the government's economic needs (Nyland & Ng, 2016). Government policy has focused on the creation of the National Quality Framework, quality assurance standards, a national learning framework and the Early Years Learning Framework for Australia (EYLF) to achieve sector improvement. The implementation of changes has been delivered in a step-approach, with different states having to reach different requirements at different points in time. All states and territories are working towards improved outcomes. However, this is achieved at different times, although a current worry in the early childhood sector is that the 5 hours of national funding for children in the year before schooling may cease for 2018. Parents may have to pay for the additional 5 hours of ECEC, making the cost of early childhood services to families even higher. Such situations are worrying, considering the research on the importance of access to high quality early childhood services.

While ECEC has in the past aimed to target the disadvantaged, it is now acknowledged as a universal need for all children, regardless of background (Nyland & Ng, 2016). Access to high-quality ECEC and affordability are two important considerations for the way forward for Australian ECEC. With almost half of the ECEC sector being operated by private business, it is hoped that current quality assurance standards and strategies will be enough to ensure increased quality for all children. Careful monitoring of the private sector, however, is needed to also ensure affordability for all parents. ECEC high-quality services should be available to all families, regardless of socio-economic status. The private sector must also be monitored to ensure that similar profit strategies for ECEC centres, such as those in the 90s, which resulted in lower staff wages and the reduction of the quality of the ECEC services, are not reintroduced.

A review of the Early Years Learning Framework may also be necessary in the future to ensure that outcomes are up-to-date and provide a holistic learning curriculum for children. Some states in Australia have created their own versions of the national Framework, such as the state of Victoria with the Victorian Early Years Learning and Development Framework for Children aged Birth to 8 Years (VEYLDF). In 2017, the Victorian state government revised the Framework to provide a more up-to-date version that had a stronger focus on learning and cultural understanding. One contention between VEYLDF and the EYLF is the age range of children. While the EYLF caters for children birth to five years, the VEYLDF caters for children aged birth to 8 years. Such differences between state and national early childhood policy may result in issues of consistency across ECEC services in the different Australian state and territories.

The Australian government has acknowledged the complicated funding structure of the early childhood sector in Australia and has made a commitment in the last federal budget to change funding and payment strategies. This is one-step forward in making the system more accessible for all, however, regular review and evaluation is needed to keep the system up to date and innovative. This is especially true for working parents and low socio-economic families who currently may not be able to afford or access full time ECEC. One important consideration for Australian policy makers is to look at ECEC policies in other countries that allow all children to participate at a reduced cost or low cost to families (such as the Nordic countries). In such countries, highly considerate ECEC policy creates opportunities for all families to work and participate in society, regardless of their socio-economic status.

The Australian Government's Productivity Commission Report released in May 2017, acknowledged that it would take further reforms to improve educational outcomes for Australian students as their performance on the international testing scene has stalled or declined (Productivity Commission, 2016). The report suggested creating an evidence-based approach to inform educational policy and teaching practices that in turn would change best practice into common practice that improves educational outcomes. The Productivity Commission recommended additional investment in collecting and reporting evidence-based research in the ECEC services, as they argued that there is a lack of research on "how the quality of ECEC services and attendance are associated with educational outcomes in Australia" (Productivity Commission, 2016, p. 79). Therefore, further research in this area is warranted, as an evidence-based approach would involve monitoring progress against objectives, diagnosis of problem areas and the creation of ways to improve ECEC and school educational outcomes, ultimately promoting transparency and accountability for policy makers (Productivity Commission, 2016).

Conclusion

This chapter aimed to present a snapshot of the ECEC landscape in Australia. A historical perspective was outlined to show the development of ECEC in Australia and highlight the changes that have occurred over time. The latest model of ECEC in Australia was also discussed, showing the complexity of access and affordability. Recent government changes were also documented, showing the government's attempts to reduce the problematic nature of funding within the ECEC sector. It is hoped that over time the Australian government will take steps to ensure all children have access to high quality ECEC, regardless of their background. Careful monitoring of the private sector is also needed to safe guard against further early childhood centre collapses that leave children, families and staff stranded. Further intervention is necessary to ensure the overall goal of being a leading country in ECEC. Overall, the Australian ECEC sector could be considered a work in progress, or as Sumsion (2012) suggested, a national experiment in corporatised early childhood education and care.

References

Adamson, E., & Brennan, D. (2014). *Financing the future: An equitable and sustainable approach to early childhood education and care.* Social Policy Research Centre, University of New South Wales.

Australian Bureau of Statistics. (2011). *Estimates of aboriginal and Torres Strait Islander Australians* (Document 3238.0.55.001). Canberra: Commonwealth of Australia. Retrieved from: www.abs.gov.au/ausstats/abs@.nsf/mf/3238.0.55.001

Australian Bureau of Statistics. (2015). *Childhood education and care* (Document 4402.0). Canberra: Commonwealth of Australia. Retrieved from www.abs.gov.au/ausstats/abs@.nsf/mf/4402.0

Australian Bureau of Statistics. (2017a). *Population clock.* Retrieved from www.abs.gov.au/ausstats/abs%40.nsf/94713ad445ff1425ca25682000192af2/1647509ef7e25faaca2568a900154b63?OpenDocument

Australian Bureau of Statistics. (2017b). *Migration, Australia* (Document 3412.0). Canberra: Commonwealth of Australia. Retrieved from www.abs.gov.au/ausstats/abs@.nsf/mf/3412.0/

Australian Children's Education Care and Quality Authority. (2017a). *National Quality Standards.* Retrieved from www.acecqa.gov.au/national-quality-framework/the-national-quality-standard

Australian Children's Education Care and Quality Authority. (2017b). *Assessment and rating.* Retrieved from www.acecqa.gov.au/educators-and-providers1/assessments-and-ratings

Australian Early Development Census. (2015). *Findings from the AEDC.* Retrieved from www.aedc.gov.au/early-childhood/findings-from-the-aedc

Barr, A., Gillard, J., Firth, V., Scrymgour, M., Welford, R., Lomax-Smith, J., & Constable, E. (2008). *Melbourne declaration on educational goals for young Australians.* Australia: MCEETYA.

Carneiro, P., Heckman, J. J., & Masterov, D. V. (2005). Labor market discrimination and racial differences in premarket factors. *The Journal of Law and Economics, 48*(1), 1–39.

Centre for Community Child Health and Telethon Institute for Child Health Research. (2009). *A Snapshot of Early Childhood Development in Australia – AEDI National Report 2009.* Canberra: Australian Government.

Cloney, D., Tayler, C., Hattie, J., Cleveland, G., & Adams, R. (2016). The selection of ECEC programs by Australian families: Quality, availability, usage and family demographics. *Australasian Journal of Early Childhood, 41*(4), 16.

Council of Australian Governments. (2009). *Investing in early years.* Australia: COAG. Retrieved from www.startingblocks.gov.au/media/1104/national_ecd_strategy.pdf

Department of Education, Employment and Workplace Relations. (2009). *Belonging, being & becoming: The early years learning framework for Australia.* Australia: Commonwealth of Australia. Retrieved from www.dss.gov.au/our-responsibilities/families-and-children/publications-articles/belonging-being-becoming-the-early-years-learning-framework-for-australia

Department of Education and Training. (2017a). *Childcare subsidy.* Australia: Australian Government. Retrieved from www.education.gov.au/child-care-subsidy

Department of Education and Training. (2017b). *Jobs for families childcare package*. Australia: Australian Government Retrieved from www.education.gov.au/jobsforfamilies

Department of Education and Training. (2017c). *Universal access to early childhood education*. Australia: Australian Government. Retrieved from www.education.gov.au/universal-access-early-childhood-education

Department of Education and Training. (2017d). *Inclusion profession support program*. Australia: Australian Government. Retrieved from www.education.gov.au/inclusion-and-professional-support-program

Dornan, P., & Woodhead, M. (2015). How inequalities develop through childhood: Life course evidence from the Young Lives cohort study. *Innocenti Discussion Paper No. 2015–01*. Florence: UNICEF Office of Research.

Elliot, A. J. (2006). *Rethinking and reshaping early childhood care and education policy: Visions and directions for the future*. Paper presented at the National Education Forum Conference, Brisbane Australia.

Ellis, K. (2009, September 15). *Ministerial statement – the future of ABC learning*.

Grieshaber, S. (2017). A changed agenda for early childhood education in the Asia-Pacific. In M. Li, J. Fox, & S. Grieshaber (Eds.), *Contemporary issues and challenge in early childhood education in the Asia-Pacific region. New frontiers of educational research*. Singapore: Springer.

Harrison, L. J. (2008). Does childcare quality matter? Associations between socio-emotional development and non-parental childcare in a representative sample of Australian children. *Family Matters, 79*, 14. Heckman, J. J. (2006). Skill formation and the economics of investing in disadvantaged children. *Science, 312*(5782), 1900–1902. doi:10.1126/science.1128898

Jokovich, E. (2002). *The selling out of children's services*. Retrieved from www.armedia.net.au/the-selling-out-of-childrens-services

Knaus, M. (2015). "Time for Being": Why the Australian early years learning framework opens up new possibilities. *Journal of Early Childhood Research, 13*(3), 221–235. doi:10.1177/1476718X14538601

Logan, H., Press, F., & Sumsion, J. (2016). The shaping of Australian early childhood education and care: What can we learn from a critical juncture? *Australasian Journal of Early Childhood, 41*(1), 64.

McKenzie, F., Glover, S., & Ross, M. (2014). *Australia's early childhood development system. What we know*. Retrieved from www.australianfutures.org/wp-content/uploads/2014/10/AFP-Early-Childhood-Development-What-We-Know-141212.pdf?COLLCC=2810728575&

Municipal Association of Victoria. (2017). *Municipal association of Victoria: Members brief*. Victoria Victorian Government. Retrieved from: www.mav.asn.au/Pages/default.aspx

Nyland, B., & Ng, J. (2016). International perspectives on early childhood curriculum changes in Singapore and Australia. *European Early Childhood Education Research Journal, 24*(3), 465–476. doi:10.1080/1350293X.2015.1102416

Organisation for Economic Cooperation and Development. (2012). *Starting strong III: A quality toolbox for early childhood education and care*. Paris: OECD Publishing.

Press, F., & Hayes, A. (2000). *OECD thematic review of early childhood education and care policy*. Sydney, Australia: Commonwealth Government of Australia.

Productivity Commission. (2016). *A national education evidence base* (Inquiry Report No. 80). Canberra.

Raban, B., & Kilderry, A. (2017). Early childhood education policies in Australia. In H. Li, E. Park, & J. J. Chen (Eds.), *Early childhood education policies in Asia Pacific* (pp. 1–30). Netherlands: Springe7r.

Sims, M., Mulhearn, G., Grieshaber, S., & Sumsion, J. (2015). *Australian national ECEC reforms, with a focus on the national quality framework and the national quality standard: Expert report for the German Youth Institute*. Munich: German Youth Institute.

Sumsion, J. (2012). ABC learning and Australian early childhood education and care: A retrospective audit of a radical experiment. In E. Lloyd and H. Penn (Eds.), *Childcare markets: Can they deliver an equitable service?* Bristol: The Policy Press.

Tayler, C., Ishimine, K., Cloney, D., Cleveland, G., & Thorpe, K. (2013). The quality of early childhood education and care services in Australia. *Australasian Journal of Early Childhood*, *38*(2), 13.

3 Early childhood education and care in Canada

Consistently inconsistent childcare policy

Brooke Richardson and Rachel Langford

Introduction

This chapter focuses specifically on the childcare aspect of ECEC in Canada, exploring what it currently looks like, how it came to be this way, and who provides services. Following a discussion of how ECEC and childcare services are broadly conceptualised, defined and governed in the pan-Canadian policy context, key historical and contemporary childcare policy developments in Canada are reviewed. The chapter concludes with a brief description of the policy actions necessary for Canada to meaningfully address the chronic childcare crisis in Canada.

The term Early Childhood Education and Care (ECEC) generally refers to inclusive and integrated services and programmes that address the care and education of young children and their families (Friendly & Prentice, 2009). The services and programmes typically include regulated childcare services, nursery schools/preschools, kindergarten within public education systems, and family support programmes, and may also encompass parental leave policies. In Canada, both defining and describing ECEC policy is highly complex since most programmes and policies operate independently of each other with little to no regard for how services and policies inevitably overlap and interact. While we acknowledge, agree and support an inclusive conceptualization of ECEC, the current fragmentation of ECEC services in the Canadian context – across jurisdictions, levels of government and ministries – makes it difficult to adequately discuss and describe all aspects of the care and education of young children. We thus focus on describing the current state of regulated childcare services at the pan-Canadian level as well as drawing on examples of contemporary policy approaches in different provinces and territories.

Historical overview of childcare policy development at the federal level

Canada has a federated governance structure, whereby the childcare policies of three levels of government (federal, provincial/territorial and municipal) interact to impact the care/education of young children and their families. In Canada, childcare falls under provincial and territorial jurisdiction, although there is general consensus among childcare researchers, advocates and even many politicians/policymakers that leadership and funding from the federal level of government is necessary to address the "mediocre" quality childcare services described by the OECD (Organization for Economic and Community Development, 2004, p. 80). Furthermore, despite the governance structure in Canada, the federal government has historically assumed a leadership role in this policy area. Notable is the Dominion-Provincial Wartime Day Nurseries Act in 1942 (Friendly & Prentice, 2009) that facilitated a 50/50 cost-sharing approach between the federal and provincial governments to open and maintain childcare centres to accommodate the influx of mothers working in essential wartime industries (Kelly-Scherer, 2001). The programme was cancelled when the war ended, and the majority of childcare centres created under the Act, also closed.

The other major federal policy initiative that played an instrumental role in the development of childcare programmes and services across the country is the Canada Assistance Plan (CAP). The purpose of CAP was not to fund childcare directly, but to reduce poverty and decrease the reliance of Canadians on social assistance (Kelly-Scherer, 2001). Through CAP, childcare received significant, "accidental" funding (Friendly & Prentice, 2009, p. 74) between 1966 and 1996. Since only not-for-profit (NFP) organizations were eligible for CAP funds, this policy contributed significantly to the growth of a NFP childcare sector across the country. In 1996, under pressure to reduce the country's deficit, Liberal Finance Minister Paul Martin replaced CAP with the Canada Health and Social Transfer (now the Canada Health Transfer and the Canada Social Transfer). The Canada Social Transfer (CST) – a lump sum, capped payment to be spent on social services at the discretion of provinces – continues to provide the overarching mechanism through which federal funds for childcare flow. Overall, this decentralizing governance shift from CAP to the CST has translated into less money going to provinces and territories to fund childcare programmes, as well as less oversight on the part of the federal government regarding how the (very limited) funds are spent (i.e. no parameters whether funds go to the NFP sector or even to regulated childcare services).

Childcare emerged on the federal policy agenda throughout the 1980s, 90s and early 2000s, although no policy was successfully pursued. The National Childcare Act of 1987 (Bill C-144), the only other national childcare legislation since 1942 to be tabled in the Canadian legislature, was rejected by childcare advocates. This rejection happened primarily because the bill included a proposal to remove childcare from CAP's open-ended funding structure. In the early 90s, a Liberal government proposed the expansion of regulated childcare services across the country, although it was dependent on a budgetary surplus that was never realised. It was not until the early 2000s that a Liberal government embraced childcare as a policy priority and followed through with action (Friendly & Prentice, 2009).

In 2003, the Multilateral Framework Agreement on Early Learning and Childcare (MFA) designated $1 billion over 5 years to *regulated* childcare services – the first funds to be ear marked for childcare since WWII (Friendly & Prentice, 2009). In 2004, Paul Martin's Liberal government built on the MFA to create the Early Learning and Childcare (ELCC) Foundations programme (Langford, Prentice, Richardson, & Albanese, 2016). The ELCC Foundations programme committed $5 billion over 5 years (with an additional $6 billion during the 2004/2005 election campaign) to ELCC programmes rooted in the principles of quality, universality, accessibility and developmentally appropriate services. Though bilateral agreements between the provinces and federal governments had been developed in several provinces and were undergoing negotiations in other provinces, the programme was never enshrined in legislation. This made it easy for Conservative leader Stephen Harper to cancel the programme after his party's victory in the 2005/2006 federal election. Instead of the inaugural ELCC Foundations programme coming to fruition, the Universal Childcare Benefit (UCCB) – a taxable $100/month payment sent directly to parents to spend on childcare of their "choice"[1] – became the only national "childcare"[2] policy in Canada for the next decade.

Friendly and White (2012) noted that the federal-provincial governance structure for childcare policy in Canada shifted from multilateralism (the MFA) to bilateralism (the ELCC Foundations programme) to no-lateralism (the UCCB) in only three short years (2003–2006). No further federal leadership on the issue for ten years, coupled with major funding cuts to social programmes that funded childcare research and advocacy, resulted in downloading the cost of care of young children primarily to the individual/family level (Findlay, 2015).

Childcare again emerged in the 2015 election campaign, although this time as an initiative of the left-of-centre New Democrat Party (NDP) (New Democratic Party of Canada, 2015). The NDP highlighted a $15/day childcare programme as a central plank of their election campaign, while Justin Trudeau's Liberals focused their campaign on the development of a new Canada Child Benefit (CCB) – a broad, tax-free payment to parents based on family income and the age of the children and designed to offset the high cost of raising children. Harper's Conservatives remained committed to an expanded version of the UCCB (an additional $60/month) alongside an income-splitting tax policy for families with young children[3] (Conservative Party of Canada, 2015). Late in the campaign, the Liberals also promised to devote $500 million to a new Early Learning and Childcare Policy framework (a fraction of what the previous Liberal government had earmarked for childcare) and to address the issue within the first 100 days of taking office (Liberal Party of Canada, 2015). After the Liberals won the election, funds previously earmarked for the UCCB were rolled into the CCB.

There does appear to be some continued commitment to childcare policy on the part of Trudeau's Liberals, as childcare policy stakeholders and government officials have met on several occasions to discuss a new ELCC policy framework. In Spring 2017 Federal Budget, the Ministry of Finance announced $7 billion in new spending "to support and create more high quality, affordable childcare spaces across the country" (Ministry of Finance, 2017, p. 132). While this financial commitment to childcare has been welcomed by childcare advocates, it remains well below the OECD's recommendation that 1% of GDP be spent on early learning and childcare. Furthermore, the bulk of the new funds do not begin to flow until 2022–2023, as this budget promises only $5 million in the next two years (and none in year 3). Advocates have thus received the budget with a degree of caution concerned about the minimal spending in the immediate future, as well as how and to whom the new ELCC framework will allocate funds (Childcare Advocacy Association of Canada, 2017).

Consistently inconsistent – a market model of childcare

In the absence of strong federal leadership, the most consistent aspect of childcare across Canada may be its inconsistency. Upwards of 98% of regulated childcare across the country (including Quebec) is provided by private for-profit (FP) and not-for-profit (NFP) organizations. Each provincial government's role is typically limited to defining and enforcing safety regulations and funding fee-subsidies for low-income parents (discussed further below). Within such a framework, or lack thereof, it is no surprise that children and families have very different experiences with access to regulated childcare across the country. Median fees for regulated childcare range from a low of under $200/month in Montreal (Quebec) to over $1300/month for a toddler in Toronto (Ontario). The most recent available data indicate that the percentage of families with children under the age of six that have access to a regulated childcare space ranges from a high of 32% in Prince Edward Island (PEI) to a low of 13% in Saskatchewan (Friendly, Grady, Macdonald, & Forer, 2015). Total spending by provinces on regulated childcare ranges from a low of about $3.4 million in the Northwest Territories to over $2.5 billion in Quebec (Friendly et al, 2015). Finally, while the majority of childcare programmes and services operate within the private sector, the proportion of for-profit (as opposed to not-for-profit) centres ranges from less than 1% in Saskatchewan, where for-profit centres are not eligible for any government funds to upwards of 55% in the Maritime Provinces (Newfoundland and Labrador, PEI, Nova Scotia, New Brunswick) and Alberta (Friendly et al., 2015). Clearly, where children live and how much their parents earn significantly affects their chances of accessing safe and regulated childcare services (Pasolli, 2015).

These gross inconsistencies across the country are fundamentally the result of the fact that childcare in Canada is currently provided and delivered predominantly through a market model (Ferns & Beach, 2015). Access to childcare is largely dependent on the ability of parents to purchase the commercial service, and the provision of high-quality childcare spaces is left to the whims of the free market economy. While provinces devote varying degrees of funding to the operational costs of individual childcare centres (the most generous being in Quebec and Manitoba), the majority of provincial/territorial spending flows through programmes providing parents with fee subsidies. This neoliberal, demand-side approach to funding reinforces childcare as the sole responsibility of individual parents, encourages competition among childcare providers, and introduces intervention only to assist the most vulnerable parents, typically based on income measures (Lloyd & Penn, 2012). This market model completely overlooks the need for long-term planning/policy to develop the programmes/services fundamental to the provision of high-quality childcare experiences (rather than commercial spaces) for young children and their families. From a gendered perspective, the Canadian childcare market contributes to the ongoing marginalization of women, mothers and the predominantly female childcare workforce, who continue to bear the brunt of the results of the lack of a funded, stable, affordable and accessible childcare system (Albanese & Farr, 2012; Albanese & Rauhala, 2015; Halfon & Langford, 2015).

Regulations

The one aspect of childcare policy and programmes in which the provincial government plays a role is in defining and enforcing regulatory standards. Within an overarching market system, regulations address the basic standards childcare centres must meet in order to legally operate. As with parent fees, the regulations differ considerably across provinces including which Ministry is responsible for the childcare portfolio (typically either social services or education). Overall, provincial regulations outline the minimum number ratios of staff to children and group sizes (i.e. 1 staff for every 10 children and a maximum group size of 20), educational requirements (i.e. one-year certificate, two-year college diploma), outdoor and indoor physical space/time requirements (i.e. square footage per child, fencing around outdoor space, adequate play structures, required time spent outdoors), behaviour management guidelines (i.e. prohibition of corporal punishment or denial of basic needs) and overarching health and safety procedures (i.e. accessible first aid kit, medications stored safety, adequate sanitization procedures).[4]

The variance in provincial regulatory requirements is significant. For example, some provinces dictate a maximum number of children who may be cared for in any one centre (Quebec, Saskatchewan, Newfoundland and Labrador, New Brunswick, and PEI) while others place no cap on the number of childcare spaces in any one centre (all other provinces and territories). Similarly, some provinces require childcare centres to prepare and provide meals and snacks for the children throughout the day (Ontario, Manitoba, Saskatchewan, Newfoundland and Labrador, New Brunswick) while other provinces do not (all other provinces and territories). Some provinces require children to spend an allotted amount of time outdoors every day (e.g. two hours a day in Ontario) while other provinces do not address outdoor time at all (PEI and Saskatchewan).

Provinces also define regulatory standards pertaining to regulated home childcare, although these are much less stringent than regulations in childcare centres, as well as set out the maximum number of children that may be cared for in unregulated childcare homes. The only law unregulated childcare providers across the country must adhere to is the cap on numbers, i.e. not caring for more children in their home than their province allows (Friendly et al., 2015). The number ranges from two children in British Columbia, to eight in Saskatchewan

(Perlman, White, Friendly, Ferns, & Donkers, 2014). Considering that upwards of 75% of Canadian mothers are in the paid labour force and regulated childcare spaces are available for fewer than 25% of children in most provinces (Friendly et al., 2015), it stands to reason that the majority of Canadian children are currently being cared for in unregulated private homes not governed by safety or public accountability mechanisms. One province (Alberta) funds unregulated childcare whereby non-immediate family members providing a minimum of 50 hours of care per month for a child between ages one and six may receive up to $400/month. Sadly, the high reliance on unregulated childcare services in Canada has led to several infant and toddler deaths across all provinces. Tragically, four children died in unregulated home childcare settings in the Greater-Toronto-Area (Ontario) across a seven month period between 2013 and 2014 alone (Monsebraaten, Marco, & Ballingal, 2014).

It is important also to recognise that not all Canadian provinces/territories have government mandated curricula, as is done in the public school system for older children. Instead, most (not all) provinces have published an optional overarching curriculum or pedagogical framework meant to communicate guiding principles and practices for understanding children, pedagogy, and working in partnership with families. Some provinces, such as New Brunswick, Ontario and most recently Alberta, have developed advanced, post-foundational curriculum frameworks (see Government of New Brunswick, 2017; Government of Ontario, 2014; Makovichuk, Hewes, Lirette, & Thomas, 2014), yet there remains a significant gap between the ideas and principles proposed in these frameworks and the resources/capacity of childcare centres to engage with new ideas and reconceptualise practices. For example, most of these frameworks emphasise the importance of creative, spontaneous and ongoing documentation of children's learning, yet the majority of the childcare workforce across the country do not have adequate time or staff to effectively carry out such documentation or the educational qualifications to work with post-foundational approaches to documentation. Furthermore, it is exceedingly rare for the workforce to have any paid professional development, planning or documentation time at all.

Childcare workforce in Canada

Data and research on the childcare workforce in Canada stalled in 2013 when the Conservative government ceased funding the Canadian Childcare Human Resources Sector Council, which had collected workforce data for a decade. The last national survey of centre-based ECEC in Canada, *You bet we still care!*, provides the most up-to-date data about the childcare workforce (Flanagan, Beach, & Varmuza, 2013). Features of the workforce mirror the inconsistencies that characterise childcare delivery across provinces and territories. Titles assigned to people who work directly with children and families in childcare centres vary from early childhood educator, early childhood assistant, childcare worker, day-care worker, to front-line staff or worker, and are often based on location (e.g. rural versus urban), professional culture, and degree of unionization. Only in Ontario, which has a self-regulatory professional college for early childhood educators, is the title "early childhood educator" (ECE) protected and limited to those who are registered with the college. In Canada, the percentage of the ECEC workforce who are immigrants (19%) is higher than for any other occupation sector, which enhances the cultural and linguistic diversity of the workforce and the potential for children to experience this diversity (Kirova, Massing, Prochner, & Cleghorn).

There is also considerable variation in the amount and type of required education of the ECEC workforce across Canada, ranging from no education or several courses to a two-year college diploma. Flanagan et al. (2013) reported that 59.1% of programme staff in Canada had completed a two-year early childhood education diploma. No province requires all staff to have post-secondary education; thus, in Nova Scotia, one-quarter of programme staff must have a one-year early childhood education certificate or equivalent and in Manitoba, two-thirds of staff must have a two-year diploma, while supervisors require additional education. In some provinces, the number of programme staff with an educational background that does not include early childhood but with equivalent credentials approved by government (as well as exemptions from having a credential at all) is increasing as centres struggle to recruit and retain certificate- or diploma-qualified staff.

The only consistent feature of the childcare workforce in Canada is that it is predominantly female, undervalued and marginalised. Factors contributing to this systemic undervaluation include a lack of national leadership in visioning an inclusive ECEC system, a childcare market model built on gender inequalities, and stereotypes of the gendered naturalism of childcare work (Halfon & Langford, 2015). This undervaluation results in poor working conditions and low compensation with a low level of access to health benefits, paid vacation and pension plans (Flanagan et al., 2013). The 2012 mean gross hourly wage for those with early childhood education credentials across provincial and territorial jurisdictions was $16.50,[5] which has additional implications for female childcare workers who are immigrants and have the lowest wages of any occupational group in Canada (Flanagan et al., 2013). Unionization of the Canadian ECEC workforce is low, with only 21.5% of programme staff respondents in the *You bet we still care!* survey belonging to a union, particularly because "small, community-based, volunteer board-run, non-profit childcare centres with limited public funding. . . [do not] . . . have the capacity to bargain with unions or meet their demands" (Halfon, 2014). ECE wages represent a key reason why programme staff are dissatisfied with their work and leave the field (Flanagan et al., 2013). Provincial governments have taken steps to remedy low wages through wage enhancement grants and some, such as Manitoba, Nova Scotia and Newfoundland and Labrador, have set out plans through consultations, task forces and commissions to support and develop their childcare workforce. However, few governments have a coordinated and comprehensive strategy with established targets to significantly increase professional education levels and wages and improve working conditions through greater public funding (Halfon, 2014).

Despite lack of movement on improving wages and working conditions, the Canadian ECEC workforce, through the work of academics, professional associations and ministry policymakers, has advanced in some areas. As mentioned above, the majority of provinces now have an early learning curriculum framework to stimulate discussion and dialogue among practitioners, families and allied professionals on their values, theories and beliefs about early learning and care. The framework also provides these practitioners with the pedagogical tools to deliver early learning experiences that reflect the framework's vision and principles (Langford, 2012). However, governments do not mandate staff to engage with the curriculum framework in their daily work. In addition, in order to advance workforce professionalization, professional associations in several provinces have sought (Ontario) or are considering (Nova Scotia) the establishment of a regulatory college for ECEs. However, there remain critical questions about the increasing regulation and accountability of the work of early childhood educators when their working conditions and compensation remains stagnant. The Association of Early Childhood Educators Ontario, in collaboration with the Ontario Coalition for Better Childcare, has launched a Professional Pay and Decent Work campaign, modelled after wage campaigns in the United States and Australia, to mobilise the ECEC workforce and develop a shared professional identity based on regulation, advocacy and the individual practitioner's own sense of professionalism.

How childcare came to be this way – highlights from provinces and territories

Despite the increasingly decentralised governance structure of childcare policy in Canada, some provinces have embraced childcare as a policy priority. Most commonly referred to is the growth of reduced-fee-contribution spaces in Quebec that has provided significantly more access to affordable, regulated childcare spaces for families (Mahon, Bergqvist, & Brennan, 2016). Up until 2016, all parents in Quebec paid just $7/day for regulated childcare services. Recently, a sliding-scale approach to fees (again based on parental income) was introduced whereby the lowest income parents pay $7/day and the highest-earning parents a maximum of $20/day. While there was a great deal of public outcry over this policy shift in the Quebec (Hendry, 2016; Plante, 2016), the price tag of upward of $70/day in neighbouring Ontario illustrates Quebec's significant progress on providing affordable, regulated childcare services in comparison with the rest of Canada.

   Less discussed is the fact that most other aspects of Quebec's system are comparable to other provinces: the workforce in Quebec has relatively low education requirements and some of the highest ratios across the country for regulated group care – 1:8 compared to 1:5 or 1:6 in most other provinces (Pasolli, 2015). The availability of reduced-fee-contribution spaces in Quebec has certainly increased access and affordability of childcare, but the *quality* of regulated childcare in Quebec has much room for improvement.

   Manitoba is another outlier in Canada's childcare policy landscape. Like Quebec, Manitoba caps parent fees at $21/day for a preschool-aged child in publicly funded NFP centres. In May 2014, Manitoba's NDP government launched a five-year plan to add 12 000 NFP regulated childcare spaces. However, a Conservative Party victory in 2016 drastically shifted this childcare policy direction. The goal of the Conservative government is to "simplify the process of governing the opening and operation of childcare facilities with a focus on home-based childcare spaces" (Progressive Conservative Party of Manitoba, 2016).

The future of childcare policy is somewhat more hopeful in other provinces. In Alberta, the NDP Party won the 2016 provincial election, marking the first time any non-Conservative government has been in power for 40 years. Outside of the territories and the maritime provinces, Alberta currently has the highest proportion of for-profit childcare centres (53%) as provincial funding models (including fee subsidy requirements) do not distinguish between for-profit and not-for-profit providers (Friendly et al., 2015). However, there appear to be preliminary signs that this province is heading in a different childcare policy direction. Alberta's current NDP government has recently launched a pilot project in which 18 not-for-profit childcare centres will receive direct funding to offer parents $25/day childcare.

Some of the most progressive and also troubling childcare policy developments are currently occurring in Canada's most highly populated province – Ontario. In addition to implementing full-day junior and senior kindergarten in the public education system between 2009 and 2014, Ontario's Liberals promised 100,000 new regulated childcare spaces in a September 2016 Speech from the Throne (Government of Ontario, 2016). The political roots of this promise can be traced back to a damning provincial ombudsman report released in 2014 that described the province (and titled the report) as *Careless About Childcare* (Jones, 2014). Four infant deaths in a seven-month period between 2013 and 2014, occurring in separate unregulated childcare homes in Ontario, prompted the Ombudsman's investigation. Ontario's Liberals are currently in the process of holding public consultations regarding the doubling of the province's regulated childcare capacity. Interestingly, there has been very little discussion about the cost or quality of the proposed spaces, raising concerns for many childcare advocates (Ontario Coalition for Better Childcare, 2016). Given that a report from the City of Toronto (Ontario) recently revealed that regulated childcare services are unaffordable for over 75% of families (Cleveland, Krashinsky, Colley, & Avery-Nunez, 2016), the importance of addressing the entire system (rather than solely cost or space or quality) is an urgent concern.

Also of concern in Ontario is the rapid expansion of large-scale, for-profit childcare chains and closure of public, municipally governed childcare centres. While for-profit care represents about a quarter of care in Ontario overall, the number of childcare centres operated by corporate childcare chains in Ontario is now comparable with Alberta. Brightpath Kids, the only corporate childcare operator to publicly trade on the stock exchange in Canada, recently bought 21 new centres in Ontario and more than doubled its presence in the province.[6]

On a more positive note, the Government of Ontario has recently released its renewed early years and childcare policy framework, which prioritises addressing the high cost of childcare services for parents and overall lack of access to regulated childcare spaces across the province. More specifically, the current Liberal government has allocated $1.6 billion to the creation of 45,000 new regulated childcare spaces in the province in the next five years. The province has also announced an expert-led affordability strategy to review current provincial funding models and answered calls from Ontario's professional association to implement a workforce strategy to support Ontario's "world-class early years and childcare professionals" (Government of Ontario, 2017, p. 1).

That it is possible for provinces to take meaningful action on childcare policy in the absence of active federal leadership is perhaps best illustrated by the small (both geographically and in terms of population) province of PEI. In 2010, PEI shifted kindergarten from the childcare sector to the public school system. Recognizing that this would be a major destabilizing force for the already fragmented and underfunded childcare sector in the province, the Liberal government commissioned a childcare policy scholar (also former PEI bureaucrat) to meet with stakeholders and propose a plan *Preschool Excellence Initiative* for childcare in the province. This initiative sought to address several aspects of the struggling childcare sector – from staff education and wages, to developing a curriculum framework, to fundamentally shifting the structure and governance of childcare programmes as well as significantly increasing funding to the sector. One of the primary components of this initiative was the introduction of publicly funded Early Years Centres that are directly accountable to the provincial government. This shift illustrated a notable move from a neoliberal ideological political orientation to an inclusive liberal one, given that many more children and families were offered access to quality, funded programmes (McGrane, 2014). Providers opting to become an Early Years Centres are required to implement the provincial curriculum framework as well as remunerate staff according to a provincial wage scale that reflects an "educator's qualifications and scope of responsibilities" (Government of Prince Edward Island, 2013, p. 2).

Canadian childcare policy directions

A strength of ECEC in Canada is the vibrant, ongoing advocacy movement that began in the 1960s. Though policy outcomes have often been less than ideal, Canadian childcare advocates continue to hold the provincial and federal governments accountable for policy (in)action in this area. To draw on one example, an ongoing $10/day childcare campaign launched in 2011 in BC has been widely broadcast and received endorsements from several labour organizations, businesses, women's groups, early childhood development organizations, municipalities, academics and politicians both within and beyond the province. This campaign successfully brought childcare into the spotlight of the 2013 election campaign and again became a front-running issue (particularly for the NDP) in the 2017 provincial election.[7]

Similarly, childcare advocates in other provinces and on the national level remain committed to highlighting affordable, accessible, high-quality childcare as a central component of citizens' wellbeing. Despite less-than-sympathetic pro-vincial and federal governments and very few resources, the Canadian childcare advocacy community remains active, vocal and committed to progressive policy action. In addition, the Truth and Reconciliation Commission of Canada has called on federal, provincial, territorial and Aboriginal governments to develop culturally appropriate early childhood education programmes for Aboriginal fam-ilies (Truth and Reconciliation Commission of Canada, 2015).

Childcare researchers and advocates are optimistic and eager to work with the federal government on their childcare policy initiative although some significant concerns remain. Outside of the significant delay in funding to the childcare sector at the federal level discussed above, there has been notable silence regard-ing what the government's role will be in the distribution of funds and govern-ance of funded programmes. As advocates have communicated in their shared vision (Childcare Advocacy Association of Canada, 2016), without a compre-hensive, overarching national framework for childcare that addresses the roles of all levels of government *as well as* access to the considerably larger tax base of the federal government, families, women and children – particularly the most vulnerable – will continue to struggle to access safe, let alone high-quality, child-care resources.

This chapter has highlighted the evolution of Canadian childcare policy illus-trating how and why childcare is currently entrenched within a market model. The chapter makes clear that childcare policy is vulnerable to shifting priorities of governments as well as changes in government. An overarching lack of sustained leadership at the federal level has resulted in a fragmented childcare system in which provinces have different licencing procedures, regulations and educational qualifications for their workforce. While early learning curriculum frameworks are in place in many provinces, these are typically not mandated and the infra-structure to support the implementation of the frameworks is lacking. Finally, this chapter has noted some provincial developments that offer modest optimism about the future of childcare in Canada.

Notes

1 "Choice" is put in quotation marks to highlight the rhetoric of Harper's Conserva-tives, rather than effectively providing childcare options for parents. It has widely been recognised that $100/month does little to enable parents to afford the high costs of childcare services let alone access high quality childcare spaces.
2 Childcare advocates question the UCCB as childcare policy at all, given that it was a cash benefit not formally tied to the care of children.
3 The proposed income-splitting policy permitted families with one high-income earner to "split" their income with a lower-earning spouse, thereby shifting the family into a lower tax bracket. Single-parent families and/or families with two earners in comparable tax brackets would see no benefit.
4 See www.findingqualitychildcare.ca for an excellent overview of childcare regula-tions by province.
5 An hourly wage of $16.50 translates into a yearly salary (before tax) of about $33,000. This can be compared to elementary school teachers in Canada who

typically make between $60,000–$80,000 per year. In Ontario, where early childhood educators (ECEs) and teachers work in "partnership" in public kindergarten
settings, ECEs get paid about 1/3 of their teaching partners.

6 In the spring of 2017, the Canadian corporation Brightpath Kids sold its shares to
Busy Bees Inc. – a larger, global corporation based in the United Kingdom.

7 At the time of writing, there is an upcoming change in government that is sympa-
thetic BC's $10/day childcare campaign opening up the possibility of significant
childcare policy changes in the province.

References

Albanese, P., & Farr, T. (2012). "I'm Lucky" . . . to have found childcare: Evoking
luck while managing childcare needs in a changing economy. *International Journal
of Child, Youth and Family Studies*, (1), 83–111.

Albanese, P., & Rauhala, A. (2015). A decade of disconnection: Childcare policies in
changing economic times in the Canadian context. *International Journal of Child,
Youth and Family Studies*, 6(2), 252–274.

Childcare Advocacy Association of Canada. (2016). *Shared framework for building
an early childhood education and care system for all.* Retrieved from Toronto, ON:
https://ccaacacpsge.files.wordpress.com/2016/01/sharedframework_jan2016.
pdf

Childcare Advocacy Association of Canada. (2017). *Multi-year funding in budget
welcome but need significant boost in annual allocations to build accessible, affordable, quality childcare system over time* [Press release]. Retrieved from https://ccaac.
ca/2017/03/22/multi-year-funding-in-budget-welcome-but-need-significant-
boost-in-annual-allocations-to-build-accessible-affordable-quality-child-care-sys-
tem-over-time/

Cleveland, G., Krashinsky, M., Colley, S., & Avery-Nunez, C. (2016). *Technical
report: City of Toronto licensed childcare demand and affordability study.* Retrieved
from Toronto, ON: http://www1.toronto.ca/City Of Toronto/Children's Ser-
vices/Files/pdf/T/Toronto Demand & Affordability Study – technical report
2016.pdf

Conservative Party of Canada. (2015). *Protect our economy: Our Conservative plan to
protect our economy.* Ottawa, ON: Conservative Party of Canada. Retrieved from
file:///C:/Users/Brooke/Documents/Dissertation/Data/party%20platforms/
conservative.pdf.

Ferns, C., & Beach, J. (2015, September 1). From childcare market to childcare system. *Out Schools, Our Selves, 53*–61.

Findlay, T. (2015). Childcare and the harper agenda: Transforming Canada's social
policy regime. *Canadian Review of Social Policy, 71*(1), 1–20.

Flanagan, K., Beach, J., & Varmuza, P. (2013). *You bet we still care, a survey of centre-
based early childhood education and care in Canada. Highlights report.* Retrieved
from Ottawa, ON: www.ccsc-cssge.ca/sites/default/files/uploads/Projects-Pubs-
Docs/EN Pub Chart/YouBetSurveyReport_Final.pdf

Friendly, M., Grady, B., Macdonald, L., & Forer, B. (2015). *Early childhood education
and care in Canada 2014.* Retrieved from Toronto, ON: http://childcarecanada.
org/sites/default/files/ECEC-2014-full-document-revised-10-03-16.pdf

Friendly, M., & Prentice, S. (2009). *About Canada: Childcare.* Winnipeg, Manitoba:
Fernwood Publishing.

Friendly, M., & White, L. (2012). No-Lateralism': Paradoxes in early childhood education and care policy in the Canadian federation. In H. Bakvis & G. D. Skogstad (Eds.), *Canadian federalism: Performance, effectiveness, and legitimacy* (3rd ed., pp. 183–202). Toronto, ON: Oxford University Press.

Government of New Brunswick. (2017). *New Brunswick curriculum framework for early learning and childcare.* Retrieved from http://www2.gnb.ca/content/gnb/en/departments/education/elcc/content/curriculum/curriculum_framework.html

Government of Ontario. (2014). *How does leanring happen: Ontario's pedagogy for the early years.* Toronto, ON: Ministry of Education. Retrieved from www.edu.gov.on.ca/childcare/HowLearningHappens.pdf

Government of Ontario. (2016). *A balanced plan to build Ontario up for everyone.* Toronto, ON: Government of Ontario. Retrieved from https://news.ontario.ca/opo/en/2016/09/speech-from-the-throne.html

Government of Ontario. (2017). *Ontario's renewed early years and childcare framework.* Retrieved from Toronto, ON: www.edu.gov.on.ca/childcare/renewed_early_years_child_care_policy_framework_en.pdf

Government of Prince Edward Island. (2013). *Prince Edward Island's preschoool excellence initiative: First year implementation report.* Retrieved from www.gov.pe.ca/photos/original/FirstYearImplem.pdf

Halfon, S. (2014). Canada's childcare workforce. *Moving Childcare Forward Project.* Retrieved from Toronto, ON: http://movingchildcareforward.ca/images/policy-briefs/MCCF_canadas_childcare_workforce.pdf

Halfon, S., & Langford, R. (2015, Summer). Developing and supporting a high quality childcare workforce in Canada: What are the barriers to change? In E. Shaker (Ed.), *Moving beyond baby steps: Building a childcare plan for today's families* (pp. 131–144). Ottawa, ON: Canadian Centre for Policy Alternatives.

Hendry, L. (Producer). (2016). *Quebec parents in for 'ugly surprise' at tax time with bill for increased daycare fees.* Retrieved from www.cbc.ca/news/canada/montreal/quebec-cpe-fee-increase-2015-1.3442846

Jones, G. (2014). *Careless about childcare: Investigation into how the Ministry of Education responds to complaints and concerns related to unregulated daycare providers.* Retrieved from Toronto, ON: www.ombudsman.on.ca/Files/sitemedia/Documents/Investigations/SORT Investigations/CarelessAboutChildCareEN-2.pdf

Kelly-Scherer, R. (2001). Federal childcare policy development: From world war II to 2000. In S. Prentice (Ed.), *Changing childcare: Five decades of childcare advocacy and policy in Canada* (pp. 171–180). Halifax, Nova Scotia: Fernwood Publishing.

Langford, R. (2012). Innovations in provincial early learning curriculum frameworks. In N. Howe & L. Prochner (Eds.), *New directions in early childhood education and care in Canada* (pp. 206–228). Toronto, ON: University of Toronto Press.

Langford, R., Prentice, S., Richardson, B., & Albanese, P. (2016). Conflictual and cooperative childcare politics in Canada. *International Journal of Childcare and Education Policy, 10*(1), 1–20.

Liberal Party of Canada. (2015). *Real change: A new plan for a strong middle class.* Ottawa, ON: Liberal Party of Canada.

Lloyd, E., & Penn, H. (Eds.). (2012). *Childcare markets: Can they deliver an equitable service?* Bristol, UK: Policy Press at the University of Bristol.

Mahon, R., Bergqvist, C., & Brennan, D. (2016). Social policy change: Work – family tensions in Sweden, Australia and Canada. *Social Policy & Administration, 50*(2), 165–182.

Makovichuk, L., Hewes, J., Lirette, P., & Thomas, N. (2014). *Play, participation and possibilties: A early learning and childcare curriculum framework for Alberta.* Retrieved from Calgary, AB: http://childcareframework.com/resources/Play, Participation, and Possibilities – An Early Learning and Childcare Curriculum Framework for Alberta.pdf

McGrane, D. (2014). Bureaucratic champions and unified childcare sectors: Neo-liberalism and inclusive liberalism in Atlantic Canadian childcare systems. *International Journal of Childcare and Education Policy, 8*(1), 1.

Ministry of Finance. (2017). *Building a strong middle class #budget2017.* Retrieved from Ottawa, ON: www.budget.gc.ca/2017/docs/plan/budget-2017-en.pdf

Monsebraaten, L., Marco, O., & Ballingal, A. (2014, October 22). Report slams 'government ineptitude'. *Toronto Star.* Retrieved from http://ezproxy.lib.ryerson.ca/login?url=http://search.proquest.com/docview/1615176487?accountid=13631

New Democratic Party of Canada. (2015). *Building the country of our dreams: Tom Mulcair's plan to bring change to Ottawa.* Ottawa, ON: New Democratic Party of Canada.

Ontario Coalition for Better Childcare. (2016). *Ontario government public town hall meetings: early year and childcare policy framework and expansion.* Toronto, ON: Ontario Coalition for Better Childcare.

Organization for Economic and Community Development. (2004). *Early childhood education and care policy: Canada country note.* Retrieved from Paris: www.oecd.org/canada/33850725.pdf

Pasolli, K. (2015). Comparing childcare policy in the Canadian Provinces. *Canadian Political Science Review, 9*(2), 63–78.

Perlman, M., White, L., Friendly, M., Ferns, C., & Donkers, M. (2014). *What do we know about unregulated and regulated family childcare in Canada, and what do we need to know? Scoping out a research agenda.* Paper presented at the Childcare by 2020: A vision and a way forward, Winnipeg, Manitoba.

Plante, C. (2016, March 4). Tax season: Quebec families say daycare hike will take bite out of their budget. *Montreal Gazette.* Retrieved from http://montrealgazette.com/news/quebec/tax-season-quebec-families-say-daycare-hike-will-take-bite-out-of-their-budget

Progressive Conservative Party of Manitoba. (2016). *Progressive conservatives pledge to increase childcare spaces.* Retrieved from www.pcmanitoba.com/progressive_conservatives_pledge_to_increase_child_care_spaces

4 Early childhood education and care in Chile

An overview of preschool education

Macarena Silva

Introduction

Early childhood education has become a key issue during the last years in Chile. The recognition of the relevance of providing quality early childhood education has led to several changes and reforms in public policies and even to the creation of a sub-secretary of early childhood. Despite these changes, there is still a strong debate around what constitutes quality in early childhood education in Chile. There is a lack of agreement among different actors involved (educators, parents, policy-makers, etc.) on the role of early childhood education. For example, is early childhood education expected to contribute to later learning and development? What is the role of play in early childhood education? Do preschool centres need to be subjected to accountability? Paralleling these points of contention are critical issues regarding preschool teacher training and teacher training in general. Currently, the provisions of quality teacher training and the role of teachers as professionals and experts in their field are questionable. This chapter thus begins with the historical perspective of early childhood education in Chile.

Historical perspective on early childhood education in Chile

The origins of preschool education in Chile date back to 1864, when the first school for young children was founded. At that time, the government aimed to promote educational initiatives and advances (Peralta, 2012). Of note, this first early school was administered by nuns who were supported by some teachers who were trained in the "Normal School for teachers".[1] Despite not having an official curriculum, these teachers introduced some pedagogical elements from Pape-Carpentier, Pestalozzi and Montessori (Peralta, 2012).

Since then, preschool education started its development in the country, which was not linear and progressive, mainly because there were no set standards in terms of providers and curriculum. This situation changed with two important events: the creation of the preschool teachers' degree in University of Chile and the first Study Plans and Programmes for early childhood education centres.

The first event, the creation of the preschool teachers' degree in University of Chile, occurred in 1944. The focus of the degree was to train teachers to work with young children and foster a comprehensive education. This approach was different from the initial attempts of preschool education, which was strongly linked to a school curriculum and had the aim of educating children to be able to work in the future (Peralta, 2012). The creation of a specific degree to address early childhood education indicated an interesting shift, as a new professional appeared: the educator, who was someone different than a teacher, with different skills, who required training for a different work setting. It also meant an implicit distinction between school aims, or schooling aims, and early years/preschool education aims, an issue that remains until today and will be discussed later.

The second event, the creation of the Study Plans and Programmes for preschool education, constituted a curricular framework to orient the work and the study of the new educational agents that were being trained. It also signified a more official recognition of the preschool educational level within the educational system.

These two events led to an expansion and greater presence of preschool education in the country. An important event occurred in 1970, where the JUNJI (national group of early childhood education centres) was founded with the aim of addressing preschool education in the country. This new institution was part of the Education Ministry, and its focus was to provide quality learning experiences for children mainly below the age of four.

During the following years, the military coup took place. Peralta (2012) reports that this authoritarian government influenced the educational system, including preschool education. Despite that, a positive was that around 1980, when a more detailed set of plans and programmes were created for three early childhood levels: medium level (children aged two to three years old) and two transitional levels (children aged four to six years old). These documents helped to maintain some of the core principles of preschool education, mainly because this educational level was less important for the dictatorship, compared to school level. Unexpectedly, during this government there was more freedom to implement the curriculum in preschool education, because the focus of the educational policies of the dictatorship were not oriented towards the initial education level.

Beginning with the return to democracy in 1990, the aim of many educational reforms was to improve coverage, that is, the expansion of education in all levels, including preschool education. In practical terms, this implied the incorporation of new modalities of preschool education, for instance, family nurseries in rural areas, distance preschool education (for instance, radio programmes), and so on (Peralta, 2012). In the same decade, a curricular reform took place in the country, and, by 1998, work began on the creation of the official document of the curricular bases of preschool education, finally released by 2002. The document was organised in three main areas: personal and social development, communication and relation with the social and natural environment. Each area includes a list of expected developments and some pedagogical orientations to accomplish them.

In 2013, a law was issued that prescribed the compulsory kindergarten in Chile (the last level of preschool education), for children ages five and six years old. However, it is important to point out that the current dominant culture about education is focused on accountability, regulations and standards (Viviani, 2016), and that culture impacts how the conceptions of quality, and other relevant topics, in preschool education are currently being addressed.

As a summary, before the military dictatorship, efforts were put into the consolidation of an early childhood and preschool education as a separate educational level, with different professionals and institutions in charge and special programmes to develop to children. Since the return of democracy, the first aim was to improve coverage, and that effort lasted many years. Nowadays, most children aged five attend preschool, and the current focus is on quality of preschool education.

Description of the current system

The current organisation of early childhood education includes two nursery levels (children from 0 to 1 year old and from 1 to 2 years old), two middle levels (2–3 and 3–4 years old, respectively), and two transition levels (4–5 and 5–6 years old, respectively).

Chile offers a mixed system of education provision. There are public institutions and private institutions, as well as mixed provision, which involves private institutions with state voucher that is given to the school directly. Thus, this system is replicated in the preschool education. In the case of the preschool provision, there are different providers. JUNJI, previously mentioned, provides free and full time preschool education for all the levels (3 months old up to 6 years old). Integra is a national foundation that also provides free preschool education for children below the age of five, giving priority to families and children in conditions of vulnerability. Private early childhood and preschool centres constitute a full paid service and they offer different arrangements, going from programmes based on what is recommended by the government, to specific curriculums, like Montessori, Waldorf and High Scope, among others. In addition, preschool education can be provided by elementary schools and they can be public, private or private with voucher. Elementary schools usually provide transition levels (children aged 4 to 6 years old), and in some cases they offer middle levels.

The institutions that provide early childhood care and preschool education can get official recognition from the government, which is now optional, but will be compulsory in 2019. Some of the requisites for this recognition are related to the education of teachers and teacher assistants, who are required to complete a four-year training degree and two-year training, respectively. Another requirement is to have an adequate adult/child ratio, established as 1 to 17 in preschool and 1 to 7 for nursery levels. In addition, the size of the groups per room should be no more than 20 children for nursery levels and 45 children for preschool levels. These requirements are thought to be related to structural aspects that are necessary to ensure quality (Slot, Leseman, Verhagen, & Mulder, 2015).

Focusing on one of these aspects of official recognition, teacher training, it is important to note that there is a current crisis of the teacher initial training in the country. Early childhood Educators are around 10% of the total number of teachers of the country (García-Huidobro, 2006). From the total number of educators, around 90% of them work in the classroom and 10% in other related functions. Fifty percent of the educators work in public provision of early childhood care and preschool centres, 28% in private with state voucher and 21% in fully private institutions. It is estimated that around 2,200 educators and 8,500 teacher assistants work in the early childhood care and preschool education provided out from schools, that is, JUNJI and Integra.

Preschool teacher training is offered in Chile by public and private institutions, some of them universities and some are professional institutes. Nowadays, it is possible to count up to 50 programmes that offer preschool teacher training. Most of the students (75%) enrol in private universities and professional institutes. García-Huidobro (2006) reported that there is a lot of diversity within the type of training received by preschool educators, and only a few areas of study are common among all the degrees offered. For instance, Adlerstein, Pardo, Diaz and Villalon (2016) reported that language, one of the important areas to be covered in the early years, shows a high variability in the amount of courses offered by different degrees, and also on the approach (e.g. content knowledge, practical knowledge, combined).

Currently, there is a national test for teachers called 'Inicia' that aims to test pedagogical and disciplinary knowledge of teachers, taking into account the curriculum demands stated in the curricular bases. Despite the test not being compulsory, it is strongly based in the curriculum; thus, it is expected that the different institutions will organise their courses' content in line with the curriculum and the test. The "Inicia" test is supposed to evaluate the core knowledge that a preschool teacher should have in order to provide a quality learning environment, and therefore it is an indirect demand for universities or training providers to cover its content, in order for their students to perform well on the test.

In addition, in 2012, the Ministry of Education created the National Standards for the Guidance of Initial Early Childhood Teacher Education. The aim of the document was to offer guidance to universities regarding teacher preparation programmes. However, there is no evidence of how these guidelines have been used for the different institutions in order to improve the quality of their programmes.

An important issue is the salary situation of the preschool teachers. Among all the education professionals, preschool teachers are the least paid, with an average salary of 957 US dollars for a full time job (44 hours per week) (Pardo & Adlerstein, 2015). The preschool teacher assistants are paid around 36% less than the preschool teacher. In addition, it is possible to notice that preschool teachers have not been fully considered when designing public policies. That is, most of reforms have not asked or included the opinion and experience of preschool teachers, considered "not knowledgeable enough to inform public policies" (Pardo & Woodrow, 2014, p. 109).

Currently, 37% of children between the ages of 3 months and 6 years attend some programme of preschool education (Cortázar, 2015), however, the distribution between the levels is not even, with 10% of the children in the nursery, 41% of the children in the medium level, and up to 80% of the children of four-year-olds. The distribution also varies depending on socio-economic status (SES), where 53% of the high SES compared to 32% of the low SES attend to preschool programmes. In a national survey aiming to study early years, parents were interviewed about the use of preschool programmes (Centro de Microdatos, 2012). The reasons parents gave not to enrol their children into early education and preschool programmes are varied. Sixty-three percent reported that they did not need it; 27% said that they did not want to enrol their children; 7% expressed that they could not access to the programmes; and 3% gave other reasons. Of note, within the parents reporting that they did not want to enrol their children in early childhood and preschool education, 15% mentioned that their children were too young to attend to preschool, 6% expressed that they did not trust the early childhood and preschool centres, and another 6% of parents reported that their children were more likely to get ill if they joined the programmes. Among the parents that reported they could not access to the early childhood and preschool programmes, 4% reported that they were too far from where they live; 2% that the service was too expensive; and 1% that the quality was not good.

The answers given by parents about the reasons for not using early childhood and preschool education facilities seems to be related to the rationale or foundations of this educational level, a question that remains unanswered: if parents can take care of children directly, what is the contribution of preschool education?

What is quality?

One of the core topics posed by preschool education is the importance of free play. However, sometimes the notion of free play is confounded by a lack of intentioned pedagogical activities. In that sense, early childhood and preschool education could become a care-centre, rather than a centre with clear learning goals or aims. In a study carried out by Strasser, Lissi and Silva (2009), some kindergarten classrooms were observed over a whole day to describe the instructional activities related to language development that occurred in that level. The results showed that the amount of time devoted to instruction was low in kindergarten, and most of the time of a preschool day was spent on activities.

The assumption that investment in preschool education produces a high economic return relies on a presumption which is that preschool education offers quality experiences (Alarcón, Castro, Frites, & Gajardo, 2015). Hence, the effect of preschool education is closely related to its quality (Rolla & Rivadeneira, 2006). There are few studies in Chile that address the impact of early childhood care and education on academic performance in further years. There are three studies that looked at the impact of attending to the transition levels, and the performance in national tests at fourth (Eyzaguirre & Le Foulon, 2001), eighth (Reveco & Mella, 1999) and tenth grade (Contreras, Reveco, & Leyton, 2007), and all the results were positive, suggesting that attending to transition levels have an effect on later academic achievement.

There is only one study that attempts to answer the question of the impact of early childhood education, that is, before transition levels, on later learning achievement, and controlling also for SES. The results of that study reported by Cortázar (2015) showed that early childhood education had a positive impact in later achievement in math, reading and social sciences. Boys and those of middle SES were the groups that benefitted the most. These results are interesting, since they show a long-term impact of early education, and that the effect is not equal on all children, an aspect that should be further investigated.

In recent years, the government has recognised the relevance of preschool education as a way to reduce future inequalities and some institutional changes have taken place to accomplish this reduction. For instance, the sub-ministry of preschool education was created with the aim of modernising the status of the preschool education and to ensure the quality of the education provided to children below six years old.

Critical points

Foundation of preschool education

There are new conceptions about the role of preschool education. The role of care has changed to a role that includes education. However, the educational aspect of preschool education is less clear in the nursery and middle levels. The high registration of children in the transition years (4 to 6 years old) could support the idea that parents think it is important to provide education outside the house at that age, although, prior to four years of age, this education seems to be considered less important. Is it necessary? In other words, if parents can take personally care of their children would it be still necessary for their children to attend a preschool centre in order to develop? Does that depend on age? Does that depend on SES? These questions remain unanswered in Chile and the debate is always implicit in the policies, that is, there is not strong encouragement for families to enrol their children in preschool programmes at a young age. As previously stated, there is a lack of studies that provide consistent and strong evidence that it is better for young children to attend preschool programmes. Further studies are needed to provide a strong rationale to address this issue.

Identity crisis

Preschool education in Chile is trying to resist schoolification. Performance demands on schools are forcing preschool levels to prepare children for elementary school, and, in some cases, to advance the development of some skills, for instance, reading. The main challenge is integration of knowledge between preschool and early elementary school, together with a focus in the transition processes that take place at that age, but in the practice that is not easy. What is the best way to materialise the articulation and appropriate transition of children between levels?

Curriculum

Regarding the curriculum, there are still different views on how prescriptive the curriculum should be. There is one side that advocates for freedom in the curriculum, which would involve having less prescribed regulations about how to teach in preschool education and allowing the teacher to develop the learning experiences that s/he considers more appropriate regarding the context and the children. On the other side, some academics and teachers advocate for having more detailed information on what and how they should teach in order to achieve the learning goals described in the curricular guidelines. For instance, currently, the teacher's national evaluation, which is optional, is strongly based on school practices (e.g. planning, assessment, etc.) and preschool teachers are evaluated with that framework, however, they do not have official documents (besides the curricular bases, which are broad) to use when planning their teaching (Yoshikawa et al., 2015). Future reforms should address these inconsistencies, and make clear the positions behind the policy decisions taken.

Conclusion

Early childhood and preschool education in Chile started 153 years ago. During the first 90 years, the focus was on growing and providing different types of preschool education, becoming more specific over time, especially with the creation of the preschool teacher degree and with the first curriculum guidelines proposed by the Ministry of Education. From the 90s onwards there was a big effort, not only in preschool education, but in the general education system, to increase the coverage of educational levels. In 2013, the government mandated compulsory kindergarten and in 2017, the sub-ministry of preschool education was created. Coverage seems to be achieved or at least is showing good progress, whereas, quality is still an issue that needs to be addressed.

More research is needed in order to obtain stronger evidence about the role of preschool education in children's development, and also regarding the role of the key actors, for instance, educators and families. In addition, it is important to make the debate about the purposes of preschool education more explicit, as now some of these purposes can only be inferred or are vaguely defined in policy documents. Hence, there is a need in Chile to openly discuss the critical aspects that are affecting early years' education with the aim of providing quality care and learning opportunities children.

Note

1 The Normal Schools were the institutions that provided teacher training from 1842 until the military regime (1973) when they were dismantled. Teacher training was mainly absorbed by the universities.

References

Adlerstein, C., Pardo, M., Diaz, C., & Villalon, M. (2016). Formación para la ense-ñanza del lenguaje oral y escrito en carreras de educación parvularia: variedad de aproximaciones y similares dilemas. *Estudios Pedagogicos*, *42*, 17–36.

Alarcón, J., Castro, M., Frites, C., & Gajardo, C. (2015). Desafíos de la educación preescolar en Chile: Ampliar la cobertura, mejorar la calidad y evitar el acoplami-ento. *Estudios pedagógicos, XLI*, 287–303.

Centro de Microdatos. (2012). *Encuesta Longitudinal de Primera Infancia (ELPI)* [Early childhood longitudinal survey]. Facultad de Economía y Negocios Univer-sidad de Chile. Retrieved from www.superacionpobreza.cl/wp-content/uploads/2014/03/documento_metodologico.pdf

Contreras, D., Herrera, R., & Leyton G. (2007). Impacto de la educación preescolar sobre el logro educacional. Evidencia para Chile. Santiago de Chile: Departamento de Economía, Universidad de Chile.

Cortázar, A. (2015). Long-term effects of public early childhood education on aca-demic achievement in Chile. *Early Childhood Research Quarterly*, *32*, 13–22.

Eyzaguirre, B., & Le Foulon, C. (2001). La calidad de la educacion chilena en cifras. *Estudios Publicos*, *84*, 85–204.

Garcia-Huidobro, J. E. (2006). Formacion inicial de educadoras(es) de parvulos en Chile. *En foco*, *80*, 1–26.

Pardo, M., & Adlerstein, C. (2015). *Informe Nacional sobre Docentes para la Edu-cación de la Primera Infancia: CHILE. Proyecto Estrategia Regional Docente.*

Pardo, M., & Adlerstein, C. (2015). *Informe Nacional sobre Docentes para la Edu-cación de la Primera Infancia: CHILE. Proyecto Estrategia Regional Docente.* Retrieved from UNESCO website: http://www.politicasdocentesalc.cl/images/stories/Biblioteca/Informe%20Primera%20Infancia%20CHILE%20WEB.pdf

Peralta, M. V. (2012). Un analisis del desarrollo curricular de la educacion parvularia chilena: cuanto se ha avanzado? *Docencia*, *48*, 59–71.

Reveco, O., & Mella, O. (1999). *El impacto de la educacion parvularia en la educa-cion basica.* Retrieved from www.isharon.files.wordpress.com/2007/06/impacto-de-la-educacion-parvularia-en-la-educacion-basica.pdf

Rolla, A., & Rivadeneira, M. (2006). Por qué es importante y cómo es una educación preescolar de calidad? *En foco*, *76*, 1–16.

Slot, P., Leseman, P., Verhagen, J., & Mulder, H. (2015). Associations between struc-tural quality aspects and process quality in Dutch early childhood education and care settings. *Early Childhood Research Quarterly*, *33*, 64–76.

Strasser, K., Lissi, M. R., & Silva, M. (2009). Gestion del tiempo en 12 salas chilenas de kindergarten: Recreo, Colacion y algo de instrucción. *Psykhe*, *18*, 85–96.

Viviani, M. (2016). Creating dialogues: Exploring the "good early childhood educa-tor" in Chile. *Contemporary Issues in Early Childhood*, *17*, 92–105.

Yoshikawa, H., Leyva, D., Snow, C. E., Trevino, E., Barata, M. C., Weiland, C., Gomez, C. J., Moreno, L., . . . Arbour, M. C. (2015). Experimental impacts of a teacher professional development program in Chile on preschool classroom quality and child outcomes. *Developmental Psychology*, *51*, 309–322.

5 Early childhood education and care in Denmark

The contested issue of quality in children's everyday lives

Pernille Juhl

Introduction

This chapter explores child participation in early childhood education (ECE) in Denmark. The Danish day-care system is rooted in a historical tradition that emphasises a child-centred approach and children's right to play and to influence their everyday lives (Jensen, 2009; Winther-Lindquist, 2017). In recent years, however, politicians increasingly view day care as a central platform for boosting the academic skills of young children. Due to this development there is a present focus on using professional methods to enhance learning and early intervention in ECE that challenges past traditions of supporting children's self-initiated activities (Kragh-Müller & Ringsmose, 2015, p. 202). The political focus on learning as enhancing children's development of academic skills tends to foster an emphasis on quality regarding the creation of learning environments and the assessment of whether learning objectives are met (Plum, 2014; Togsverd, 2015), consequently producing a hierarchy between academic learning activities and holistic approaches to children's learning and development.

Based on the theoretical analysis of empirical examples from an ongoing research project at a nursery in Copenhagen, I will explore the meanings of the dominant understandings of learning and quality in ECE. I will also demonstrate how these meanings are ambivalent and contradictory in the face of the complexity of everyday life for children and professional child minders. The aim of this chapter is to problematise how the importance of fostering young children's development by supporting their self-organised activities has become a blind spot, due to a narrow political understanding of learning. In order to furnish context for the empirical examples presented later, the next section provides an overview of some of the historical and societal developments that have influenced methods currently in play in ECE.

Historical and societal development of ECE in Denmark

Historically, day care in Denmark dates back to the beginning of the last century, and since the 1980s, the number of day-care centres has multiplied. In 2014, approximately 90% of 1 to 2 year olds and 98% of 3 to 5 year olds were enrolled in public day care in Denmark (Statistics Denmark, 2014). Only a small percentage of children are enrolled in private day care. Consequently, this chapter will only treat the three most common public day-care options in Denmark: public nursery, public family nursery and public kindergarten. Table 5.1 provides a summary of these three options.

ECE in Denmark has traditionally been child-centred, with an emphasis on valuing and respecting children's democratic rights and their right to play (Jensen, 2009; Winther-Lindquist, 2017). In recent years, political interest in day care as a context for learning and preparation for school has challenged these traditions. This change in political interest grew in the wake of several transnational comparative studies and assessments of children's school performance in the late 1990s and in the 2000s, e.g. the Programme for International Student Assessment (PISA). These assessments indicated that Danish children were falling behind academically compared to other European countries (Egelund & Mejding, 2004), and subsequent research findings focused on day care (initially kindergartens and later nurseries) as potential resources for enhancing children's learning skills to ensure a higher level of school readiness (Ramey & Ramey, 2004). Consequently, during the late 1990s, day-care legislation explicitly underlined that one of the main purposes of day care was to support the development of certain skills, e.g. language and early understandings of natural phenomenon. Scholars describe this change in focus as a transformation from the core task of care to what they term educare (Broström & Hansen, 2010). During the 2000s, this trend was reinforced in 2004 by the implementation of a national education curriculum comprising six areas of learning (Table 5.1). The learning areas are currently under revision in 2017, further emphasising that a core pedagogical task is to create high quality learning environments and to evaluate and reflect on learning indicators. In addition, play and children's self-organised activities are stressed as important (Ministry for Children, Education and Gender Equality, 2016a). The result is that ambiguous interests and demands are put on professional day-care child minders who are responsible for implementing and conducting these changing and highly politically influenced tasks.

Contemporary day care is considered a resource for fighting social inequality, which is why political demands concerning early preventive interventions influence ECE in Denmark (Jensen, 2009). Research associating school performance with early learning and skills training, especially with regard to disadvantaged children (Heckman & Masterov, 2007; Heckman, 2006), has led to the prevalence of evidence-based methods and programmes intended to enhance learning in early childhood (Bjørnestad & Samuelsson, 2012). Scholars argue that early intervention is the most efficient approach, and provides the greatest economic return. At the same time, maintaining the enhancement of, literacy and concept formation very early in life is the best way to improve later school performance and, that didactics should play a larger role in day care in general, and in ECE in particular (Heckman, 2006; Jensen & Bullard, 2002; La Paro, Williamson, & Hatfield, 2014). Some studies reject these arguments, emphasising that the best way to support child learning in school is to prioritise children's self-organised

Table 5.1 Provision of ECE in Denmark

ECE day-care options	Public nursery (infants and toddlers)	Public family nursery (infants and toddlers)	Public kindergarten (preschoolers)
Financing	Subsidy and self-payment	Subsidy and self-payment	Subsidy and self-payment
Child's age	26 weeks to 2.10 years old; most commonly start at age 1	26 weeks to 2.10 years old; most commonly start at age 1	2.10 to 6 years old
Opening hours	Monday – Friday, 7 am – 5 pm	Monday – Friday, 7 am – 5 pm	Monday – Friday, 7 am – 5 pm
Provider	Local authorities	Local authorities	Local authorities
Staff	Approximately two professional child minders and one untrained assistant assigned to 12 children; not all the staff assigned to the group is always at work during opening hours.	One caretaker with short training for 3–5 children.	Approximately three professional child minders and one untrained assistant assigned to 24 children; not all the staff assigned to the group is always at work during opening hours.
Location and number of children	Municipal building; one or more groups of 12 children.	Child minder's home; minimum of one weekly outing at another minder's home.	Municipal building; one or more groups of 24 children.
Average daily number of hours spent in care	7–9	7–9	7–9
Mandatory curriculum/ pedagogical objectives (Retsinformation, 2017)	Six areas of learning: 1) personal skills, 2) social skills, 3) language, 4) body and exercise, 5) nature and natural phenomenon, 6) cultural values and forms of expressions. No specific theoretical framework or method required but assessment and documentation of the learning environment is required.	Six areas of learning: 1) personal skills, 2) social skills, 3) language, 4) body and exercise, 5) nature and natural phenomenon, 6) cultural values and forms of expressions. No specific theoretical framework or method required but assessment and documentation of the learning environment is required.	Six areas of learning: 1) personal skills, 2) social skills, 3) language, 4) body and exercise, 5) nature and natural phenomenon, 6) cultural values and forms of expressions. No specific theoretical framework or method required but assessment and documentation of the learning environment is required.

* In Denmark there are no minimum limits for staffing or specifications for the number of educated child minders and untrained assistants.
Source: Ministry for Children and Social Affairs, 2017.

play in day care (Sommer, Samuelsson, & Hundeide, 2013). Winther-Lindquist (2017, p. 111) argues, for instance, that children's self-organised play activities have significant importance in the personal and social development of children. The prevailing academic debate reflects major political interests, and despite the conflicting perspectives in research on how to best support children, the focus on improving early academic learning unambiguously dominates the current political agenda on ECE in Denmark (Plum, 2014; Togsverd, 2015). The following section illustrates how this change, from considering day care as play-based to being an arena for education, influences the current debate on how to define and achieve high quality ECE.

Conflicting perspectives on quality

Political debate in Denmark on quality is highly influenced by international research and best practices. The Danish Evaluation Institute (EVA), in addition to conducting literature reviews on the ways in which day care is organised in other countries, also performs quality assessments of ECE in Denmark. In a recent report on international research (EVA, 2016), structural quality, process quality and outcome quality were the three defining aspects of quality (p. 4). First, structural quality covers parameters such as the staff and their training (Loeb, Fuller, Kagan, & Carrol, 2004) and the physical environment (Nordtømme, 2012). Second, process quality involves parameters such as the relationship between professional child minders and children (Dalli et al., 2011), available learning environments (Heckman, 2006; Nordahl et al., 2012; Sylva et al., 2006) and which activities are conducted and how (e.g. play and learning). The third aspect is outcome quality, which entails the learning outcome in the form of the academic skills children develop in day care (Heckman, 2006), e.g. literacy (Hilbert & Eis, 2014) and numeracy (Van Luit & Toll, 2015).

International research distinguishes between quality for older preschoolers and under 2 year olds. In a literature review, Dalli et al. (2011, p. 4) report, that the curriculum for under 2 year olds is relationship building between the adults and the children. Danish discussions on the quality of ECE centre on the development of learning environments, regardless of the age group. A 2016 EVA report concludes that: "structured and explicit learning activities enhance children's academic cognitive skills . . ." (p. 29, author's translation). Additional research perspectives on quality stress other parameters. For instance, Kragh-Müller and Ringsmose (2015, p. 199) discuss how quality day care, in its own right, also involves enjoying childhood here and now. Moreover, play and the right of children to influence their own lives are highlighted as important quality parameters (Pellegrini, 2009; Sommer, Samuelsson, & Hundeide, 2013; Winther-Lindquist, 2017). These research perspectives, however, are not given much attention in the political arena (Plum, 2014; Togsverd, 2015), indicating that a hierarchy apparently exists in which learning activities designed to enhance academic skills are placed higher at the expense of a broader understanding of child development and learning (Fenech, 2011). This hierarchy specifically manifests itself at the municipal level in the growth of requirements for day cares to use methods and learning programmes designed for enhancing children's early knowledge of natural science, numeracy and language (Bjørnestad & Samuelsson, 2012), as well as manuals for how to asses learning environments (Danish EVA, 2015). Fenech (2011) contends that the result of this hierarchy is that: "what we understand to be quality [. . .] may well be confined to what has been measured" (p. 110).

In the following, the presentation and analysis of two empirical examples illustrate how the understanding of quality as closely related to enhancing academic skills through structured and documentable learning activities influence children's everyday lives. The aim of presenting the empirical examples is to: 1) illustrate how an understanding of learning as mainly a matter of children acquiring skills as a result of measureable, didactic activity manifests itself quite concretely in how learning activities are organised in the nursery and to 2) direct attention toward the potential for supporting human development and learning that is encompassed by children's self-organised activities, when learning is understood as related to processes of being a participant in a social world. Before undertaking these analyses, the following section supplies a brief introduction to the underlying analytical framework.

Analytical framework

Employing cultural-historical research traditions (e.g. Hedegaard, 2015; Rogoff, 2003) and German-Scandinavian critical psychological conceptualisations (e.g. Dreier, 2008; Højholt, 2008), I analyse children's development as situated in concrete historical and cultural contexts. In other words, children develop by participating in social practices (e.g. in day care and family life) that are located in a concrete, historical and societal context (Hedegaard, 2015; Rogoff, 2003). Consequently, children's development is closely related to their *opportunities* for *participating in* and *contributing to* social situations that are situated in changing historical and cultural contexts (Højholt, 2008). In this analytical framework, the concept of participation highlights how children, through their actions, are active contributors in processes of co-creating and developing the conditions under which they live (Dreier, 2008). Accordingly, my analytical focus is what children are doing, what they are trying to achieve, and what they engage in, in addition to how children and staff, as co-participants, act together and thus open up as well as delimit one another's opportunities for action (Juhl, 2015).

Opportunities for children to participate are related to processes of orientation (Højholt, 2008; Juhl, 2015) that take place when children look at each other and adults to discover what is at stake in a given situation and how they can participate and contribute to what is going on (Juhl, 2015). On the one hand, analysing the nursery as a social practice entails focusing on the societal and historically developed aims and scopes of everyday life in day care. Whereas, on the other, centring on how the people who inhabit the nursery (children, professional child minders and assistants) are active participants with different interests, engagements and tasks in relation to day care.

The following sections examine empirical examples of everyday practices in a Danish nursery in order to illustrate what everyday situations in a nursery are typically like.

The nursery as a context for ECE

The empirical data derives from participatory observations of a group of 12 children at a nursery and the two professional child minders and one assistant assigned to the group. I conducted the empirical work in relation to a research project exploring children's wellbeing during everyday life in a Danish nursery.

After all of the children in the group have arrived, a typical day begins by sitting in a circle on the floor to sing a couple of songs. Afterward the children sit at two or three small tables to eat a light snack. By 9:30, all three staff members are ideally present and a planned activity takes place. These activities, anchored in the six areas of learning listed in Table 5.1, involve planned, adult-initiated activities, such as excursions, painting, music, dialogical reading, numeracy or geometry activities. Around 10:30 the staff tidy up, get the children ready for lunch, and later have them nap from noon to 2 pm. At this point, some of the staff finishes with their shift. Around 2:30 pm, the children are up, have a light snack and play, until their parents pick them up between 3–5 pm.

The following section contains a description of how two planned activities were organised. One of the activities is the regular morning circle time and the other is a planned learning activity corresponding to one of the six areas of learning (nature and natural phenomenon). Note that planned learning activities take place in the morning, when all of the staff is ideally present, allowing them to be given high priority and the staffing to support them.

At 9:30 am, after their morning snack, 10 children, aged 10 months to two years, are gathered and sitting on a big mattress in a circle before starting the daily planned activities. One of the professional child minders begins the circle time in the usual way by saying: "Now, let's see who's here today first". Each child is then asked the name of the person sitting next to them. If they have difficulties saying the name, the child minders help. All of the children smile when their name is said and appear to concentrate carefully on looking around at all of the faces. Circle time concludes with singing a few songs. When the singing is over, the minder gets out coloured blocks shaped as circles, triangles and squares. The activity is designed to enhance children's early recognition of various colours and shapes. The minder lays blocks on the floor and asks a boy, Peter, if he knows the colour of a circle-shaped block. Another boy, Simon (22 months), takes some square blocks and tries to pile them up. A girl, Olivia (18 months), watches him for a little while and then accidently topples his pile when she reaches for a block, causing him to point at her and scream. The assistant takes the blocks away from the two children and tries eagerly to get them and the rest of the children to focus on the colour of the blocks – for example, by asking what colour the sun is, varying her voice and trying to achieve eye contact with the children. A boy, David (10 months), is eagerly sucking on a triangle while observing the activities going on around him. Olivia tries to take the triangle out of his mouth.

The staff planned both of these activities, which appear to have entirely different objectives. The usual morning greeting during circle time appealed to the children, who sat quietly on the mattress. The next activity, however, did not seem to sustain their attention. Why is this the case? A more careful look at the first activity reveals that it is familiar to the oldest children, who have been attending the nursery for a long time. Part of the aim of the activity is for the children to see who, i.e. which potential playmates, are at nursery that day. For the most recently enrolled children, this activity allows them to become familiar with the faces and names of the other children and the staff. This daily activity provides the opportunity for the children to sit quietly and observe their co-participants, who move around constantly at other times. As a result, the situation constitutes an opportunity for orientation (Højholt, 2008) as part of, and premise for, participating in the nursery. The observations recorded concerning the children above and other activities in the nursery show that they keenly observe each other and appear to be constantly occupied with exploring how they can participate in shared activities, e.g. getting a hold of the same toy other children want and exploring what and how they can play together. Seen in this light, the repeated morning activity with the names supports the children in their mutual engagements.

The second activity involved the staff trying to engage the children in focusing on colours and shapes. The children, however, were engaged in exploring the social aspects of the activity, for example by negotiating the right to the blocks. The staff made an effort to distract the children from the social aspects, e.g. the conflicts that arose, and tried to keep the children focused on the planned activity. In a subsequent interview, the staff explained that they were very well aware that the children were engaged in the social aspects of the situation and that the situation entailed the potential for working with other learning areas as well, for instance social skills. The staff, however, was supposed to evaluate the learning outcome and to document what they did to create optimal learning opportunities for the children in relation to the six areas of learning (Ministry for Children, Education and Gender Equality, 2016b). The professional child minders explained that the requirements of documenting the children's recognition of various colours and shapes, in correspondence with the learning area is too difficult if mixed with other emerging aspects, for instance, the children's social conflicts. As a result, they tried to concentrate only on the colour/shape-related activities. However, as the example illustrates, attempts to detach the social aspects from the activity seemed to diminish the children's interest and they apparently failed to pay attention to the colours and shapes of the blocks. Moreover, the staff did not focus on nor support the children's way of approaching one another.

The point that I wish to make is not that the children, per definition, are uninterested in shapes, colours or other adult-initiated activities, but that, if they are to be of relevance to the children, they must be anchored in and support the children's endeavours to participate in the social situation, just as the circle time activity with their names did. As explained earlier, the societal and political changes that have taken place in appraising learning inform discussions on quality.

Activities that enhance the early recognition of colours and shapes represent high quality, for instance, since they help improve later school performance (Danish EVA, 2013). However, the actions and engagements of children in the concrete situation demonstrated that exploring shapes and colours and their meaning is a ubiquitous part of children's exploration of the complexity of the social practices that they participate in, what other children are doing and how to take part in it. Another important point is that everyday life becomes vexed due to the many different, and sometimes contradictory, tasks that professional child minders are required to solve. For example, there are narrow requirements for organising learning activities in certain ways, combined with historical traditions for including children's perspectives and following and supporting their own engagements. Additionally, the varying perspectives on quality intermingle with the concrete situations anchored in the complexity of everyday life in the nursery, where children are active subjects already involved in self-organised activities.

The next section presents an empirical example from a different situation with the same group of nursery children to demonstrate how other notions of learning are also at stake in the everyday life of the nursery. The main point I wish to make by presenting the example is to highlight the potential for learning embedded in the complexity of child-initiated activities that unfold in the everyday life of the nursery.

The nursery as a context for children's participation

It is 8:00 am and children are arriving at the nursery. A girl, Sarah (23 months), sits at a table doing a puzzle after emptying all of the pieces out on the table. She is focused on trying to make the pieces fit together. Another girl, Melanie (20 months), who just arrived in the nursery, looks at Sarah, climbs up on a chair and sits at the table. After Melanie takes some of the puzzle pieces, Sarah shouts "No!" and points at her while trying to take a piece out of Melanie's hand. Sarah lays her upper body on top of the puzzle pieces in an attempt to protect them from Melanie's grasp. The professional child minder, who is sitting nearby on a chair with another girl on her lap, asks Sarah whether she minds if Melanie helps her with the puzzle. Sarah looks from the minder to Melanie, glances down at all the puzzle pieces and nods. The minder helps the girls cooperate, which requires ongoing input. After a while, Melanie puts a puzzle piece up to her mouth and pretends it is a cup, simultaneously tilting her head back while making drinking sounds. Sarah stops doing the puzzle and looks at Melanie closely, following her every move with her eyes. Then she takes another piece and imitates Melanie, who smiles at Sarah. Melanie takes another puzzle piece and pours an imaginary drink into Sarah's cup while saying "Coffee". Sarah drinks again and holds the cup towards Melanie, saying "Cocoa", after which Melanie replies "Yes". The minder occasionally steps in to support their play.

In the example, there is no planned learning activity and no learning objectives, since the girls' activity is self-organised and spontaneously generated (Winther-Lindquist, 2017). Nevertheless, when conceptualising learning as related to participating in changing social practice (Højholt, 2008), important learning is going on. Through their joint activities the girls learned about possibilities, limitations and contradictions in relation to engaging in shared activities. Protecting the puzzle pieces by lying on top of them, for instance, made it impossible for Sarah to do the puzzle. Sharing the puzzle helped the children gain important experiences with being a participant in a shared social practice (Dreier, 2008), for example, how to make cooperation work and include other participants' contributions. Imagining that the puzzle pieces were cups and saucers comprised as-if aspects, allowing the children to experiment with how to influence a given situation (Winther-Lindquist, 2017). Melanie initiated the play and Sarah noticed it, leading both girls to experience how they contributed to developing the shared activity (Hedegaard, 2015, Juhl, 2015). Taking part in changing social practices require children to orient, re-orient and adjust their way of participating. Such complex situations comprise the developmental conditions for children, which is why they possess important potential for children's learning and development.

Together, with the girls, the professional child minder explored the options made available by the situation. In the case of the example, the child minder suggested working on the puzzle together, instead of fighting over the right to the pieces, helping the girls to expand and develop their play. Providing support was only possible when the girls' own engagements are explored concurrently. For instance, by noticing how the girls used the puzzle pieces as imaginary cups and saucers, the minder supported their change in activity. Even though the minder succeeded in supporting the girls, she also had to attend to numerous other responsibilities, like welcoming arriving children, talking to parents and helping other children becoming part of activities. Hence, it is important to point out that the girls' activity unfolded in the morning when not all the staff was at work yet. As a result, supporting pivotal processes for the children that involve dealing with social life was not scheduled at a time of the day when it can be given high priority, in contrast to standardised activities with a learning goal. Due to the conflicting perspectives in research and policy about what quality is, stressing on the one hand the documentable enhancement of children's academic skills, and on the other hand holding on to former traditions, including children's right to influence their own lives, professional child minders are left to prioritise and organise activities in the everyday life of day care. In addition, where children's mutual engagements, interactions and conflicts are integral aspects of all activities, including adult-initiated ones, results into quality becoming a contentious issue of everyday life in the nursery.

Conclusion

This chapter focused on the change in political focus on day care and ECE in Denmark from being a context for children's play to a context for early education. I illustrated how this change influences the understandings of quality as related to creating optimal conditions for children's learning. I then exemplified how these dominant understandings of learning and current quality indicators tend to reveal themselves as contradictory conditions in the everyday childcare practice for both children and professional child minders. Anchored in cultural-historical conceptualisations of child development, my analysis illustrated how nursery life and children's self-organised and shared activities contain the potential for children to gain crucial experience with being a person among other persons (Winther-Lindquist, 2017). The child minders are left juggling with multi-faceted political interests, tasks, requirements and considerations related to everyday life in the nursery and the narrow political understanding of quality appears to de-emphasise important potential for supporting children's development and learning. The analysis illustrated how children's engagements and subjectivity cannot be discarded and ignored in academic learning activities without putting aside the learning potentiality embedded in the children's interactions and conflicts with each other. Doing so means missing out on opportunities to support children's development as related to participating in and influencing a shared life with co-participants.

References

Bjørnestad, E., & Samuelsson, I. P. (2012). *Hva betyr livet i barnehagen for barn under tre år? En forskningsoversikt*. Retrieved from www.regjeringen.no/globalas sets/upload/kd/vedlegg/barnehager/rapporter20og20planer/forskningsover sikt_barn_under_tre_aar.pdf

Broström, S., & Hansen, O. H. (2010). Care and education in the Danish crèche. *International Journal of Early Childhood*, *42*(2), 87–100. doi:10.1007/s13158–010–0010-x

Dalli, C., White, E. J., Rockel, J., Duhn, I., Buchanan, E., Davidson, S., . . . Wang, B. (2011). *Quality early childhood education for under-two-year-olds: What should it look like? A literature review*. Retrieved from http://thehub.superu.govt.nz/sites/default/files/41442_QualityECE_Web-22032011_0.pdf

Danish Evaluation Institute (EVA). (2013). *Natur og naturfænomener i dagtilbud*. Retrieved from www.eva.dk/projekter/2013/natur-og-naturfaenomener-i-dagtilbud

Danish Evaluation Institute (EVA). (2015). *0–2 årige børns læring. Tæt på det læringsorienterede arbejde i dagtilbud*. Retrieved from www.eva.dk/projekter/2015/arbejdet-med-laering-for-de-0-2-arige-born

Danish Evaluation Institute (EVA). (2016). Kvalitet i dagtilbud. *Pointer fra forskning*. Retrieved from www.eva.dk/projekter/2016/forstaelse-og-maling-af-kvalitet-i-dagtilbud

Dreier, O. (2008). *Psychotherapy in everyday life. Learning in doing: Social, cognitive and computational perspectives*. Cambridge: Cambridge University Press.

Egelund, N., & Mejding, J. (2004). *OECD PISA: Programme for international student assessment*. Copenhagen: Danish School of Education Press.

Fenech, M. (2011). An analysis of the conceptualisations of "quality" in early childhood education and care empirical research: Promoting "blind spots" as foci for future research. *Contemporary Issues in Early Childhood*, *12*(2), 102–117. doi:10.2304/ciec.2011.12.2.102

Heckman, J. J. (2006). Skill formation and the economics of investment in disadvantaged children. *Science, New Series*, *312*(5782), 1900–1902.

Heckman, J. J., & Masterov, D. V. (2007). The productivity argument for investing in young children. *Review of Agricultural Economics*, 29(3), 446–493.

Hedegaard, M. (2015). A cultural historical approach to children's play: Play as a leading activity across cultural communities. *International Perspectives on Early Childhood Education and Development*, 1, 1–17.

Hilbert, D. D., & Eis, S. D. (2014). Early intervention for emergent literacy development in a collaborative community pre-kindergarten. *Early Childhood Education Journal*, 42(1), 105–113.

Højholt, C. (2008). Participation in communities: Living and learning across different contexts. *Australian Research in Early Childhood Education*, 15(1), 1–12.

Jensen, B. J. (2009). A Nordic approach to Early Childhood Education (ECE) and socially endangered children. *European Early Childhood Education Research Journal*, 17(1), 7–21.

Jensen, B. J., & Bullards, J. A. (2002). The mud centre: Recapturing childhood. *Young Children*, 57(3), 16–19.

Juhl, P. (2015). Toddlers collaboratively explore possibilities for actions across contexts: Developing the concept conduct of everyday life in relation to young children. In G. B. Sullivan, J. Cresswell, A. Larraín, A. Haye, & M. Morgan (Eds.), *Dialogue and debate in the making of theoretical psychology* (pp. 202–210). Toronto, ON: Captus Press Inc.

Kragh-Müller, G., & Ringsmose, C. (2015). Educational quality in preschool centers. *Childhood Education*, 91(3), 198–205.

La Paro, K. M., Williamson, A., & Hatfield, B. (2014). Assessing quality in toddler classrooms using the CLASS-Toddler and the ITERS-R. *Early Education and Development*, 25(6), 875–893.

Loeb, S., Fuller, B., Kagan, S. L., & Carrol, B. (2004). Childcare in poor communities: Early learning effects of type, quality and stability. *Child Development*, 75, 47–65.

Ministry for Children, Education and Gender Equality. (2016a). *Master for en styrket pædagogisk læreplan*. Copenhagen: Ministry for Children, Education and Gender Equality.

Ministry for Children, Education and Gender Equality. (2016b). *Børns tidlige udvikling og læring i dagtilbud. Udviklingsprogrammet Fremtidens dagtilbud*. Copenhagen: Ministry for Children, Education and Gender Equality.

Ministry for Children and Social Affarirs. (2017). Retrived from www.english.sm.dk/

Nordahl, T., Kostøl, A., Sunnevåg, A., Knudsmoen, H., Johnsen, T., & Qvortrup, L. (2012). *Kvalitet i dagtilbuddet*. Frederikshavn: Dafolo.

Nordtømme, S. (2012). Place, pace and materiality for pedagogy in a kindergarten. *Education Inquiry*, 3(3), 317–333.

Pellegrini, A. (2009). *The role of play in human development*. New York: Oxford University Press.

Plum, M. (2014). A "globalised" curriculum: International comparative practices and the pre-school child as a site of economic optimisation. *Discourse – Studies in the Cultural Politics of Education*, 35(4), 570–583. doi:10.1080/01596306.2013.87 1239

Ramey, C. T., & Ramey, S. L. (2004). Early learning and school readiness: Can early intervention make a difference? *Merrill-Palmer Quarterly*, 50(4), 471–491.

Retsinformation. (2017). *Dagtilbudsloven*. Retrieved from www.retsinformation.dk/forms/r0710.aspx?id=182051

Rogoff, B. (2003). *The cultural nature of human development.* Oxford: Oxford University Press.

Sommer, D., Samuelsson, I., & Hundeide, K. (2013). Early childhood care and education: A child perspective paradigm. *European Early Childhood Education Research Journal, 21*(4), 459–475.

Statistics Denmark. (2014). *Statistikbanken.* Retrieved from www.statistikbanken.dk/statbank5a/SelectVarVal/Define.asp?MainTable=PAS22&PLanguage=0&PXSId=0&wsid=cftree

Sylva, K., Siraj-Blatchford, I., Taggart, B., Sammons, P., Melhuish, E., Elliot, K., & Totsika, V. (2006). Capturing quality in early childhood through environmental rating scales. *Early Childhood Research Quarterly, 21*(1), 76–92. doi:10.1016/j.ecresq.2006.01.003

Togsverd, L. (2015). *Da "kvaliteten" kom til småbørnsinstitutionerne.* Doctoral dissertation, Roskilde University.

Van Luit, J. E. H., & Toll, S. W. M. (2015). Remedial early numeracy education: can children be identified as having a language deficiency benefit? *International Journal of Language & Communication Disorders, 50*(5), 593–603.

Winther-Lindquist, D. (2017). The role of play in Danish childcare. In C. Ringsmose & G. Kragh-Müller (Eds.), *Nordic social pedagogical approach to early years: International perspectives on early childhood education and development* (pp. 95–114). Switzerland: Springer International Publishing. doi:10.1007/978-3-319-42557-3_6

6 Early childhood education and care in Estonia

The organisation and reforms of preschool education

Tiia Õun, Aino Ugaste and Tiina Peterson

Introduction

Several economic, cultural and other changes have taken place in Estonia after the regaining of independence, and these have affected the field of education. By the constitution, access to education is a right people have since birth, regardless of their place of residence, nationality, language or other specificity. It is important for all children that teaching would be based on their needs and would meet their capabilities. Increasing attention is paid in Estonia to the organisation of education and its quality and the curricula of educational institutions starting already from preschool education. Preschool pedagogy in Estonia has developed in the context of European education. In 1840, the first establishment offering day childcare was opened in Estonia, the work of which was based on the ideas of Friedrich Fröbel. The first national, Estonian-language kindergarten was opened in 1905. After Estonia regained its independence in 1991, all legal acts valid in the Soviet time became invalid, and the whole Estonian educational system started to be democratised. The field of preschool education is regulated by the Preschool Childcare Institutions Act (Koolieelse lasteasutuse seadus, 1999) and the National Curriculum of Preschool Childcare Institutions (Koolieelse lasteasutuse riiklik õppekava, 2008).

Quality goals and regulations of early childhood education and care in Estonia

According to the Estonian Lifelong Learning Strategy, flexible opportunities need to be developed for all children to participate in early childhood education (Eesti elukestva õppe strateegia, 2014). According to the Estonian Education Information System (EHIS), 93.6% of children between the age of 4 to 6 years and 77% of children between the ages of 18 months to 3 years attended the early childhood education institutions in 2014. The majority of children who participate in preschool education attend preschool childcare institutions that fall under the responsibility of the Ministry of Education and Research. All children between 18 months and 7 years are legally entitled to a place in preschool education. For local governments, it is compulsory to provide a place, if a parent wishes so. Parents have the right to choose preschool educational programmes either in municipal or private preschool institutions. All parents have to make a financial contribution towards the costs for pre-primary education. Legally, the costs are capped on the level of 20% of minimum wage. According to the Preschool Childcare Institutions Act (Koolieelse lasteasutuse seadus, 1999), and with the objective of ensuring a safe educational environment for children, the work organisation of the staff of a preschool institution shall be based on the principle that during the whole working time of a group, there is a person employed in the field of learning and teaching or an employee assisting a teacher for up to 7 children. This includes a maximum of 1:8 in the nursery groups and 1:12 in the kindergarten groups. Teachers have 35 working hours in their working week, of which, five hours are assigned to preparation and reflection with their team. The promotion of a child's development, including inclusive education, is teamwork, for which the leader of the childcare institution is responsible. For children with special needs, conditions have to be created for learning in integration groups together with other children. If there are no possibilities to establish an integration group in a local childcare institution, the local municipality or city government creates special groups or establishes special preschools. Children attending preschool childcare institutions have a guaranteed access to speech therapists and special education teachers. According to the Estonian Education Information System (EHIS), such support systems are made available to nearly 16% of children attending mainstream preschool childcare institutions. Local governments and preschool childcare institutions also use the services provided by regional counselling centres (speech therapists, special education teachers, psychological and social-pedagogical counselling) that receive state support.

Based on the Preschool Childcare Institutions Act, the criteria for the internal evaluation of the provision of preschool education have been set through regulation from the Minister of Education and Research (Koolieelse lasteasutuse seadus, 1999). These criteria include leadership and management, personnel management, cooperation with interest groups and stakeholders, resource management, the education process and the children's results; statistics for the preschool institution (covering children aged between 18 months to 7 years), including children-to-adult ratios, the size of the group and the salary level of the teachers. Advisory activities which support internal evaluation are organised and coordinated by the Ministry. This advice provides support to the leaders of the preschool institutions.

Based on reports commissioned by the Eurydice network (2014) and the European Commission (2014), the professionalism of preschool teachers is a key factor in ensuring the quality of early childhood education. In Estonia, a strong feature of the teaching force is that it is highly educated, also in pre-primary institutions. Estonia considers preschool teacher education as holistic, consolidating three levels of the teacher education system (initial training, induction year, in-service training) that creates opportunities for preschool teachers' professional development. 67% of teachers and 98% of principals have higher education degree equivalent to the bachelor's degree. Tallinn University and the

University of Tartu provide higher education in the specialised subject of early childhood education for bachelor's, master's and doctorate studies, and pursue research in educational sciences. Preschool childcare institutions have centrally allocated budgets for professional development. Support is also allocated from the state budget to local governments for the salaries of the teachers of preschool institutions, since September 1, 2017 (about 61 MEUR during the years 2017–2021). A European Social Fund programme (EDUKO) was launched in 2009 to help to make teachers' professional preparation more open, more flexible and more focused on practice. As part of the EDUKO project, three studies were conducted which were highly influential in designing the professional training. According to Peterson et al. (2016) and Peterson et al. (2014), the professionalism of teachers in Estonia is described by seven processes: interaction, family involvement, the planning of education and the evaluation of children's development, the use of teaching strategies, support for professional development, the creation of a growth environment and the development of values. The same aspects are important in the "Proposal for Key Principles of a Quality Framework for Early Childhood Education and Care" report by the European Commission (2014). Based on these studies, professional standards for preschool teachers in Estonia are prepared and the teacher-training system in Estonia will improve.

The implementation of curricula in preschool education

The quality of preschool childcare institutions is helped by the national curriculum for kindergartens. After Estonia regained its independence, one of the central tasks of the educational system was to develop new curricula that would meet the needs of a democratic society. In 1999, the new Framework Curriculum of Preschool Education (Alushariduse raamõppekava, 1999) was adopted which defined the aims, principles, content and temporal organisation of educational activities. The curriculum was renewed and the National Curriculum of Preschool Childcare Institutions (Koolieelse lasteasutuse riiklik õppekava, 2008) adopted in 2008 also defines the aims, principles, content and organisation of educational activities, as well as the principles of child assessment. The curriculum of 2008 consists of six chapters, in which a general part and a subject-specific part can be distinguished. The general part includes the aims, principles and organisation of educational activities, and the subject-specific part consists of seven specialty areas: language and speech, mathematics, environment, arts, exercise, music, Estonian as the second language. While the curriculum of 1999 described the temporal organisation and volume of educational activities, in the curriculum of 2008 this has been replaced by an emphasis on an integrated approach. While the 1999 curriculum described the outcomes of child development at different ages, the 2008 curriculum presents only the expected outcomes of the development of the 6- to 7-year-old child. Differently from the framework curriculum, the 2008 curriculum emphasises an approach to learning where learning is understood as a lifelong process, as a result of which there appear changes in behaviour, knowledge, attitudes, skills and the relationships between these aspects. Children's skills of play have been stressed separately, and more attention has been paid to the consideration of children's individuality and development potential. Based on the national curriculum, every childcare institution develops its own curriculum, and all teachers as well as the healthcare worker participate in the development of the curriculum. Thus, the development of the curriculum of childcare institutions based on the national curriculum has considerably changed the role and meaning of the preschool teacher in curricula-related activities. Preschool teachers participate in the development of the general principles of the curriculum of their childcare establishment and take responsibility for following these principles and completing the curriculum.

The national curriculum for preschool childcare institutions addresses the evaluation of children's development as cooperation between teachers and parents (Koolieelse lasteasutuse riiklik õppekava, 2008). Focusing on each child's individual needs, special qualities for supporting his or her positive self-esteem and development has been the cornerstone of these assessments. Teachers can get needed guidance by the centrally prepared methodological and support materials for assessing the children's development in cooperation with parents. The evaluation of a child's development is a part of everyday process of education and schooling, by observing free play situations and activities led by teachers. It also part of the teachers' experiences to conduct, at least, once a year, a development-oriented interview with parents, giving them feedback about the child's development and exploring parents' views and expectations. Pursuant to the Preschool Childcare Institutions Act (Koolieelse lasteasutuse seadus, 1999), a preschool institution issues a readiness for school card to children who have completed the curriculum of the preschool institution. A parent submits the readiness for school card to the school where the child commences his or her compulsory school attendance. A readiness for school card describes the child's achievements in the development of general skills and in fields of learning and educational activities, following the national curriculum for preschool childcare institutions. The child's strengths as well as aspects that need development are outlined. The evaluation of readiness for school and the compilation of the readiness for school card support the smooth transfer of a child from preschool to school. The readiness for school card helps the class teacher to understand the child's individuality and development and to plan cooperation with parents and support specialists. The class teacher takes account of the child's previous experiences and creates, in cooperation with the family, opportunities to support the child's individual development.

The views of Estonian preschool teachers on the curricula of the Soviet period and those adopted after the regaining of independence as well as their views on the ideal curriculum have been studied (Tuul, Ugaste, & Mikser, 2011). The findings revealed that preschool teachers generally perceived the Soviet-time curricula as thorough and detailed prescriptions that had to be followed precisely. Although some teachers felt fine with such curricula (since following detailed instructions provided a sense of certainty about one's activities), there were also teachers among those studied who thought that too many prescriptions limited considerably the creativity and initiative of teachers. The curricula adopted after the regaining of independence were described as documents that provide a general framework, but leave enough freedom for teachers to make decisions and act. Although most teachers liked that the curriculum had become more general in wording, some teachers expressed doubts about the capability of teachers to organise their work according to the framework curriculum. A particular worry was expressed about young, inexperienced teachers who, in the opinion of the study participants, need more specific instructions at the start of their work than those provided by the curricula of the newly independent Estonia.

The study about the general satisfaction of teachers about the changes in the curricula and about the views on the ideal curricula, which involved 383 teachers, revealed that the ideal curriculum as described by teachers was very similar to the current national curriculum of preschool childcare institutions (Tuul, Mikser, Neudorf, & Ugaste, 2015). The general part of the curriculum was assessed particularly highly, as well as the great freedom the curriculum provides for teachers. It appeared that teachers' views about the ideal curriculum were not related to their pedagogical work experience or the level of education. Since teachers have to develop the curriculum of their preschool childcare institution based on the national curriculum, the responsibility of teachers in the development of the curriculum has become more important and the feeling of ownership regarding the curriculum has increased. Ugaste, Tuul, Mikser, Neudorf and Jürimäe (2016) studied the experiences of Estonian preschool teachers in developing the curriculum of preschool childcare institutions and their assessment of the curriculum development process on their professional development and on increasing democratic professionalism. Semi-structured interviews conducted with 32 preschool teachers revealed that, in teachers' views, participation in the development process of the curriculum of their preschool childcare institution contributed to their understanding of the nature of the curriculum, increased their motivation of participating in curriculum development and supported the teachers' general professional development. It appeared in the interviews that cooperation with colleagues was, on the one hand, the indisputable precondition for the development of the preschool curriculum. On the other hand, the experience of cooperation and increased ability to cooperate with others were the most valuable outcomes of the curriculum development process. This, in turn, added to the increase in democratic professionalism. The findings of the study confirmed that the current national and political approach in preschool education has been justified, and supported teachers' cooperation in curricula development. It also appeared in the study that teachers wish to educate themselves in the development of curriculum, and that more attention should be paid to the organisation of the curriculum development process in the preschool establishment, primarily in the fields of management and teachers' cooperation.

The National Curriculum of Preschool Childcare Institutions (Koolieelse lasteasutuse riiklik õppekava, 2008) emphasises the importance of implementing a child-centred approach to learning in kindergartens. The approaches to learning of Estonian preschool teachers were studied through observation, whereby teachers' everyday learning activities with children were assessed. It appeared that teachers primarily apply the principles of a child-centred approach to learning, but not in all learning activities, and sometimes they apply an adult-centred approach (Kimer, Tuul, & Õun, 2016). The observations revealed that teachers put more emphasis on creating a positive mood for children and making the material understandable for children, and that they paid less attention to children's choices and independent learning. Thus, teachers were mainly following the approach to learning defined in the national curriculum of preschool childcare institutions, but they still need support in implementing the principles of child-centred education. A more precise definition of the content of the approach to learning, as well as specific examples of implementing the approach to learning in practice, is necessary.

Multiculturalism in Estonian preschool education

Contemporary education requires that the principles of cooperative learning are followed with the aim to create, in the process of learning, natural connections between citizenship, work places, social integration, lifelong learning and cultural diversity (Olssen, Codd, & O´Neill, 2004). Estonia is a multicultural society, and therefore, attention needs to be paid to understanding the educational needs of non-Estonians and to offering opportunities for coping in the society already from the preschool age. The educational process is multi-layered, starting from the preschool age and continuing as lifelong learning on different educational levels. During the past 20 years of independence, socio-economic conditions in Estonian society have changed and the influence of these changes also appears in education. Currently, the aim regarding learners who do not speak Estonian is that they achieve functional bilingualism by the end of the basic school, and are then competitive in the Estonian labour and educational market. Year after year, attention has increased towards other early learning opportunities for the national language. One of the most promising and effective of the learning opportunities in Estonia is considered to be the language immersion programme (Mehisto & Asser, 2007). In Estonia, the early language immersion programme has been implemented in kindergartens since 2000, in order to support the integration of children of other nationalities into Estonian society. The language immersion programme is a form of study where subject teaching is done in a language different from the learners' native language, and its central aim is to give children equally good skills both in their native language and in other languages. In Estonia, children can join the early language immersion programme in their two last preschool years (ages 5 and 6) or in the first grade at school. The aim in early language immersion is to support the studies of the national language to non-Estonian children, so that they acquire good skills both in their native language and in Estonian, and that they could continue their education in an Estonian-language school. The need for starting to learn Estonian in the first grade or at preschool age is based on studies of second language acquisition, which suggest that the most productive language learning period in a person's life is between the age of 5 and 10. Between these ages, the child acquires the second language faster, with more correct pronunciation and better results (Shrum & Glisan, 1994). Thus, the main focus in teaching the second language needs to be put on the primary level, and linguistic preparations need to be already started in the preschool education.

Studies on language immersion in Estonia have demonstrated that children who have studied by the language immersion methodology are well prepared for school, but children's age plays a major role (Kukk, Õun, & Ugaste, 2014). In the views of teachers and parents who participated in the study, the achievement of the aims of the preschool curriculum did not cause any trouble for children who had participated in the language immersion programme. The children had also acquired the basics of writing in both languages. The views of teachers and parents were mainly similar, which creates favourable preconditions for mutual cooperation. The children who participated in the language immersion programme in the kindergarten have also been studied further at school (Kukk & Õun, 2014). Regardless of their further language of study, those children who participated in the language immersion programme have, in the opinion of teachers, a very good understanding of values, respect for good manners, the skills to accept people's differences and the existence of responsibility. The average learning outcomes of children who had studied in the language immersion programme were very good in grades 1–3. On the 5-point scale, the average academic achievement was over four points. The study confirmed that regardless of the fact that in the kindergarten preparation for school took place in Estonian, it did not hinder successful coping with studies either in the Estonian-language school or in a Russian-language school.

Current reforms and future directions

A new act of early childhood education in Estonia is under preparation. The purpose of the new act is to ensure access to high-quality early childhood education and care for all children between 18 months and 7 years of age, and to establish an integrated approach instead of two parallel systems (preschool childcare institutions act and social welfare act) that exist today. The planned changes will give local governments more flexibility in organising the high-quality provision of early childhood education and care possibilities based on the needs of children and families. With the help of the European Social Fund, local governments have the possibility to create around 3,200 new kindergarten or childcare places. About 47 MEUR will be invested during the years 2014–2020. Estonia participates in the Organisation for Economic and Cooperation Development (OECD) Early Learning (for Child Wellbeing) study 2016–2020. The aim of participation is to get more information on contextual factors in children's learning processes and to improve the national curriculum for preschool childcare institutions (OECD, 2017).

The Estonian lifelong learning strategy defines its central aim as the creation of learning opportunities for people in Estonia, which meet their needs and capabilities in order to ensure people's opportunities for self-realisation within society, work life and in family life (Eesti elukestva õppe strateegia, 2014). The strategy addresses five major areas, which also need to be considered in preschool education. First, educational institutions need to implement the new approach to learning, which means supporting the individual and social development of every learner. In preschool education, the child-centred approach to learning is supported by a more precise definition of the approach to learning, as well as examples of implementing the approach in practice (Kimer, Tuul, & Õun, 2016). Second, it is emphasised in the strategy that educational institutions should have professional teachers and leaders. In Estonian childcare institutions, it is important to ensure that the salary and status of preschool teachers is equal to teachers in schools. Starting from autumn 2017, the equalisation of preschool teachers' salaries will be a nation-wide priority in Estonia. The third aim in education is the correspondence of lifelong learning opportunities to the needs of the labour market. In Estonia, preschool teachers are required to have higher education and teacher training has to take place at universities. Currently, 83% of preschool teachers meet the qualifications required by law. Thus, suitable opportunities need to be created for already working preschool teachers for acquiring higher education. The fourth strategic aim is the use of digital technology on every level of education. This means that modern digital technology is used in learning and teaching. In Estonia, several discussions and conferences have taken place where the opportunities for broader use of digital technology in kindergartens have been discussed. Research has demonstrated that teachers and parents need additional knowledge about children's use of digital technology and knowledge of how to teach children the skills to manage in the digital environment (Siibak & Vinter, 2010; Vinter & Siibak, 2012). The fifth strategic aim is the creation of equal opportunities for lifelong learning for all children and adults. In Estonian preschool education, the challenge involves ensuring a kindergarten place for all children. There are a lack of kindergarten places in rural municipalities near towns where the population has increased fast, and the need is greatest for places for children under 3 years of age (Riigikontroll, 2015). Also, the unification of preschool childcare institutions and childcare provisions is planned, which would ensure accessibility of high-quality preschool education to all children and would not put families in an economically unfair situation.

A new challenge lies in enabling preschool education to the children of immigrants. In Estonia, there have not appeared to be problems related to migration and refugees, but the attitudes of the population and the willingness and preparedness of teachers to deal with children from other cultures needs to be developed. Estonia has long-term experience in offering language immersion programmes to Russian-speaking children starting from preschool education. This experience can be used in providing preschool education to refugees' children. The language immersion programme has helped to support the teaching of national language to children of other native languages, helping them to acquire good skills both in their native language and in Estonian, so that they could successfully participate in the political, economic and cultural life of Estonian society in the future (Kukk & Õun, 2014; Mehisto & Asser, 2007). The central aim of

Estonian preschool education is to ensure democratic education that is supportive of every child in preschool childcare institutions and to ensure the accessibility
to education for all children and families. In Estonia, preschool education is available to all children in the preschool age, and the quality of preschool education is
supported by the national curriculum and qualified teachers. The main challenges
of preschool education include the preparedness of teachers to manage multicultural education, the unification of preschool childcare institutions and preschool
childcare provisions and the equalisation of preschool teachers' salaries with the
salaries of school teachers to ensure professional and highly valued teachers in all
childcare institutions.

References

Alushariduse raamõppekava. (1999). [Framework curriculum of preschool educa-
tion]. *Riigi Teataja I, 80,* 73.
Eesti elukestva õppe strateegia 2020. (2014). [The Estonian lifelong learning strategy
2020]. Retrieved from www.hm.ee/sites/default/files/estonian_lifelong_strategy.pdf
European Commission. (2014). *Proposal for key principles of a quality framework
for early childhood education and care.* Report of the Working Group on Early
Childhood Education and Care under the auspices of the European Commission,
Brüssels.
EURYDICE. (2014). *Key data on early childhood education and care in Europe.* Brus-
sels: Education, Audiovisual and Culture Executive Agency.
Kimer, M., Tuul, M., & Õun, T. (2016). Implementation of different teaching appro-
aches in early childhood education practices in Estonia. *Early Years, 36*(4), 362–
382. doi:10.1080/09575146.2015.1118443
Koolieelse lasteasutuse riiklik õppekava. (2008). [National curriculum of preschool
childcare institutions]. *Riigi Teataja I, 23,* 152.
Koolieelse lasteasutuse seadus. (1999). [Preschool Childcare Institutions Act]. *Riigi
Teataja I, 27,* 387.
Kukk, A., & Õun, T. (2014). Meeting the objectives of the curriculum at the first
stage of basic school by the child having left the language immersion kindergarten.
Education 3–13, 42(4), 357–368.
Kukk, A., Õun, T., & Ugaste, A. (2014). Readiness for school of children having
attended language immersion kindergarten in their teachers' and parents' opinions.
International Journal of Early Years Education, 22(2), 156–168. doi:10.1080/09
669760.2014.900475
Mehisto, P., & Asser, H. (2007). Stakeholder perspectives: CLIL programme man-
agement in Estonia. *International Journal of Bilingual Education and Bilingual-
ism, 10*(5), 683–701.
Organisation for Economic and Cooperation Development. (2017). *Early learning
matters.* Paris: OECD Publishing.
Olssen, M., Codd, J., & O'Neill, A. (2004). *Education policy: Globalization, citizenship and democracy.* London: Sage.
Peterson, T., Veisson, M., Hujala, E., Härkönen, U., Sandberg, A., Johansson, I., &
Kovacsne Bakosi, E. (2016). Professionalism of preschool teachers in Estonia, Sweden, Finland and Hungary. *European Early Childhood Education Research Journal,
24*(3), 136–156.

Peterson, T., Veisson, M., Hujala, E., Sandberg, A., & Johansson, I. (2014). The influence of leadership on the professionalism of preschool teachers in Estonia, Sweden and Finland. In A. Liimets & M. Veisson (Eds.), *Teachers and youth in educational reality* (pp. 119–142). Frankfurt am Main: Peter Lang Verlag.

Riigikontroll. (2015). *Lasteaiakohtade kättesaadavus valdades ja linnades* [The availability of kindergarten places in the municipalities and cities]. Tallinn: Riigikontroll. [National Audit Office in Estonia].

Shrum, J. L., & Glisan, E. W. (1994). *Teachers handbook. Contextualized language instruction.* Boston, MA: Heinle & Heinle.

Siibak, A., & Vinter, K. (2010). Making sense of the virtual world for young children: Estonian pre-school teachers' experiences and perceptions. *Journal of Virtual Worlds Research. Virtual Worlds for Kids, 3*(2), 3–27.

Tuul, M., Mikser, R., Neudorf, E., & Ugaste, A. (2015). Estonian preschool teachers' aspirations for curricular autonomy – the gap between an ideal and professional practice. *Early Child Development and Care, 185*(11–12), 1845–1861.

Tuul, M., Ugaste, A., & Mikser, R. (2011). Teachers' perceptions of the curricula of the Soviet and postSoviet eras: A case study of Estonian preschool teachers. *Journal of Curriculum Studies, 43*(6), 759–781.

Ugaste, A., Tuul, M., Mikser, R., Neudorf, E., & Jürimäe, M. (2016). Koolieelse lasteasutuse õpetajate kui õppekava arendajate kogemused, ootused ja hinnangud. *Eesti Haridusteaduste Ajakiri, 4*(1), 92–118. Retrieved from http://ojs.utlib.ee/index.php/EHA/article/viewFile/12891/7974

Vinter, K., & Siibak, A. (2012). The role of parents in guiding pre-school children's use of computers and the Internet: Analyzing perceptions of Estonian children and parents. In J. Mikk, M. Veisson, & P. Luik (Eds.), *Lifelong learning and teacher development* (pp. 78–94). Frankfurt am Main: Peter Lang Verlang.

7 Early childhood education and care in Finland

Compassion in narrations of early childhood education student teachers

Antti Rajala and Lasse Lipponen

Introduction

Emotions are a salient topic in contemporary research of early childhood education (Madrid, Fernie, & Kantor, 2015). Yet research addressing such a fundamental emotion or phenomenon as compassion is still scarce. The significance of compassion is nicely stated by Nussbaum (2014): it is the basic sentiment of a democratic community without which people lack the motive to respect others, protect them from harm and respond to their undeserved sufferings. Compassion and its attributes, such as social responsibility and emphatic concern, are essential competences and cultural practices that are needed, not only to build a future society, but also to thrive in everyday lives (Adamson & Darling-Hammond, 2016; Nussbaum, 2011). In the Organisation for Economic Co-operation and Development (OECD) 2016 report, *Global competency for an inclusive world*, empathy and compassion are regarded as essential global competences, and these competences are increasingly being foregrounded in the curricula of different countries. Moreover, compassion results from and is a condition for secure attachment of children (Gillath, Shaver, & Mikulincer, 2005). Taggart (2016) proposes that compassion should form the foundation for ethical practices in early childhood education and care.

In this chapter, we present and elaborate a new perspective for researching compassion in early childhood education and care (ECEC) settings, which we call the Cultures of Compassion perspective (see also Lipponen, Rajala, & Hilppö, in press). In this perspective, compassion is defined as an action that seeks to alleviate another person's suffering and involves empathic concern for the other's wellbeing (Lilius, Worline, Dutton, Kanov, & Maitlis, 2011). Our perspective goes beyond the more conventional psychological and pedagogical perspectives on compassion that address such questions as to how children develop capacities to display compassion or how compassion can be fostered through pedagogy. While recognising the importance of these questions, the Cultures of Compassion perspective conceptualises compassion in broader terms, that is, as an integral aspect of the daily lives of both adults and children (see also Lilius et al., 2011; Lipponen, in press; Madrid, Fernie & Kantor, 2015). In other words, compassion is embedded in the relationships and everyday practices of ECEC settings. Furthermore, the perspective discussed in this chapter draws upon research in the social sciences that considers compassion in its socio-political context and as a contested phenomenon (for an overview, see Ure & Frost, 2014). Thus, compassion may involve balancing different agendas and potentially conflicting interests. It can also take the form of not only alleviating the immediate suffering, but acting to transform the social circumstances that damage people or cause them distress.

The purpose of this chapter is to explore how the Cultures of Compassion perspective can help us to understand ECEC educators' lived experiences of compassion in their work. In particular, we explore narratives of compassion collected from master degree students of early childhood education, most of whom have worked or work as qualified ECEC professionals.

Firstly, we outline our perspective for researching compassion in ECEC settings and distinguish it from other perspectives on compassion. After that, we discuss how narratives can be used to research compassion. We then outline the Finnish ECEC system and elaborate our conceptualization of compassion by analysing narratives of Finnish ECEC educators. In addition to grounding our theoretical claims, our examples demonstrate the import and relevance of our theoretical conceptualisations for research of compassion in ECEC settings. Finally, we will pose some practical implications based on our analysis for developing ECEC practices.

The cultures of compassion perspective for researching compassion in ECEC settings

The existing research and pedagogical programmes related to compassion in ECEC settings has mainly been conducted from psychological perspectives. From a psychological perspective, compassion is understood as an emotion, or as an individual skill or trait. As an emotion, it is seen as a part of an emotion family of distress, pity, sadness, sympathy and love. However, as pointed out by Goetz, Keltner and Simon-Thomas (2010), evolutionary analysis has shown that compassion is a distinct emotion and should not be confused with these other emotions or with empathy, which is perhaps the closest to compassion. Compassion depends not only on the noticing of suffering, but also on the extent to which a focal actor feels empathic concern (Dutton, Workman, & Hardin, 2014; Kanov, Maitlis, & Worline, 2004). This is defined by Batson as "other-oriented feelings that are most often congruent with the perceived welfare of the other person" (1994, p. 606). This emotional sub process is the dominant way that psychologists have studied and defined compassion (Goetz, Keltner, Simon-Thomas, 2010). Empathic concern involves feelings of sympathy that tend to be other-oriented and altruistically, as opposed to egoistically, motivated (Batson, 1987). These feelings are a "potent source of motivation to help relieve the empathy-inducing need" (Batson, Eklund, Chermok, Hoyt, & Ortiz, 2007, p. 65). As a trait, compassion can be understood as a general pattern of behaviour, thought, or styles of emotional responses to act on the behalf of a distressed or suffering other. These patterns or styles persist across contexts and over time. They also differ across individuals and influence one's behaviour.

One central limitation of a psychological perspective is that while exclusively focusing on those who express compassion, it has mainly ignored the perspectives of those who receive compassion or witness it as bystanders. Furthermore, there is a lack of studies that treat compassion as a culturally constructed phenomenon, especially in early childhood settings.

Informed by a social practice theory (Lilius et al., 2011; Orlikowski, 2002), this study seeks to overcome the limitations of the psychological perspectives and conceptualise compassion as a multi-dimensional process composed of three elements: 1) noticing another person's suffering, 2) having other-regarding empathic concern and 3) acting to alleviate the suffering (Kanov et al., 2004). Whereas empathy means the capacity to understand what another person is experiencing, compassion goes further in leading to actions such as helping, including, caring, comforting, sharing and protecting others from harm and injustice. By suffering, we refer to "a wide range of unpleasant subjective experiences including physical and emotional pain, psychological distress and existential anguish" (Lilius et al., 2011, p. 874).

Drawing on a practice perspective, research in workplaces, such as a hospital or a university, has shown that compassion increases positive emotions and commitment to work (Frost, Dutton, Worline & Wilson, 2000; Lilius et al., 2008). Compassion, or lack thereof, also shapes people's sense making about themselves, others, as well as the workplace. In the context of institutional education, Lipponen (in press) studied the formation of compassion, related to rules that govern how it is and should be expressed in early childhood settings. In particular, the study focused on acts of compassion and their constitutive practices in a Finnish kindergarten. Lipponen found that rules for compassion were clearly inscribed in the kindergarten's curriculum, and they had significance in everyday practices, even if the teachers and children did not explicitly refer to them, and did not thereby justify their situational acts. The most common rule, inscribed in the curriculum was 'including', which probably implies that the kindergarten aimed to be an inclusive space in which everybody is accepted, and everyone's needs are recognised. Observing everyday interactions, Lipponen (in press) found that most of the concrete acts of compassion were acts of comforting and caring. This is perhaps not surprising, given that the need for comfort and care is very visible in everyday life. A crying child missing its parents or a child who has hurt himself or herself is easy to recognise. Most of the acts of compassion were directed by teachers towards children.

Whilst acknowledging the importance of the psychological and practice perspectives, we, however, argue that understanding such a complex phenomenon as compassion, requires us to go beyond the psychological and practice perspectives. As a solution, we will offer a third approach, which we call the Cultures of Compassion perspective. The basic idea of our approach is that we further elaborate and develop the practice perspective with ideas from the 'politics of compassion' (Ure & Frost, 2014), and Cultural Historical Activity Theory (CHAT)

(Engeström, 1987). Both approaches share the idea of transforming and expanding existing institutional or organizational practices and structures.

One central question in the 'politics of compassion' is to where, or towards what are acts of compassion directed. Whitebrook (2014) advocates the nature of compassion, arguing that compassion becomes political when it identifies systemic or institutional causes of collective suffering, and then acts against these causes. In a similar way, Nussbaum (2014) argues that compassion is the basic sentiment of a democratic community: without it, we lack the motive to respect others, protect them from harm and respond to their undeserved sufferings. As a building block of a democratic community, compassion should operate beyond the individual emotions as well as the relationship of the sufferer and the one who is trying to alleviate the pain.

From an activity theoretical (Engeström, 1987; Stetsenko, 2016) point of view, tracking structures or institutional causes of collective suffering and acting against them requires exploring and understanding the historical development of these institutions or systems and their practices. These systems are shaped and transformed over long periods of time, and their problems and capacity to develop into something new in the future can only be understood against their own history. Moreover, human beings do not live in a vacuum, but our activities are mediated by the cultural symbol systems and artefacts we use, and social mediators, such as rules and division of labour. Thus, to understand compassion, and following the principles of activity theory, one should explore, for instance, historical developments of an organization, formation of rules as well as practical and symbolic tools that mediate how compassion can be, and should be expressed in early childhood settings.

Compassion narratives

To illustrate our theoretical claims, we analyse examples derived from narratives collected from master degree students of early childhood education (N=24) in the University of Helsinki. The master's degree programme in early childhood education is based either on the Bachelor of Education or other at least first-cycle university degrees. The master's degree of early childhood education is comprised of 300 ECTS credits, including orienting studies, major subject studies and optional studies.

All students participating in this study were women (aged between 22–50 years), and many of them had experiences of working as a kindergarten teacher before or during their master degree studies, or both. As a part of one of their courses, "Perspectives on Early Childhood Pedagogy and Learning", we asked them to write a short narrative about compassion. The narratives were solicited with two open-ended questions, using the following instruction (see also Lilius et al., 2008): "Please provide a one-page long story of a time when you either (a) experienced compassion in everyday life and at work, or (b) witnessed compassion in everyday life or at work".

Narratives provide a good starting point for researching compassion and sense making about compassion since they capture and convey participants' lived experiences and emotions (Bruner, 1986). For the most part, the descriptions were stories in which the respondents had received compassion from colleagues, leadership, or the children, or stories in which compassion was denied. Some of the respondents reported events that they had witnessed or in which they were themselves giving compassion. A frequent trigger of compassion in the narratives was a tragic event or a difficulty in the respondents' personal lives. These triggers included family or personal issues, serious illness of oneself or loved one, home fire, or problems in combining working life and personal life. Other triggers included difficulties to fulfil the demands of work (many of the respondents occupied a novice position in their working community), conflicts between the employees, or children's suffering. The compassionate acts most often took the form of provision of emotional support (comforting, hugging, listening), giving time or flexibility, or material support.

In the following, we show in more detail how compassion was structured in the narratives. We also show how compassion (or its denial) was not merely described as individual isolated instances but as a recurrent feature of how the social and cultural practices were organised in the ECEC communities.

Finnish early childhood education

Finnish ECEC is guided by two national level documents prepared by multi professional expert groups consisting of administrators, researchers and trade union representatives: National Core Curriculum for Early Childhood Education and Care (2016, to be implemented for the first time in August 2017) and National Core Curriculum for Pre-Primary Education (2014). These documents serve as a basis for the curricula devised at the municipality and day-care unit levels. Early childhood education staff is responsible for drafting unit-specific curricula. Early childhood education and care, pre-primary education that is part of it and basic education form an entity proceeding consistently in relation to the child's growth and learning and build a foundation for life-long learning. The municipalities are responsible for arranging the ECEC services, as well as for their quality and supervision. At the national level, ECEC is the responsibility of the Ministry of Education and Culture.

The Finnish ECEC curricula emphasise compassionate orientation to other people. Mutual respect, empathy and a caring attitude towards others and the environment are seen as important educational goals and should be a visible part of the ECEC activities. Children are encouraged and instructed to recognise, express and regulate a variety of emotions. Moreover, the ECEC curricula instruct educators to foster children's capacity to take others into account in various conflict situations.

In general, Finnish early childhood education can be characterised in terms of a holistic approach that encourages play, relationship and curiosity. It builds on children's interests, and resists the 'school preparation approach'. The daily practices of Finnish early childhood education include adult-initiated activities, such as reading to children and presenting hands-on activities. Activities such as eating lunch, dressing for outdoor activities, and taking naps are also considered educationally valuable, and educators play an important role in these activities by guiding and helping children. In addition, during the day in the centre, children receive three meals, have a rest break, and take part in outdoor activities around the year.

Furthermore, the Finnish ECEC is characterised by a multi professional work community with a varying combination of professional qualification levels and job descriptions, as well as cooperation with professionals in other sectors. The cooperative work is usually organised in multi professional teams. The ECEC staff members responsible for children are required to have appropriate training. One in three in ECEC centres must have a higher education degree. The minimum requirement for a kindergarten teacher is a Bachelor's degree in Education or in Social Science. Other staff members in ECEC centres are expected to have at least a vocational upper-secondary qualification in the field of social welfare and health care. The Finnish early childhood education teacher is considered to be an autonomous professional who is committed to continuous personal development and is assumed to have an inquiry-oriented approach to uphold the quality of their work. This development orientation usually takes the form of reflection through discussion, observation and documentation within the professional community, families and the child (Kopisto, Salo, Lipponen, & Krokfors, 2014).

Compassion as a recurrent aspect of daily practice in Finnish ECEC settings

In the first narrative, the respondent describes how difficulties in her personal life spilled into the workplace, and how the situation was collectively handled among the colleagues and leadership.

Narrative 1

I had been in a difficult personal relation and when it ended, I was really broken mentally. Tears flowed from my eyes when I gave the children their meals. My team mates noticed this and said that I could take the time to go to the rest room. They came to substitute me. The situation made me sleepless, so after several nights of staying awake I could not do anything else than cry when I came to work. The vice principal and my team related to the issue well and they were okay with it when I took a three-day sick leave. Part of the work community were perhaps a bit unaware of what was the reason of my sick leave but when I came back to work they asked how I felt. My own team at that time (now I am in a different team) was really encouraging and compassionate, not only towards me, but towards all team members. I feel that one needs to be able to trust in one's own team and to feel that team members encourage one to cope at work. While I was in the sick-leave, I felt that it was crucial that my team communicated to me that I should take the time to rest. But also, that they miss me. :).

The basic structure of compassion can be observed in the narrative. Compassion is *triggered* by an overt suffering due to a difficulty in personal relationships. The difficulty spilled to the workplace and eventually took away the narrator's ability to work. Through the uncontrollable display of emotions (i.e. crying), the narrator's team *notices* that everything is not okay. Noticing the suffering triggers *an empathic response* on the part of the others. *The compassionate acts to alleviate the suffering*, then, take the form of making flexible work arrangements to allow for the narrator to recover from the difficult situation (i.e. taking a pause from work, sick-leave). In addition, the colleagues provided understanding, assurance and encouragement that were instrumental for overcoming the hardship.

Moreover, the narrative describes compassion in the narrators' workplace as a recurrent and reliable feature of the way of working of the community that was equally made available for all members of the community (Lilius et al., 2008). The narrative also evidences that compassion was experienced as a crucial aspect of a well-functioning work community. Furthermore, the trust in others' willingness to respond to hardships in a compassionate way appeared to strengthen the sense of belonging that the narrator experienced towards the community while being in a vulnerable position (Pinson, Arnot, & Candappa, 2010).

Denial of compassion as a recurrent aspect of daily practice

In the following narrative, compassion was denied by colleagues but given by the children.

Narrative 2

I had not worked in a kindergarten. I only have done my practicum studies during the bachelor studies. I felt that every adult working in the kindergarten were old ladies tired of life. I only received compassion from the children, they were authentic and joyful. For example, when I had personal worries, I told the children, that I have gone through sad things and I will survive. At the same time, we discussed about different emotions and their significance. Somehow, I felt that the adults did not have compassion and everyone was afraid that I would steal their place in the children's hearts. I thought that was strange.

The narrator describes her experiences of a teaching practicum. She depicts a contrast between the authentic and joyful children and the old and tired adults working in the kindergarten. By doing this, she construes an in-group and out-group configuration (Nussbaum, 2014) in which compassion is shared within the in-group but denied for members of the out-group. Thus, how compassion was given and received in this working community is described in the narrative to be within fragmented and self-contained social circles.

The following narrative illustrates another example in which compassion was denied, this time by the kindergarten leadership.

The compassion between adults was strongly and unfortunately associated with a bad supervisor. I experienced compassion when I felt being treated unfairly. One example of this must do with substituting in the Forest club in our house. The contract says, 'and the other tasks assigned by the supervisor', so I had to substitute in the Forest club although because of being pregnant (it was no secret, the supervisor and other staff members knew about the pregnancy) I went to pee every hour, without exaggerating. The supervisor gave me a hint not to drink. (In the forest, it is not possible to go to the toilet unless one goes to the bush to do it). In our house, there was another person who was also pregnant, who was exempted from the Forest club because of pregnancy. My team gave me compassion and the nods and words saying it was unfair. Apparently, the Forest club was for those whose face did not please the boss.

In this narrative, the narrator facing a personal difficulty (i.e. pregnancy) is denied the flexibility to accommodate the working arrangements to this condition. The suffering in this casje is not caused by the pregnancy but the difficulty to carry out the assigned work tasks, which involved directing outdoor activities in forest. The suffering is made worse by the sense of being treated unfairly by the supervisor. Here the team members notice the suffering and show compassion by giving emotional support. Thus, we can notice a similar phenomenon as in the previous narrative: sharing of compassion is fragmented into disjoint social groups. Moreover, the lack of compassion from the supervisor appears to be associated with a declining sense of commitment and belonging to the work community.

Narratives 2 and 3 point not only to a single, isolated instance of compassion but also to a recurrent feature of the social practice. In narrative 3, this is indicated in presenting the case as one example of being treated unfairly ("*One example* of this . . ."). Another indication is the assertion that the flexibility was granted unfairly in the workplace depending on whether the face of the employee pleased the supervisor. Moreover, the acts of compassion of the team members help the narrator in coping with the situation instead of raising voice to question the unfair treatment that caused the distress.

Next, we show how compassionate acts can not only help people who suffer in adapting to their difficult situations but also in questioning and trying to transform the social circumstances that cause suffering.

Questioning daily practices that may cause suffering

The next narrative tells about a development workshop in which the narrator raises her voice to call into question the way in which the adults in the kindergarten supervise children's free play in outdoor situations.

Our kindergarten staff was having a development workshop on the topic of "the development of a child's language capacities" . . . Together with one of the nurses, I discussed the significance of small, quickly passing pedagogical moments and how important it is for adults to be present for the children. We both had made an observation that especially when being outside, some of the adults tend to gather into adult groups leaving the children's doings without attention, although they are simultaneously doing a bit of controlling . . . When collectively sharing our experiences and thoughts, my group encouraged me to bring forward our observation about the pedagogical moments and their significance. I described the situation in a nice way and said that I also myself can sometimes be blamed for 'standing' in the yard. Without offending or pointing to anyone we wanted to get our kindergarten community to reflect on their activity, to which the principal replied a bit offended that she does not recognise this problem. As a new and recently graduated kindergarten teacher I felt very embarrassed and uncomfortable. I was also irritated because I knew the problem existed. Nevertheless, approving facial expressions and nods of some of the colleagues were expressions of compassion in my opinion. One kindergarten teacher commented and supported our group's view of the situation. Having experienced the compassion by a few persons of our community, I was left feeling strong, and the principal's comment did not feel so bad any longer. Even a small gaze, nod, and approving comments meant a lot after the comments and gestures of the principal.

The narrator first describes how she was discussing the relevance of fleeting pedagogical moments with children and how opportunities to create these moments were lost when the adults gather amongst themselves in the yard. This empathic concern for the children's needs and wellbeing can be interpreted as an act of compassion towards the children. The narrator was encouraged by her small group to raise this issue in the collective discussion. However, the kindergarten leader was less than pleased with this remark and denied the existence of the problem. The narrator was a recent graduate and new recruit to the kindergarten and was thus in a vulnerable position when she dared to question the social practices of the kindergarten. She felt embarrassed and uncomfortable as well as irritated by being treated in an unjust way by the leader. In the situation, compassion was also shown by the colleagues who openly showed their support by nodding and making approving comments. In a sense, the subject of the compassionate act towards the children was gradually expanded to include more people. The narrator experienced this social support as essential for her wellbeing.

Discussion

In this chapter, we have unpacked compassion as a practice-related phenomenon, illuminating how compassion is embedded in the social relationships and practices of ECEC settings. In particular, we showed how compassion was supported or hindered by the way the work was organised in the kindergartens. Our analysis also illuminates a distinction between compassionate acts that help others to adapt to their difficult situations and more transformative acts that question and seek to transform the undesirable practices. Notably, no one can make a social change alone; it requires a collective effort and shared agency (Archer, 2000; Virkkunen, 2006). We showed how questioning taken-for-granted practices was risky and resulted in irritating people who oversaw organizing the work. This risk was decreased by caring others who showed their compassion by giving social support for the dissident person. Our analysis also underscores the important role that giving, receiving and witnessing compassion plays in shaping people's sense-making about themselves as persons and educators, as well as about significant others and the work organisation.

The cultures of compassion perspective discussed in this chapter helps to rethink how compassion can be promoted in ECEC settings. We argue that working towards cultures of compassion involves designing inclusive spaces, spaces where dignity and safety are norms, diversity is recognised and accepted, and everyone feels encouraged, supported and included. Designing inclusive spaces is in line with the European Commission's (2015) "new policies for fairness in education from early age". Moreover, the practices of compassion and their enactment constitute the potential to answer to the polarization in contemporary society by increasing the opportunities on what people are actually able to do and to be. Compassion is a necessary part of social interaction in terms of facing societal challenges of increasing diversity, unpredictability and complexity.

In sum, while there is a growing attention to the role of emotions in early childhood education, little research exists on compassion. Moreover, the existing research is often premised on individualistic assumptions (Madrid, Fernie, & Kantor, 2015; Vadeboncoeur & Collie, 2013) and fail to address compassion as constituted in and constituting social practices. Our explorative research guides further research on the topic. Future research needs to produce research-based information for practitioners to support the development of cultures of compassion. There is a need to develop proactive models and scripts for educational practice that can contribute to the development of compassion on institutional and cultural levels. For policy makers, there is a need to produce tools for capitalising knowledge on constitution of cultures of compassion in terms of both preschool level activities and national and municipal level policymaking in increasing social justice in the society.

Acknowledgements

The research reported in this article was funded by the Academy of Finland (the project no. 299191).

References

Adamson, F., & Darling-Hammond, L. (2016). The critical choice in American public education: privatization or public investment? In F. Adamson, B. Åstrand, & L. Darling-Hammond (Eds.), *Global education reform: How privatization and public investment influence outcomes* (pp. 131–168). New York: Routledge.

Archer, M. S. (2000). *Being human: The problem of agency*. Cambridge: Cambridge University Press.

Batson, C. D. (1987). Prosocial motivation: Is it ever truly altruistic? *Advances in Experimental Social Psychology, 20,* 65–122.

Batson, C. D. (1994). Why act for the public good? Four answers. *Personality and Social Psychology Bulletin, 20,* 603–610.

Batson, C. D., Eklund, J. H., Chermok, V. L., Hoyt, J. L., & Ortiz, B. G. (2007). An additional antecedent of empathic concern: Valuing the welfare of the person in need. *Journal of Personality and Social Psychology, 93,* 65–74.

Bruner, J. (1986). *Actual minds, possible worlds*. Cambridge, MA: Harvard University Press.

Dutton, J., Workman, K., & A. Hardin, A. (2014). Compassion at work. *The Annual Review of Organizational Psychology and Organizational Behaviour, 1,* 277–304.

Engeström, Y. (1987). *Learning by expanding*. Helsinki: Orienta-Konsultit.

European Commission. (2015). Retrieved from https://ec.europa.eu/programmes/horizon2020/sites/horizon2020/files/13.%20SC6_2016–2017_pre-publication.pdf

Frost, P. J., Dutton, J. E., Worline, M. C., & Wilson, A. (2000). Narratives of compassion in organizations. In S. Fineman (Ed.), *Emotions in organizations* (pp. 25–45). Thousand Oaks, CA: Sage.

Gillath, O., Shaver, P. R., & Mikulincer, M. (2005). An attachment-theoretical approach to compassion and altruism. In P. Gilbert (Ed.), *Compassion: Its nature and use in psychotherapy* (pp. 121–147). London: Routledge.

Goetz, L., Keltner, D., & Simon-Thomas, E. (2010). Compassion: An evolutionary analysis and empirical review. *Psychological Bulletin, 36,* 351–374.

Kanov, J., Maitlis, S., & Worline, M. (2004). Compassion in organizational life. *American Behavioral Scientist, 47,* 808–827.

Kopisto, K., Salo, L., Lipponen, L., & Krokfors, L. (2014). Transformations and tensions in Finnish early childhood education and care. In L. Kroll & D. Meier (Eds.), *Crossing borders of reflection: Educational change in international early childhood contexts* (pp. 141–154). New York: Routledge.

Lilius, J., Worline, M., Dutton, J., Kanov, J., & Maitlis, S. (2011). Understanding compassion capability. *Human Relations, 64,* 873–899.

Lilius, J., Worline, M., Maitlis, S., Kanov, J., Dutton, J., & Frost, P. (2008). The contours and consequences of compassion at work. *Journal of Organizational Behavior, 29,* 193–218.Lipponen, L. (in press). Constituting cultures of compassion in early childhood educational settings. In S. Garvis & H. Harju-Luukkainen (Eds.), *Nordic children and families*. Routledge.

Lipponen, L., Rajala, A., & Hilppö, J. (in press). Compassion and emotional worlds in early childhood education. In C. Pascal, A. Bertram, & M. Veisson (Eds.), *Pedagogic innovations in early childhood education in crosscultural contexts*. Routledge.

Madrid, S., Fernie, D. E., & Kantor, R. (2015). Introduction to reframing emotions. In S. Madrid, D. Fernie, & R. Kator (Ed.), *Reframing the emotional worlds of the early childhood classroom* (pp. 1–15). New York: Routledge.

Nussbaum, M. C. (2011). *Creating capabilities*. Boston: Harvard University Press.

Nussbaum, M. C. (2014). Compassion and terror. In M. Ure & M. Frost (Eds.), *The politics of compassion* (pp. 89–207). New York: Routledge.

Organisation for Economic Co-operation and Development. (2016). *Global competency for an inclusive world*. Retrieved June, 22, from www.oecd.org/education/Global-competency-for-an-inclusive-world.pdf

Orlikowski, W. J. (2002). Knowing in practice: Enacting a collective capability in distributed organizing. *Organization Science*, *13*, 249–273.

Pinson, H., Arnot, M., & Candappa, M. (2010). *Education, asylum and the 'non-citizen' child: The politics of compassion and belonging.* Hampshire: Palgrave Macmillan.

Stetsenko, A. (2016). *The transformative mind: Expanding Vygotsky's perspective on development and education.* New York: Cambridge University Press.

Taggart, G. (2016). Compassionate pedagogy: The ethics of care in early childhood professionalism. *European Early Childhood Education Research Journal*, *24*, 173–185.

Ure, M., & Frost, M. (Eds.). (2014). *The politics of compassion.* New York: Routledge.

Vadeboncoeur, J. A., & Collie, R J. (2013). Locating social and emotional learning in schooled environments: A Vygotskian perspective on learning as unified. *Mind, Culture, and Activity*, *20*, 201–225.

Virkkunen, J. (2006). Dilemmas in building shared transformative agency. *Activités*, *3*, 19–42.

Whitebrook, M. (2014). Love and anger as political virtues. In M. Ure & M. Frost (Ed.), *The politics of compassion* (pp. 21–36). New York: Routledge.

Worline, M., & Dutton, J. E. (2017). *Awakening compassion at work: The quiet power that elevates people and organizations.* Oakland, CA: Berrett-Koehler Publishers Inc.

8 Early childhood education and care in Germany

Policy, key data, quality and pedagogical approach

Claudia M. Ueffing

Basic information about Germany, the educational system and law regarding ECEC

To understand the German educational system, first and foremost it is important to know that Germany is a federal republic and education both covering schooling and ECEC is under the responsibility of the 16 federal states (Arbeitsgemeinschaft, 2006). Schools are under the responsibility of the 16 ministries of education, whereas ECEC belongs to the 16 ministries of social affairs. These facts cause a huge variety of curricula and legal regulations, both in the school system as well as in ECEC. The average age for children to enrol at school is 6 years, but could be 5 or 7 depending on the children's skills and on the parents wish.

All 16 federal states guarantee a place for each and every child at the age of one year. In terms of fees, Germany is highly diverse. In six states, day-care is free of charge covering the last year before school up to three years or even from the second birthday of the child onwards. In the ten remaining states, parents have to pay related to their income and to the number of children attending day-care. Hence, the common basis for the stated diversity is laid in Book Eight of the Social Code – Services for Children and Young People (Sozialgesetzbuch SGB VIII – Kinder – und Jugendhilfe). In Chapters 3–5, principles of funding as well as support for families, children and children with special needs are regulated. The focus lies on participation, gender, prevention of child endangerment and inclusion.

Further relevant legal regulations are fixed in the "Tagesbetreuungsgesetz" (TAG) and "Gesetz zur Weiterentwicklung der Kinder- und Jugendhilfe" (KICK). In TAG, for the first time the extension of day-care facilities has been put on the political agenda in Germany. Quality indicators have also been defined. The Children's and Youth Aids Development Act (KICK, Law on the further development of child and youth welfare assistance) is a German October, 2005 and led to changes in SGB VIII, which concern inter alia, full-time care, which concretises the existing protection order for children in danger. It is also intended to underpin the daily support system for children, parents and families.

Investment and funding for day-care provision

Since 2000 and the first publishing of PISA results, ECEC has been a boom sector. Due to European targets, the quantity of day-care provision has been raised (BMFSJ, 2008). Investment in ECEC has increased permanently up to 2.18 bn €. But again, the investments also differ from state to state. The range covers about 4.3% of the net expenditure into day-care per child in one state up to 8.9% in another state. This of course raises the question of equal chances for each and every child. The overall costs for ECEC are covered by multiple funding:

1   Financing and investment on a federal level for all Germany by Federal Ministry for Family Affairs, Senior Citizens, Women and Youth
2   The federal states – the regional level
3   The municipalities – the local level
4   The NGOs
5   The parents who pay fees.

(Bock-Famulla et al. 2015)

The subsidiary principle

A key element of ECEC in Germany is the subsidiary principle, which was implemented in 1949 when the German Federal Republic was founded. This means that NGOs have to be prioritised, and only in the case that a municipality cannot find a volunteering NGO, it has to be in charge of a new day-care-centre itself. Before 1990, in Eastern Germany most day-care centres were run by the state. After 1990, the system in the eastern states was adapted to the western German system, and in the eastern states, an increasing number of day-care centres is now run by NGOs as well. Therefore, nationwide, approximately 67% of all day-care centres are under the responsibility of NGOs and only approximately 33% are municipal day-care centres (Bock-Famulla et al., 2015).

Types of day-care provision in Germany

Different types and forms of day-care provision exist in Germany. All types of day-care have in common that children are not split up in age groups, but stay together to learn from each other like siblings.[1] In Germany, three different types of institutional day-care facilities exist:

1   The "Kinderkrippe", equivalent to a crèche is for children 0–3 years of age.
2   The German word "Kindergarten" covers day-care provision for 3–6-year-old children. It also includes preschool, which is integrated and usually covers special activities for children to up-skill them for school, e.g. in fine motor skills.
3   Primary school in Germany mainly covers teaching in the morning. Due to an increasing number of both parents in the labour market, afterschool-care

is also provided to the children and their parents. The so called "Hort" is a traditional institution for afterschool-care.

Nowadays, most day-care centres cover all three or at least two types of day-care provision under one roof.[2] In addition, afterschool clubs organised by parents themselves and often located in the school building are very common. Normally the opening hours of the afterschool clubs are shorter compared to the ones in a "Hort". For children aged 0–6 parents might also like to choose private childcare. This is provided at the nanny's home and she might take two or three children in. Bigger groups of private childcare are called "Großtagespflege". Here, two or three members of staff take care of max. 10 children, for example in a flat especially equipped for children (Diller, Jurczyk, & Rauschenbach, 2005). All forms of day-care are subsidised on national level and by the federal states.

Data on enrolment of children

As of March 1, 2015, one and a half years after the entry into force of the legal claim, nationwide a total of 32.9% of all 3-year-olds were enrolled in a crèche or children's day-care centre. The participation rate among the 3-year-olds increased in 2009 to 20.4%. This growth is almost exclusively due to rising participation rates for 1-year and 2-year-olds, that is, the two age-related years to which the newly introduced legal claim relates. While 20.4% of the 1-year-olds have already attended a children's day-care facility or children's care in 2009, more than one-third (35.8%) are in 2015.

From 1996 to mid-2013, only children who had completed their third year of age were entitled to a place in a Kindergarten, regardless of the educational and occupational situation of their parents. Correspondingly, the participation of these older children in institutional childcare is a self-evident component of their life and education biography. In 2015, for example, a large proportion of children aged under 6 (95.3%), who are not yet at school, will be looked after in a Kita, a children's day-care facility or a (preschool) institution. Hence the participation range varies around Germany, depending on the region, the rate differs between 90 to 98%. But almost every child aged 4 and 5 years attends Kindergarten in Germany (Bertelsmannstiftung, 2015).

Quality matters – education of staff, child-adult-ratio and national initiatives and projects

Quality now matters in ECEC in Germany since the quantity has been a target from 2000 to 2015. Besides the resources in general, human resources play a key role regarding quality in ECEC.

Both cross-sectional and longitudinal studies converge to say that qualifications matter. Higher levels of preparation correlate positively with better childcare quality as well as with better developmental outcomes for children (Clarke-Stewart, Vandell, Burchinal, O'Brien, & McCartney, 2002; Early, Maxwell, Burchinal, Bender, Ebanks, Henry, 2007; Fukkink & Lont, 2007; Sylva, Melhuish, Sammons, Siraj-Blatchford, & Taggart, 2004). Moreover, the 2006 Starting Strong report from the Organisation for Economic and Cooperation Development (OECD) concludes that: "Research from many countries supports the view that quality in the early-childhood field requires adequate training and fair working conditions. Research shows the link between strong training and support of staff and the quality of ECEC services. In particular, staff who have more formal education and more specialised early-childhood training provide more stimulating, warm and supportive interactions with children.

(OECD, 2006, p. 158; CoRe, 2009)

In Germany, national standards and indicators have been set up based on current research. They cover "Orientierungs-, Struktur- und Prozessqualtiät" (Tietze & Viernickel, 2016), which is a set of structural and process indicators. Staff have to be trained and educated, otherwise they cannot be hired to educate children. Also, study programs have been implemented for the academic education of staff for around 20 years. Furthermore, all federal states have implemented curricula in ECEC and they have implemented quality standards in the day-care centres. Based on these national or regional standards most of the providers, municipalities or even day-care centres themselves have worked out a curriculum on local level (Viernickel, Fuchs-Rechlin, Strehmel, Preissing, Bensel, & Haug-Schnabel, 2015).

Education of staff and professions

Staff in ECEC are qualified both on vocational (VET) and academic levels, with BA and MA diplomas. Hence, a strong tradition in Germany exists to educate future staff for ECEC in vocational education and training. Since 2004, academic study programs have been implemented due to a high pressure put on Germany in the European Union and by the Bologna Process. In VET, the assistants and the German 'Erzieherin' are trained for the job. This refers back to Friederich Fröbel, who in 1840 opened his first Kindergarten and attached a School of Education to it to support mothers in the upbringing of their children. In 1911 in Prussia, the first education act had been launched and the education of staff in ECEC was formulised (Berger, n.d.; Nagel, 2000).

Special VET schools provide on the job training on ISCED Level 3B for the 'KinderpflegerIn/SozialassistentIn'. The prerequisite for enrolment at a VET institute is graduation from general school after class 10. The training lasts two years and the focus is very much on practical skills, e.g. preparing the room for activities and assist staff in charge of them. Assistants cannot be responsible for a group or class. The 'Erzieherin', however, is trained to be in charge of a group of children. Education takes place in a VET institute for five years covering two years of guided preparatory internship, two years of theoretical training in school leading to exams each student has to take plus one year of on the job training combined with decent mentoring leading to an exam as well. This education is recognised as ISCED level 5b and nationwide leads to the profession of a states approved childcare worker.

Since 2004, students can also study ECEC programs at university. Two types of study programs exist:

1   regular BA programs with 7 semesters and 210 ECTs
2   and those who validate and recognise the VET education up to 90 ECTs so that the study program at university only last 4 semesters.

All study programs in Germany are provided by universities and universities of applied sciences, and lead to a BA-or MA-qualification called 'Kindheitspäda-goge/in". Supporting and safeguarding a child's learning and development involves a range of complex duties and demands on employees. Meeting these demands requires specialist professional training that links methodological exper-tise with teaching and organisational skills and further develops competencies in relation to specific duties. This includes:

•   Initiate, promote, accompany, document, reflect and evaluate educational processes with particular attention to gender issues, intercultural and ethical challenges and in collaboration with relevant persons and institutions
•   Social networking of different learning and living places
•   Interface management (for example, transition of children's day-care to school)
•   Planning, management, organization and management of educational and educational institutions
•   Evaluation and quality development
•   Organisation and management.

In addition, students who study social work might head for an employment in the field of ECEC. They also have the permission to work as special teacher or as deputy head or director of a day-care centre. Further professions, except those stated above, do not have the permission to work in day-care centres. This is part of the quality management regulated by the state. Hence, nationwide there is a huge research based debate about whether this regulation makes sense, because it does not open doors for other professions, e.g. artists, speech therapists or even psychologists. This raises the question whether the strict regulation meets both children's and society's demands in terms of high quality education. Although, unions and other stakeholders plead for multi-professional teams.

Child-adult ratio

One of the key indicators for quality in ECEC is the staff-child-ratio. Here, again, a huge variation can be stated across Germany. In some regions, the ratio is 1:6

for under-3-year-old children, and in others it is 2.9 children per adult. For the 3- to 6-year olds, the variation ranges from 1:7.7 up to 1:14.4, with a national median of 9.5. This shows the challenge Germany faces in terms of quality in ECEC, because research requires ratios of 1:3 and 1:7.5. In addition, these figures do not include any non-contact time, sickness leave or holidays for staff. Therefore, the realistic staffing ratios are even higher.

Regarding the additional fact that lots of pedagogues work part time, go on maternity leave or change job due to health problems, Germany has to rethink staffing and salaries in ECEC. In addition, Germany faces a retirement wave of staff at the moment, and has difficulties in recruiting specialists for ECEC. Furthermore, like in many other countries, the ratio of men working in this sector is rather low, at around 5%. Gender is an important consideration for the future.

In most German day-care centres, leadership and management have to be done on top of the daily routine in a group. Only about 37% of all directors nationwide are employed to only manage the day-care centre, 8% to cope with the management in a team and to share non-contact time for these duties, whereas 57% have to do it as a manager with a few extra hours or even on top (17.1%) of their job as a pedagogue in class. This can be considered critical in terms of quality management in ECEC (Bock-Famulla et al., 2015).

National initiatives and projects to enhance quality in ECEC in Germany

Further national initiatives and projects have been launched. Under the umbrella of 'Frühe Chancen' launched by the Federal Ministry of Education and Research (BMBF) the following projects are the most important national initiatives since 2009: WIFF – Weiterbildungsinitiative Frühpädagogische Fachkräfte, Bildung durch Sprache und Schrift (BISS) and Sprachkitas. All programs strongly focus on continuous professional development:

WIFF

The professionalisation initiative was founded in 2009 and is a project of the Federal Ministry of Education and Research (BMBF), the Robert Bosch Stiftung and the German Youth Institute. WIFF is funded by the BMBF. The project promotes the professionalisation of the specialists in various ways:

- The project provides expertise on current topics in early education.
- It promotes professional, competency-oriented further education and monitors and analyses the ongoing professionalisation process.
- It is committed to better interlinking of vocational and higher education skills, so that educational paths can be connected.
- It involves the actors of education and training, the subject of policy, including sponsors and associations, as well as science. In this way, WIFF keeps the discourse on quality in children's day-care alive.

BISS

More than 600 educational institutions from all federal states are involved in elementary education, primary and secondary education in BISS. They have formed a total of 100 alliances. A network consists of three to ten children's day-care centres or schools, as well as other partners, such as universities or libraries. In the coming years, the alliances will further develop their concepts and measures for language promotion, language diagnostics and reading promotion, and in some cases will work together across countries. Almost 30 associations are active in the field of child day-care: the main focus of their work is the language stimulation, linguistic and literacy education. This approach is also pursued in the federal program "Language Kitas: Because Language is the Key to the World".

Sprachkitas

All children should benefit from good education opportunities right from the start. In January 2016, therefore, the new federal program "Language Kitas: Because Language is the Key to the World" of the Federal Ministry for Family, Senior Citizens, Women and Youth was launched. With the new program, the Federal Ministry of Family Affairs supports daily integrated language stimulation, linguistic and literacy education as an integral part of ECEC. This is considered an important step towards equal chances for each and every child. To ensure a sustainable impact on daily routines, in day-care centres staff receive specialist guidance, counselling and on the job training.

Besides these projects to enhance quality in ECEC in Germany, socio-economic long-term targets are discussed in round table discussions of experts both with research and working-life background in ECEC. Further relevant issues, as well as challenges for society in 2016, like a successful integration of children with refugee background or the threatening of poverty for families with children, are on the agenda as well.

Curricula in Germany

The curricula in ECEC in Germany is located on the interface of quality management, on the one hand, and pedagogy on the other hand. Again, Germany is marked by high diversity. As each federal state holds responsibility for education, 16 curricula exist in Germany (Deutscher Bildungsserver). This raises the question about what they all share and have in common. Primarily, a trend towards learning experience and child's exploration can be seen. The focus on learning objectives is getting less important. All curricula are based on a holistic and child-centred approach and share a number of learning fields, including:

- personal and social development, interaction and social skills
- language acquisition, literacy and communication
- mathematics and natural sciences

- aesthetic and music education, arts and crafts
- ethical values, norms and religion
- physical education, health and wellbeing
- cooperation with parents and networking for children's demands.

In addition, in Germany a common understanding of ECEC has been developed during the last 20 years by international cooperation and research, for example, through implementing and improving the Bavarian Curriculum.

The image of the child and the pedagogical approach

German ECEC staff have a triple mandate for '*Bildung, Betreuung & Erziehung*'. Unlike in English, *Bildung & Erziehung* have different connotations, although both are translated to just one English word: education. Whilst *Bildung* has a more academic connotation and implies the active process a child undertakes to explore the world, *Erziehung* covers the aspect of upbringing, behaviour and adults' intervention. *Betreuung*, however, can be translated with care and covers both child's wellbeing and health (Fthenakis, 2006; Fthenakis, 2009; Schäfer, 2011).

The image of the child

The image of the child, the philosophical basis, is that of an active human being right from the start. Even the youngest children are equipped with rich potential in order to adapt themselves to the world in a manner appropriate to them, and are in a lively exchange with their environment. They strive to participate in everything their environment provides to them. Already, infants have versatile cognitive abilities. They, by themselves, strive for experiences and participation. They explore, understand and influence their life and assert themselves, if there are any possibilities. Language acquisition, ways of thinking, problem-solving strategies and role-play are not solely learned by the child by themselves, but by the interaction with adults or more competent children. These persons, for example, alternately take over all the roles during the role-play and present it to the toddler. Hereby the child gradually becomes a more active participant in the play, and step by step adapts more aspects of the role models, and under this influence finally turns into a full "role player". This theoretical basis of the image of a child refers back to Piaget and Vygotsky and has recently been elaborated and adapted for Germany by Fthenakis (2006) and Schäfer (2011).

In Germany, ECEC, including *Bildung, Betreuung & Erziehung*, is strongly play based. In early childhood, the essential form of exploring the world is to play. Unlimited and free play is, apart from planned intervention and stimulation, essential for the positive development of a child. Play is the childlike form of learning, and both playing and learning go hand in hand. Play, however, also means an exercise field for emotions, encourages children to make social experiences or to process, discover and shape the individual child's world. Therefore, the child needs a lot of space and time to play because it has a fundamental importance for a physical and mental health development. For the child to play is not merely leisure time, as often assumed, but the form of children's acting. For this reason, for example, Fröbel (n.d.) and Montessori (1969) emphasised the importance of the play and demanded a "play management" of staff in ECEC. The German attitude towards playing and learning has also been influenced by the so-called Nordic Approach in Europe, Pramling et al. (2008) explains:

> Play, as well as learning, are natural components of children's everyday lives. When children are asked what they like to do best, the answers are unanimous: to play. On the other hand, education for children is, on the whole, organised to promote learning rather than play. However, while school is traditionally seen as a place of learning and not of play, preschool is more often associated with play rather than learning, from the child's perspective.
> (Pramling et al., 2008)

However, the basis of the above-mentioned learning of children in the day-care centre is, first of all, the welbeing of the child. If staff work with children aged between 0 and 6 years, all aspects of communication should be taken into consideration. A positive body language and active communication can lead to an enormous learning growth in children. The active attachment to the child, a loving charisma, accepting gestures and genuine interest in the child positively build up the relationship with the child. The child feels at the same time independent and perceived and develops an emotional stabilization. This is considered to be the essential basis for learning the growth for all children at an early age in a day-care centre in Germany.

Core issues in ECEC in Germany

The composition of the children in a day-care centre reflects the diverse world of today. There are many dimensions of heterogeneity in German society, which also manifest themselves in day-care centres, such as migration, disability, religion, socio-economic conditions of families and gender. Linguistic diversity and peculiarities of the child's language development are also included. It is therefore a question of regarding diversity as new normality rather than striving for homogeneity and monolingualism, in order to meet not only the children's, but also families' and society's, demands.

In German conurbations, about 50% of all children come from multilingual families who have either immigrated only recently or grown up as part of an immigrant family throughout the generations. This high percentage of children have not only got an immigrant background but are also brought up in families practising a mother tongue different to German and/or might be brought up under challenging socio-economic conditions.[3] Recently children's language skills have been a core issue in public and political discussion due to the Pisa results published in 2000, and a high immigration rate of immigration, especially in 2015 with the refugee influx.

The above-mentioned image of the child is closely linked to the idea of children's language acquisition. Successful language acquisition at early age is considered an indicator for future performance in school and both social and working life. Again, due to the children's way of learning, staff focus on stimulation rather than on learning objectives or vocabulary and grammar. The accepted method both for monolingual children with German as their mother-tongue or bi- or trilingual children, is language immersion. The linguistic accompaniment of everyday activities, which staff perform in a daily routine, should be emphasised at this point. Even during a walk to the bathroom, a teacher actively promotes language growth. For example, the child learns: sweaters, sleeves, upwind, water, faucet, warm, cold, wash hands, soap, towel, paper-towel, dry-off, trousers, skirt, zipper, button, close up, toilet paper, clean, rinse, tighten and get dressed. Through the repeated use of the same message and syntax, the child unconsciously learns the grammar and adapts pronunciation and prosody.

To enhance literacy education, story-telling and reading books in a cosy setting are recommended. Through this, children are encouraged to listen, to develop and design their own stories and are stimulated to expand their language skills. In order to provide all children with as many chances as possible, the so-called "Dialogisches Lesen" (dialogic reading) is recommended as a method. It is characterised by the teachers actively listening while looking at a picture book, a positive bonding and relationship and the possibility of the participation of all children on the basis of their welbeing. Their behaviour is characterised by open questions. To address children with German as a second language, bilingual books should be available, e.g. to support traumatised refugee children (e.g. Stein, 2017).

The last point shows that children might have special needs with regard to their physical or psychological development. To consider all children as part of a day-care community is anchored in the UN Convention on the Rights of the Child, as well as in the UN Convention on the Rights of Persons with Disabilities as well as in the Children's and in the German Youth Protection Act. With the entry into force of the UN Conventions in Germany, social participation of children with disabilities has entered a new development stage. With the ratification of the UN convention, Germany has committed itself to an inclusive education system at all levels. It can be assumed for the children's day-care centres that the idea of inclusion, in the sense of a comprehensive and self-determined participation, is no longer questioned in principle. It is no longer a question of whether inclusion in children's day-care facilities is useful, but rather the question of how inclusion in children's day-care facilities can be put into practice in the most productive way possible. Children's day-care centres, as part of an inclusive education system, and as required by the UN Convention, are faced with the task of understanding inclusion as supportive and appropriate for all children.

The recognition of heterogeneity seems to be challenging and staff in ECEC has to gain new elaborated skills to cope positively, rather than fostering prejudice and stereotypes. This is a big issue on political, educational and provision level in German ECEC. Though this is a global issue, it is it is somehow typical for Germany regarding the percentage of immigrant children in bigger cities. The UN convention calls for a change of perspectives from early education specialists in several ways. First of all, it is necessary for them to discuss and reflect their own perception of barriers, power balance and professional performance. The aim is to identify and overcome barriers and obstacles to the comprehensive participation of all children. With the demand for inclusive education, the UN Convention also places special emphasis on early education specialists on their own value system. One of the most important resources for inclusive education is seen in the attitude of the professionals to inclusion. Good structural conditions and stable support systems are also among the indispensable resources for the development of an inclusive education system at all levels. In this development dimension, early-education specialists will be given greater responsibility in the future cooperation with other specialists both on the internal as well as on the external level of the cooperation.

Assessment of a child's developmental progress

To ensure that no child is left behind, it is also important to examine the child's developmental progress, e.g. language skills, by appropriate and research based means that meet scientific criteria, since the mission of day-care provision is also a preventive one. Educational disadvantage, for example, lower language competency, should by all means be prevented. From the Bertelsmann Foundation and the Staatsinstitut für Frühpädagogik (State Institute of Early Childhood Research), KOMPIK was developed, which is available free of charge on the Internet and which maps all development areas of the child. It offers many advantages in terms of manageability in day-care centres. If, for example, a more detailed assessment seems to be required, it can be combined with other assessment tools. A huge variety of tools exist in Germany and some federal states recommend some of them. In 13 out of 16 federal states it is mandatory to carry out the monitoring, and in only three of them it is optional. From the results of the assessment, knowledge about developmental state of the art of the child can be gained and the next steps of professional intervention and stimulation can be planned. Thus, a quality circle of observation, planning, targeted developmental stimulation, re-assessment of the child's progress and further planning can be implemented. This ensures a reflected professional performance of staff in ECEC and is closely linked to the target of professional quality management in German ECEC.

Cooperation with parents and networking

Assessment results are a crucial part of talks with the parents to build up a partnership between professionals in a day-care centre and parents. They are considered experts for their own child and staff regularly meet with parents to build up a good relationship and report to the parents about their child. All day-care centres do have a parents' board elected by the parents themselves. They meet with the head of the day-care centre regularly.

In addition, some demands of children and their families may only be responded to by networking and external co-operation, e.g. psychologists or speech-thera-pists, because they are far beyond the scope of responsibility of a day-care cen-tre. At the level of networking with the environment, additional specialists are involved in the pedagogical work of the day-care centre. The construction of a regional network in the sense of a support system has proved to be helpful. Good children's day-care facilities have a wide range of relationships to the imme-diate environment, including social space orientation. In addition, the support of supervisors or specialist for family care and counselling, organizational and administrative social services and further programs, special educational institu-tions like social paediatric centres and primary schools have to be mentioned. All these institutions form a network and partnership to offer early intervention if needed.

ECEC in Germany: work in progress in a changing society and world

This article has provided a brief overview about German ECEC. As a conclusion it can be stated that the sector has shifted completely during the last 20 years towards a growing and very professional one. ECEC is now strongly is on the political agenda with a new focus where quality matters. Though quality as a whole has increased, Germany as a country still has to rethink ECEC in terms of:

- steering, because the diversity caused by the responsibility of the federal states does not allow any obligatory national quality standards both for day-care provision and education of professionals,
- education of staff, because society changes, ECEC is no longer just care but also education and so far only a small percentage is educated on BA- or MA- level,
- the actual child-staff ratio, which is not good enough to ensure quality in ECEC and to respond to the demands of children,
- monitoring of children's developmental and learning progress to stimulate the child professionally, to report properly to the parents and to build a good partnership as well as to monitor staff performance,
- access to day-care in *all* regions – rural areas and big cities – and for all chil-dren, including refugees.

This leads to the conclusion that Germany, as a wealthy country, has to con-sider an increase in spending of GNP on ECEC as an investment in the future to address the challenges mentioned above.

Notes

1 Some exception might exist, e.g. in Reggio day-care centres.
2 Therefore in the following text only the phrase *day-care centre* will be used, which in this sense does not include day care for children after enrolment at school.
3 This does not mean that all children with immigrant background live under these condition or have problems in learning German. Yet the number of good and excellent performers, though it is increasing, still has to be higher, because it is still underscores that of native German children.

References

Arbeitsgemeinschaft für Kinder- und Jugendhilfe (Ed.). (2006). *Auswirkungen der Föderalismusreform auf die Kinder- und Jugendhilfe*. Berlin, Germany.
Berger, M. (n.d.). *Friedrich Fröbel – Sein Lebensweg und sein erzieherisches Wirken*. Retrieved from www.kindergartenpaedagogik.de/131.html
Bertelsmannstiftung (Ed.). (2015). *Ländermonitor Frühkindliche Bildungssysteme – Übersicht/Grafiken*. Retrieved from www.laendermonitor.de/uebersicht-grafiken/indikator-4a-bildungsbeteiligung-von-kindern-in-kindertagesbetreuung/indikator/4/indcat/15/indsubcat/40/index.nc.html
Bock-Famulla, Kathrin. Länderreport Frühkindliche Bildungssysteme. (2015). *Transparenz schaffen – Governance stärken*. Gütersloh: Bertelman Stiftung.
Clarke-Stewart, K., Vandell, D., Burchinal, M., O'Brien, M., & McCartney, K. (2002). Do regular features of child-care homes affect children's development? *Early Childhood Research Quarterly, 17*(1), 52–86.
CoRe. (2009). *Competence requirements in early childhood education and care* (Public open tender EAC 14/2009). Issued by the European Commission Directorate-General for Education and Culture. Research Documents. Retrieved from https://download.ei-ie.org/Docs/WebDepot/CoReResearchDocuments2011.pdf
Deutscher Bildungsserver. (n.d.). Bildungspläne der Länder (n.d.). Retrieved from www.bildungsserver.de/Bildungsplaene-der-Bundeslaender-fuer-die-fruehe-Bildung-in-Kindertageseinrichtungen-2027.html
Diller, A., Jurczyk, K., & Rauschenbach, T. (2005). *Tagespflege zwischen Markt und Familie. Neue Herausforderungen und Perspektiven*, DJI-Fachforum Bildung und Erziehung (2), München, Germany.
Early, D., Maxwell, K., Burchinal, M., Bender, R., Ebanks, C., Henry, G., et al. (2007). Teachers' education, classroom quality, and young children's academic skills: results from seven studies of preschool programs. *Child Development, 78*(2), 558–580.
Fröbel, F. (n.d.) *Entwurf eines Planes zur Begründung und Ausführung eines Kindergartens*. Leipzig. Retrieved from https://books.google.de/books?id=SwUZB YgEJnMC&printsec=frontcover&dq=inauthor:%22Friedrich+Fr%C3%B6bel%22& hl=de&sa=X&ei=5YGOUe-dBePy4QTz0ICYCA&ved=0CDIQ6AEwAA#v=onepage&q&f=false
Fthenakis, W. E. (2006). *Der Bayerische Bildungs- und Erziehungsplan für Kinder in Tageseinrichtungen bis zur Einschulung*. Weinheim & Basel: Cornelsen.
Fthenakis, W. E. (2009). Bildung neu definieren und hohe Bildungsqualität von Anfang an sichern. Ein Plädoyer für die Stärkung von prozessualer Qualität, Teil 1. *BETRIFFT KINDER – Das Praxisjournal für ErzieherInnen, Eltern und*

GrundschullehrerInnen heute. Retrieved from www.fthenakis.de/cms/Betrifft-Kinder_01-09.pdf

Fukkink, R. G., & Lont, A. (2007). Does training matter? A meta-analysis and review of caregiver training studies. [Review]. *Early Childhood Research Quarterly, 22*(3), 294–311.

Gesetz zur Weiterentwicklung der Kinder- und Jugendhilfe (Kinder- und Jugendhilfeweiterentwicklungsgesetz – KICK). (2005). Retrieved from www.bgbl.de/xaver/bgbl/start.xav?startbk=Bundesanzeiger_BGBl&jumpTo=bgbl105s2729.pdf

Montessori, M. (1969). *Die Entdeckung des Kindes*. Freiburg, Germany.

Nagel, B. (2000). Der Erzieherberuf in seiner historischen Entwicklung. In *Bildung, Erziehung, Betreuung von Kindern in Bayern 2000*, Heft 1, S. 11–13. Retrieved from www.kindergartenpaedagogik.de/95.html

OECD. (2006). *Starting strong II: Early childhood education and care*. Paris, France: OECD Publishing.

Pramling, I., & Asplund Carlsson, M. (2008). The playing learning child: Towards a pedagogy of early childhood. *Scandinavian Journal of Educational Research, 52*(6), 623–641.

Schäfer, G. E. (2011). *Was ist frühkindliche Bildung?* München/Weinheim, Germany

Sozialgesetzbuch (SGB) – Achtes Buch (VIII) – Kinder- und Jugendhilfe – (Artikel 1 des Gesetzes v. 26. Juni 1990, BGBl. I S. 1163) Retrieved June 10, 2017, from www.gesetze-im-internet.de/sgb_8/index.html

Staatsinstitut für Frühpädagogik (IFP). (2008). *Jahresbericht*. Retrieved from www.ifp.bayern.de/imperia/md/content/stmas/ifp/jahresbericht_2008.pdf

Staatsinstitut für Frühpädagogik (n.d.). *KOMPIK*. Retrieved from www.kompik.de/kompik.html

Stein, S. (2017). *Das Kind und seine Befreiung vom Schatten der großen, großen Angst*. Retrieved from www.susannestein.de/VIA-online/traumabilderbuch

Sylva, K., Melhuish, E.C., Sammons, P., Siraj-Blatchford, I. and Taggart, B. (2004). *The Effective Provision of Pre-School Education (EPPE) Project: Technical Paper 12 –The Final Report: Effective Pre-School Education*. London: DfES / Institute of Education, University of London.

Tietze, W., & Viernickel, S. (Ed.). (2016). *Pädagogische Qualität in Tageseinrichtungen für Kinder. Ein Nationaler Kriterienkatalog. Pädagogische Qualität in Tageseinrichtungen für Kinder*. Weimar/Berlin: Verlag das Netz.

Viernickel, S., Fuchs-Rechlin, K., Strehmel, P., Preissing, C., Bensel, J., & Haug-Schnabel, G. (2015). *Qualität für alle. Wissenschaftlich begründete Standards für die Kindertagesbetreuung*. Freiburg: Herder.

9 Early childhood education and care in Greece

Looking back and moving forward

Maria Birbili and Ifigenia Christodoulou

Introduction

Georgeson, Payler and Cambell-Barr (2013, p. 3) argue that early years settings hold "important and revealing positions" in society. They are as Tobin, Hsueh andd Karasawa (2011, p. 2) explain, "sites where a variety of domains, interests, and social actors interact".

Early childhood provision in Greece may not have the long and rich history of other European early education systems, but it presents an interesting case example of the challenges involved in developing early childhood care and education services that meet European requirements, while responding to the needs and current circumstances of the Greek society.

Greek early childhood education and care: the European influence

The people who set up the first 'schooling establishments' in Greece came mainly from Europe or had the so-called 'European education' (Charitos, 1998). In 1831, not long after the liberation from the Turkish occupation, the German August Frederic Hildner, sent by the Church Missionary Society, established the first 'school' for children 2 to 6 years old (nipiako scholio) on the island of Syros (Charitos, 1998). Hildner was one of the many missionaries who came to Greece to assist the newly established state to build an educational system. In his school, following the teaching methods used in English and American kindergartens of the time, children learned "holy history, various [learning] subjects, elements of Geography and handiwork" (Charitos, 1998, p. 89).

In the same year (1831), the American missionary John Hill and his wife Francis established the first school for girls in Athens, which included children 2 to 8 years of age. In the history of Greek early childhood education, the Hills are considered those who first introduced the idea of systematic and organised pre-school education (Charitos, 1998). According to Hill, his school did not differ from primary school as they shared the goals of learning "the elementary knowledge (the alphabet, spelling, writing and arithmetic)" and "cultivating children's religious sentiment" (Charitos, 1998, p. 93). The children were also exposed to 'school discipline'. Both establishments also served as teacher training institutions for Greece's first female preschool and primary teachers.

As more educated people were inspired by the success of the first preschool institutions in Athens, more private 'nipiagogia' (kindergartens) began to 'pop up' around the country – typically in large urban centres (Doliopoulou, 2006). Their primary goal was to prepare young children for primary school, borrowing from pedagogical trends that flourished in Europe at the time, like the ideas of the French pedagogue Mari Pape-Carpentier and Friedrich Froebel from Germany. Overall, however, preschool institutions during the 19th century remained relatively few and available primarily to citizens of a high social class. It was not until 1929 that the state recognised that 'nipiagogia' were important for "the whole Greek state and all the social classes, especially the low ones (working class)" (Charitos, 1998, p. 219). A law that was passed that year which integrated 'nipiagogia' into primary education, making them accessible to all children for two years. Their purpose was stated, for the first time, as follows: "to help children's physical and intellectual development through simple and enjoyable activities and exercises in order to prepare them for primary school" (Charitos, 1998, p. 222).

The Greek kindergarten was perceived as a preparatory stage for primary school from its establishment until 1980, when the third official preschool curriculum was introduced. Until that time, kindergartens' daily programs were full of "exercises" and followed the "general principles" of primary school curricula (Kitsaras, 2004, p. 42). The 1980 curriculum, keeping up with developments in the field of psychology, described the young child as an "independent, distinctive and dynamic [human] being" and defined the purpose of kindergarten as "fostering the physical, emotional and intellectual health of the young child" (Kitsaras, 2004, p. 46). Despite the criticism that it has received, it remains the first curriculum that tried to put the child at the centre of the educational process.

The first childcare centre was founded in 1901 in Athens by a philanthropic organization. Like kindergartens, the first childcare centres owe their existence to private initiatives, mainly charities and philanthropists. Unlike kindergartens, however, childcare centres were generally associated with low-income working families and as the 'names' they were given suggest, "children's nest', "children's roof", "asylum for children", their mission was primarily to protect/take care of poor children while their mothers were at work, and only secondarily to 'educate' them (Charitos, 1998, p. 238).

The institution of childcare centres was first acknowledged by the Greek state in 1926, an act that lead to the establishment of a small number of "trial national childcare centers" (Charitos, 1998, p. 238). In 1935, another law defined their purpose as "the daily care and education of impoverished minors" and their operation as 'philanthropic institutions" (Charitos, 1998, p. 239). As welfare institutions, childcare centres were put under the auspices of the Department of Child Protection at the Ministry of Health and Social Welfare and remained there until 2001 when their responsibility was transferred to local authorities (and their supervision to the Ministry of Interior), following the European Union's directive to decentralise the education system.

The first 'daily program' for national childcare centres was introduced in 1937. In 1977, the Ministry of Health and Social Welfare issued an Operation Regulation (or else Operating Rules), a document that, among other things, defined the scope of childcare centres and described "children's daily occupation". The Operation Regulation still exists today, with amendments in 1988 and 2002. Changes in its content show that the purpose of childcare centres has moved from being children's "habitation, discipline and recreation" (in 1977) and children's "daily nutrition, discipline and recreation" (in 1988) to being "primarily a place for education and a safe place for children of preschool age" (FEK, 2002, p. 6665).

As this brief historical account shows, for many years, the Greek state was just 'watching' the efforts of individuals and associations to take care and educate young children. Unable to support it financially and having other priorities (wars, the refugees from Minor Asia etc.), it put early childhood provision in its agenda rather late and in a piecemeal way. It also becomes evident that early childhood provision in Greece developed along two tracks: care and education.

Types and structure of early childhood services

Today, formal early childhood education and care (ECEC) in Greece is still provided in separate settings: kindergartens and infant/childcare centres. The two types of institutions are typical of the split management approach to early childhood education where funding, regulation and governance are divided between different authorities. *Kindergartens (nipiagogia)* provide education for children 4 to 6 years. Since 2006, attendance has become compulsory for children 5 to 6 years old (children who on the 31st of December of the enrolment year have reached the age of 5 years).

Kindergartens, both in the private and the public sector, are supervised and regulated by the Ministry of Education, Research and Religious Affairs (MoE). Public kindergartens include 'experimental kindergartens' (which are monitored by a scientific committee) and kindergartens for children with special education needs which follow a 'Special Education Curriculum framework'. Public kindergartens are free of charge, but often parents are asked, unofficially, to contribute to the cost of educational supplies.

Until very recently, public kindergartens were divided into half-day and full-day programs, which operated from 8 am to 1 pm and 8 am to 4 pm respectively. Since August 2016, there is a 'single type of full-day kindergarten' with a compulsory and an optional program. The compulsory program starts at 8.30 am and finishes at 1 pm, while the optional program ends at 4 pm. There are also kindergartens, which operate in the afternoon from 2 pm to 6 pm.

All kindergartens, public and private, follow a national preschool curriculum developed by an advisory body to the MoE (the former Pedagogical Institution and current Institute of Educational Policy). The current curriculum (*Cross-thematic Curriculum Framework – DEPPS*) was implemented in 2002 (14 years after the previous one) and introduced early childhood educators to concepts and practices, such as the cross-thematic approach to learning, the project approach and the use of portfolio for assessing children's learning. According to it, the purpose of kindergarten is "to help children develop physically, emotionally, mentally and socially within the context of the overall goals of primary and secondary education" (MoE, 2002, p. 586). The learning outcomes and the curriculum content are organised around five learning areas: language, mathematics, human and physical environment, creation and expression (includes physical education) and computer science. As is the standard practice in the Greek education system, the curriculum is accompanied by an educator guide. The Greek preschool curriculum is described as "an organised system of work which prescribes what children should/ought to learn [. . .] and what the educator should/ought to do" (MoE, 2002, p. 586). Although this is perceived by the educators as "open and flexible enough to be adapted to the children's needs and interests and the teachers' work contexts" (Sofou & Tsafos, 2009, p. 419).

Kindergarten educators are graduates of a four-year degree offered in one of the nine university departments of early childhood education in the country (Petrogiannis, 2013). Each department has its own program of studies depending on the expertise and research interests of its academic staff. Since 1994, to be employed in a public kindergarten, graduate teachers have to go through a national competition organised by an independent board (accountable to the Greek Parliament and not to the Ministry of Education), the Supreme Council for Civil Personnel Selection (ASEP).

Childcare centres accept children from 6 months (or two months for the private sector centres) to 6 years of age. More specifically, centres with infants and toddlers (Vrefikos Stathmos) provide principally nursery care and education services for children from 6 months up to two and a half years. 'Child centres' (Pedikos Stathmos) are a similar form of care for children aged from 2 and a half years to 6 years old (Petrogiannis, 2013). Until 2001, public childcare settings were under the auspices of the Ministry of Health and Social Welfare. Since then, they are run, funded and supervised by the local authorities (municipalities) with the support of the Ministry of Interior. Private centres are still supervised (and licenced) by the Ministry of Health and Social Welfare.

Families have access to public childcare settings from 7.00 a.m. to 16.00 p.m., five days a week. They are open to all children, irrespective of their socio-economic background, but the law stipulates that children with working parents, families with low economic resources and children who need care because of various 'social causes' (orphans, single-parent families, parents with disabilities etc.) have priority. Public childcare settings are funded by local authorities but, depending on their income, some parents must pay an additional fee on a monthly basis.

There is no national curriculum for children attending childcare settings. In the academic year 2008–2009, the Ministry of Interior appointed a team of experts from National and Kapodistrian University of Athens to develop a "pedagogical-educational" program for public childcare settings. The proposed program was an adaptation of the "official pedagogical program" of the city of Berlin, Germany, for children 0–6 years (Varnava-Skoura, 2009). Although the program was successfully piloted in a small number of childcare centres, it was never adopted nationally due to the reaction of interest groups who resented the fact that they were not consulted. There is, however, as mentioned earlier in the chapter, an Operation Regulation which defines "the broad goals" of the centres (e.g. to "provide a unified preschool education, according to the most current scientific evidence", "help children develop holistically", "eliminate, as much as possible, the differences that may exist among children due to the cultural, economic and educational level of parents") and suggests "a flexible daily program of creative engagement that secures a harmonious psychosomatic development" (FEK, 2002, pp. 6665). The absence of a curriculum for childcare settings has been identified "by many as a major concern" and an indication of the status that childcare has in the Greek education system (Evangelou & Cortessis – Dafermou, 2005, p. 123).

Childcare centres' staff is often a mixture of people with different levels of qualification and from different disciplines: social workers, nurses, kindergarten educators, nursery assistants and childcare workers (pedagogues). The latter graduate from the Technological Educational Institutions, (TEIs) (Departments of Early Childhood Education) after 3.5 years of study and 6 months of practicum. Nursery assistants usually hold a post-secondary education college diploma following a two-year training course (Petrogiannis, 2013). The law allows local authorities to hire educators who are secondary education graduates if there is a scarcity of educators with higher education degrees (European Commission's Expert Group on Gender and Employment Issues, 2009).

Alternative types of childcare

Centre-based provision is the main type of childcare arrangement in Greece. Efforts to introduce alternative types of childcare, like child-minding, (piloted in the 1990s with European Union funding) were both ignored by policy makers and opposed by early childhood educators' unions on the grounds that the State would not be able to regulate and supervise properly the child-minders.

This lack of variety in childcare provision is also due to a tradition of "strong family ties and a high reliance on the extended family for supporting childcare needs", a tradition that is shared by the Mediterranean countries (Petrogiannis, 2013, p. 2). As Petrogiannis (2013) puts it,

> four decades ago it would have been inconceivable for a Greek mother to leave her child in someone else's care. Children's needs would have been met by a close relative or neighbour [. . .] This has always been a core component of the Greek social structure and a characteristic feature of the family care regime (or "familism") prevailing in this country.
>
> (p. 2)

Although childcare centres have served working parents for many years now, interestingly, in-home care remains that most common form of childcare in

Greece (European Commission's Expert Group on Gender and Employment Issues, 2009; Petrogiannis, 2013). As a recent statistical report prepared for the European Union points out, with the exception of Romania, nearly 60% of Greek children are being cared for a substantial amount of time by grandparents, relatives, friends, neighbours and other household members, the so-called 'kin network' (Mills et al., 2014). This type of informal care seems to be the preferred option for parents with children under 3 (Melhuish, 2016). As children get older, they are more likely to find themselves in formal care in the morning and with a grandparent or a young student teacher working as a nanny in the afternoon, until their parents return from work. These observations have led Mills et al. (2014, p. 36) to include Greece in the group of countries which are "falling behind by neither meeting nor coming close" to meeting the Barcelona targets.

Greek early childhood education and care: a case example of a split system

Bennett (2011) argues that a country's approach to early childhood education governance "says much about how early childhood is understood in a country and the relative value given by governments to policy-making, funding and regulation in this field" (p. 1).

Greek early childhood care and education provision has most of the characteristics that Bennett (2011, p. 2) describes as "the consequences of split system governance". Similar to other European countries that operate a split system of governance, the sector that suffers the most from the fragmentation of the early education system is childcare. As Bennett explains, the split between care and education usually weakens state investment and regulation for childcare. This means that the quality of the learning environment in childcare services and the work conditions for staff are often poor. In the last 10 years, Greek research indicates that public childcare services 'suffer' in critical areas such as regulation, funding, adult-child ratio, workforce and curriculum (Petrogiannis, 2013; Rentzou, 2010; Rentzou, 2015).

Kaga, Bennett and Moss (2010) add that the split between care and education also weakens the value of care while overemphasizing the value of education. When childcare as a service and a profession is devalued, then not only will governments spend less money on it, but also less people will choose it as a profession and will devote time and energy to their professional development. Overemphasizing education of young children, on the other hand, often encourages a "junior school" or "schoolification" approach to early childhood education (Bennett, 2011, p. 3; Moss, 2011). Research conducted in kindergarten settings confirms that Greek children spend little time in play (Rentzou, 2015) and that teachers follow a predetermined curriculum (Kakana & Mavidou, 2015). Studies also show that there is an overreliance on closed-ended worksheets, especially in the context of language and mathematics, and that interaction between teachers and children is very often based on closed-ended questions that aim to check children's knowledge (Birbili, 2013).

Lack of coherence between care and education provision also creates discontinuities for children and their families (Moss, 2011). If a Greek child enters the early education system, for example, at the age of 2, they will experience at least two transitions between institutions with different aims, programs and learning environments, until they enter primary school (a third transition).

"Falling behind . . ."

There is international consensus that Greece has much work to do to meet the established targets for ECEC (Eurydice, 2014; Mills et al., 2014; Organisation for Economic Cooperation and Development [OECD], 2011). Four recurring themes – challenges emerge in monitoring and evaluation reports: the centralisation of education policy, the absence of an evaluation culture, the lack of information on the quality of early childhood education and care and a cultural commitment to education that overshadows childcare provision. We discuss these in turn.

1. A highly centralised education system with a top down approach to policy and decision making that goes back to the Bavarian Monarchy in 1832. The 2011 OECD report "Education Policy Advice for Greece" states that "Greece remains one of the most centrally governed education systems in Europe" (p. 14)

Four years later, in another report, the European Union (2015) gives the following example to illustrate the degree to which centralisation of decision-making affects education in Greece:

> While in most European countries teachers in primary education can act relatively autonomously in matters related to teaching, Greece is the only country where the relevant education authorities take decisions nearly on all matters relating to teaching, including the choice of teaching methods.
>
> (p. 5)

Perhaps the worst consequence of a centralised education system is that reforms usually do not survive changes in political leadership. A case example is the development of a new curriculum for kindergartens in 2011, as part of an intended comprehensive reform of compulsory education, that never reached classrooms due to change of government. As the 2011 OECD report suggests, based on lessons from other European countries, Greece needs to establish educational 'units' or 'entities" that have the legal status to carry through reforms and changes. At the same time, decentralised units need to assume their responsibilities and learn to coordinate their tasks. For example, local authorities have not yet (since 2001) set up an inspection mechanism for the childcare centres under their auspices (Petrogiannis, 2013).

2. Absence of a culture of evaluation. The OECD (2011) points out that "Greece faces a major challenge in developing a culture of evaluation, as external evaluations have historically been distrusted, particularly by the teaching profession" (p. 45).

In 2011, as a step towards developing a comprehensive evaluation policy framework, a "culture of evaluation" and a "culture of trust between the state, educators and society", the Ministry of Education and its advisory body (IEP) proposed a pilot project entitled "Evaluation of the Educational Work of Schools: The Process of Self-Evaluation" (Pasias, et al., 2012, p. 4). School units (including public kindergartens) were asked to submit at the end of the school year a report that assessed, among other things, the performance of the school as a whole and its success in achieving the educational goals set in the action plan. The report also included suggestions for improvement in the next school year. The project, which was funded by the European Structural Funds, was conducted for two years amidst protests by teachers' unions and opposing political parties and stopped when the funding ran out in 2013. In 2016, the European Union expressed its concern about the suspension of "the procedures for evaluating schools and teachers, given the positive influence that autonomy and accountability can have on education performance" (p. 5).

The discussion on evaluation opens up another topic: that of the available information on important components of educational performance (e.g. teaching staff, students, school characteristics, enrolment rates, expenditures etc.). Often, as reports on Greece indicate with an asterisk at the end of the page, data are not available. Lack of systematically collected data on schools, students and teachers has implications not only on the administration of the Greek education system but also on the effectiveness of changes and reforms. Ikonomidis (2010) gives the example of the institution of compulsory attendance in kindergarten, which was implemented without enough information on the current infrastructure. Lack of data also hinders cross-national work.

3. Poor regulation of quality in early education. Discussing the issue of quality in early childhood education and care, Petrogiannis (2013) points out that "despite the improvements that have been made in the last decade with the aid of European funds, in Greece "high quality' is a notion under question" (p. 4). He goes on to say:

> even the term quality is scarcely met in the relevant legislative texts. The preferred term is typically 'operational standards' and these are referred principally to premises, the staff employed, its tasks and qualifications, the child/staff ratio, conditions of hygiene, safety and feeding requirements.
>
> (p. 4)

The lack (or avoidance) of discussion about quality in ECEC (and therefore the silence around perceptions, responsibilities, expectations), combined with the absence of official evaluation procedures and inspection mechanisms (see previous point), has as a result given a very limited picture of the quality of early education provision in the country (Petrogiannis, 2013; Tsatsaroni, Vrettos, Kyridis, Katsis, & Linardos, 2011). Furthermore, the split system of governance, the confusion of responsibilities and the lack of cooperation between services "hinder any initiatives to capture a unified picture in Greek ECEC" (Grammatikopoulos, Gregoriadis, Tsigilis & Zachopoulou, 2017, p. 2).

What we know about the quality of Greek early education services comes from the work of individual researchers or university research teams. A case example, and probably the most recent study on the topic, is one conducted by Gregoriadis, Tsigilis, Grammatikopoulos and Kouli in 2016 with the support of the European Union Social Fund. The researchers evaluated the quality of 535 early childhood classrooms from kindergarten and childcare programs using the Early Childhood Environment Rating Scale-Revised edition (ECERS-R). Focusing on two specific aspects of ECEC process quality, 'Activities' and 'Program Structure', the researchers found "an overall picture of medium quality for these two subscales, a little below the good quality cut-off point as it is set by the developers of the scale" (Gregoriadis, Tsigilis, Grammatikopoulos, & Kouli, 2016, p. 1147). Older studies also show a "low to medium level of quality" in indicators like learning and teaching, style of care, building and equipment, educator-child ratios and family – school relationships (see Petrogiannis, 2013 and Rentzou, 2015).

4. A cultural commitment to education that overshadows childcare provision (OECD, 2011). While education is seen as a public good, childcare is still viewed as a family (or a local community) issue. As part of the public educational system, early childhood education has not only government support, subsidy and regulation but also a national curriculum which, in the Greek context, is an indication of the value attached to its role. Childcare provision, on the other hand, as a 'private' and temporary issue – as Shlay et al. (2002, p. 90) put it, "its salience ends when children enter school" – seems to be treated more as an economic issue than an educational one. Moreover, lack of a national curriculum does not help childcare services to escape their history as places that support working mothers.

At this point, it is worth noting that despite the importance Greek families place on their children's education, parents never acted as a pressure group for higher quality early childhood education. This may suggest that although early childhood education is considered to have higher status than childcare, it is always one step behind from primary education, the 'real' education.

Looking into the future . . .

In the current economic crisis, with the percentage of extreme poverty standing at around 15%, (Georgakopoulos, 2016) and a constant flux of immigrants, Greek early childhood education and care services are facing both old and new challenges. For example, the demographic changes are putting pressure on Greek early childhood settings to function as sites of both continuity and change (Tobin, Hsueh & Karasawa, 2011).

From the EU Member State with the least developed formal childcare system in 1997, Greece has gone a long way on the path of change (Petrogiannis, 2013). However, like in other countries, reforms in early education have to deal with what Willekens, Scheiwe and Nawrotzki (2015, p. 13) call "vested interests and crystallised ways of doing things". The division between early childhood education and care may have its roots in the history of Greek education system but it is also a reflection of the policies that the state has adopted – or not – for early education. Since their transfer to local authorities, childcare services stopped being the concern of policy makers at the government level. Changes and reforms are mostly geared towards early childhood education and more specifically to kindergartens, thus solidifying their role in the education system. Local authorities on the other hand, with notable exceptions (e.g. the Municipality of Athens), find it hard to introduce changes to childcare centres as they struggle with limited funding from the Ministry of Interior and their own problems. As the political climate does not change for childcare, childcare workers feel that they constantly have to defend their role in young children's lives and education.

Before the economic crisis, the tension between the two sectors seemed to be mostly about pedagogical issues (e.g. which institution serves best the needs of 4 and 5 years old, when education begins and care stops etc.). During the economic crisis, the tension revolves mainly, albeit covertly, around employment opportunities (who is going to work with the 4 and 5 years old?). As kindergartens are closing down, due to the state's efforts to rationalise the public sector, both kindergarten educators and childcare workers feel threatened and insecure. The tension intensified when attendance to kindergarten became compulsory for 5 year olds and suggestions about lowering even more compulsory attendance age began to circulate.

Despite the picture painted above, there are indicators of a growing social awareness that things need to change deeply and fast. Although the European Union is an important force pressing for change, real change can only come from within the country. There are significant steps being made by university departments of Early Childhood Education and non-profit organizations (e.g. the Society for the Development and Creative Occupation of Children – EADAP), in collaboration with educators in both sectors. A discussion that began recently between academic staff and representatives of childcare workers shows that both sides are open to changes, provided that the state is willing to initiate a genuine dialogue with all stakeholders and takes into consideration that integration is a multilevel effort.

Universities also influence the quality of early childhood provision through professional training, research collaborations with early childhood professionals and participation in advisory committees and bodies attached to the Ministry of Education. Research collaborations in particular, help practitioners transform ideas and practices borrowed from abroad into practices that fit well in the Greek cultural context. In Greece, where 'educational borrowing' is very common university researchers can help early childhood professionals reflect on what is unique to the Greek context and worth keeping and what needs changing in order to meet the needs of the next generation of Greek citizens.

Although university departments cannot work miracles, international experience shows that they can, through "sound and persuasive" research, influence policy development on early years education (Taggart, Siraj-Blatchford, Sylva, Melhuish, Sammons, 2008, p. 17). In Greece, however, where policymaking is slow moving, universities and practitioners together may be able to achieve conceptual integration of ECEC sooner than structural integration.

References

Bennett, J. (2011). Early childhood education and care systems: Issue of tradition and governance. In *Encyclopedia on early childhood development*. Retrieved from www.child-encyclopedia.com/sites/default/files/textes-experts/en/857/early-childhood-education-and-care-systems-issue-of-tradition-and-governance.pdf

Birbili, M. (2013). Developing young children's thinking skills in Greek early childhood classrooms: curriculum and practice. *Early Child Development and Care, 183*, 1101–1114. http://dx.doi.org/10.1080/03004430.2013.772990

Charitos, X. G. (1998). *To Elliniko nipiagogio ke i rizes tou. Simvoli stin istoria tis proscholikis agogis* (The Greek kindergarten and its roots. Contribution to the history of preschool education). Athens: Gutenberg.

Doliopoulou, E. (2006). *System of early education/care and professionalization in Greece*. Commissioned report by the State Institute of Early Childhood Research (IFP), Munich, Germany. Retrieved from www.ifp.bayern.de/imperia/md/content/stmas/ifp/commissioned_report_greece.pdf

Eurydice. (2014). Eurydice policy brief. *Early Childhood Education and Care*. Retrieved from http://eacea.ec.europa.eu/education/eurydice/documents/thematic_reports/Eurydice_Policy_Brief_ECEC_EN.pdf

European Commission's Expert Group on Gender and Employment Issues (EGGE). (2009). *The provision of childcare services. A comparative review of 30 European countries*. Retrieved from www.fruehe-chancen.de/fileadmin/PDF/Archiv/the_provision_childcare_services.pdf

European Union. (2015). *Education and training monitor 2015 – Greece*. Retrieved from http://ec.europa.eu/dgs/education_culture/repository/education/tools/docs/2015/monitor2015-greece_en.pdf

Evangelou, D., & Cortessis – Dafermou, H. (2005). Contemporary perspectives in early childhood education. The case of Greece. In O. Saracho & B. Spodek (Eds.), *International perspectives on research in early childhood education* (pp. 119–136). Greenwich, CT: Information Age Publishing.

FEK (2002). *Protipos kanonismos litourgias dimotikon ke kinotikon nomikon prosopon dimosiou dikeou pedikon ke vrefikon stathmon* (Operation Regulation of public and community child- and infant care centres) (FEK B' 497/22.4.2002). Athens: Ministry of Public Administration.

Georgakopoulos, T. (2016). *Extreme poverty in Greece*. Retrieved from www.dianeosis.org/en/2016/06/extreme-poverty-greece-survey/

Georgeson, J., Payler, J., & Cambell-Barr, V. (2013). The importance of international perspectives. In J. Georgeson & J. Payler (Eds.), *International perspectives on early childhood education and care* (pp. 3–8). Berkshire, England: Open University Press.

Grammatikopoulos, V., Gregoriadis, A., Tsigilis, N., & Zachopoulou, E. (2017). Evaluating quality in early childhood education in relation with children outcomes in Greek context. *Early Child Development and Care*, 1–10. doi:10.1080/03004430.2017.1289192

Gregoriadis, A., Tsigilis, N., Grammatikopoulos, V., & Kouli, O. (2016). Comparing quality of childcare and kindergarten centres: the need for a strong and equal partnership in the Greek early childhood education system. *Early Child Development and Care, 186*(7), 1142–1151. doi:10.1080/03004430.2015.1077820

Ikonomidis, V. D. (2010). I thespisi tis ipochreotikis proscholikis ekpedefsis stin Ellada (The institution of compulsory preschool education in Greece). In I. E.

Pirgiotakis & V. D. Ikonomidis (Eds.), *Peri Pedias Dialogos* (Dialogue on Education) (pp. 99–113). Rethimno, Greece: University of Crete.

Kaga, Y., Bennett, J., & Moss, P. (2010). *Caring and learning together: A cross-national study on the integration of early childhood care and education within education.* Paris, France: UNESCO. Retrieved from www.lefuret.org/projets/outils/VIII1UNESCO2010.pdf

Kakana, D. M., & Mavidou, A. (2015). Myth and antinomy in early childhood education: Formal vs. applied curricula and professional development. *US-China Education Review B, 5*(12), 780–793. doi:10.17265/2161–6248

Kitsaras, G. D. (2004). *Programmata. Didaktiki methodologia proscholikis agogis* (Curricula. Teaching methodology in preschool education). Athens: Kitsaras.

Melhuish, E. (2016). *Provision of quality early childcare services: Synthesis report.* Retrieved from http://eprints.bbk.ac.uk/16446/

Mills, M., Präg, P., Tsang, F., Begall, K., Derbyshire, J., Kohle, L., Miani, C., & Hoorens, S. (2014). *Use of childcare services in the EU Member States and progress towards the Barcelona targets.* Retrieved from http://ec.europa.eu/justice/gender-equality/files/documents/140502_gender_equality_workforce_ssr1_en.pdf

Ministry of Education, Research and Religious Affairs (MOE). (2002). *Cross-thematic curriculum framework – DEPPS.* Athens: Pedagogical Institute.

Moss, P. (2011). *Introducing continuity and equality into a "split" system of early child education and care: An international perspective* [Power Point slides]. Retrieved from http://drees.social-sante.gouv.fr/IMG/pdf/PPT_Moss_P_14-09-11.pdf

OECD. (2011). *Education policy advice for Greece, strong performers and successful reformers in education.* Retrieved from http://dx.doi.org/10.1787/9789264119581-en

Pasias, G., Lamnias, K., Mattheou, D., Dimopoulos, K., Papachristos, K., & Merkouris, S. (2012). *I afto-axiologisi se mia matia* (Self-evaluation in one look). Retrieved from http://aee.iep.edu.gr/sites/default/files/iep_files/AEE μια ματιά/H AEE μια ματιά_τελικό.pdf

Petrogiannis, K. (2013). Early childhood education and care in Greece: In search of an identity. *Nordic Early Childhood Education Research, 6*(29), 1–9.

Rentzou, K. (2010). Using the ACEI global guidelines assessment to evaluate the quality of early childcare in Greek settings. *Early Childhood Education Journal, 38*(1), 75–80.

Rentzou, K. (2015). Reflections on the quality of the dichotomous early childhood education and care system in Greece. *Childhood Education, 91*(4), 250–258.

Shlay, A. B., Jaeger, E., Weinraub, M. Murphy, P., Shaw, K., & Gottesman, L. (2002). *Making a case for childcare: An evaluation of a Pennsylvania-based based intervention called childcare matters.* Retrieved from http://williampennfoundation.org/sites/default/files/reports/child%20care%20matters%20eval.pdf

Sofou, E., & Tsafos, V. (2009). Preschool teachers' understandings of the national preschool curriculum in Greece. *Early Childhood Education Journal, 37*(5), 411–420.

Taggart, B., Siraj-Blatchford, I., Sylva, K., Melhuish, E., & Sammons, P. (2008). Influencing policy and practice through research on early childhood education. *International Journal of Early Childhood Research, 14*(2), 7–21.

Tobin, J., Hsueh, Y., & Karasawa, M. (2011). *Preschool in three cultures revisited: China, Japan, and the United States.* Chicago, IL: University of Chicago Press.

Tsatsaroni, A., Vrettos, I., Kyridis, A., Katsis, A., & Linardos, P. (2011). *OECD project. Overcoming school failure. Policies that work. Country background report.* Athens: Ministry of Education, Life Long Learning and Religious Affairs.

Varnava-Skoura, T. (2009). *Programma gia tin kaliergia, tin agogi ke ti frontida pedion proscholikis ilikias* (Program for the development, the education and the care of preschool age children). Retrieved from www.ppps.ecd.uoa.gr/

Willekens, H., Scheiwe, K., & Nawrotzki, K. (2015). Introduction: The longue durée – Early childhood institutions and ideas in flux. In H. Willekens, K. Scheiwe, & K. Nawrotzki (Eds.), *The development of early childhood education in Europe and North America. Historical and comparative perspectives*. New York: Palgrave Macmillan.

10 Early childhood education and care in Iceland

The origin, influences, curriculum reforms and possible paths

Kristín Dýrfjörð

Introduction

Iceland is one of the lesser-known Nordic countries. It shares many similarities with its fellow Nordic countries, but the most striking one is the importance it bestows to its social welfare system. Education and children's right to preschool are an important part of these countries' shared roots and values. In Iceland, the concept of *playschool* is used in all official early childhood programs and pre-schools[1]. Notably, in the country, education in the early childhood system is not provided according to children's age, and the same laws and rules apply to all children under the age of six years.[2] This means, for example, that the same standards on teacher education and curriculum are used for all age groups under six. To understand Iceland and the Icelandic preschool system, we need to examine the society that shaped the system and, hence consider some key statistics.

Some facts about the Icelandic society

Iceland has a small population. As of the end of 2015, Iceland had a population of 332,529 people, and on the same year, a total of 4,129 living infants were born. The fertility rate in Iceland has been one of the highest in Europe but has been declining over the last few years; it was around 1.9 infant per woman in 2014 (Eurostat, 2017). According to the World Economic Forum's Global Gender Gap Report (2016), Iceland is ranked number one in their list as the country with the smallest gender gap, with the participation of women in the Icelandic labour market currently being one of the highest. Iceland's performance was based on its achievements in improving gender equality in the area of education, political participation and women's role in the labour force (Centre for Gender Equality Iceland, 2012). The participation in the labour market by both men and women has been at a high level in Iceland for most of the 20th century.

In 1970, women started entering the labour market at a greater rate, which translated into a greater need for preschools and childcare. Most municipalities with help from women groups responded to this need, but full coverage was not provided[3]. At the same time, the legal right for parents to return to their jobs after childbirth and a generous parental leave system were introduced, similar to the practice in other Nordic countries. At present, more and more women have a full-time job, and their level of education is increasing.

In 1993, 53% of women in the labour market had a full-time job. In 2008, 65% of working women had a full-time job, whereas 90% of men worked full-time. On average, the *rate of participation* among women in the workforce has been just under 80%, whereas among men, it is about 86% (Arnalds, Eydal, & Gíslason, 2013; Centre for Gender Equality Iceland, 2012). According to the then head of the organisation Business Iceland (BI) and now the current Minister of Welfare, Þorsteinn Víglundsson, the current living standards in Iceland are better because of the high participation of women in the workforce. According to the BI, if women in Iceland followed the average participation in the labour market for women in the EU, a 15% – 20% decrease in the country's gross domestic product (GDP) and worse living conditions for the whole country would result (Auðunsdóttir, 2014).

BI is advocating for more childcare spaces for children starting at the age of nine months, rather than giving more parental leaves, which is society's clamour, because it believes that this will promote equal rights, strengthen the labour market, and increase the country's GDP (Samtök atvinnulífsins, 2017). As is evident, women are an essential part of the workforce, and they help improve living standards and foster the wellbeing of Icelanders. The labour market needs all able hands, and the realisation that women contribute to a productive economy may have led to the focus on childcare within the country. However, this realisation did not happen overnight; it had to be fought for. Examining the past, particularly the history and development of Iceland as a country and the nation is henceforth important to understand its preschool system. The next section discusses the historical roots of ECE in Iceland and how it headed towards urbanisation.

Historical roots of early childhood education in Iceland

The history of Icelandic early childhood education follows the same track as that in many other countries (Burman, 2016; Kamerman, 2000). With urbanisation at the beginning of the 20th century, new problems emerged, such as the neglect of children from poor families. Upper-class women, many of whom were connected to recently formed women groups at that time, promoted the idea of educational places that were focused on improving the lives of the poorest children and to promote the idea they established an organisation (Friðriksson, 1991; Guðmundsson, 1949). At that time, an Icelandic male primary schoolteacher was studying at Columbia University in New York under W. H. Kilkpatrick, a follower of John Dewey, and he was asked to lead new organisation (Arason, 1953; Guðmundsson, 1949). The first preschool built in Iceland, however, was based on a blueprint from the English McMillan sisters; it was an open-air nursery, involved play inside and outside, required participation in the daily caretaking of the school (Guðmundsson, 1949). The first preschool teachers in Iceland were educated in the 1930s in Denmark (at that time, Iceland was still a colony of Denmark and remained so until 1944) and in Sweden (Thorsteinsson, 2010).

> **Parental leave**. In 2000, the law regulating parental leave changed radically. Icelanders now have a parental leave scheme that can be considered unique. Parents' total leave period is nine months. Each parent is entitled to a three-month leave that is non-transferable. In addition, the parents can divide the three months as they like. According to statistics, fathers have used this opportunity, and around 90% use their paternal leave. Commonly, one of the parents stay at home with the child for over a year and receive a part of the salary.
>
> (Arnalds et al., 2013)

In Denmark, the pedagogues attended Froebel College, but in Sweden, the first preschool-teachers attended the then new and somewhat radical college that Alva Myrdal founded and directed; it was a college that was based on child developmental models and a strong sociologic view on the importance of preschools in society and of women's rights (Bremberg, 2009). In a way, Myrdal's ideas can be considered a counter-ideology to that of the Froebelians' middle-class ideology (Balke, 1990). Myrdal visited the US, where she became familiar with the progressive movement and Dewey's ideology. She promoted the active role of the state in early childhood education and in social welfare. Her ideas may be reasoned to have shaped the Nordic model of early childhood education, and are still strong and evident in the Swedish system. Alva Myrdal and her husband Gunnar proposed many ideas to improve the living standards in Sweden. For example, the idea that the government should treat the country as a home and, that the population should consider themselves as living in a common home is strongly connected to the Myrdals. They also believed that the parents should be offered paid parental leaves during their child's infancy, that day care and education should be available, that families receive financial support, and that universal child health services be offered (Burman, 2016). These ideals are a part of people's perceptions of the Nordic welfare system today and have become the shared roots of Nordic countries. The other shared Nordic values that remain strong within the Nordic preschool system are those of preschools being *loci of democracy*, the emphasis on outdoor education and the concept of free play, as well as the belief that children develop their abilities and democratic skills by belonging to a group and by playing with other children in what has been labelled as "free play" in the Nordic countries.

With independence, Icelanders wanted to be self-sufficient, both educationally and politically. Shortly after the country gained independence (1946), a special college for preschool teachers was established in Iceland, and the person who strongly influenced this decision and who worked on the blueprint for the new college was Alva Myrdal's former student, Þórhildur Ólafsdóttir (Guðmundsson, 1949). Chosen to lead the college was a young woman, Valborg Sigurðardóttir, educated at Smith's Colleges in the US. Her background in child psychology and child development made these areas integrated into the curriculum (Sigurðardóttir, 2010).

Geographically, Iceland is situated on the Mid-Atlantic ridge and uniquely occupies a part of the Eurasian plate and a part of the North American plate. Culturally, Iceland belongs to Europe. Historically, it has a strong relationship with Nordic countries (Iceland, Denmark, Sweden, Norway and Finland) and a shared value base with these countries, with emphasis on social welfare, gender equality and human rights. For the most part of the 20th century, however, Iceland also had a rather close relationship with the US and was influenced by events in the US. The pedagogical development in preschools is a proof of this. The three national curricula that have been published show that education in Iceland has its roots in Myrdal pedagogy and Myrdal's focus on the role of the social environment in the preschool, on the one hand, and in the Froebelian pedagogy and Froebel's emphasis on free play, on the other hand. At the same time, the US has influenced pedagogy in Iceland through the educational philosophy of John Dewey, the Progressive Movement, child development studies, the High Scope approach, Howard Gardner's intelligence theory, the Project Approach developed by Lillian Katz, and the methods developed from Vygotskian ideology in the US; in fact, many preschools refer to these on their websites as their main influence. Over the last decades, the influence of the philosophy of Loris Malaguzzi and the city of Reggio Emilia in Italy has also been evident, such as in the national curriculum and related documents in which pedagogical documentation (as well as learning stories) is recommended as a method to understand children's learning. Although, many of the founders of the preschool system were strongly influenced by Americans, an examination of the current and older national curricula shows that the Icelandic preschool model has a strong kinship to the Nordic models, in which play (outside and inside schools), social competency, the children's right to a good childhood, and the children's welfare are highly valued. As mentioned previously, preschools are called playschools in Iceland.

In the last part of this historical journey, understanding how preschool teachers' education has evolved is also essential. In the beginning, preschool teachers completed two years in the college run by the organisation that founded the first schools. This practice changed in 1968 when preschool teachers' two-year education became a three-year one, and in 1973, their college became a government college. In 1996, teachers' education became a university degree (B.Ed.) after a long fight led by the preschool teachers' union (Bjarnason, 2010), and since 2008, all new teachers in Iceland are required to have a master of education degree. This change has been controversial, especially as it led to fewer people applying for teacher education (Ríkisendurkoðun, 2017). Some politicians have openly discussed the need to revise this decision.

The preschool system: laws and the national curricula

The Icelandic early childhood education system is considered a high-quality one both in terms of the education, it provides and its affordability for families. Its coverage is almost 100%, so it includes all children. The concept of quality, however, is problematic, as it has many different meanings and is also contested by many (Moss, 2016). Nevertheless, a certain consensus exists among those who have developed the national curricula in other countries that quality education involves the recognition of the importance of child centredness; integration of learning, a holistic view of the child, and the importance of play; and social and emotional development, empowerment of the child to be an autonomous learner, and inclusiveness and equal opportunities (Bertram & Pascal, 2002, p. 35). All these concepts are at the core of the Icelandic national curriculum for preschools and are based on laws governing preschools. To understand how the preschool system has developed, let us examine the development of relevant laws and the national curriculum.

In 1976, Iceland had its first law called as Act of Law on Childcare concerning preschools, but it mainly focused on the building of schools and the cost associated with it, and less about the educational or pedagogical aspect. According to this law, the state was required to finance a part of the cost of building preschools. The preschool was considered an educational institution under the responsibility of the Ministry of Education. In 1985, Iceland developed its national curriculum for preschools. At the time, the concept of the curriculum was not yet used, and, instead, it was called "A Program for Upbringing in Day Care/Preschool Settings" (Icelandic Ministry of Education, 1985). This first formal national curriculum was both very normative and strongly connected to child developmental ideas from a physiological point of view. In the first part of the curriculum, a special chapter was devoted to Piaget and Erikson. Another characteristic of the curriculum at that time was that it was more like a manual than a policy plan.

The year 1991 was a historical year for the community of early childhood education in Iceland. During this year, new laws regarding the early childhood education system were passed in the Parliament after a long battle between groups that took different stands on the role of preschools and how the preschool system should be developed (Acts of Law on Preschool, 1991). Some members of the government wanted preschools to be a part of the social welfare system, with an emphasis on the preschools as a component of a wide social network directed at families, under the administration of social workers. Others wanted the preschool system to continue being a part of the education system, as it had been from the time of the first law on it; it should be, first and foremost, an educational institution based on the right of children to attend preschool, regardless of their parents' status. The proponent of this viewpoint was the preschool teachers' union, which organised public and private debates on this issue, as well as actively lobbied at the Parliament and within political parties (Jónsdóttir, 2010). The union was pushing for a preschool system that should be for all and that is based on the right to education of all children. The Preschool Act of 1991 is among the first in the world to define young children's right to education and a preschool place, regardless of their parents' status.

Just a few years later, the Parliament decided that the system should not only be based on the right of children but should also be defined as the first part of Iceland's formal school system. Preschool attendance should be every child's right, and municipalities should provide placement for all children. In reality, this is not the case, as complete coverage for all children aged between age 9 and 18 months has yet to be achieved (Act of Law on Preschool, 1994).

In connection to the then new bill, the next curriculum reform was carried out in 1997–1999, and the result was a new national curriculum. One of the main changes was how language was used in the new curriculum; it focused on the vocabulary used in primary schools, was based on individual children's rights, and, in retrospective, reeked of a neoliberal ideology.

However, an attempt was made to eradicate the normative language of the 1985 curriculum and make the psychological trends less prominent. Instead, concepts, such as curriculum and evaluation, emerged, as well as subject learning in the form of defined learning fields for preschools; this change led to schoolification in many preschools. Notably, although the ideology in the national curriculum changed and moved away from care toward education and individualisation, it was not as normative as the former was (Icelandic Ministry of Education, 1999). The dominance of child development in the field of early childhood education, however, has been so strong that more than one curriculum reform is needed to eradicate or decrease its influence substantially. From the beginning, a binary storyline within the Icelandic curriculum has existed – one connected to child development and another associated with children's right to free play. The legacy of the second curriculum is probably a vision indicating that each child is an able citizen who can and shall participate in shaping his or her own world.

In 2008, a new law for the entire Icelandic school system was passed by a right-wing government, and it included many changes that resonated with neoliberalism; among them was an emphasis on deregulation, auditing, school choices, and standardisation (Dýrfjörð, 2011a; Dýrfjörð & Magnúsdóttir, 2016). For example, regulations concerning child – teacher ratio and square meters per child were fully removed, although in practice, most municipalities still used the previous criteria. The new law enabled the government to revise simultaneously the national curricula for all school levels and use new neoliberal ideas, on which the law was based. The work on the new curriculum had just started when Iceland was severely hit by the financial crisis of 2008, leading to the collapse of the economy. The curriculum, which was in the making at that time, focused on measurement and goals, and it emphasised skills, unlike the case in the UK (Clausen, 2015). The curriculum was actually based on "policy borrowing" (Lingard, 2010). More or less, it would have been an experiment with a neoliberal school system (Dýrfjörð & Magnúsdóttir, 2016).

Shortly after the financial crisis, the political system crashed, and a new left-wing government was voted in. The financial and moral breakdown of the country in 2008 led many people and politicians to re- evaluate their value base and reconsider the market values that were the main driving force in Icelandic society prior to the financial crisis. A part of the re-evaluation of society was an investigative committee, set up by the Parliament, which researched what led to the crisis. The committee concluded, among other factors, that the school system failed in educating young people on the role of citizenship and critical thinking (Rannsóknarnefnd Alþingis, 2010). This finding found its way into the new curriculum by the left-wing government (Icelandic Ministry of Education, 2011). A part of the new curriculum reform for all school levels was to base the curriculum on the following six fundamental pillars: *democracy and human rights, sustainability, equality, literacy* (multimodal), *creativity* and *wellbeing and welfare*. The goal was for schools to make these values the foundation of their curriculum. Since the Enlightenment, education has been viewed as a possible agent of change, and this fundamental belief has persisted among left-wing politicians. With the financial crisis, these politicians were given another opportunity to redirect the system away from the neoliberal path. However, they may have won a small battle, but not the war. After four years in government, the left wing lost to the right wing, which just picked up where it left off (Dýrfjörð & Magnúsdóttir, 2016). As a result, schoolification is on the rise, attention has been focused on preschool children's *reading skills*, and *evidence-based* is the new buzzword. In preschools, many are worried that more and more municipalities are moving five-year-olds into primary schools, particularly separate classes for five-year-olds, to make space for children under 18 months in preschool.

According to the national curriculum, the concepts of upbringing, caring, and education are supposed to be integrated. Showing respect and concern to children, encouraging them, and giving them appropriate responsibilities are mandatory. They are considered legitimate participants and active citizens in the preschool community (Icelandic Ministry of Education, 2011). Some aspects of the new national curriculum stand out, such as the idea that all preschool activities should be integrated and that democracy and play are highly valued. The individualism that was so obvious in the curriculum from 1999 has mostly been eradicated. However, having a democratic curriculum in place is inadequate if, at the same time, the Ministry of Education and its institutions produce white papers that actually go against what is stated in the national curriculum (Dýrfjörð & Magnúsdóttir, 2016). At a teacher conference on the education of five-year-olds in April 2017, some primary schools with classrooms for five-year-olds gave examples of how they developed and organised their curriculum. Much focus was given to reading and preparing children for "real" school; preschools evidently encountered problems with integrating subjects and incorporating free play into classrooms, although all stated that the national curriculum was their guideline (RannUng, 2017). Another part of the same phenomena is a booklet published by the Directorate of Education and lists words and concepts that should be a part of all three- and five-year-olds' vocabulary (Pálsdóttir, 2017). The booklet is an indication of plans to transform the early childhood education system, and it even represents the first step toward a baby PISA and governmental standardised tests in Icelandic preschools.

Other positive signs on the horizon can be seen. In smaller municipalities around the country, the gap between parental leave and preschool is being closed; as of the end of March 2017, Reykjavík, the largest provider of preschool places in the country, is opening baby classrooms (crèche) in a few preschools next autumn, but it has decided not to send five-year-olds to primary schools to make space for younger children (The Icelandic social democratic party, 2017). These are baby steps, but they are all steps toward the right direction. What is perhaps most remarkable about this decision, which is unusual for Iceland, is that the country has a plan of action concerning both the financial and educational aspects of this expansion.

Possible stories

Hursh and Martina (2016) wrote about the rise of the neoliberal social imaginary, how we are lured to see the world from a certain perspective, and little by little, we cannot imagine it anymore in any other way. This new way becomes the way. A few years ago, I wrote an article (in Icelandic) about the dangers that preschools could be facing in their close encounters with primary schools – dangers that emerge when minor changes that we hardly notice take place, when concepts and vocabulary become the same, when children become students, when play becomes learning, and so on. In this chapter, the metaphor of the *black hole* in space was used, in which primary schools are the black hole with such a strong gravitational pull that they could easily swallow preschools and their uniqueness (Dýrfjörð, 2011b). This issue is worrisome, especially that just recently, the current (right-wing) Minister of Education discussed about the possibility of teachers moving between school levels, so this means that a preschool teacher can teach in primary schools and vice versa. Sweden adopted this practice but reversed it a few years later because the result was disastrous for preschools (Dahlberg, 2013). Between 1,200 and 1,500 preschool teachers are needed in Iceland over the next few years so that the law on preschools, which states that 2/3 of the staff working with children should be educated teachers, could be met (Ríkisendurkoðun, 2017). In the preschool sector, a key concern is that the movement of teachers between school levels will, in fact, be popular with preschool teachers and encourage their move to primary schools, among other because of the higher social status associated with teaching in primary schools. The value of preschools as an important part of the education system, as well as the professional status of preschool teachers, is therefore undermined.

Another possible and predictable storyline is that of the neoliberal with a focus on evidence-based-education, measurement, standardisation and the making of a commodity. This view considers education as a product that can be bought and sold in an open market, and that childcare (and preschool education) is neither a form of education nor care but is more of an industry for others to mine and inject with technical solutions and languages. This perspective is evident in many programs and kits, with promises of quick fixes (often as behavioural modification programs), sold to Icelandic preschools, and it is an idea that many preschools have bought into. Having such programs listed as a part of the curriculum has become a selling point for some preschools and has given them a competitive advantage in that they are in a better position to attract new parents and enrolees (Dýrfjörð & Magnúsdóttir, 2016).

The last storyline presented is slightly more positive, one in which preschool teachers actively participate in changing the world. Concepts, such as criticality, agency, feminism, sustainability, democracy, creativity and multimodal literacy, are the principal pillars. This storyline aims to create spaces where preschools can possibly be places of hope and a meeting of minds. However, the problem is that it needs to become *the storyline, the imaginary place*, as the neoliberal one has been for some decades. As Dahlberg (2013) expressed, the development of a preschool system with two legs, so to speak, one that serves as an ethical meeting place with a strong self-identity, is important. For example, sustainability is becoming the way of living and is affecting preschools in multiple ways. Sustainability and creativity are concepts that are easy to connect to the concept of *makerspaces*. A good preschool has been argued to be a place where connectivity is the focus, where there are spaces *to make, to be* and *to try* out new things, where a connection between humans, the digital, making, and creating can grow. Perhaps, in the future, this closeness and the attention that makerspaces are receiving from mainstream education will help build an understanding and enforce the status of the preschool

Notes

1 Playschool is a legal concept, and it applies to institutions for children up to primary school level (six years). In the text, I use the better known word for it, preschool, which includes educational institutions for children aged 1–6 years.
2 Preschoolers: Preschool attendance in Iceland is universal. The starting age of children for beginning preschool is related to the parent's maternity leave. Most children start preschool around the age of 18–24 months, with the gap being minded by family day care. According to Statistics Iceland (2016, 2017), around 97% and around 80% of children aged 2½ to 6 years and between 1½ year and 2 years, respectively, attend preschools. All preschools have full-day classes, and most children attend school for around 7 ½ to 8 hours, with the longest stay of around 9 hours.
3 The preschool system is mainly financed and managed by municipalities. All parents pay for preschool services on a sliding scale, according to their income, between 12% and 15% of the actual cost of running the schools (Icelandic Association of Local Authorities, 2011).

References

Act of Law on Childcare, 112/1976. Retrieved from www.althingi.is/lagas/140a/1976112.html

Acts of Law on Preschool, 48 (1991). Retrieved from www.althingi.is/altext/stjt/1991.048.html

Act of Law on Preschool, 78 (1994). Retrieved from www.althingi.is/lagas/119/1994078.html

Arason, S. (1953). *Ég man þá tíð*. *Reykjavík*. Reykjavík: Hlaðbúð.

Arnalds, Á., Eydal, G., & Gíslason, I. N. (2013). Equal rights to paid parental leave and caring fathers- the case of Iceland. *Icelandic Review of Politics and Administration*, 9(2), 323–344.

Auðunsdóttir, S. D. (2014). Konur standa undir góðum lífskjörum þjóðarinnar, News. *Fréttatímin*, p. 6.

Balke, E. (1990). Kvinner som tolkere av barnehagepedagogikk. In U. Bleken (Ed.), *Barnet viste veien: Festskriv til Eva Balke* (pp. 25–34). Oslo: Barnevernsakademie i Oslo.

Bertram, T., & Pascal, C. (2002). Early years education: An international perspective. *International Review of Curriculum and Assessments Framework Internet Archive (INCA)*. Retrieved from London: www.nfer.ac.uk/research/centre-for-informa tion-and-reviews/inca/TS%20Early%20Years%20Education%202002.pdf

Bjarnason, B. (2010). Menntun flutt á háskólastig. In A. Jónsson & O. Helgadóttir (Eds.), *Spor í sögu stéttar*. Reykjavík: Skrudda.

Bremberg, S. (2009). A perfect 10: Why Sweden comes out on top in early child development programming. *Paediatr Child Health*, 14(10), 677–680.

Burman, A. (2016). *Pedgogikens idÉhistoria: Uppfostrings idéer och bildningsdeal under 2500 år*. Lund: Studentlitterature.

Centre for Gender Equality Iceland. (2012). *Information on gender equality issues in Iceland*. Akureyri: Centre for Gender Equality Iceland.

Clausen, S. B. (2015). Schoolification or early years democracy? A cross-curricular perspective from Denmark and England. *Contemporary Issues in Early Childhood*, 16(4), 355–373. doi:10.1177/1463949115616327

Dahlberg, G. U. (2013). A dialogue with the co-author of "the vision of a meeting place". In P. Moss (Ed.), *Early childhood and compulsory education: Reconceptualising the relationship*. London: Routledge.

Dýrfjörð, K. (2011a). Áhrif nýfrjálshyggju á íslenskt leikskólastarf. *Íslenska þjóðfélagið*, 2, 47–66.

Dýrfjörð, K. (2011b). Er leikskólinn sólkerfi, reikistjarna eða tungl? Eftirnýlenduvæðing leik- skólahugmyndafræðinnar. In Á. Ásgeirsdóttir, Björnsdóttir H & H. Ólafsdóttir (Eds.), *Rannsóknir í félagsvísindum XII* (pp. 381–388). Reykjavík: Félagsvísindastofnun Háskóla Íslands. Félags- og mannvísindadeild..

Dýrfjörð, K., & Magnúsdóttir, B. R. (2016). Privatisation of early childhood education in Iceland. *Research in Comparative and International Education*, 11(1), 80–97.

Eurostat. (2017, March 8). *Fertility statistics*. Retrieved from Eurostat explained: http://ec.europa.eu/eurostat/statistics-explained/index.php/Fertility_statistics

Friðriksson, G. (1991). *Saga Reykjavíkur. Bærinn vaknar 1870–1940. Fyrri hluti.* Reykjavík: Iðunn.

Guðmundsson, G. (1949). *Barnavinafélagið Sumargjöf 25 ára*. Reykjavík: Barnavinafélagið Sumargjöf..

Hursh, D., & Martina, C. A. (2016). The end of public schools? Or a new beginning? *The Educational Forum*, 80(2), 189–207. doi:10.1080/00131725.2016.1135380

Icelandic Association of Local Authorities. (2011). *Leikskólar – gjaldskrár – reglur.* Reykjavík: Icelandic Association of Local Authorities.

Icelandic Ministry of Education. (1985). *Uppeldisáætlun fyrir dagvistarheimili: Markmið og leiðir.* Reykjavík: Menntamálaráðuneytið.

Icelandic Ministry of Education. (1999). *Aðalnámskrá leikskóla* [The national curriculum for preschool]. Reykjvík: Mennta- og menningarmálaráðuneytið.

Icelandic Ministry of Education. (2011). *Aðalnámskrá leikskóla* [The national curriculum for preschool]. Reykjavík: Mennta- og menningarmálaráðuneytið.

The Icelandic Social Democratic Party. (2017). *Borgin opnar ungbarnadeildir og fjölgar leikskólaplássum* [Press release]. Retrieved from http://xs.is/borgin-opnar-ungbarnadeildir-og-fjolgar-leikskolaplassum/

Jónsdóttir, A. (2010). Selma Dóra Þorsteinsdóttir. In A. Jónsson & O. Helgadóttir (Eds.), *Spor í sögu stéttar* (pp. 201–203). Reykjvík: Skrudda.

Kamerman, S. (2000). Early childhood education and care: an overview of developments in the OECD countries. *International Journal of Educational Research, 33*(1), 7–29.

Lingard, B. (2010). Policy borrowing, policy learning: Testing times in Australian schooling. *Critical Studies in Education, 51,* 129–147.

Moss, P. (2016). Why can't we get beyond quality? *Contemporary Issues in Early Childhood, 17*(1), 8–15. doi:10.1177/1463949115627895

Pálsdóttir, E. (2017). *Orðaforðalistinn.* Kópavogur: Mennamálastofun [Directorate of Education].

Rannsóknarnefnd Alþingis. (2010). *Bindi 8: Siðferði og starfshættir í tengslum við fall íslensku bankanna.* Reykjavík: Alþingi.

RannUng. (2017). *Afmælisráðstefna RannUng – Hvernig menntun þurfa 5 ára börn?* Retrieved from http://menntavisindastofnun.hi.is/rannung/afmaelisradstefna_rannung_hvernig_menntun_thurfa_5_ara_born

Ríkisendurkoðun. (2017). *Kostnaður og skilvirkni kennaramenntunar. Háskóli Íslands og Háskólinn á Akureyri.* Retrieved from http://rikisendurskodun.is/wp-content/uploads/2017/02/SU- kostnadur_og_skilvirkni_kennaramenntunar_HI_og_HA.pdf

Samtök atvinnulífsins. (2017). *Umsögn um breytingu á lögum nr. 10/2008, um jafna stöðu og jafnan rétt kvenna og karla, mál 437, þingskjal 570.* Reykjavík: Samtök atvinnulífsins.

Sigurðardóttir, V. (2010). Valborg Sigurðardóttir [Þróun menntunar leikskólakennara] In A. jónsson & O. Helgadóttir (Eds.), *Spor í sögu stéttar* (pp. 17–25). Reykjavík: Skrudda.

Thorsteinsson, J. (2010). Þórhildur Ólafsdóttir. In A. Jónsson & O. Helgadóttir (Eds.), *Spor í sögu stéttar* (pp. 205–210). Reykvík: Skrudda.

World Economic Forum. (2016). *The Gglobal Ggender Ggap Rreport 2016.* Retrieved from Geneva: http://reports.weforum.org/global-gender-gap-report-2016/

11 Early childhood education and care in Korea

History, current trends and future challenges

Sojung Seo

Introduction

In recent decades, Korea has made tremendous investments in early childhood education and care (ECEC) services influenced by a stream of studies pertaining to the significance of education and care for early years. Related research using cost-benefit approaches has supported the claim that providing quality care for young children brings greater returns from government investments than does making these same investments in adulthood (Cunha, Heckmen, Lochner, & Masterov, 2005). The findings across studies have generally agreed that early childhood is a critical time for providing a variety of developmentally appropriate stimuli through continuous, quality interactions with primary caregivers because these affect young children's development (Seo & Moon, 2012).

In accordance with a great deal of attention and support from the academic arena, much broader social and economic sectors have directed government initiatives to develop ECEC policies in Korea. This expansion of childcare provision has mainly been the result of the Korean government's response to Korean women's increased participation in the paid labour market. However, it is generally considered that workplace culture and practices interfere with the employment of women with young children because few workplaces offer parental leave or other family-friendly measures. The most recent data reveal that the labour participation rate for women aged 15–64 was 52.7%, increasing from 49% in 2000, but 67.1% of married women in the workforce reported that they carried the dual burden of child-rearing at home as well as paid employment outside the home (Korean Statistics, 2016). The data report that the high demand for early childhood education and care (ECEC) services among working mothers with young children is caused by the unsatisfactory parental leave (institutionalised in 2001), though ECEC services in Korea still appear inadequate in both structural and pedagogical quality (Lee & Lee, 2014).

In the midst of the rapid societal changes in Korea, ECEC policy and practice development is a cooperative process that involves diverse voices and perspectives. The aims are to address a number of serious challenges in the country: 1) tackling the problem of the low-birth rates of 1.21 children per family on average over the past decade; 2) increasing women's labour market participation; 3) reconciling family and work responsibilities; and 4) providing young children, particularly from economically disadvantaged backgrounds, with better starts in life (Korean Institute of Childcare and Education [KICCE], 2015).

From the perspective of the 'best interests of young children', most researchers and practitioners agree that all children can learn and should have the equal opportunity to reach their highest potential. As opposed to the rhetorical approach, however, the primary Korean stakeholders in ECEC have developed diverse political perspectives over the last decade. ECEC is often considered a dynamic, changing discipline that has solid roots but is currently under keen debate about how to provide quality ECEC services to all eligible populations.

This chapter is divided into four sections. The first describes the social and political contexts of ECEC services in Korea, focusing on why these services matter in the midst of the radical changes that Korean society has been experiencing in recent decades. The next section presents national-level research and policy documents that demonstrate the ECEC policy development at critical points in time, followed by a presentation of the beliefs or perceptions about ECEC services which have emerged in recent studies to illustrate the gaps between ECEC policy and ECEC practice in Korea. This chapter concludes with some of the main challenges to be solved for developing potential ECEC practices and policies in Korea.

Contexts

This section presents the historical context of development in Korea from 1900 to the 1960s and the more radical developments from the 1980s to the present within the dynamics of the country's social, economic and political interfaces. In particular, the section provides a short description of the so-called 'picture of ECEC' within the context of the political and social upheavals that is necessary for understanding the deep historical split between childcare and education (kindergarten), that is still evident in the disparities in ECEC arena today.

Currently, Korea has a dichotomised Early Childhood Education and Care (ECEC) system with two distinct authorities in charge: kindergartens for 3–5 year olds and childcare centres for 0–5 year olds, under the supervision of the Ministry of Education and the Ministry of Health and Welfare, respectively. Historically, policies for the childcare and education of the two age groups have been developed separately, with different conceptualisations and understandings of young children (Organisation for Economic Cooperation and Development [OECD], 2006). Because of this conceptual divide, ECEC policies fractured the Korea's governance system. As was the case in the United States, childcare in Korea was considered a private responsibility for parents, not a public one, though the Korean government generally acknowledged its responsibility for children from socially marginalised or at-risk backgrounds, but less so for children under age three. In general, younger children (aged 0–3) were considered to need childcare rather than early education, and depending on household income and/or efforts to stimulate women's participation in the labour market, parents might or might not be provided public assistance. Table 11.1 displays the organisational and conceptual divide under the current split auspices divide between early education (i.e. kindergarten) and childcare (i.e. childcare centres).

Table 11.1 Early childhood education and care (ECEC) services in Korea[*]

	Early education	*Childcare*
Governance	Ministry of Education	Ministry of Health and Welfare
Legal Base	Early Childhood Education Act (2005. 1. 30 Enforced)	Childcare Act (1991, Enacted)
Target Age	Age 3–5	Age 0–5
Goal	Education (major) + Care	Care (major) + Education
Operation Hours	4–5 hours + After school	12 hours(7:30~19:30) +extended hours
Teacher Qualification (minimum criteria)	Kindergarten teacher level 1–2 (College graduate (2yrs))	Nursing teacher level 1–2–3 (High school graduate + 1 year training)
Teacher-to Child Ratio	Varied by each province (the ratio is decided by superintendent of education). In case of Seoul, Age 3 (1:18), Age 4 (1:24), Age 5 (1:28), Mixed age class (1:23)	Based on Article 10 of Childcare Act Age 0(1:3), Age 1(1:5), Age 2(1:7), Age 3(1:15), Age 4–5(1:20)
Tuition Fees Public	Varied by each province (the amount of funds is determined by superintendent of education)	Varied by each province (the amount of funds is determined by provincial or city governor within the nursery unit cost)
Private	Autonomous (under administrative guidance)	Determined by provincial or city governor (Article 30 of Childcare Act)
Budget	Approx. 5.3 trillion won[**]	Approx. 9.64 trillion won
Financial Support	Age 3–5 Nuri Curriculum: 220,000 won After-school program: 50,000~70,000 won	Age 0: 406,000 won Age 1: 357,000 won Age 2: 295,000 won Age 3–5: 220,000 won +40,000~50,000 won
Curriculum	Nuri Curriculum (Age 3–5)	Standardised Childcare Curriculum(Age 0–2) Nuri Curriculum (Age 3–5)

[*]Korea Institute of Childcare and Education (KICCE, September, 2015): ECEC Statistics of Korea.
[**]1$ (USD)=1,142won(Korea)

History of early years practices

It was 1914 when the first kindergarten for Korean children was established by the Ewha Woman's University, influenced by a female American Methodist missionary named Charlotte Brownlee (Choi, 2006) during the Japanese colonisation of

Korea. At that time, the curriculum was mainly influenced by pedagogical ideas and principles of Froebel, and trained kindergarten teachers applied his core ideas and principles by providing various activities and lessons for both large and small group sessions on a daily basis (Park & Yang, 2016).

Influenced by a western scholar, John Dewey, who advocated a child-centred philosophy and a hands-on experiences approach, the first National Kindergarten Curriculum was developed in 1969, with new editions being developed about every five years (OECD, 2006). Kindergartens experienced tremendous growth between 1980s and the 1990s, and the 1980s was the hub of the momentum for a wide range of progressive ideas from cognitive development theories and philosophical and educational frameworks such as those of Piaget, Vygotsky, and Montessori, imported from Western countries (Rhee, Rhee, & Lee, 2005; Park & Yang, 2016). Kindergarten was regarded as the bedrock of the education system, with the purpose of educating children to prepare them for primary school, though Froebel's core educational beliefs about "*learning through play*" was embedded in practice (Park & Yang, 2016). As pedagogy came to be more teacher-centred rather than child-centred, kindergarten teachers were advised to instruct children in purposeful and structured ways in the 1980s.

A new era of reform

The Early Childhood Education (ECE) Supporting Act in 1982 marked the first reform, in that the kindergartens and childcare centres were temporarily integrated under the governance of the Ministry of Internal Affairs to align the fragmented ECEC system to centralised government control. The ECE Supporting Act of 1982 is noteworthy in ECEC history because for the first time it issued a three-year action plan at the national level to lay a legislative foundation for kindergarten education, and provide guidance for kindergarten practitioners (OECD, 2006).

Curriculum and pedagogy

Before the 1990s, the term *pedagogy* and *curriculum* were applied synonymously without discretion, but researchers and practitioners in Korea began to distinguish the terms in the 1990s. The premise was put into practice that young children are learning all the time, and the content of that learning is always determined by the adults who care for them. In alignment with their understanding of the term curriculum, Korean practitioners came to widely accept the term pedagogy as referring to the full set of instructional techniques and strategies that enable learning and other types of development to take place in early childhood (Siraj-Blatchford, 2009).

As the numbers of young children being cared for by the non-maternal caregivers' in-group programs increased rapidly, the need strengthened for greater clarity about teaching and learning best practices and standards in the late 1980s and 1990s. In response to this need for curricular reform in ECEC, the concept 'Developmentally Appropriate Practice' (DAP), and the guidelines by the

National Association for the Education of Young Children (NAEYC) in the United States were extensively adopted by the educators in Korea (Bredekamp, 1987). Integrating thematic, unit, and project approaches into curricula became an emerging focus in practice, and general academic and early childhood associations were paying more attention to both content and process goals for early childhood in the national curriculum (Park & Yang, 2016).

Lee (2003) conducted a cross-cultural study and found that among the curricular and pedagogical trends in the early 2000s, the U.S. kindergarten teachers had the weakest overall DAP beliefs among the countries of interest (Korea, China, Taiwan and Turkey). Nevertheless, the study showed the highest levels of engagement in actual DAP practices than those in any of the other nations. It was also interesting that Korea held the strongest beliefs, but showed the second lowest engagement in actual DAP practices (China showed the least engagement). In line with the claim by Tobin, Hsueh and Karawawa (2009), the success of curriculum reform might depend upon the degree to which teachers understand why and how to teach their children in the ways the guidelines suggest. There appeared to be a disparity between the ideals imported from the West, and actual kindergarten practices. On the one hand, there was an emerging need for and focus on curriculum reform including integrated curricula and DAP, but paradoxically, kindergarten teachers felt pressured to follow the standardised, subject-centred curricula, particularly in literacy and mathematics.

From the 2000s to the present

Over the last ten years, there has been considerable ECEC policy development in Korea. The most radical development during this period, perhaps, would be the overall revision of the Childcare Act of 2004, along with the government funding to ensure the quality of ECEC services. The ground-breaking 2004 revised Childcare Act was enacted to introduce new mechanisms to ensure high- quality care, moving from "reporting-based" to "licensing systems" for running childcare centres. Regulatory requirements for establishing and operating childcare centres were to be stricter, and a National Accreditation System for the childcare centre was introduced in 2005 (OECD, 2015).

In parallel, the Early Childhood Education Act was also established in 2004. In the past, the full legal base of early childhood education was in the Primary and Secondary Education Act, but the new independent ECE Act provided a legal foundation for spending public funds on private kindergartens and day-long programs (OECD, 2015). Since 2004, the notion of early education and care as a public good has been widely accepted, though government provision and entitlements to access differ widely across the nation.

Transforming ECEC policy

Korea's extremely low fertility rate during the last decade (e.g. a historic low of 1.09 in 2005, the lowest among 34 OECD members) has pushed the Korean government to invest in early child education and care. During the past decade, the government has spent more than 150 trillion won, and ECEC expenditures from 2010 to 2014 increased from 0.52% to 1.01% of overall GDP, including not only financial support for child rearing and tuition, but also quality enhancement of ECEC services such as disseminating the Nuri Curriculum (KICCE, 2015).

Accelerated by the speculation that the early childhood period provides an unequalled opportunity for investment in human capital (Cunha, Heckmen, Lochner & Masterov, 2005), ECEC policy in Korea shifted from a selective to a universal approach with particular attention to young children aged three to five. The Nuri Curriculum was designed to offer free preschool education and care to equally prepare young children from all families for primary education. To enhance the quality of ECEC services, the curriculum was also integrated during 2012 and 2013 to meet the new primary goals of ensuring an equal start for all children, increasing access for parents and children, and improving the quality of ECEC services and teachers' working conditions (KICCE, 2015). The national standard curriculum entitled Nuri Curriculum has been implemented since 2013, and the core of this Nuri Curriculum is to guide a common set of early child-hood learning goals for all 3–5-year-old children who receive early childhood education and care (ECEC) services in Korea. Since the introduction of the Nuri Curriculum in 2013, the Korean government has continuously supported early childhood education and care by implementing free infant care (aged 0–2 years old) in 2012 and extending free ECEC services to children aged 0–5 in 2013.

Current status of the Nuri curriculum

Given that the free Nuri childcare curriculum was implemented nationwide in 2012–2013 as part of a pledge by incumbent, President Park (later impeached) to strengthen the nation's responsibility for early education and care, the pro-gram has created severe budgetary conflicts every year between regional educa-tion offices and the central government. Because of the curriculum's skyrocketing annual state budget for expanding the program to children aged 0–5, the gov-ernment ordered regional education offices to assume the burden of funding the program in 2015 (Choi, Park, Ha, & Kim, 2016). The regional offices have strongly refused to support the free childcare program by claiming they are not responsible for providing this care, especially for the day-care centres, which are under the jurisdiction of the Ministry of Health and Welfare. Although kin-dergartens are under the control of the Ministry of Education, some municipal councils have also refused to fund their kindergartens, citing fairness with the day-care centres within the same districts (Choi, Park, Ha, & Kim, 2016).

In the latest national survey, nearly 40% of respondents preferred income-based support for childcare and education for children (aged 3–5) to the current free care, whereas only 29% of respondents supported the current free system regard-less of family income (KEDI, 2015). The survey results seem to reflect people's doubt that the current free childcare program could be operated without cur-rent and sustainable government funding. It appears that the Nuri Curriculum is being swayed by the winds of politics in the midst of the current economic and political downturns, not meeting the best interests of young children in Korea.

Through lenses of primary stakeholders

The organisational and conceptual divides between the ECEC services are still prevalent, even since the integrated Nuri Curriculum was implemented in 2012–2013. Researchers from a variety of disciplines examined how primary stakeholders in Korea perceive the country's ECEC, but it has been challenging to integrate their findings because some researchers have focused on practitioners as the ECEC providers, whereas others have focused on the family-practice interfaces or interconnections through the lens of family as ECEC users.

In the following section, a review of research that examines the family-practice interfaces through both lenses is presented to discuss the strengths, limitations, and unexplored domains in each. Such initiative is imperative because we are at a time in ECEC history when early childhood education and care has become a public good. This is a relatively new development, and there are a lack of models and guidelines about how to conceptualise and structure the family and practice that share child-rearing responsibilities in society.

Mismatch between ECEC providers and users

Before the implementation of the Nuri Curriculum, the cultural norm was still dominant in Korea that children, especially very young children, should be cared for by their mothers, but a broader ideology of gender and family expanded to concur with the results of studies on the types of childcare parents of young children in Korea were locating.

The findings from a recent study by Seo and Ha (2014) lend empirical support for explaining the potential influences on how mothers as the main ECEC decision-makers locate particular types of childcare. The main results revealed that mothers preferred centre-based subsidised childcare over others, and the mothers on waiting lists reported difficulties in receiving the subsidised care they wanted owing to the lack of access to and availability of these publicly subsidised facilities (Seo & Ha, 2014). The mothers whose infants were cared for in family home care settings were more likely to emphasise learning achievement and maturity over personality or character education than were their counterparts who used childcare centres. The results from logistic regression analysis found that mothers were more likely to locate family home care over centre-based public subsidised care when they were employed, had younger infants, had spent more time on waiting lists, and emphasised the structural dimensions of infant care (Seo & Ha, 2014). That finding clearly indicates a considerable gap between the types of childcare mothers want and what they actually have access to choose (Seo, 2003). However, it is possible that mothers would report different beliefs or perceive differently before they had actually made a childcare choice, but later their beliefs or perceptions were changed to rationalise their choice of childcare (Barnes et al., 2004; Seo, 2003).

There has also been persistent debate regarding the quality and appropriateness of available ECEC quality services. ECEC services are often out of reach for eligible families under the current system. Data from the National Childcare Survey showed that 35% of households with infants (aged 0–2) and 33.2% of those with young children (aged 3–5) utilised in-home non-maternal childcare (Suh, Kim, Choi, Yoo, Son & Lee, 2012). More than 50% of respondents reported that they preferred relatives because family members were the most reliable, but care quality cannot be ensured (Lee, Do, Kim, & Na, 2012). Thus, there has been a mismatch between ECEC users and providers. Less often, but of great significance, is the influence of the gaps between what parents want and the actual childcare they must use on their children's outcomes, such as social and emotional adjustment, entirely separate from any economic effects.

Quality matters

It is widely accepted that ECEC quality cannot exceed the quality of the teachers who provide the education and care. ECEC quality has been directly related to the preparation and compensation of early childhood educators (Seo & Moon, 2013). In theory, better compensation and working conditions for early childhood educators can decrease provider turnover, but in practice, the greatest hindrances to enhancing quality in ECEC are low salaries and low education levels for these educators. These outcomes relate to the facts that in Korean culture, young children's care and education have traditionally been unpaid women's work, and that the young children themselves have no political right to vote.

Professionalism is usually defined by high standards in professional practice and distinct characteristics in common, such as ethics, mastery of specialised knowledge and skills, autonomy and control regarding entry into the profession, and commensurate compensation (Karz, 1987, p. 3). Under these criteria, research finds no professional status for ECEC in Korea. The current dual ECEC systems further compound the problem in that teachers at childcare centres receive lower salaries than kindergarten teachers, and teachers at private institutions receive lower salaries than those employed by publicly subsidised centres (Kim & Seo, 2010; Seo, 2016). It has also been consistently reported that staff at private childcare institutions report less job satisfaction and show lower teaching efficacy than their public sector counterparts (Seo, 2016).

With regard to pedagogy, there has been a distinct unevenness because of the differences in the initial training of employees in the kindergarten versus early childcare sectors. On average, kindergarten teachers have at least three years of higher education, whereas early childhood care workers receive two years of childcare and development educational training, and these deep-rooted discrepancies have resulted in differing perceptions of the nature of early childhood education by the different ECEC stakeholders (Seo, 2016).

The integrated ECEC curriculum discussed earlier was introduced in 2012–2013 as a common set of early childhood learning goals for children (aged 3–5). However, in terms of its implementation, the research shows that ECEC teachers perceive differing levels of difficulty, depending on factors such as their own education backgrounds and teaching experience, as well as the institution type (Seo, 2016; Tae & Hwang, 2013). Given the inequality in ECEC services, this is not surprising, although it is debatable, given that kindergarten teachers have had more experience with implementing the Nuri Curriculum. These more experienced kindergarten teachers have felt more efficacious in teaching than their counterparts at government subsidised childcare centres (Tae & Hwang, 2013). The gap between kindergarten teachers and teachers from the subsidised centres remains evident, and its ramifications should be taken into consideration in attempts to improve ECEC quality.

Looking ahead: challenges but opportunities

Despite the noticeable progress over the last decades, there remain significant challenges for the future that can serve as promising opportunities for developing ECEC policy in Korea. This section begins with some of the current paradoxes in ECEC policy that needs to be addressed.

Missing voices of young children

Korean has no national definition of ECEC quality, but the only indicators for ECEC accreditation and evaluation are national (OECD, 2015). The indicators consist of environmental dimensions, curricula (the Standardised Childcare Curriculum for ages 0–2 and the Nuri Curriculum for ages 3–5), interactions, health and safety, and management, and settings that meet these minimum quality criteria are accredited or pass evaluation. In the current situation of the deep rooted conceptual and organisational divide in ECEC services, a united evaluation system with unified quality standards for both kindergartens (ages 3–5) and centres (ages 0–5) should be enacted in the near future.

What is, however, still missing in the equation of quality, along with the lack of an integrated monitoring system, is young children's perceptions of their own experiences in ECEC. Children's perceptions not only can provide useful information on their own developmental outcomes, but also are important in staff evaluations regarding pedagogical practices, which in turn positively affects children's early development (Garvis, Ødegaard, & Lemon, 2015). As the recipients of ECEC services, young children should be heard and considered seriously, and their voices could help provide policy makers and ECEC staff with new insights into enhancing ECEC quality, as in Finland, which currently monitors children's views on their own ECEC experiences (OECD, 2015).

Paradox of professionalism

As mentioned earlier, socially, early childhood education is considered more amateur than professional, compared with other public professions such as medicine and the law. The socially recognised professions require ongoing professional development, which is distinctly different from other professions. In reality,

ECEC teaching in South Korea does not specify the knowledge or philosophical premise on which teacher preparation is based. It is paradoxical that there is often unnecessary regulation of what is considered reasonable professional behaviour, in the context of the lack of support for professional standards that could ensure higher-quality educational services for young children (Fromberg, 2003). Ethical considerations should also be part of developing standards for preparing teaching personnel. This lack of preparation contributes to high teacher attrition rates and becomes a disincentive to long-term teaching commitments.

Over the last decade, the Korean government has increased the regulations and duration of pre-service teacher programs, but the majority of ECEC educators have completed two years of college education or only have a high school diploma, whereas some researchers contend that professional teacher education should entail four years of college education that includes initiation and apprenticeship. These requirements would in turn, lead to the licensing and advanced accreditation that mark, other socially recognised professions. Furthermore, with strong professional organisation, ECEC teachers can potentially engage in autonomous practice.

In the same vein, the government's initiative to integrate early education and childcare services has resulted in a burgeoning of policy and programming for professional development in ECEC services across the nation. This, in turn, has raised awareness across the nation about the importance of teachers' professionalism to ensure optional learning and development in the years prior to entry into formal schooling. However, under the current conditions in which quality, affordability and professional compensation are contradictory or antithetical rather than integrated elements, this paradox in professionalism cannot be resolved. Thus, the inequality in qualifications, conditions of service and remuneration should be readdressed in the area of job training and professional development.

The most recent data indicate that there was a great deal of variation in both the training offered and what staff were able to access (Seo, 2016). Studies found a stronger emphasis on education when teachers were well trained, and these teachers played a leading role in curriculum planning and served as positive pedagogical role models to less qualified staff (Seo, 2016; Sosinsky, Lord, & Zigler, 2007). Similarly, Baek (2016) found that ECEC teacher's perceived professionalism, which referred to their self-regulation and autonomy, salary satisfaction and perceived respect for their profession, significantly influenced their job satisfaction. Such findings suggest practical alternatives for enhancing ECEC teachers' professionalism by providing them with opportunities to participate in decision-making. Although the time is ripe for reforming teaching practices in ECEC, the counter-argument is that without better training and higher qualifications, teaching quality cannot be ensured.

The inherent paradox in ECEC professionalism is that it is a profession that cannot regulate itself. In contrast with the law, for example, in terms of compulsory job training and an on-going career development, comprehensive ECEC career development should encompass a range of appropriate levels, education content and materials, new technologies, job structuring and enrichment and the facilitation of relevant personal skills and interpersonal relationships for both the pre-service and in-service ECEC teachers (Seo, 2016).

Sustainable ECEC policy development

As addressed herein, from the perspective of the 'best interests of young children', few early childhood practitioners and researchers disagree that all children can learn and should have equal opportunities to reach their highest potential. Although the ECEC development in Korea has undergone dramatic changes in both policy and practice, its magnitude is well beyond what was addressed in the arena of politics. Political perceptions of ECEC among primary stakeholders have diversified over the last decade, and ECEC is a dynamic, changing discipline that is part of current debate about the provision of free childcare to all in need. Under the current split system, kindergartens and childcare centres have separate evaluation systems, resulting in different quality standards and less unification in ECEC.

In 2015, a move was scheduled toward developing a coherent, explicit and comprehensive monitoring framework and standardised tools, but it has not yet taken effect, primarily because ECEC policy has been under the sway of politics rather than the best interest of young children. In the evolution of ECEC policy development, the pendulum had swung to universalism, but is now is moving backward toward selectivism in the upcoming 2017 Korean presidential and general elections. The new chapters of ECEC history should be written by more coherent and sustainable child-related family policies, not swayed by the dynamics of politics, but firmly anchored to "the best interests of young children". This revised focus would provide the momentum for the nation to get back on track for reforms in ECEC services.

References

Baek, S. H. (2016). A research on the childcare teachers' recognition of professionalism and job satisfaction. *Journal of Future Early Childhood Education, 23*(3), 47–63.

Barnes, J., Leach, P., Sylva, K., Stein, A., Lars-Erik, M., & Families, Children and Childcare Team. (2004). Infant care in England: Mothers' aspirations, experiences, satisfaction and caregiver relationships. *Early Child Development and Care, 176*(5), 553–573.

Bredekamp, S. (Ed.). (1987). *Developmentally appropriate practice in early childhood programs serving children from birth through age 8.* Washington, DC: National Association for the Education of Young Children.

Choi, W. G. (2006). *The traditional education of Korea.* Seoul: Ewha press.

Choi, Y. K., Park, C. H., Ha, Y. S., & Kim, H. S. (2016). *Implementing strategies for ECEC integration and its settlement in Korea.* Seoul: KICCE.

Cunha, F., Heckmen, J., Lochner, L., & Masterov, D. V. (2005). *Interpreting the evidence of life-cycle skill formation* (IZA Discussion Paper Series, No. 1575). Bonn, Germany: Institute for the Study of Labour.

Fromberg, D. P. (2003). The professional and social status of the early childhood educator. In J. P. Isenberg & M. R. Jalongo (Eds.), *Major trends and issues in early childhood education: Challenges, controversies, and insights* (2nd ed., pp. 177–192). New York: Teachers College Press.

Garvis, S., Ødegaard, E., & Lemon, N. (2015). *Beyond observations: Narratives and young children.* The Netherlands: Sense Publishers.

Karz, L. G. (1987). The nature of professions: Where is early childhood education? In L. G. Katz & K. Steiner (Eds.), *Current topics in early childhood education* (Vol. 7, pp. 1–16). Norwood, NJ: Ablex.

Kim, S. Y., & Seo, S. J. (2010a). Teachers' professionalism, teaching efficacy, and their perceptions about the integration of kindergarten and childcare centres in the current early childhood professional training system: A comparison across subjects by college major degree and work place. *Korean Journal of Child Studies, 31*(3), 215–233.

Korea Institute of Childcare and Education. (2015). *ECEC statistics of Korea: Access to service, participation and financial resources* (Policy Brief, Issue 8). KICCE.

Korean Statistics. (2016). *Annual Korean family household research report.* Seoul: Korean Government Department of Statistics.

Lee, J. W., Do, N. H., Kim, S. H., & Na, J. H. (2012). *Recommendation for policy proposals for improving fertility rate and reconciling work and family life (II): A focus on in-home care for infants and suggested support measures.* Korean Institute of Childcare and Education.

Lee, J. W., & Lee, H. M. (2014). *Outcomes and challenges of child caring policy.* KICCE.

Lee, S. M. (2003). Relative strength of adoption of developmentally appropriate practices in preprimary early childhood professionals: Comparing Korea to four other countries. *Journal of Future Early Childhood Education, 10*(3), 377–403.

Organisation for Economic Cooperation and Development. (2006). *Starting strong II: Early childhood education and care.* Paris: OECD Publishing. doi:http://dx.doi.org/10.1787/9789264035461-en

Organisation for Economic Cooperation and Development. (2015). *Starting strong IV: Monitoring quality in early childhood education and care.* Paris: OECD Publishing. doi:http://dx.doi.org/10.1787/9789264233515-en

Park, Y. J., & Yang, Y. J. (2016). The continuing influence of Froebel's kindergarten system in current early childhood education in the USA and South Korea. *Asia-Pacific Journal of Research in Early Childhood Education, 10*(3), 125–140.

Rhee, U., Rhee, W., & Lee, Y. (2005). Early childhood care and education in Korea: Current state and research. In B. Spodek & O. Saracho (Eds.), *International perspectives on research in early childhood education* (pp. 161–190). Charlotte, NC: Information Age Publishing.

Seo, S. J. (2003). Early childcare choices: A theoretical model and research implications. *Early Child Development and Care, 173*(6), 637–650.

Seo, S. J. (2016). Teaching efficacy belief as a new paradigm for teacher career development and professionalism in Korea. In S. Garvis & D. Pendergast (Eds.), *Asia-Pacific perspectives on teacher self-efficacy* (pp. 53–69). The Netherlands: Sense Publishers.

Seo, S. J., & Ha, J. Y. (2014). Effects of variables on mothers' choices of infant care. *Journal of Korean Childcare and Education, 10*(2), 319–335.

Seo, S. J., & Moon, H. J. (2012). Do Korean children's daily routines and their mothers' parenting stress differ according to socioeconomic status? *Social Behavior and Personality, 40*(3), 481–500.

Seo, S. J., & Moon, H. J. (2013). A comparative study of teaching efficacy in pre-service and in-service teachers in Korean early childhood education and care (ECEC). *Asia-Pacific Journal of Teacher Education, 41*(4), 363–376.

Siraj-Blatchford, I. (2009). Conceptualizing progression in the pedagogy of play and sustained shared thinking in early childhood education: A Vygotskian perspective. *Educational and Child Psychology, 26*(2), 77–89.

Sosinsky, L. S., Lord, H., & Zigler, E. (2007). For profit/non-profit differences in centre-based childcare quality: results from the National Institute of Child Health and Human Development Study of Early Childcare and Youth Development. *Journal of Applied Developmental Psychology, 28*, 390–410.

Suh, M. H., Kim, E. S., Choi, Y. K., Yoo, H. M., Son, C. G., & Lee, H. M. (2012). *The 2012 national childcare survey: A household census.* The Ministry of Health and Welfare & Korean Institute of Childcare and Education.

Tae, S. R., & Hwang, H. J. (2013). A study on the practicing level of the NURI curriculum for early childhood teachers. *Journal of Korean Childcare and Education, 9*(3), 253–272.

Tobin, J., Hsueh, Y., & Karawawa, M. (2009). *Preschool in the three cultures revisited.* Chicago, IL: The University Press.

12 Early childhood education and care in Aotearoa/New Zealand

History and features

Gaye Tyler-Merrick, Joanna Phillips,
Claire McLachlan, Tara McLaughlin,
Karyn Aspden and Sue Cherington

Introduction

Aotearoa New Zealand has a long history of both formal and informal provision of early childhood education (ECE) services for children and their families, beginning with the introduction of kindergartens in 1889 (Stover, 2016). In the intervening 120 years, the provision of services has grown to include not-for-profit, community-based and private (for profit) ownership. This diversity has become a hallmark of the sector and caters for the different needs and preferences of families (Shuker & Cherrington, 2016).

Alongside the diversity of services, the ECE landscape has been characterised since the mid-1980s by rapidly shifting government policy and educational reforms that have impacted on the regulatory environment and on provision of services at the local level (May, 2014; McLachlan, 2011). Stover (2016) described these shifts as a *Unity Agenda* (1975–1989) and an *Education Agenda* (1989–2010) (p. 527). The *Unity Agenda* saw the integration, in 1989, of all education and childcare services under the former Department of Education. This agenda removed the administrative and philosophical dichotomy between *childcare* and *education* and was the catalyst for an increasingly unified ECE sector in terms of regulations, qualifications and funding requirements. The *Education Agenda* was significant for its pattern of shifting policy direction and distinct periods of advancement and retrenchment. The aim of this chapter is to identify the key shifts in early childhood provision since the unification of all early childhood services in 1989. Drawing on Moss and Dahlberg (2008), we argue that the changes in early childhood provision are the result of shifting and often competing discourses, highlighting the tensions between neoliberal, managerial government policies and the demands of a complex early childhood sector serving multiple and diverse needs of a multicultural and multilingual population within a bicultural curriculum framework. The following discussion illustrates and critiques the main shifts in policy and direction since 1989, including regulations and licensing, the development of the early childhood curriculum,

Te Whāriki (Ministry of Education, 1996) and its recent 2017 revision. The chapter concludes with critique of the current state of early childhood in New Zealand and explores the implications for future development of early childhood research and policy.

Policy changes over time

Early childhood services in New Zealand cater for children from birth to school entry (typically at five years of age), and are licensed as teacher-led, family-led and whānau[1]-led. In addition, children may attend informal parent-led playgroups or be enrolled in the Correspondence School, which provides ECE programmes for children with health, isolation or transience needs. Table 12.1 indicates the different ECE services, the type of programme offered to different aged children and the ownership model of Aotearoa New Zealand early childhood services.

The amalgamation of all these ECE services in 1986 was the precursor to significant change in the nature of ECE teaching qualifications. The three-year Diploma of Teaching in ECE, introduced in the early 1990s across six Colleges of Education, brought parity between ECE and primary teaching qualifications. Significant deregulation of the tertiary education sector since 1986 has meant initial teacher education programmes for ECE are now delivered by 19 providers (TeachNZ, 2017). Providers include universities, polytechnics, childcare organisations and private training providers; all are recognised for teacher registration.

In 2002, the Ministry of Education, in close consultation with the ECE sector, developed a 10-year ECE Strategic Plan – *Pathways to the Future: Ngā Huarahi Arataki*. This plan established clear goals to improve the quality of ECE services, increase child participation rates and foster the development of collaborative relationships between ECE services and families, schools and broader social and health services. Specific initiatives included equity funding for services in low socio-economic communities; setting progressive targets to increase the proportion of qualified and registered teachers in teacher-led services to 100%; financial incentives to support provisionally registered teachers to gain full registration and establishing the Centres of Innovation programme to "showcase excellence and innovation in ECE" (Ministry of Education, 2002, p. 15). Alongside the Strategic Plan, the introduction of a new funding policy to increase participation and reduce costs to families made three- and four-year-old children eligible for up to 20 hours of free ECE per week from 2007 (Bushouse, 2008).

A change in government in 2008 saw the dismantling of many of these policy initiatives (May, 2014; Stover, 2016). The Strategic Plan was disestablished in 2010 and, as a result, there was a reduction in minimum requirements for the proportion of qualified teachers required for teacher-led services and a significant reduction in the provision of Ministry of Education funded professional learning for ECE teachers. The *20 hours free ECE* policy was re-framed as *20 hours ECE*, with services allowed to impose surcharges on parents for optional extras such

Table 12.1 Overview of Aotearoa/New Zealand early childhood education service types, programme delivery and ownership structure

Licence-type	Service type	Programme	Caters for children:	Ownership and management structures
Teacher-led	Kindergarten	Predominately school-day sessions	Predominantly 3–4 year olds	Not-for-profit, community-based; managed at local level within umbrella Association
	Education and care services	Mix of sessional & full-day programmes. Includes services with varied philosophies, e.g. Montessori, Steiner & Pasifika language nests	Birth – five years; programmes may cater for mixed-aged groups, infants & toddlers, or 2–5 year olds	Mix of ownership models: not-for-profit, community-based; employer-subsidised; private owner-operated; corporate ownership
	Home-based services	Part or full-day programme	Birth – five years	Mix of ownership models: not-for-profit, community-based; employer-subsidised; private owner-operated; corporate ownership
Parent-led	Playcentre	Sessional programme	Predominantly 2–5 year olds	Not-for-profit, community-based; managed at local level within umbrella Association
Whānau-led	Te Kōhanga Reo	School- or full-day programme. Programme aims to revive & maintain Māori language & culture	Birth – five years	Not-for-profit, community-based; managed at local level within umbrella of National Kōhanga Reo Trust

as the provision of meals or outings beyond the usual programme offered. Furthermore, a freeze on the government funding rates for ECE services occurred and the capping of funding for qualified teachers to 50% of a service's workforce has collectively seen funding reduced in real dollar terms by $58,000 per annum for each ECE service between 2010 and 2017 (NZEI: TE Riu Roa, 2017). The impact of these changes has been a marked change in the demographics of ECE service types and governance structures between 2000 and 2015. There has been a 4% decrease in the number of community-based services, but a 132% increase in the number of privately owned ECE services. Moreover, the largest increase in services has been in the privately owned home-based sector, with a 690% increase (Education Counts, 2017). The changing nature of the regulatory framework is considered next.

Regulations and licensing

There is a robust regulatory framework for ECE services. All licensed ECE services must meet the minimum standards specified in the Education (Early Childhood Services) Regulations 2008 (SR 2008/204). Responsibility for the regulation and licensing of ECE services rests with the Ministry of Education, while the quality assurance function rests with the Education Review Office: *Te Tari Arotake Mātauranga* [ERO]. Established in 1989 as part of a significant reform of the wider New Zealand education system (Stover, 2016), ERO is responsible for reviewing, evaluating and publicly reporting on the quality of education and outcomes for children and students in every New Zealand school and early childhood service. Reviews are undertaken in a cyclical rotation and are based on the quality of the service. Services deemed to be *well placed* to meet key quality indicators are reviewed every 3–4 years, or more frequently if there are risks in performance or compliance or risks to the education or safety of children, and additional supports, interventions and requirements are put into place.

An emerging ERO focus is on outcomes for children as the key determinant of quality, which is arguably part of a larger government focus on return on investment in early childhood. ERO (2013a, p. 1) states, "The focus of ERO's reviews in early childhood services is on the capacity of the service to promote positive learning outcomes, with the purpose of contributing to improved wellbeing and learning for all children". To support this aim, the review guidelines *He Pou Tātaki* (Education Review Office, 2013a) were introduced, marking a significant update and revision of the 2004 *Evaluation Indicators for Education Reviews in Early Childhood Services* document. ERO's stated intention is to build the capacity of early childhood services to be self-managing and for improvements to be grounded in robust processes of self-review. Alongside its review functions, ERO also publishes national evaluation reports across areas of key educational importance, which contribute to government policy making, such as the revision of the ECE curriculum, which will be examined next.

The early childhood curriculum: *Te Whāriki: He Whàriki Màtauranga mò ngà Mokopuna o Aotearoa Early Childhood Curriculum*

Te Whāriki (Ministry of Education, 1996, 2017) is a bicultural national early childhood curriculum framework that embraces both Māori and dominant Western worldviews. Development of *Te Whāriki* started in the early 1990s and was led by two University of Waikato academics, Helen May and Margaret Carr, with Tamati and Tilly Reedy from Te Kōhanga Reo Trust. Curriculum development involved extensive consultation with the ECE community, including teachers of infants, toddlers and preschoolers, special education services, home-based care, Pacific Island and Māori stakeholders (Te One, 2003). Consultation cumulated with a draft curriculum released in 1993 (Ministry of Education, 1993). Based on further consultation, a revised document was released for general use in 1996. *Te Whāriki* became the gazetted curriculum for ECE in the revision of the regulations in 2008.

Te Whāriki has had a significant influence on ECE in New Zealand, as well as being respected internationally for being the first bicultural curriculum to honour indigenous cultures (Tesar, 2015). *Te Whāriki* has the aspiration that all children are "competent and confident learners and communicators, healthy in mind, body and spirit, secure in their sense of belonging and knowledge that they make a valued contribution to society" (Ministry of Education, 2017, p. 6). The curriculum highlights the role of family/whānau and culture in ensuring this aspiration is achieved, which is evidenced in the four *Principles* of Empowerment, Holistic Development, Family and Community, and Relationships, and five *Strands* of Welbeing, Belonging, Contribution, Communication and Exploration. Across these strands there are 18 *goals* to describe the environment children should experience and, in the 1996 version, 118 *learning outcomes* that describe skills, knowledge and attitudes that children should develop from their ECE experiences. The goals and learning outcomes provide broad statements for curriculum planning and a framework for assessing children's progress.

Under the revision of the regulations in 2008, it became compulsory for centres to deliver the gazetted parts of the curriculum: the principles, strands and goals. However, apart from the licensing requirement, *Te Whāriki* is not a prescribed curriculum. Each early childhood service in collaboration with their children, families and community creates a curriculum to reflect their own philosophy and beliefs. *Te Whāriki* is constructed as a *whāriki*, a 'mat' where curriculum is woven together by the local stakeholders. The weaving of experiences created by the teachers, children, families and community is designed to build on children's strengths, dispositions and interests, as well as family and community aspirations.

Like curriculum, assessment is also not prescribed. Guidance for assessment, planning and evaluation indicates that each ECE service develop their own distinctive approach. General recommendations include the use of on-going observations to inform assessment and planning and ensure that information gained is helpful to understand and inform children's learning. Although there is no mention of any specific assessment method(s), teachers typically assess children's learning via a unique narrative approach, called a '*learning story*' (Carr & Lee, 2012). This form of narrative is used to inform parents of their child's disposition for learning rather than identify what their child can or cannot do. To support teachers' use of learning stories, the Ministry of Education (2004, 2007, 2009) created a resource called *Kei Tua o te Pae: Assessment for learning: Early childhood exemplars.*

There has been strong support for *Te Whāriki* since its introduction, to the point where it has gained "gospel like status" (Cullen, 1996, p. 123). Te One (2003) suggests the durability of *Te Whāriki* is because it enabled teachers and communities to weave curriculum specific to their own philosophy of how children learn.

Surprisingly, given *Te Whāriki's* widespread acceptance, there has been a notable lack of research and critical review of its content and implementation. Nuttall (2003) suggests that the early lack of critique may have been due to teachers being reluctant to criticise the developers and/or teachers viewing *Te Whāriki* as supporting their current practice. More recently, some critiques have suggested that the generalised nature of the principles, strands, goals and learning outcomes may result in a limited range of curriculum experiences (Blaiklock, 2010; McLachlan, Carvalho, de Lautour, & Kumar, 2006) and subject knowledge (Cullen, 1996; Hedges & Cullen, 2005) provided to children. Recent ERO reports highlight concerns regarding the consistency and quality of curriculum implementation and teaching practices across the sector (ERO, 2011; 2013a; 2013b; 2015). In their separate analyses from this period, ERO (2016) and McLaughlin, Aspden and Snyder (2016) identified the variability of quality across the sector, with specific concern about the lack of guidance given to teachers on how to implement a quality curriculum. This is of concern, especially when changing policy requires only 50% of the teaching staff in teacher-led services to have a teacher qualification, and professional development opportunities have decreased over time.

It was against this backdrop that the Organisation for Economic Co-operation and Development (OECD) (2015) and the Ministry of Education Advisory Group on Early Learning (AGEL) (2015) both signalled the need for a review of *Te Whāriki* and advocated for practical strategies and tools to support its implementation. In July 2016, the Ministry of Education finally announced a review. Their intention was to "refresh and enrich the curriculum in response to societal change, shifts in policy and respond to the educational research on curriculum, assessment, pedagogy and practice for a new generation of children" (Ministry of Education, 2016, p. 8).

In July 2016, the Ministry called for expressions of interest to revise the curriculum and appointed a team of four ECE academics and three teachers, who collectively had knowledge and skills in Western, Māori and Pasifika theory and practice. They were supported by the original writing team of *Te Whāriki* and a team of Ministry of Education selected advisors. The brief for revision did not include the gazetted principles, strands and goals; instead it had an update of everything else was in scope and included a reduction in the number of learning outcomes to follow OECD and AGEL recommendations. The revision process started in August and a draft completed in November. The preliminary draft was discussed with Ministry ECE Advisory committees and original writers and then 28 consultation meetings were held around the country during a one-month period, with feedback submissions closing online in mid-December. The curriculum was revised in light of consultation and submissions. It was then reviewed by Ministry Advisory committees, advisors and original writers, revised again and released in April 2017. A summary of submissions posted on the Ministry website reveals that reception was mixed: many liked the increased clarity, reduced learning outcomes and greater inclusion of different perspectives on learning. Others were strident that the update would limit their ability to express philosophical beliefs about children's learning and said photos detracted from content. In addition, many people took to social media to express their concern over the lack of time for consultation, although it was signalled consultation was constrained by Ministry budgets and the Minister's agenda to have the curriculum revised within her term of office.

To critique successive drafts and revisions of the curriculum over the last 25 years, key features of each document are highlighted in Table 12.2.

As noted in Table 12.2, the aspiration for children, the principles, strands and goals have remained much the same over successive versions. Notably, the foreword to *Te Whāriki* originally celebrated the connections with Kōhanga Reo and Māori. The update offers the first inclusion of the role of Te Tiriti o Waitangi as a foreground to the importance of culture, cultural responsiveness and cultural competence in early childhood. In addition, there is reference to the changing nature of New Zealand as a multi-cultural nation. Consistent with previous versions, the update provides an English and Māori version. The Māori version is not a literal translation but while closely related, different cultural "*connotations mean the two are not equivalent*" (Ministry of Education, 2016). Differences in the presentation have occurred, with the 2017 Māori version separate to the English. Likewise, learning outcomes have reduced from 118 to 20, with these now written in more definitive terms (children become increasingly capable of) rather than the open-ended (children develop). Visually, there are several changes. The most notable was the inclusion of photos to the 2016/17 document. The 2017 document is half the size of the original, with photos reflecting children and adults engaging in a range of curriculum activities.

There are some similarities between the 1996 and 2017 versions. The metaphor of the *whāriki*/mat has been retained, but the 2017 version has less reference to the structures that might influence the pattern of the woven *whāriki*. Similarly, the definition of curriculum has been slightly altered but still refers to "experiences, activities and events, both direct and indirect, which occur within the early learning setting" (p. 7). The addition of the term "learning need" (p. 13) is a difference and marks a change for a sector that has long focused on children's strengths and interests and avoided a focus on needs or concerns about children's learning and development. This changed focus will help ensure a

Table 12.2 A comparison of successive changes to *Te Whāriki* from 1993 to 2017

Te Whāriki: Early Childhood Curriculum
(Ministry of Education)

	1993	1996	2016	2017
Title	Te Whāriki: He Whāriki Mātauranga mō ngā Mokopuna o Aotearoa Draft Guidelines for Developmentally Appropriate Programmes (DAP) in Early Childhood Services	Te Whāriki: He Whāriki Mātauranga mō ngā Mokopuna o Aotearoa Early Childhood Curriculum	Te Whāriki: He Whāriki Mātauranga mō ngā Mokopuna o Aotearoa Early Childhood Curriculum Draft for Consultation	Te Whāriki: He Whāriki Mātauranga mō ngā Mokopuna o Aotearoa Early Childhood Curriculum
Foreword	Description of development & consultation, including consultation with Kōhanga Reo & Māori immersion to understand DAP for all services	Introduces first national curriculum for ECE and first bi-cultural curriculum for New Zealand. Acknowledge the consultation to be responsive to all services.	Left un-written	Description of importance and of valuing early learning; foundation of the whāriki/mat; bi-cultural framework and responsive to all services
Statement on Te Tiriti o Waitangi	None (Mentioned in at least one location in document)	None (Mentioned in four locations in document)	Introductory statement provided to foreground curriculum, inclusive of new settlers and a multi-cultural nation	Wording changed Intent the same as 2016
Aspiration for children	1996 Aspiration for children: to grow up as competent & confident learners & communicators, healthy in mind, body, & spirit, secure in their sense of belonging, and in the knowledge that they make a valued contribution to society (p 9). 2016: Aspiration that all children will grow up as competent . . . (p 7). 2017: Underpinning *Te Whāriki* is the vision that children are competent . . . (p. 6).			
Curriculum Envisaged or Curriculum Metaphor	Envisaged as a whāriki or mat, woven from the principles, aims and goals defined in this document. Distinctive patterns come from different programmes,	Envisaged as a whāriki or mat, woven from the principles, aims and goals defined in this document. Distinctive patterns come from different programmes,	The whāriki (woven mat) is used as a metaphor . . . settings weave together the principles and strands in the whāriki to create a holistic, child-	The whāriki (woven mat) is used as a metaphor. Principles & strands interwoven & give expression to the vision for children

Description of curriculum	Experiences which are humanly, nationally, culturally, developmentally, individually, and educationally appropriate	Sum total of the experiences, activities, & events, direct or indirect which occur within an environment to foster children's learning	All the experiences, activities and events, both direct and indirect, that occur within the early learning setting. . . . responsive to the strengths, interests and learning needs of the children in the setting and to the aspirations of the parent community.	Interprets the notion of curriculum broadly, . . . to include the experiences, activities & events, both direct and indirect, that occur within the ECE setting. It provides a framework of principles, strands, goals and learning outcomes that foregrounds the mana of the child and the importance of respectful, reciprocal and responsive relationships. . . . weave a local curriculum that reflects its own distinctive character and values.
Principles	1. Empowerment – empowers the child to learn & grow. 2. Holistic Development – reflects the holistic way children learn & grow. 3. Family & Community – family & community integral part. 4. Relationships – responsive & reciprocal relationships with people, places, & things.			
Strands[a]	1. The health & **welbeing** of the child are protected & nurtured. 2. Children & their families feel a sense of **belonging**. 3. Opportunities for learning are equitable, & each child's **contribution** is valued. 4. The languages & symbols of their own & other cultures are promoted & protected (**communication**). 5. The child learns through active **exploration** of the environment.			
	Assessment should start from the children's needs and from the aims and goals of these guidelines. Assessment should focus on individual children rather than making comparisons between children.	. . . obtaining, and interpreting, information that describes a child's achievements and competence. The purpose of assessment is to provide pertinent information to contribute to improving learning opportunities for children.	Assessment is used to find out about what children know and can do, what interests them, how they are progressing, what new learning opportunities may be appropriate, and where additional support may be required.	Assessment makes valued learning visible . . . find out about what children know and can do, what interests them, how they are progressing, what new learning opportunities are suggested and where additional support may be required.
Learning Outcomes	None	118	20	20

(Continued)

Table 12.2 (Continued)

Te Whāriki: Early Childhood Curriculum
(Ministry of Education)

	1993	1996	2016	2017
Description of pedagogy	No	No	No	No, although mention is made in section on child dispositions and working theories
Reference to teachers	Adults	Adults	Kaiako (defined as teacher, educator)	Kaiako (defined as teacher, educator)
References to theories and theorists	None specifically mentioned in text. Footnotes to cite Bruner, Gerber, Erickson, Mahler, Bronfenbrenner, & Piaget	Bronfenbrenner's Ecology of human development described in text	Section on theories: socio-cultural, Kaupapa Māori, Pasifika, bioecological systems, and critical theory. Specific mention Vygotsky & Bronfenbrenner. Mention neuroscience research. Positioned at beginning of document	Positioned at end of document. Repositioning of theorists with Bioecological placed first. Deletion of neuroscience section but now included in Emerging research and theory section. Connections made to curriculum principles and pedagogy.
Connections to school curriculum	Detailed description of connections with examples of connections between learning outcomes from both curriculums	Brief description of connections with overview of links between strands and essential learning areas and skills	Detailed description of connections with overview of links between learning outcomes in strands and key competencies and learning areas	Extended further to include Te Aho Matua philosophy (Kura) and a 'weaving' column to connect the two curriculums
Children with special needs	Specific section to describe commitment to inclusion with examples provided for each aim (strand).	Specific section to describe commitment to inclusion	No mention. Reference to inclusive curriculum for all children	Extended to state removing any barriers to participation &working with families. Strength based.

References to literature	Foot notes with references	No	Bibliography 5 pages No references in text	One page bibliography at end including references to ECE policy documents. No references in text.
Presentation	Integrated within sections	Presented as one section within the document	Māori -English Split/ Reverse document; separate table of contents	Māori -English Split/Reverse document; separate table of contents
Pictures of children	No	No	Yes 32 pictures often taking up whole page with little focus on curriculum. No diversity	Yes, smaller photos showing more diverse range of adults and children – curriculum focused
Questions for Reflection	Included with each Strand.	Included with each Strand.	No	Included with each Strand.
Consideration for Leadership, organisation & practice	In each Aim (later known as Strand): Titled 1. Management & organisation of the environment 2. Adults' Responsibilities	In each Strand: Titled Adults' responsibilities in management, organisation and practice	In each Strand: Titled Consideration for leadership, organisation & practice.	In each Strand: Updated & more inclusive

Note: Where possibly text taken directly from documents; ¹ referred to as aims in the 1993 version.

child's strengths and interests, as well as their learning needs and progress can be identified through assessment. The description of assessment supports this focus, with an increased focus to both spontaneous and planned assessment to support children's learning.

Of continued concern is the lack of specific information about pedagogy and teaching. The update still lacks guidance or "clear standards of practice" for curriculum implementation (see ERO, 2016), although there is increased guidance on teaching practices to promote learning outcomes in each strand, and an overarching statement on the responsibilities of kaiako (p. 59). This lack of guidance has been noted by Meade and Cullen for many years and was recently re-emphasised by McLaughlin, Aspden and Snyder (2016) in their comparison of the New Zealand and Australian early childhood curriculums, which showed the Australian curriculum provides clearer guidance for intentional teaching in the context of play, consistent with international trends. Moreover, Cherrington (2016) suggests a pressing need in New Zealand to examine how teachers understand and enact intentional teaching.

This relative silence on pedagogy may reflect the eclectic theoretical underpinnings of the curriculum. *Te Whāriki* has long been viewed as a socio-cultural curriculum based on the work Vygotsky and other social-cultural theorists (Blaiklock, 2010; Hedges & Cullen, 2005). Yet, there is no mention of Vygotsky in the 1993 draft or 1996 version. The multiple theorists referenced through footnotes in 1993 were limited to just Bronfenbrenner in 1996. Despite this absence, socio-cultural theory has been long accepted as the foundational underpinning to *Te Whāriki* (Blaiklock, 2010; Hedges & Cullen, 2005). Teachers' interpretations of how this might guide their teaching are complex, as many teachers stand back and let children self-direct their learning through play. Meade describes this practice as "a hangover from the days when developmentally theory dominated" (2002, p. 16). For the first time, there is specific reference to some theoretical underpinnings, such as the bio-ecological systems model, sociocultural, Kaupapa Māori, Pasifika, critical theory and emerging theories to inform teaching. While some different theories are now identified, there is still no explicit linking of theory to practice, which is problematic as teachers consistently report they struggle to use theory to inform practice (Hedges & Cullen, 2005). This continued lack of guidance may limit teachers' ability to think critically about how to improve practice.

Feedback from the consultation process appeared to have influenced the 2017 version. For example, there was a move away from the generic position of 'curriculum for *all*' to specific mention to how children's needs could be addressed. Both the 1996, 2016 and 2017 versions were intended to be inclusive, but the 2017 version is more inclusive by stating:

> Inclusion encompasses gender and ethnicity, diversity of ability and learning needs, family structure and values, socio-economic status and religion. *Te Whāriki* holds the promise that all children will be empowered to learn with

and alongside others by engaging in experiences that have meaning to them. This requires kaiako [teachers] to actively respond to the strengths and needs of each child and at times provide them with additional support in relation to learning, behaviour, development or communication.

(Ministry of Education, 2017, p. 13)

Specific reference to "learning, behaviour, development or communication needs" and "additional support" is in line with delivering a *curriculum for all* and should assist teachers address the needs of the most at-risk children. In addition, the connections between ECE and school is updated and strengthened. Excluded from the 2016 draft, but included in 1996 and the now updated 2017 draft is the inclusion of 'Examples of practice' and 'Questions for reflection'. Of note, also in each Strand, is an updated version of 'Management, organisation and practice' and 'Adults' responsibilities', now called in the 2016/17 versions 'Considerations for leadership, organisation and practice'. This section provides teaching points for teachers to consider in relation to the environment, teaching and working with families/whanau, which encourage kaiako to reflect on their own use of theory and practice for infants, toddlers and young children.

A large bibliography was included in the 2016 draft but this was considerably reduced in 2017, with only a one-page bibliography, which includes references to policy documents. There are no citations in text, thus diminishing the importance of where information comes from; although stylistically this is consistent with the New Zealand Curriculum, which also does not include references.

Implications for practice and future research

The next epoch of ECE in Aotearoa New Zealand will build on recent changes in policies, regulations and curriculum requirements. *Te Whāriki* has been used for the past 20 years and was due for revision. However, we need to be cautious about implementation and attempt to avoid the challenges identified with the original. Some implications for the future include:

1. The implementation of the revised curriculum must be regularly evaluated; with findings used to strengthen guidance for teaching practice.
2. The Ministry of Education and ECE services should provide substantive and ongoing professional learning and development opportunities for all ECE teachers and parent-led services so that learning outcomes for children are achieved.
3. Future research could investigate the following:

    a. If the 2017 curriculum meets the needs of all children, specifically those with additional learning and development needs.
    b. How intentional teaching impacts on children's learning outcomes.

Conclusions

Over the past 40 years, there has been considerable change in the ECE sector in Aotearoa New Zealand. Political and economic factors played an important role in shaping ECE in this country. The amalgamation of the education and childcare sectors, upgrading of teacher qualifications to degree status, teacher registration, the decrease in not-for-profit services and commensurate increase in private services and home-based care have all impacted on the nature of ECE. Many changes have been in response to changes to families' need for different types of services, and in response to global trends concerning quality of ECE services (OECD, 2015). The recent revision of *Te Whāriki* signals the beginning of another epoch in the history of ECE in this country. It will be interesting to follow how the changes in *Te Whāriki* influences teachers' practices and the learning outcomes for our young children in the future.

Note

1 Whānau is the Māori word for extended family.

References

Blaiklock, K. (2010). Te Whāriki, the New Zealand early childhood curriculum: Is it effective? *International Journal of Early Years Education, 18*, 201–212.

Bushouse, B. K. (2008). *Early childhood education policy in Aotearoa/New Zealand: The creation of the 20 hours free programme.* Wellington: Fulbright New Zealand.

Carr, M., & Lee, W. (2012). *Learning stories. Constructing learner identities in early education.* London: Sage.

Cherrington, S. (2016). Early childhood teachers' thinking and reflection: A model of current practice in New Zealand. *Early Years*, 1–17. doi:http://dx.doi.org/10.1080/09575146.2016.1259211

Cullen, J. (1996). The challenge of Te Whāriki for future developments in early childhood education. *Delta, 48*(1), 113–125.

Education Counts. (2017). *Early childhood education statistics: Services.* Retrieved March 30, 2017, from www.educationcounts.govt.nz/statistics/early-childhood-education/services

Education Review Office. (2011, October 30). *Positive foundations for learning: Confident and competent children in early childhood services.* Wellington: New Zealand Government. Retrieved from www.ero.govt.nz/National-Reports/Positive-Foundations-for-Learning-Confident-and-Competent-Children-in-Early-Childhood-Services-October-2011

Education Review Office. (2013a). *He Pou Tātaki: How ERO reviews early childhood services.* Wellington, NZ: Author.

Education Review Office. (2013b, November 1). *Priorities for children's learning in early childhood services: Good practice.* Wellington, NZ: New Zealand Government. Retrieved from www.ero.govt.nz/National-Reports/Priorities-for-Children-s-Learning-in-Early-Childhood-Services-Good-Practice-November-2013

Education Review Office. (2016). *Early learning curriculum. What's important and what works.* Retrieved from www.ero.govt.nz/assets/Uploads/ERO-Early-Learning-Curriculum-WEB.pdf

Hedges, H., & Cullen, J. (2005). Subject knowledge in early childhood curriculum and pedagogy: Beliefs and practice. *Contemporary Issues in Early Childhood, 6*(1), 66–79.

May, H. (2014). New Zealand: A narrative of shifting policy directions for early childhood education and care. In L. Gambaro, K. Stewart, & J. Waldfogel (Eds.), *An equal start? Providing quality early education and care for disadvantaged children.* Bristol, UK: Policy Press.

Meade, A. (2002). Remembering: Knowing the moment cannot be repeated. *Childrenz Issues, 6*, 12–17.

McLachlan, C. (2011). An analysis of New Zealand's changing history, policies and approaches to early childhood education. *Australasian Journal of Early Childhood, 36*(3), 36–44.

McLachlan, C., Carvalho, L., de Lautour, N., & Kumar, K. (2006). *Literacy in early childhood settings in New Zealand: An examination of teachers' beliefs and practices.* Retrieved from http://web.b.ebscohost.com.ezproxy.canterbury. ac.nz/ehost/pdfviewer/pdfviewer?vid=2&sid=5685a067-5007-46f6-ac9d-a806405f8985%40sessionmgr120

McLaughlin, T., Aspden, K., & Snyder, P. (2016). Intentional teaching as a pathway to equity in early childhood education: Participation, quality, and equity. *New Zealand Journal of Educational Studies, 51*(2), 175–195. doi:10.1007/s40841-016-0062-z

Ministry of Education. (1993). *Te Whāriki: He Whàriki Màtauranga mò ngà Mokopuna o Aotearoa Draft Guidelines for Developmentally Appropriate Programmes (DAP) in Early Childhood Services.* Wellington, NZ: Learning Media.

Ministry of Education. (1996). *Te whāriki mātauranga mō ngā mokopuna o Aotearoa: Early childhood curriculum.* Wellington, NZ: Learning Media.

Ministry of Education. (2002). *Pathways to the future: Ngā huarahi Arataki. A 10-year strategic plan for early childhood education.* Wellington, NZ: Learning Media.

Ministry of Education. (2004, 2007, 2009). *Kei Tua o te Pae: Assessment for learning: Early childhood exemplars.* Wellington, NZ: Learning Media.

Ministry of Education. (2015). *Report of the advisory group on early learning.* Retrieved from https://education.govt.nz/assets/Documents/Ministry/consultations/Report-of-the-Advisory-Group-on-Early-Learning.pdf

Ministry of Education. (2016). *Te Whāriki: He Whàriki Màtauranga mò ngà Mokopuna o Aotearoa Early Childhood Curriculum. Draft for consultation.* Wellington, NZ: Author.

Ministry of Education. (2017). *The early childhood curriculum: Te Whāriki: He Whàriki Màtauranga mò ngà Mokopuna o Aotearoa Early Childhood Curriculum.* Wellington, NZ: Author.

Moss, P., & Dahlberg, G. (2008). Beyond quality in early childhood education and care – Languages of evaluation. *New Zealand Journal of Teachers' Work, 5*(1), 3–12.

Nuttall, J. (2003). Introduction. In *Weaving Te Whariki: Aotearoa New Zealand's early childhood curriculum document in theory and practice* (pp. 7–15). Wellington, NZ: New Zealand Council for Educational Research.

NZEI: TE Riu Roa. (2017). *Media release: Government cuts cost ECE $260 million this year.* Retrieved from http://nzei.org.nz/NZEI/Media/Releases/2017/03/Government_cuts_cost_ECE__260_million_this_year.aspx#.WNxXyfp96Ul

NZ Government. (2008). *The regulatory framework for ECE.* Retrieved from https://education.govt.nz/early-childhood/running-an-ece-service/the-regulatory-framework-for-ece/

Organisation for Economic Co-operation and Development (OECD). (2015). *Starting strong IV: Monitoring quality in early childhood education and care.* Paris,

France. Retrieved from www.keepeek.com/Digital-Asset-Management/oecd/education/starting-strong-iv_9789264233515-en#.WSKYA-uGPs0

Shuker, M. J., & Cherrington, S. (2016). Diversity in New Zealand early childhood education: Challenges and opportunities. *International Journal of Early Years Education*, 1–16. doi:10.1080/09669760.2016.1155148

Stover, S. (2016). The educationalising of early childhood in Aotearoa New Zealand: tracking "free play" 1940s–2010. *Paedagogical Historical International Journal of the History of Education*, 52(5), 525–541.

Te One, S. (2003). The context of Te Whāriki: Contemporary issues of influence. In J. Nuttall (Ed.), *Weaving Te Whāriki: Aotearoa New Zealand's early childhood curriculum document in theory and practice* (pp. 17–49). Wellington, NZ: New Zealand Council for Educational Research.

TeachNZ. (2017). *Teacher education providers.* Retrieved from www.teachnz.govt.nz/thinking-of-teaching/qualifications-information-for-2017/QualificationSearchForm

Tesar, M. (2015). New Zealand perspectives on early childhood education: Nāku te rourou nāu te rourou ka ora ai te iwi. *Journal of Pedagogy*, 6(2), 9–18.

13 Early childhood education and care in Norway

Cultural historical context, new regulations and perceived quality

Alicja R. Sadownik and Elin Eriksen Ødegaard

Introduction

Norway's Early Childhood Education and Care (ECEC) system has experienced significant growth in recent years. While the age for compulsory school entry is 6 years old, nearly all children in Norway between the ages of 1 and 5 are enrolled in ECEC institutions, called kindergarten. Paid parental leave is available for parents of children up to the age of 1, so it is common for children to begin attending a kindergarten early. A cash-for-care benefit is also available for the few families that do not enrol their children in a kindergarten. Public funding for early childhood education has significantly increased over the past 15 years, enabling a fast expansion of this sector. As a result, the related fields of research have also grown. In addition, since Norway is becoming an increasingly diverse society, the government has devoted a portion of this funding to ensure that the early childhood education sector is addressing the needs of migrant children and their families (Engel, Barnett anders, & Taguma, 2015).

This chapter describes Norwegian early childhood education from a cultural-historical perspective that emphasises the mutual influences of a broad historical mentality (culture); governance through the state, municipalities and institutions; and individuals participating in these contexts (Hedegaard, 2009). Therefore, this chapter first presents a broad background for why a democratic and holistic approach has become so strong in Norway, particularly as reflected in the new early childhood education regulations and curriculum. Next, this chapter focuses on central features of the Norwegian ECEC system and the way it is organised to describe the new regulations and goals of institutional practice. Third, this chapter seeks to provide a deeper understanding of the challenges that Norwegian ECEC programmes face in an increasingly complex and heterogenic society that is comprised of families with diverse cultural and ethnic backgrounds (Hedegaard, 2005).

Here, the quality of kindergarten practices is understood as a multidimensional concept that includes structural characteristics, process quality and a more in-depth, perceived quality. Structural quality, such as group size, teacher-child ratios, formal staff qualification levels and available space and materials, is governed by the state through laws, regulations and economic support. Municipalities support and monitor this quality at the local level for both public and private kindergartens. Process quality refers to the nature of pedagogical practice; e.g. the relationships between staff and children, peer interactions, cooperation with families and the use and availability of space and materials. One form of process quality can be referred to as *perceived quality*, which refers to the way that parents perceive (experience) the quality of a kindergarten attended by their children (Bjørnestad, Gullbrandsen, & Johannson, 2013; Bråten, Hovdenak, Haakestad, & Sønsterudbråten, 2015; Engel et al., 2015).

After discussing the background, curriculum and quality features of Norway's ECEC, we present results from a new empirical study of the *perceived quality* of Polish migrant parents whose children attend Norwegian kindergartens. The largest migrant minority group in Norway is Polish; therefore, analysing how these parents' experience of Norwegian kindergartens will provide insight into the complexity and dynamics of process quality in this education sector.

A cultural historical background – democratic, egalitarian roots as well as old heterogeneity

Norway became a nation state in 1905 after the dissolution of the union between Norway and Sweden to avoid war. Negotiations between the two governments led to Sweden's recognition of Norway as an independent constitutional monarchy. The new Norwegian government organised the county into municipalities with local political authorities; these communities included, for example, farmers, teachers, fishermen and church priests. This approach was similar to the way Sweden was organised and resulted in an early version of local, municipal welfare societies, which Sejersted has referred to as "municipality socialism" (2005, p. 63). Folk movements, such as grassroots movements concerning language and religion, the anti-alcohol movement and labour unions, nominated individuals to serve as politicians in the national government. These politicians were then trained in organising and solving problems at the local level. This may be an explanation for the development of democratic public- mindedness in Norway, as well as the high level of trust in authorities, politicians and the government. This is a distinctly different approach to establishing and experiencing democracy, contrary to other democratic countries, which have historically recruited their politicians from the ranks of the educated or economic elite. Politicians with whom the average citizen can identify, along with long-term stability in the political sphere, facilitates the development of social trust that, in turn, serves as a guarantor of the welfare state.

The Norwegian society has traditionally had a weak upper class, with a nascent welfare state since right after World War II. The country's history of a rapid increase in wealth due to offshore oil is a short one, but in the past century, many Norwegians have worked in the shipping and oil industries. Along the long coastline, the fishing industry also provides many jobs, often in combination with small-scale farming. The metal industry has employed workers in Western

Norway for the past 100 years, and many small communities have been built near the tall waterfalls that generate electricity through power plants. Due to Norway's rich natural resources spread over a large geographic area on land and in the sea, a forceful policy promoting economic growth has been possible. Consequently, continued improvements in the local infrastructure, such as in the fields of education, health and transportation (e.g. tunnels, bridges and roads), have been prioritised by the public sector.

We can therefore see that a widespread localisation of power, freedom and self-realization is possible through the welfare state, as it creates a *habitus* of public-mindedness as an ideal. From early on, this perspective has included women and children as equal human beings in both thoughts and ideas (Sejersted, 2005). However, while Norway has its roots in an egalitarian approach to society, it has also traditionally been a heterogeneous culture. For example, it is home to an indigenous minority group, the Sami, and including their presence and cultural traditions in a recounting of Norway's history allows for a more holistic understanding of the broader cultural perspective.

The Sami mostly live in the circumpolar regions in the Nordic countries. They have fully relied – and to a certain extent still rely – on natural resources like fishing, hunting and herding reindeer. In the Sami tradition, no distinction is made between man and nature. In direct opposition to Western cultures, their child rearing is based on learning by experience; children observe themselves, and the adults trust that they will draw their own conclusions instead of being taught by means of direct communication (Stordjord, 2008). Over the years, in the education sector and in other facets of society, the Sami people have been subjected to paternalism, ignoring their language and cultural identity. The law in Norway did not even officially recognise the Sami until 1987.

Society's views toward children, especially regarding early childhood education, have also evolved over the years. Based on a European model, orphan asylums were established in the largest cities in 1837 as a way to cope with widespread poverty. At the time, the dominant features of child rearing were health, obedience and handicrafts. Beginning around 1930, Fröbel kindergartens were opened in urban areas for children whose parents could afford to pay for early education. In these schools, singing, playing and handicrafts were emphasised. Full-day childcare became popular after World War II as more parents entered the workforce. The first kindergarten act came into force in 1975 to regulate this diverse sector and, one term was chosen to refer to all institutions in the ECEC sector, i.e. *kindergarten*. According to Korsvold, this term was chosen because of the persistent cultural idea of the importance of a 'good childhood', its association with outdoor peer play and the ambivalence regarding separating children from their mothers. Beginning in the late 1960s, there has been a steady increase in the number of women employed outside the home due to the growing acceptance of gender equality, and therefore the need for all-day childcare has also grown (Korsvold, 2011). A sparsely populated nation such as Norway particularly needs a workforce in both the private and public sectors, such as industry, service trades, health and education.

In sum, with a few exceptions, such as the Sami people group, a long tradition of local democracies in sparsely populated areas; a strong national 'folkedannelse' (popular education); and many decades of centrifugal forces (e.g. one national broadcasting station for educating people and disseminating stories about national and local heroes) has fostered a strongly governed Norwegian society, in which every citizen receives free, standardised public education and health services. However, despite the strong public welfare services and a national strongly governed education system, Norway has never been completely homogeneous because of the strong local policy. From being one of the last countries in Europe to have more than one national radio and television station, the country today has several state and private channels and the global media is a powerful force penetrating nearly every aspect of society. In the new era of globalisation, Norwegian policy- and curriculum-making processes are closely linked to the global discourse and other countries' economies. Kindergarten is increasingly viewed as an arena for social mobility and life-long learning, but this education sector is still centrally governed. Indeed, since 1996, a national framework plan has served as a national mandate and regulating instrument of all kindergarten owners and staff (Ministry of Education and Research, 2017).

Regulations and curriculum

In 2006, the responsibility for the kindergarten sector was transferred from the Ministry of Children and Family Affairs to the Ministry of Education and Research. This move points to a growing emphasis on the educational dimension of kindergarten and the idea of life-long learning. However, the ideals of play, care, development and 'bildung' (in Norwegian, bildung is translated as 'danning'; in English, it is translated as cultural formation) are still highly valued and seen in their own right as forms of education. Therefore, there is an ongoing debate and negotiations concerning what education should mean in Norwegian kindergartens, including the questions 'What is the role of a teacher within a more holistic framework?' and 'How can a teacher balance children's interest with supporting them discover the world they live in'?

In the past few years, the Ministry of Education and Research has been working on a new kindergarten framework in response to the rapidly changing Norwegian and global societies. This plan is currently being introduced in kindergartens across the country. It is organised into nine chapters: foundations and values, responsibility and roles, aims and content, children's participation, cooperation between families and kindergartens, transitions, kindergarten as a pedagogical institution, kindergartens' forms of working and kindergartens' seven knowledge areas.

The most fundamental values of this framework are 'childhood as its own right' and 'experienced democracy'. These values are introduced in the first paragraph:

> Childhood has a value of its own, and kindergartens should have a holistic approach to children's development. The kindergartens' mandate is to

cooperate in close understanding with the home, to protect children's need for care and play and to promote learning and 'danning' as a basis for multipurpose development.

(Ministry of Education and Research, 2017, p. 7)

The plan emphasises democracy as a value: "It shall be experienced by all children through a variety of opportunity to express themselves, as well as experienced by being included in activities and peer groups" (2017, p. 9). This is, as can be seen in the cultural and historical backgrounds of Norwegian kindergarten, a persistent and fundamental value.

A new value in the 2017 plan is 'sustainability as a value'. It is stated that, "The children shall learn to take care of themselves, each other and nature. Sustainable development includes nature, economy and social conditions and is a condition for taking care of life on earth, as we know it" (Ministry of Education and Research, 2017, p. 10).

Democratic values and a closeness to nature are considered to be special features in the Nordic kindergarten model. Wagner (2006) tried to 'translate' the Nordic kindergarten universe for American readers. When discussing democracy and participation issues, she confronted the American focus on *boundary setting* with the Nordic modus of *cooperation with children*. She writes, "The Nordic notion of democracy as an essential feature of a good childhood requires that children experience democracy directly as an integral and consistent aspect of their daily lives at home, in school and kindergarten" (Wagner, 2006, p. 292). She continues: "The "because I said so" mentality does not exist in Nordic settings . . . A key difference is that American preschools and schools are not conceptualised as democracies, but rather, as places where students learn about democracy. It is often said that the purpose of education in America is to *prepare* children to participate in a democracy and to teach them to use freedom when they are adults. In contrast, Nordic people expect that children should experience democracy directly from their earliest days" (Wagner, 2006, p. 294).

The OECD confirmed this perspective when referring to the earlier framework and areas of learning:

> The framework does not impose instructions on the implementation of the learning areas nor does it specify activities to be performed. Moreover, it recognises each kindergarten as free to adapt the learning areas to the interests of individual children, the group, and the local community.
>
> (Engel et al. 2015, p. 78)

In both the old and new early childhood frameworks, the child is seen as a social actor in his own right – an individual who has right to participate in and influence his own conditions to a degree appropriate for his age and maturity (Grindheim, 2011). Physical and emotional expressions are interpreted as children's views and expressions and, it is noted that children should be supported in understanding the views of others by considering these. Children should also be given opportunities to be active participants in planning and evaluating institutional life and to raise a critical voice, as critical thinking is seen as an important skill. The Norwegian guidelines emphasise learning and play; the distinctive characteristic in a traditional Nordic comparison is denoted by the term 'bildung' (German word). In the latest version of the framework, the concepts of 'bildung' and education for a sustainable future are made explicit as a basis for prioritising the values of the kindergartens. In the Norwegian framework, the concept of 'bildung' is close to the central European roots of acting a critical, participatory citizen with responsibilities to society and to nature (Ødegaard & White, 2016).

As was previously earlier pointed out, the cultural and language diversity that has resulted from migration in recent decades and the recent influx of refugees is a major concern in enhancing the quality of Norwegian kindergartens. In the new framework, this addressed as follows "The kindergartens should use diversity as a resource in pedagogical work and support [and should] strengthen and follow up with the children based on their own cultural and individual conditions" (Ministry of Education and Research, 2017, p. 9). All children are therefore, exposed to curriculum content that acknowledges national minorities, such as the Sami and other ethnicities.

New demands – the diverse Norwegian society and the diverse ECEC community

Today, 90.4% of Norwegian children aged 1 to 5 attend kindergartens. More precise figures from the Directorate of Education (2016) indicate that 69% of all 1-year-olds and 97% of all 5-year-olds attended kindergarten in 2016. That means that children from all social categories attend kindergarten. This is the direct result of a political agreement and promise in 2003 that all families who wanted their child to attend a kindergarten should have access to reasonably priced schools near their homes by 2005. As a result of this pledge, kindergartens are generously subsidised by the state. A historical glance back to 1990 indicates that only 15% of 1-year-olds and 36% of all children under the compulsory school age attended kindergarten. This means that during the period of only a few years, there has been a huge change in Norwegian society that has challenged the established practices and traditional knowledge of how to cooperate and build partnerships with families.

The growing cultural diversity in Norway has been officially acknowledged. For example, a government white paper (Ministry of Children, Equality and Inclusion of 2012–2013) articulated that everybody, regardless of their cultural background, should experience full membership in their local communities and trust in the authorities, as well as participate in a just society. Kindergartens as well as other educational institutions are recognised as significant social arenas in the multicultural landscape. They are expected to collaborate with their students' families to safeguard the children's overall development and to develop inclusive communities where all children and parents – regardless of their level of functioning, age, gender or family background – feel that they and everyone else in the group belong (Ministry of Education and Research, 2017, pp. 29–30).

An OECD review of migrant education in Norway acknowledged an increase in the ability to tackle challenges, but they pointed to the need to further develop practices that are even more responsive to linguistic and cultural diversity (Taguma, Shewbridge, Huttova, & Hoffman, 2009). This was later followed up by the Ministry by identifying more key challenge points, some of which addressed early childhood education, early efforts in general, multilingualism as a positive value, the need for competence building in the education sector and implementation challenges (Ministry of Education and Research, 2015).

The issues of diversity and multicultural environments in Norwegian kindergartens have also been discussed in the professional literature (Gjervan, Andresen, & Bleka, 2006; Giæver, 2014; Nilsen, 2016). In published research as well as argumentative papers, the cultural, religious and linguistic diversity among children, parents and staff in Norwegian kindergartens has been recognised as a normal condition and as a resource for cultural understanding and learning. Nevertheless, migrant and minority children are still viewed as an at-risk group that has a strong effect on the current goals for Norwegian ECEC. Heterogeneity is addressed as both a resource (as an ideal) and as a challenge for potential misunderstandings, conflicts and pedagogical dilemmas.

A need for new competencies in cultural diversity and working with all kinds of families has been noted by both the government and professionals. Kindergarten staff face new challenges related to negotiating between different – and sometimes conflicting – institutional discourses. And despite good intentions, kindergarten staff can end up treating children from different backgrounds unequally (Nilsen, 2016). Therefore, in order to safeguard all children's rights to care, play, 'danning' and participation, parental cooperation needs to be increased.

According to the Directorate of Education (2016), 38% of all Norwegian kindergartens have minority parents who are struggling with language acquisition, while 16% of kindergartens never involve those parents in such work. The same source shows that 97% of kindergartens ensure that they talk with all parents individually twice a year and that 78% arrange meetings for the community of parents. A recent study of the teacher education curriculum after the latest reform (Ministry of Education and Research, 2012) found that there were only a few pages on the theme of family work/parent cooperation (Ødegaard & Sataøen, 2016). Therefore, there is a growing concern as to whether themes such as cooperation with diverse families has been taken into consideration in the teachers' education (Garvis, 2015; Garvis & Ødegaard, 2018).

Norwegian ECEC quality perceived by Polish migrant parents

The findings presented below were reconstructed from an analysis of research material from semi-structured interviews with 20 Polish parents (16 mothers and 4 fathers) living permanently in Norway. The interview guide included questions on reasons for migration, experiences within Norwegian society/culture, perception of Norwegian kindergartens, experiences with Norwegian kindergartens and trust developed (or not) with childcare institutions in Norway. Four of the interviews were recorded and transcribed. The other 16 were written in the form of researchers notes as the informants did not permit their interviews to be recorded.

The informants represented different educational backgrounds (vocational to university level), different ages (29 to 39 years) and different amounts of time spent in Norway (1 to 9 years). All of the interviewed parents had Polish spouses. The Polish group of parents was chosen because it is the biggest migrant minority group in Norway and because the researcher spoke Polish and would therefore be able to interview them in their first language. The data analysis, inspired by Goodson's narrative inquiry, was focused on reconstruction of the dynamics of meanings that change over time (Goodson, 2008).

The first impressions of the Norwegian kindergarten were shared by all the participating informants. They referred to the low-quality food served to the children on a daily basis, the narrow pedagogical approach focused on motor skills and outdoor activities, limited engagement among the staff and children sleeping outside in their prams. This latter observation caused them to conclude that the kindergartens either lacked resources or lacked caring attitudes among the staff.

However, their first impressions, which were grounded in the Polish ideals of high-quality care and a good childhood, changed over time. Parents with university degrees who had been in Norway over three years and had already had one or more positive experience with other public services (police, health system, etc.) were the most open to the Norwegian way of running an ECEC centre. Parents with higher levels of education and bad or no experiences with other public services were more sceptical at the beginning but changed their perception over time. Parents with lower levels of education but who had good experiences with other public services tended to also change their feelings about the kindergartens over time.

The changes in their first impressions were facilitated by formal meetings with the pedagogical leaders as well as informal chats when dropping off and picking up their children. Other influences turned out to be weekly or monthly newsletters sent to the parents as well as the use of digital tools to provide parental insight in the schools' daily activities (e.g. a closed Facebook group or the MyKid app).

The changes in these parents' perceptions went from 'Why do they do it this way?' to finding the good in practices that initially seemed strange. The 'low-quality food' started being seen as food that the children simply liked and would eat. The 'narrow pedagogical approach' started being seen as rich. The outdoor activities started being seen as healthy and not only connected to motor skills, but also to gaining social competencies, friends, language skills, mathematical skills and creativity. The limited engagement of the staff turned into conscious 'holding back' in order to let the children be agents in free-play situations. Moreover, the work that lay behind good playing situations started being seen and appreciated (by some of the parents). They started to see sleeping in the prams as being good for the immune system, and it was 'transformed' into an activity that required a lot of care. For example, putting the children in warm clothes before they went to sleep, standing in the rain to ensure that the children were safe while they slept and stroking and caressing those toddlers who needed help falling asleep.

The parents with higher levels of education pointed out that reasons given by kindergarten staff for different activities were more convincing than 'national' ones (e.g. 'In Norway, all the kindergartens do it this way'). They also emphasised the kindness that they were met with.

However, not all of the parents had changed all of their first meanings/impressions before the interviews. Many of them (12) seemed to still be in this process. For example, some of them saw the healthiness of sleeping outside and the focus on free play but remained insecure about the pedagogical approach as a whole as it still seemed too narrow.

The group of parents with lower levels of education and with no or negative experience with other public services in Norway were those who tended to take their feelings about the kindergartens in another direction. They started by accepting that 'this is how Norwegian kindergartens are run' and focusing on the fact that kindergartens gave them 'some hours of freedom', self-realisation and/or time for the parents his/herself. This was in line with the informants' expectations towards their own migrations (i.e. for economic benefits) and was experienced as appreciated by the kindergarten staff. This empirical example shows the dynamics and complexity of the *perceived quality* and its dependence of other social factors (i.e. educational background, time spent in the country of destination and experiences with other public services).

A category that appears to be significant for *perceived quality* is the teachers' competence. The ways that some of the teacher's expressed their points of view and the kindness that they showed the parents can be viewed through Van Manen's (1991) concept of 'tact of teaching', this is centred at the intersection of the professional and personal competences of the (kindergarten) teachers. It includes the ability to judge, to make quick decisions and to direct situations with sensitivity and alertness that involve strong feelings and emotions. The 'tact of teaching' is therefore a significant dimension of pedagogical leadership as well as of process and *perceived quality.*

Summary

In this chapter, Norwegian early childhood policies and practices have been explained from a cultural and historical perspective. Experienced democracy is still a dominant feature of the new framework plan for kindergartens, which also includes a focus on sustainability and diversity as a teaching resource. Nevertheless, the cultural and language diversity due to the increase in migration and refugee families is a major concern for enhancing the quality of Norwegian kindergartens. In the new framework, minorities are paid special attention, and it mandates the fostering of a critical and new citizen with agency. The concept of 'danning' embraces the European tradition of 'bildung'. In order to further problematise and understand new forms of diversity, this chapter has disseminated original results from a study of how Polish migrants experience quality in Norwegian kindergartens. This study provides important insight into understanding the complexity and challenges that kindergartens face in an increasingly heterogeneous Norwegian society.

References

Bjørnestad, E., Gullbrandsen, L., Johannson, J.-E., & Os, E. (2013). *Metodiske idealkrav og nødvendige tilpasninger: Foreløpig tilstandsrapport fra prosjektet* [Better provision for Norway's children in ECEC: A study of children's well-being and development in ECEC]. Oslo: Høgskolen i Oslo og Akerhus (HiOA).

Bråten, B., Hovdenak, I. M., Haakestad, H., & Sønsterudbråten, S. (2015). *Har barn det bra i store barnehager?* [Do children benefit from large kindergartens?] Fafo-rapport. Retrieved from www.fafo.no/index.php/nb/zoo-publikasjoner

Engel, A., Barnett, S., Anders, Y., & Taguma, M. (2015). *Early childhood education and care policy review – Norway*. Paris: OECD.

Directorate of Education. (2016). *Utdanningsspeilet – Tall og analyse av barnehager og grunnopplæring i Norge 2016* [Figures and analysis of kindergartens and basic education in Norway 2016]. Retrieved from http://utdanningsspeilet.udir.no/2016/

Garvis, S. (2015). Vurdering av praksis – en fortellingsmontasje om hvilke stemmer vi gjør gyldige. In E. E. Ø. Ødegaard & M. S. Økland (Ed.), *Fortellinger fra praksis – Trøbbel vendepunkt og stolthet* [Accounts from practicum – turning points and pride] (pp. 217–237). Bergen: Fagbokforlaget.

Garvis, S., & Ødegaard, E. E. (2018). *Nordic dialogues on children and families*. London: Routledge.

Gjervan, M., Andresen, C. E., & Bleka, M. (2006). *Se mangfold! Perspektiver på flerkulturelt arbeid i barnehagen*. [Look! Diversity – Perspectives on multicultural practice in kindergarten]. Oslo: Cappelen Akademisk Forlag.

Giæver, K. (2014). *Inkluderende språkfelleskap i barnehagen* [Inclusive language community]. Bergen: Fagbokforlaget.

Goodson, I. (2008). *Investigating the teacher's life and work*. Rotterdam: Sense Publishing.

Grindheim, L. T. (2011). Barnefelleskap som demokratisk danningsarena. Kva kan gje høve til medverknad i leik i barnehagen? [A community of peers as democratic arena for cultural formation] *Nordisk Barnehageforskning, 4*(2), 91–102.

Korsvold, T. (2011). The best interest of the child – early childhood education in Norway and Sweden from 1945. In K. Hagemann, K. Jarauch, & C. Allemann-Gionda (Eds.), *Children, families, and states: Time policies of childcare, preschool, and primary education in Europe*. Oxford, UK: Berghan Books.

Hedegaard, M. (2005). Strategies for dealing with conflicts in value positions between home and school: Influences on ethnic minority students' development of motives and identity. *Culture & Psychology, 11*(2), 187–205.

Hedegaard, M. (2009). Children's development from a cultural-historical approach: Children's activity in everyday local settings as foundation for their development. *Mind, Culture, and Activity, 16*, 64–82.

Ministry of Children, Equality and Inclusion. (2012–2013). *En helhetlig integreringspolitikk* [A holistic integration policy]. Oslo: Ministry of Children, Equality and Inclusion.

Ministry of Education and Research. (2012). *Forskrift om rammeplan for barne-hagelærerutdanning* [Regulations on the national curriculum for kindergarten teacher training]. Oslo: Ministry of Education and Research.

Ministry of Education and Research. (2017). *Rammeplan for barnehagen: Innhold og oppgaver.* [Framework plan for kindergartens content and tasks]. Oslo: Ministry of Education and Research.

Ministry of Education and Research. (2015). *Country background report for the OECD ECEC review.* Oslo: Ministry of Education and Research.

Nilsen, A. C. (2016). In-between discourses: Early intervention and diversity in the Norwegian kindergarten sector. *Journal of Comparative Social Work, 11*(1), 1–22.

Ødegaard, E. E., & Sataøen, S. O. (2016). *A reform in the making. The new kinder-garten teacher education program – background, study model and challenges.* Paper presented at the NERA, Helsinki.Ødegaard, E. E., & White, J. E. (2016). Bildung: Potential and promise in early childhood education. In M. Peters (Ed.), *Encyclope-dia of educational philosophy and theory* (pp. 1–7). Dordrecht: Springer.

Sejersted, F. (2005). *Sosialdemokratiets tidsalder – Norge og Sverige I det 20. Århun-dre* [Social democratic era – Norway and Sweden in the 21st century]. Oslo: Pax Forlag.

Stordjord, M. H. (2008). *Barnehagebarns liv i en samisk kontekst – En arena for kul-turell meningsskaping* [Kindergarten children's lives in a Sami context – an arena for cultural meaning-making] Dissertation. Tromsø: University of Tromsø.

Taguma, M., Shewbridge, C., Huttova, J., & Hoffman, N. (2009). *OECD reviews of migrant education: Norway.* Retrieved from www.oecd.org/edu/school/43723539.pdf

Van Manen, M. (1991). *The tact of teaching. Meaning of pedagogical thoughtfulness.* New York: State University of New York Press.

Wagner, J. T. (2006). An outsider perspective: Childhoods and early education in Nordic countries. In J. Einarsdottir & J. T. Wagner (Eds.), *Nordic childhoods and early education: Philosophy, research, policy and practice in Denmark, Finland, Ice-land, Norway, and Sweden* (pp. 289–306). Greenwich: IAP.

14 Early childhood education and care in Russia

Different contexts of the cultural-historical theory

Igor Shiyan, Olga Shiyan, Alexander Veraksa and Nikolay Veraksa

Introduction

The Russian preschool education system has a long history. The first nursery institutions in Russia were established at the end of the 19th century and were inspired by the ideas of Friedrich Wilhelm, August Fröbel and Maria Montessori. In the 1930s, the state preschool education system was formed, and the "Program for the Work of Nursery Institutions" as well as preschool teachers' guidelines were approved. Over 2 million children attended kindergartens in the USSR by the late 1940s. Since establishment until now, the state preschool education system is designed for 3–7 year olds. It mostly consists of full-day kindergartens with three hot meals and an obligatory daytime nap included.

The first "Program for Mentoring in a Kindergarten" was presented in the early 1960s. It was presented as a single obligatory guiding document for the functioning of all nursery institutions around the country. It was slightly amended in 1978, and in 1984, was renamed as the "Standard Program for Education and Mentoring in a Kindergarten" (1984). These programs included explicit description of the content and methods of organization of classes for physical education, intellectual development, moral development, labor skills, artistic development and play. The programs also contained calendar planning, so that preschoolers in all parts of the country easily could have had very similar math or art lessons on the same day.

Many of the principles and ideas of cultural-historical approach (in particular, the idea of age-based child's abilities, or of adult's position as a bearer of cultural norms) were included into the "Standard Program". The most influential theoretical works belonged to Lev Vygotsky (1982, 1983) and his students and followers: Daniil Elkonin, Alexander Zaporozhets, Leonid Venger and Nikolay Poddyakov. However, daily practice of the program implementation was mostly teacher-focused (i.e. an adult was the only translator of the norms), and often copied school ways of educational work. The program was aimed at the acquisition of object knowledge, skills and capabilities. In an educational process of this kind, the major initiative belongs to a teacher; the educational process is founded on the basis of examples of actions which are demonstrated by the teacher and then repeated by children. The content of education is strictly stipulated and provides limited possibilities for teacher's creativity in process of education.

Alternative educational programs appeared in the late 1980s to early 1990s. Among others, one can name "Razvitie" ("Development") program based on the ideas of cultural tools acquisition, which was created under the guidance of Leonid Venger (2000), and the "Zolotoy Kliuchik" ("Golden Key") program by Elena and Gennady Kravzov (Kravzov, 2014), with special attention to play as a foundation of child development. At the same time, programs for the development of preschoolers' dialectical thinking (Veraksa, 1990), creative imagination (Kudryavtsev, 2011), etc., were proposed. Moreover, some foreign programs also gained popularity, such as the "Step by Step" program by Montessori and the Waldorf program. Nevertheless, a profoundly revised version of the "Standard Program" – "From birth to school" (2010) – remains the most abundantly used one. The new edition continues to provide preschool teachers with highly detailed instructions.

In the early 1990s, the first private preschool institutions were created in Russia but they are still in minority compared to municipal institutions. On the other hand, some private preschool communities are quite influential (for example, the Montessori approach, which is applied mostly in private preschool kindergartens).

In national republics (Tatarstan, Yakutia-Sakha, Buryatia, etc.) bilingual (Russian plus second national language) preschools are quite widespread. In recent years, the network of trilingual (Russian, Tatarian and English) preschools was developed in Tatarstan. In the 2000s, the inclusive education movement started.

The standard of preschool education

According to the Federal Law of the Russian Federation "On Education" (2012), the state took up the obligation to provide all 3- to 7-year-old children with the opportunity to receive preschool education. After official statistical data as of August 1 2015, various forms of preschool education cover 96.4% of the target population. The government pays no less than 20% of the cost of supervision and care for the first child, no less than 50% for the second child, no less than 50% for the third child, no less than 70% for the fourth child. The education is free of charge. Preschool institutions are generally financed by local budgets. Relevant regulations oblige preschool teachers to obtain a specialised education. Most of them graduate from teacher colleges and some from universities. Proceeding to the child-adult ratio, normally it approximates to 12–15. The common group size is usually around 30 children, and they are taken care of by one main teacher and one supporting teacher. This supporting teacher also performs technical duties (cleaning, serving food, etc.). Another document which regulates the educational system is the Federal State Educational Standard for Preschool Education (2013), which frames the requirements imposed on the structure of educational programs, the conditions of its implementation and educational performance (i.e. each preschool institution gets the right to create its own educational program).

The core point of the Standard lies in the requirements for implementation of the educational program in kindergartens, including psychological and pedagogical conditions. The conditions for the implementation of educational programs must support full-scale development of a child's personality in all educational areas: social, communicative, cognitive, speech, artistic, esthetical and physical development, all based on emotional wellbeing and a positive attitude to the world, themselves and other people. Indicated requirements are designed to create a social context of development for participants of educational relations – a context in which the child develops with the upmost efficiency and with adult assistance.

The psychological and pedagogical requirements for the implementation of educational programs are as follows:

1) Adults respect the human dignity of children; they form and support their positive self-esteem, confidence in their own abilities and skills;
2) Teaching and methods applied in an educational activity match children's age and individual characteristics (both artificial acceleration and deceleration of child development is unacceptable);
3) Educational activity is built on the basis of interaction between children and adults, focused on interests and abilities of each and every child, and takes in consideration social situation of his/her development;
4) Adults support a positive attitude of children to each other and their collaboration within different activities;
5) Initiative and independence of children in specific kinds of activities is supported;
6) Children can choose materials, kinds of activities, participants of joint occupation and communication;
7) Children are protected from physical and psychological abuse of all kinds;
8) Parents receive support in the upbringing of children, protection and strengthening of their health; families get directly involved in educational activities.

The conditions required for the creation of a social situation of child development are described by the Standard, as below:

1) Emotional wellbeing is provided via direct communication with each and every child, respectful attitude towards each and every child, and attention to his/her feelings and needs.
2) Individuality and initiative of children is supported through providing conditions for children's free choice of activities, participation in joint occupations, creation of conditions for children to make decisions, express their feelings and thoughts; non-directive assistance for children, support of child initiative and independence in various activities (play, exploration, etc.).
3) Establishment of interactional norms in different situations: providing conditions for positive, friendly relations between children, including those

belonging to various national, cultural and religious communities and social groups and those with distinct (among others, limited) physical abilities; development of such communication abilities of children that allow resolving conflict situations with their peers, and development of the ability to work in a group of age-mates.

4) Development education focused on the level of development acquired by children in joint activity with adults and more experienced peers, but not actualizing in their individual activity (furthermore – the zone of proximal development of every child), through providing conditions for mastering cultural means of activities; organization of activities promoting the development of thinking, speech, imagination and child creativity, personal, physical, artistic and aesthetical development; support for spontaneous play and its enrichment, provision of playtime and space; evaluation of individual development of a child.

5) Interaction with parents concerning educational issues, direct involvement of them into educational activities, including creation joint educational projects together with families basing on revealing special needs and supporting family educational initiatives.

Thus, the Standard contains requirements both for the character of the communication between a teacher and a child and for the content of this communication, which, from our point of view, determines the space for development of preschool educational system in Russia.

Traditionally, education quality measurements were based on formal data (teacher qualifications, frequency of children's sicknesses, etc.) and children's achievements. However, the Federal Law of the Russian Federation "On Education" (2012) prohibited the usage of children's achievement scores for measurement of the quality of preschool education. From that time on, it is the evaluation of the quality of the environment that forms the most influential tendency in preschool education quality assessment. In 2016–2017, several major research studies applying Russian translation of the Early Childhood Environment Rating Scale Revised (ECERS-R) were completed (Harms, Clifford, & Cryer, 2016).

Zone of proximal development and foundations of preschool education

Cultural-historical theory by Vygotsky determined the main findings in Soviet and Russian early child education theory and practice. The concept of the zone of proximal development (ZPD) allowed Lev Vygotsky to separate developmental education from education focused on the child's existing achievements, which became the cornerstone for the theory of developmental education. Regarding junior preschoolers, one can say that ZPD is created if learning is aimed at the child's mastering of the system of scientific concepts. It is understood that the content of education is transmitted by teachers, who help children to learn. Although it was Lev Vygotsky who introduced the concept of ZPD, the questions related to this concept in the context of analysis of the problem of learning and development were addressed in various ways.

One of the approaches to understanding the processes that occur within ZPD was presented in the works of Daniil Elkonin (Elkonin, 1960) and Vasiliy Davydov (1972). In these work,s the theory of developmental education found further development. Herewith the developmental education of primary-school children has continued to be understood as learning aimed at formation of the system of scientific concepts. According to Daniil Elkonin, mastering of the scientific concept is not limited to simply learning its definition. The main goal is to reveal the system of relations with a variety of objects and other concepts in which that scientific concept exists. In order to identify this system of relations, the child must rely on the guidance of the adult, who directs his/her activity and transforms it into the learning activity. Thus, certain specificity of content distribution, which is learnt by the child and by the adult, shows itself in ZPD. On behalf of the child, these are actions with objects, diagrams and various models; on behalf of the adult, it is the management and direction of these actions towards the definition of essential properties revealing the diversity of relations embodied in the concept.

The important aspect of this approach implies that reality, with which the child deals, corresponds to the reality which goes beyond the content already learned by that child. In other words, the system of relations underlying the concept does not form part of the relations known by the child. Davydov approached this problem by modeling the most common and extremely abstract relations. Davydov suggested,

> Every important thematic segment of the program begins with a special full-scale introduction of children into such situations where a need for relevant concepts of theoretical nature exists. While performing certain objective actions indicated by the teacher, young students find and register some important features of objects, orientation on which allows solving any problem of the specific class associated with this or that similar situation.
>
> (Davydov, 1972, p. 375)

For example, through interaction with real objects, a child learns to compare them according to particular characteristics. Herewith, he/she discovers their equality or inequality. Defining the generalised relations and capturing them in their "pure" form permits studying the properties of these relations. Therefore, an educational program was elaborated as a consecutive specification of studied material when the process of development was understood as a process of formation of generalizations taking place during the studies under that program, though not coinciding with it.

Another direction of approaching ZPD can be found in the context of works of Alexander Zaporozhets and his students (Leonid Venger and Nikolay Poddyakov, among others). Zaporozhets (1986) advanced and promoted the concept of "amplification", within which development could proceed along two lines: the line of acceleration, which is the fastest transition from one level of development to another and the line of enrichment, meaning ultimate saturation of each level via certain types of activity, intrinsic for this level. In the latter case, ZPD can be characterised not only by the difference between the levels of actual and potential development, but also by completion of these levels. This idea is most clearly elaborated in the works of Poddyakov (1977) who discusses two types of learning. The first type represents studying taking place on a regular basis and being organised by adults, where all forms of activity of the child are thought through, by adults, and aimed at mastering of the program content that is supposed to ensure development. The second type represents unstructured, spontaneous learning, which is implemented by the child and mostly has a nature of spontaneous experimentation. During the learning process of the first type, children develop the means of mental activity (for example, concepts) with the properties planned by adults in advance, and the scope of which is clearly defined. According to Poddyakov, in the second case, indistinct, overlapping and syncretic concepts are developed. They are not system-based, but they represent the ground for the formation of mental tools appearing during the task-oriented learning. In fact, indistinct concepts are the means of transfer to ZPD – from pre-cultural forms of psyche to the cultural ones. The task of an adult acting in the zone of proximal development is to provide the child with a developing environment for his/her spontaneous exploratory activity.

If we compare the approach of Davydov and Poddyakov, the difference between them is that, in the first case, the past experience of a child is eliminated, and the basis for identification of the common relation and movement is searched in accordance with the basis in ZPD; and in the second, the indistinct knowledge is the mean of assimilation of mental formations with the determined properties. Both approaches set the same task of mastering the objectivity of the content, which provides the development, but they solve it differently. In one case, it is achieved through the search for universal grounds, and in the other one, through assimilation of the new content with the help of already existing syncretic concepts.

Quite a special understanding of ZPD can be discovered in the context of play activity and the studies dedicated to it. According to Alexey Leontiev (2000), any activity has two sides: operational and motivational. Let us review the motivational side first. The motives are associated with the objects that satisfy relevant needs. In addition, this activity in itself can be a motive. Therefore, the development of motivation is, first, connected with the change of the leading activity.

However, in the play activity, in addition to the development of motivation, one can also find the operational side. It was shown that preschool children involved in one game preserve the ability to "read" the context of usage of the same objects in the games of other children. Research works by Olga Diachenko demonstrated that the usage of substituent objects is connected with the development of imagination (Diachenko, 2011). The operational side of activity is systematically connected with the implementation of symbolic mediation in childhood (A. Veraksa & Veraksa, 2015).

These data make it possible to look at the understanding of the processes taking place in ZPD from a new angle. If according to the first two approaches, transformations take place within a one-dimensional field of relations (within qualificatory relations) then the third approach implies that in play activity transformations take place in the space of two dimensions: the symbolic space and the space of object relations. It would be justifiable to say that the play activity not only creates a child's ZPD associated with the mastering of social roles and meanings of human activity, but also a special space of objects transformation from the symbolic space into the qualificatory one. In the system of play activity, every new object becomes available to a child due to its symbolic interpretation, and the objective of the adult becomes slightly different if compared with previous approaches: now it consists of transformation of a symbolic image into an image reproducing qualificatory relations, with the help of the system of analogies and metaphors. This approach is associated with the movement of the child's consciousness from the symbolic to the rational reflection of reality.

Another direction in understanding of ZPD is associated with the studies of dialectical thinking of children and its role in the construction of modern systems of education. As it was shown in our studies (Veraksa et al., 2013), the mechanism of dialectical thinking is being made up during the preschool years. It represents a complex structure of information processing based on dialectical transformations. This mechanism is the basis of the dialectical thinking, making it possible to manage the relations of the opposition. Formation of dialectical thinking is associated with the development of imaginative anticipation and transformation of contradictory problem situations. The simplest contradictory situations can arise even among young children. However, dialectical transformations of contradictory situations associated with the formulation of the dialectical problem, are for the first time systematically implemented in the senior preschool age. During the preschool years, the basis of the mechanism of dialectical thinking is made up of the transformations of the situation, which have been identified as actions of dialectical seriation, conversion and transformation. The ability of preschoolers to use these actions is conditioned upon the formation of complex images reflecting the same object together with its various properties and relations, including contradictory ones. Any content can be represented as a complex structure of opposing units that make up its elements that is providing the child with the possibility to make dialectical transformation. Because of children's intellectual activity, even the most complex content, regardless of the peculiarities of its objectivity, can become a field for child's movement within it.

We turn to another line of ZPD understanding related to the problem of subjectivity. In one way or the other, it appears in all the approaches described above. In the works by Elkonin and Davydov, it is expressed in the concept of "learning activity". The idiosyncrasy of the learning activity is that in this activity the child is not the subject of the movement in the content, but the subject of the organization of the own activity on the mastering of this content (for example, control over the learnt things and those which were not). In the works by Zaporozhets and Poddyakov, the child becomes the subject in the content movement, but this content is not objective, meaning it is not directly related to the scientific paradigm. Within the context of exploration of the play activity, it should be noted that the child becomes the organiser of the activity and its content, which is not educational, yet, as long as the spontaneous play activity is in process. Within the dialectical approach, the presence of dialectical relations in the objective content provides the child with the opportunity to take the subject position not only in relation to the content given in the metaphorical form, but also to the immediate objective content, that is to produce objective content managing the relations of opposites. In the latter case, the process of development appears as a filling of dialectical structures with the specific content, and as a formation of a more detailed and integral picture of the world.

Conclusion

Thus, the understanding of the psychological processes that occur in the zone of proximal development is connected with the structure of the content mastered by a child. It is clear that the processes of development and education are different, and the understanding of the very nature of development changes depending on the type of education. In general, the content mastered by the child is given in three forms: alphabetic (standard), symbolic (metaphorical), and transformational (dialectical). Depending on the aspect of the education content, the understanding of the processes of ZPD development changes, too. In the first case, it appears as the formation of the learning activity (normative, objective content), in the second, as a play activity (metaphorical content, amplification) and in the third, as a creative activity (dialectical, content transformation). Herewith, each form determines the degree of subjectivity: the subject of the learning activity is aimed at mastering of the objective content; the subject of the play activity is aimed at mastering of social roles and meanings through the creation of the game theme; the subject of creativity is aimed at the creation of a new objective content.

In other words, we can say that different approaches to understanding of the zone of proximal development set up different context of adult-child communication in this space. On the one hand, ZPD became a powerful impulse for the creation of preschool educational programs. On another hand, it resulted in ignoring specifics and inherent value of the childhood, expansion of education of the school type to preschool institutions and, consequently, to the dominance of traditional way on interaction between a child and an adult, where an adult sets an example and a child is meant to follow it. In this context, one can see a distinct significance of a special research line in Russian psychology of education that explores the problem of neo formations specific for preschool childhood as an age of establishment of initiative and autonomy, and implying a different way of interaction with an adult, supporting a child's initiative and autonomy (A. Veraksa & Veraksa, 2015). This refers to a search for a content that, due to its unique "childishness", is crucial and interesting for an adult, too. Moreover, insofar as children may surpass adults while solving problems involving imagination or creative thinking, adults, in their turn, can perceive communication with a child as a resource for their own development.

References

Davydov, V. V. (1972). *Types of generalization in education*. Moscow: Pedagogica.

Diachenko, O. (2011). On major developments in preschoolers' imagination. *International Journal of Early Years Education, 19*(1), 19–25.

Elkonin, D. B. (1960). *Child's psychology*. Moscow: GUPI MP RSFSR.

Federal Law of the Russian Federation "On Education". (2012, December 31). Retrieved from https://rg.ru/2012/12/30/obrazovanie-dok.html

Federal State Educational Standard of Preschool Education. (2013, November 25). Retrieved from https://rg.ru/2013/11/25/doshk-standart-dok.html

Harms, T., Clifford, R., & Cryer, D. (2016). *Scales for comprehensive assessment of the quality of education in pre-school educational organizations (ECERS-R)*. Moscow: Natsionalnoye obrazovanie.

Kravzov, G. G. (Ed.). (2014). *The preliminary main educational program in preschool age*. Moscow: Lev.

Kudryavtsev, V. T. (2011). The phenomenon of child creativity. *International Journal of Early Years Education, 19*(1), 45–53.

Leontiev, A. N. (2000). *Lectures in general psychology*. Moscow: Smysl.

Poddyakov, N. N. (1977). *Child's thinking*. Moscow: Pedagogica.

Veraksa, N. E. (1990). Dialectical thinking and creativity. *Voprosy psikhologii, 4*, 5–14.

Veraksa, N., Belolutskaya, A., Vorobyeva, I., Krasheninnikov, E., Rachkova, E., Shiyan, I., & Shiyan, O. (2013). Structural dialectical approach in psychology: Problems and research results. *Psychology in Russia: State of the Art, 6*(2), 65–77.

Veraksa, A., & Veraksa, N. (2015). Symbolic mediation in cognitive activity: Acquisition of complex notions. *European Early Childhood Education Research Journal, 4*, 668–683.

Veraksa, N., & Veraksa, A. (2015). Project activity of preschool children. *Psychology in Russia: State of the Art, 8*(2), 73–86.

Vygotsky, L. S. (1982). *Collected works in 6 vol.* (Vol. 2). Moscow, Pedagogica.

Zaporozhets, A. V. (1986). *Selected psychological works: In 2 vol. Vol.1. Mental development of the child*. Moscow: Pedagogica.

15 Early childhood education and care in Serbia

Current challenges and policies

Tijana Bogovac

Introduction

In Serbia, the term used for organised early education and care of children from 6 months to 6 years is "predškolsko vaspitanje i obrazovanje" (preschool upbringing and education). It implies a holistic approach to education and includes upbringing, education and care (Government of the Republic of Serbia, 2010; Ministry of Education, 2006). The term portrays a specific educational philosophy that follows traditions of pedagogy as an educational science developed in Germany, starting from the 19th century. Pedagogy focuses on education as a holistic support to the development of children, where care and education intertwine (Petrie et al., 2009; Moss, 2006). The professionals that work with children in ECEC in Serbia are named "vaspitači", from the word upbringing, "vaspitanje" (Banković, 2014).

The Curriculum framework for preschool education in Serbia is based on a humanistic understanding of children. The child is perceived as a holistic being and play as an authentic mean of expression and learning of preschool children is seen as the most important method of work with children in the early years (Ministry of Education, 2006). Children are perceived as a value *per se* and as carrying developmental propositions and being agents of their own development, socialisation and upbringing (Ministry of Education, 2006). However, traditionally in Serbia, children were perceived as vulnerable, in need of protection and guidance, and they were at the lowest position in the hierarchy of the family (Trebješanin, 2008). The traditional view of the child is changing (Trebješanin & Jovanić, 2015). Consequently, even though the teacher-centred approach was traditionally present, the emphasis is shifting towards more child-centred practice.

ECEC in Serbia is organised as a system of preschool institutions with the aim to provide children and families with holistic education and care of children (Gavrilović, 2006; Government of the Republic of Serbia, 2010). Recently, there has been a growth in the number of private kindergartens, which is a novelty in the context, as most of the kindergartens are public (European Commission/EACEA/Eurydice, 2015). Even though the programmes of the institutions are predominantly all-day programs, and the ECEC system is stated to be uniformed (Krnjaja & Breneselović, 2013; The Government of the Republic of Serbia,

2012), in recent years there has been a movement towards more diversified, inclusive and decentralised system (The Government of the Republic of Serbia, 2012; UNICEF, 2017).

The ECEC context in Serbia is dynamic, as the country is in transition, a post-socialist country aspiring to enter the European Union. There are projects being carried out in cooperation with international organisations, aiming at building the system on democratic premises. Current challenges are evident, with the issues of low coverage, inequality of access and uneven distribution of institutions being just a few (The Government of the Republic of Serbia, 2012; UNICEF, 2012).

The historical background of ECEC in Serbia

Early childhood education and care started developing in Serbia with the emergence of the first kindergartens in the 19th century (Gavrilović, 2003). The kindergartens were developed based on the traditions of Froebel and Maria Montessori, but were reshaped in time in accordance with the need of the society (Gavrilović, 2003, 2006). The kindergarten was named "zabavište" and the role of the teachers was to have enough patience and skills and to work in a manner that makes the day for the children easy and fun (Gavrilović, 2003). The context of care was brought about by situations of war, poverty and need of organised care in the time of First and Second World War. This is how the first idea of kindergarten, "zabavište", was broadened with the idea of "obdanište", whose functions were to give food and care to children from poor families and whose parents were working all day, as well as to help children learn. The predominant function of "obdanište" was social (Gavrilović, 2006). After the Second World War, "zabavište" and "obdanište" were integrated in the concept of a preschool institution, in which social care, health-preventive and education were joint (Gavrilović, 2003). From then on, the preschool institution developed as a public institution, which carries a broad understanding of early childhood education and care.

The legal framework for preschool education in Serbia

Preschool education in the Republic of Serbia is a part of the formal system of education. The legal framework for preschool education is based on two laws: The Law on the Fundamentals of the Education System and the Law on Preschool Education, which are further specified through sub-laws (Government of the Republic of Serbia, 2010, 2013). The Law on Preschool Education, which was adopted in 2010, defines preschool education as an activity of direct public concern and a public service. Preschool education in Serbia is regulated and monitored by the state.

The objectives of preschool education, amongst the rest, are to support the full development and wellbeing of children of preschool age, building and expanding on their experience and learning about themselves, others and the world. In addition, it aims to support the educational function of the family and the involvement of the community (Government of the Republic of Serbia, 2010; IBE-UNESCO, 2011). The principles of preschool education set by the law are: availability, democracy, openness, holistic approach to children development, authenticity as approach to play as a mean of expression and learning of preschool children, development of various forms of preschool provision. This in accordance with the needs of the children and their families, as well as the continuous improvement through evaluation and pedagogical innovation (Government of the Republic of Serbia, 2010).

Curriculum framework

In Serbia, there is the Curriculum framework as a base for development of curriculum at the level of kindergarten (Ministry of Education, 2006). The document is a framework base on which preschool teachers develop curriculum in line with the needs of children, family and specificity of the context (IBE-UNESCO, 2011). Preschool teachers plan the programme for the actual group of children based on continual monitoring of their development, and individualisation is a leading principle. Curriculum framework is a document with two models, model A and model B, and preschool teachers choose which one to follow (Ministry of Education, 2006).

Even though Model A and Model B have shared starting values, they conceptualise practice differently. Model A conceptualises preschool education as an open system where the programme is developed on the level of educational group based on the interest of children, while Model B is conceptualised as a cognitive-development programme, with specific educational aims, tasks for the teacher and types of activities (Ministry of Education, 2006; IBE-UNESCO, 2011). In both the cases, the development of the programme is conceived as a continual, dynamic process that should be developed based on evaluation, participation of all the partners in the context allowing for the specificity to be achieved (Ministry of Education, 2006). However, the fact there are two conceptualisations is stated not to be giving clear base for the practice and the document itself is considered outdated (Krnjaja, 2014; Breneselović & Krnjaja, 2015). Currently, the process of production of the new Curriculum framework for ECEC is taking place, with the aim to make an integral vision of preschool education in the Republic of Serbia.

Preschool institutions

Preschool institutions are places where preschool education is being organised and they provide children of preschool age with food, nursing, health and social care (Government of the Republic of Serbia, 2010). Therefore, the functions of preschool institutions are complex, integrating social, educational and health functions. The way in which this is conducted is set up in the agreement between the Ministry of Education, Ministry of Health Care and Ministry of Social Affairs, which is one of the challenges in the system. The main jurisdiction on ECEC is within the Ministry of Education, as preschool education belongs to the formal system of education from 2002 (IBE-UNESCO, 2011).

Preschool institutions consist of a certain number of kindergartens (see Figure 15.1), organised on a municipal level (Government of the Republic of Serbia, 2010). Kindergartens usually consist of "jasle" (nursery) and "vrtić" (kindergarten). Nursery represents organised education and care for children from 6 months to 3 years and kindergarten for children from 3 to 5 years. There is also a preparatory preschool programme, which is compulsory in the year before entering school (Government of the Republic of Serbia, 2010). It lasts for at least 9 months in the year prior to enrolling in primary school and is free of charge as a half-day programme (Government of the Republic of Serbia, 2010). In the Republic of Serbia, as in some other European countries, like Bulgaria, Estonia, Finland and Sweden, school starts at the age of 7 (Commission/EACEA/Eurydice, 2015).

The number of children per group is set by the law (see Table 15.1) (Government of the Republic of Serbia, 2010). However, the number goes beyond what is projected in congested urban areas and is linked with another issue, the lack of facilities. The group size can be 20% more than the set number, which is still in accordance with the law. This is said to be negatively corresponding with the quality (Krnjaja & Breneselović, 2013).

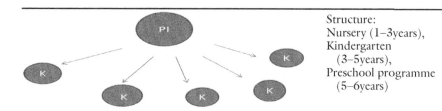

Structure:
Nursery (1–3years),
Kindergarten
(3–5years),
Preschool programme
(5–6years)

Preschool institution (PI) consists of several kindergartens (K) as its organisational unit. Kindergarten as a term is used to imply 1) kindergarten as a unit and 2) kindergarten as a group range from 3–5 years of age.

Figure 15.1 Preschool institution

Table 15.1 Number of children per age group in kindergartens in Serbia as defined by law

Number of children per group	Under 1	1 year olds	2 year olds	3 year olds	4 year olds	5 year olds
	7	12	16	20	24	26

Source. Government of the Republic of Serbia, 2010.

Financing of preschool education

Average expenditure on preschool education in Serbia is 0.43% of the GDP, lower than the average in Europe, which is 0.5% of GDP (UNICEF, 2012). Concerning the costs of kindergartens, local governments are bearing 80% of preschool education costs, while the parents cover 20% (Government of the Republic of Serbia, 2010). The Budget of the Republic of Serbia covers expenses for the preschool preparatory program. Preschool education is financed according to the number of educational groups. The price of the programme is further determined based on the average net salary in Serbia for the accounting month and the price of energy products, utilities and transportation (UNICEF, 2012). Children without parental care, children with special needs and children from financially disadvantaged families have priority in enrolment and are to be exempt from paying (Government of the Republic of Serbia, 2010). This is one of the ways in which the issue of the low coverage of children, especially from vulnerable groups, is approached as a measure to promote inclusive education and increase coverage (IBE-UNESCO, 2011).

The ownership of preschool institutions

Preschool institution can be funded by the Republic of Serbia, autonomous provinces, local authorities and other legal entity or natural person (Government of the Republic of Serbia, 2010). Most kindergartens are public, although the number of private kindergartens rose significantly in recent years, as there is need for available spaces in kindergartens. The need for kindergartens is greater than the number of available spaces (see Table 15.2). In 2017, there are 2,479 kindergarten facilities that are state funded and 203 that are private (Statistical Office of the Republic of Serbia, 2017). The physical conditions, requirements for professionals working in private institutions and the quality of these kindergartens are regulated by the state and are specified with the sub-law (Government of the Republic of Serbia, 2010).

Table 15.2 Preschool institutions by ownership, enrolled children, children not enrolled due to limited capacities and children enrolled more than the maximum norm

Republic of Serbia	*Ownership*	*Number of institutions*	*Number of facilities*	*Number of enrolled children*	*Children not enrolled due to capacities at full*	*Children enrolled in excess of the maximum norm*
	Total	334	2682	206170	4200	10466
	State-owned	162	2479	195092	4124	10401
	Private	172	203	11078	76	65

Source: Statistical Office of the Republic of Serbia, 2017, p. 2.

Quality assurance

The quality assurance in preschool education in Serbia implies external and self-evaluation of preschool institutions based on nationally developed quality standards at least once in a five-year period (Ministry of Education, 2012a, 2012b). External evaluation is implemented in cooperation between the Ministry of Education and Institute for Evaluation of Educational Quality. During external evaluation, the quality is described in line with the quality standards and the preschool institution is given a mark and suggestions for improvements. Self-evaluation is carried out by the professional bodies, parent councils, managers and managing authorities of the institution, in line with the quality standards (Ministry of Education, 2012a, 2012b). Moreover, the activities of the preschool institution are supervised by inspection and professional and pedagogic supervision of the work of preschool institutions (Government of the Republic of Serbia, 2010).

ECEC professionals in Serbia/division of work within ECEC institution

The multifaceted function of preschool education (Gavrilović, 2006) leads to diverse staff working in preschool institutions. Professionals directly engaged in working with the children are preschool teachers (nurse-teachers, preschool teachers and special educators). They are supported by expert associates (pedagogues, psychologists, teachers of art, music, physical education and speech therapists), who have advisory roles. This is perceived as one of the comparative advantages of preschool education in Serbia compared to other countries, as the expert associates' role is to support the quality development of ECEC in curriculum improvement, quality of children-adult relations, building relations with the family and local community, to introduce new approaches to learning, play and creativity (Krnjaja & Breneselović, 2013). The activities regarding food, nurture, health and social care are carried out by the dietitians, nurses for preventive health care, social workers and special educators (Government of the Republic of Serbia, 2010).

Preschool teachers

In Serbia, the professional name for a preschool teacher is agreed in correspondence to the specific understanding of ECEC. The term "vaspitač" comes from the word "vaspitanje" (upbringing), from which it derives its meaning (Banković, 2014). Banković (2014) explains that the emphasis in work of "vaspitač" (preschool teacher) is pedagogical, which differentiates it from the teacher working in primary schools, "učitelj", where the emphasis is on teaching. Nurse-teachers work with children from 6 months to 3 years and they possess at least the appropriate secondary education. Kindergarten teachers can have the same level of educational requirements as teachers in other parts of the education sector, degree education, and they are paid equally (Government of the Republic of Serbia, 2010).

There are different programmes of initial education for preschool teachers in Serbia; some are of academic nature, others vocational, and they last for different time periods, from three to four years (Government of the Republic of Serbia, 2010). Even though this causes difficulties in practice, for instance with salaries, conceptual differences within these programmes are the biggest challenge (Krnjaja & Breneselović, 2013). The question of initial preschool teachers' education is one of the core questions for future quality development in Serbia that needs to be linked and based on future conceptual framework.

Once they start working, preschool teachers, as well as the expert associates, go through a year-long mentoring program. During this period, they are supported by a mentor, a professional who possesses the licence, after which the preschool teachers take the national exam, in order to obtain their professional license (Ministry of Education, 2008). During this period, all the segments of the professional role are practised and evaluated with the mentor, all of which is documented. After acquiring the licence, the teacher's professional development includes ongoing training (Ministry of Education, 2016).

Gender disparity

There is gender inequality in relation to the ECEC professionals in Serbia (see Table 15.3). In 2017, there are 26,755 professionals working in the ECEC sector in Serbia, 25,398 of which are women, which makes about 94.9% of working population, while men constitute only 5.1%. More precisely, female teachers form 98%, 5% of preschool teachers, while there are only 1.5% of male preschool teachers in Serbia (Statistical Office of the Republic of Serbia, 2017). This shows that the profession is still perceived as a maternal one, which is in line with the traditional view of preschool teachers (Banković, 2014).

The challenges and strategy projections

There are a number of challenges within the ECEC area in Serbia, but low coverage, lack of facilities, inequality in access and uniformity are often highlighted (Krnjaja & Breneselović, 2013; The Government of the Republic of Serbia,

Table 15.3 Employees in pre-primary education by type/title of occupation and sex

Territory		Total	Teachers				Other professions
			Total	Teachers	Nurse-teachers	Special education needs teacher	
Republic	Total	26755	17765	13415	4254	96	8990
of Serbia	Women	25398	17501	13163	4248	90	7897

Source: Statistical Office of the Republic of Serbia, 2017, p. 4.

2012; UNICEF, 2012). The ECEC system in Serbia tends to be described as uniformed, as all day programs are dominant and, there are few alternative programs (Krnjaja & Breneselović, 2013, The Government of the Republic of Serbia, 2012; UNICEF, 2012).

The coverage of children with ECEC in Serbia is low, compared to other European countries (UNICEF, 2012). Multiple Indicator Cluster Surveys (MICS) from 2014 in Serbia shows that attendance in early childhood education programmes for children 36–59 months old was 50.2%, while for children from Roma settlements it was only 5.7% (Statistical Office of the Republic of Serbia & UNICEF, 2012). The coverage is lowest with the youngest age and grows with the age of children. At the nursery level, the coverage was about 20% in 2012, at the kindergarten age it was around 48%, while in the preparatory programme the coverage went up to 95%, being obligatory (UNICEF, 2012). The enrolment in 2017 is 97% of children in the preparatory programmes (Statistical Office of the Republic of Serbia, 2017).

The issue with the coverage of children from the sensitive groups was emphasised in previous research as only 29% of rural, 22% of poor and only 8% of Roma children were covered in 2012 (UNICEF, 2012). It is acknowledged that the children who need the preschool education the most are the least covered (The Government of the Republic of Serbia, 2012; UNICEF, 2017). Coverage is further characterised by high territorial differences, where mostly developed municipalities have the highest coverage of children with preschool education and under-developed municipalities have the lowest (UNICEF, 2012). This portrays that the system is unfair as the children that need the kindergarten the most lack the opportunity to be enrolled (UNICEF, 2012).

One of the measures developed to tackle the issue of inequality in the coverage is the positive discrimination in the enrolment policy by which children from the vulnerable groups have priority in enrolment (The Government of the Republic of Serbia, 2012). Moreover, children without parental care, children with special needs and children from financially disadvantaged families are excluded from payment obligations for full-time and half-day stay in kindergartens. This leads to the conclusion that the lack of facilities is one of the major issues in Serbia currently, as available capacities are not sufficient to cover the total number of children with preschool education Serbia (UNICEF, 2012).

Children are mostly enrolled in the full-day programmes, as opposed to the half-day three-hour programmes (Commission/EACEA/Eurydice, 2015). In that sense, the ECEC in Serbia remains quite uniformed, as the predominant type of programmes are all-day programmes. This is an issue that is endeavoured to be resolved with the development of diversified programs, which could also allow for the greater coverage of children and more equity (The Government of the Republic of Serbia, 2012; UNICEF, 2012). Diversification of preschool programmes implies starting alternative programmes to achieve greater coverage as a response to the needs of family and children. The half-day programs are organised in alternative spaces such as schools, community centres, specialised programmes in preschool institutions after the working hours of all day programs such as playrooms, workshops and family nurseries, travelling kindergartens, travelling kindergarten teachers and parent counselling (The Government of the Republic of Serbia, 2012).

The Strategy for the Development of Education in Serbia until 2020 (The Government of the Republic of Serbia, 2012) determines the development focus of the education system. The main aim of public care and preschool education, as defined in the Strategy, is to create conditions for quality living, holistic and harmonious development, upbringing and socialisation of children in line with needs of every child and in the spirit of children's rights conception. By 2020, the projections are made towards the educational system being more democratic, decentralised and with better internal cohesion, quality and equality. Preschool education in Serbia aims towards increasing accessibility, righteousness of the system, development of quality education, better responsiveness to the needs of family and parents, especially from the vulnerable groups (UNICEF, 2017).

In recent years, many national projects are being organised in collaboration with international organisations, which focus on building the system on democratic premises, diversification and inclusion. For example, the Improvement of Preschool Education in Serbia (IMPRES project), Kindergartens without borders 1, 2 and 3, Inclusive Early Childhood Education and Care Project for Serbia and other (Improvement of Preschool Education in Serbia, 2011; Inclusive Early Childhood Education and Care, 2017; Early years last throughout life, Kindergartens without Borders 3, 2017). The project "Kindergartens without Borders" is developed in cooperation between the Centre for Interactive Pedagogy, UNICEF and the Ministry of Education, which aims to build innovative solutions to create better coverage and quality of preschool education for children from 3 to 5 years old, with the focus on children from vulnerable groups.

Future developments of the ECEC system can also be projected based on the contemporary literature in Serbia. The researchers suggest, as the next developmental steps, a move towards the paradigm of children's rights and values of participation (UNICEF, 1989; Woodhead, 2006), as well as the respect for the culture of the community. However, the children's rights perspective is not yet operationalised and, therefore, only declarative (Krnjaja & Breneselović, 2013; Krnjaja & Breneselović, 2014; Miškeljin, 2014, 2015). The need for research and evaluation studies as a base to develop the strategies is also highlighted (Krnjaja & Breneselović, 2013; The Government of the Republic of Serbia, 2012). Mostly important, the societal consensus on education as the base for reforms and future developments has been highlighted by the researchers (Krnjaja & Breneselović, 2013).

Summary

This chapter gave an overview of preschool education in Serbia. The specific conception of the ECEC, preschool upbringing and education, as a holistic approach to education with a long tradition, was explained (Gavrilović, 2003, 2006). Correspondingly, the professionals that work with children in ECEC in

Serbia, named "vaspitači", from the word upbringing, "vaspitanje", were revisited (Banković, 2014). Preschool education, as an activity of direct public concern and public service, dedicated to children from 6 months to 6 years of age, was portrayed (Government of the Republic of Serbia, 2010).

In addition, the legal and the conceptual framework of ECEC in Serbia based on the long tradition of preschool education was also described (Government of the Republic of Serbia, 2010, 2013; Ministry of Education, 2006). Preschool education, organised through the work of preschool institutions, multifaceted institutions providing social, educational and health functions, was explained (Gavrilović, 2006; Government of the Republic of Serbia, 2010). Although predominantly state-governed (Banković, 2014), recent growth in the number of private kindergartens was acknowledged, as a way to tackle one of the major issues of ECEC in Serbia, the coverage of children with preschool education.

The chapter gave an overview of the structure of preschool institutions, number of children per group, issues of financing and ownership of preschool institutions, ECEC professionals as well as the quality assurance system. The multifunctional character of preschool education was explained, as a reason for different professionals being engaged in preschool institutions. It showed that all the professionals possess appropriate education, which was considered one of the strengths of preschool education in Serbia (The Government of the Republic of Serbia, 2012). The existence of expert associates working on the level of institution, responsible for improvement of educational quality, was also highlighted as one of the strong points of ECEC in Serbia.

Even though preschool education in Serbia is often characterised as uniform, there has recently been a movement towards a more diversified, inclusive and decentralised system as projected within Strategy (The Government of the Republic of Serbia, 2012, Krnjaja & Breneselović, 2013). The number of challenges have been emphasised, such as the low coverage, lack of facilities and the inequality in coverage. National projects in cooperation with international organisations, aiming at building the system on democratic premises, also make the context dynamic. The need for a systematic approach to the ECEC in Serbia, based on national evaluations, research and reflection on the values of the ECEC, was emphasised by the researchers (Krnjaja & Pavlović Breneselović, 2013). Finally, it can be concluded that the current context of ECEC, with its strengths, challenges and strategy projections, set the question of the shape of ECEC in Serbia moving forward in the 21st century.

References

Banković, I. (2014). Early childhood professionalism in Serbia: current issues and developments. *International Journal of Early Years Education*, 22(3), 251–262.

Breneselović, P. D., & Krnjaja, Ž. (2015). Examining a quality of preschool education in Serbia: Curriculum framework analysis. In *Research and education quality development in Serbia – state, challenges and perspectives*. University of Belgrade, Faculty of Philosophy, Institute for Pedagogy and Andragogy.

European Commission/EACEA/Eurydice. (2015). *Early childhood education and care systems in Europe* (National Information Sheets – 2014/15). Eurydice Facts and Figures. Luxembourg: Publications Office of the European Union.

Gavrilović, A. (2003). Nastanak i razvoj predskolskih ustanova u Srbiji. [Emergence and the development of preschool institutions in Serbia]. *Beograd: Službeni glasnik*, 305–329.

Gavrilović, A. (2006). Multifunkcionalna delatnost predškolskih ustanova [Multifunctional Work of Preschool Institutions]. *Nastava i vaspitanje*, 55, 57–69.

Government of the Republic of Serbia. (2010). *Law on preschool education*. Belgrade: Official Gazette.

Government of the Republic of Serbia. (2013). *Law on the foundations of the education system*. Belgrade: Official Gazette.

IBE-UNESCO. (2011). *World data on education VII Ed. 2010/11 Serbia*. Retrieved from www.ibe.unesco.org/sites/default/files/Serbia.pdf

Improvement of Preschool Education in Serbia. (2011). Retrieved from http://europa.rs/mapa/map/projectdetail/78ae47.html?project_id=134

Inclusive Early Childhood Education and Care. (2017). Retrieved from http://projects.worldbank.org/P157117?lang=en

Krnjaja, Ž. (2014). The curriculum ideologies: What to expect from education current state and perspectives in Serbia. *Sociologija*, 56(3), 286–303.

Krnjaja, Ž., & Breneselović, P. D. (2013). *Gde stanuje kvalitet – Politika uspostavljanja kvaliteta u predškolskom vaspitanju Knjiga 1* [Where does the quality live. Policies of buliding early childhood education quality]. Belgrade: Institute for Pedagogy and Andragogy, Faculty of Philosophy, University of Belgrade.

Krnjaja, Ž., & Breneselović, P. D. (2014). Politika obezbeđivanja kvaliteta predškolskog vaspitanja u Srbiji [A policy for quality assurance and improvement of preschool education in the Republic of Serbia]. *Pedagoški modeli evaluacije i strategije razvijanja kvaliteta obrazovanja [Pedagogical models of evaluation and strategies of educational quality development]*. Belgrade: Faculy of Philosophy, the Institute for Pedagogy and Andragogy.

Ministry of Education. (2006). *Opšte osnove predškolskog programa* [General foundations of the preschool programme]. Serbia: Official gazette.

Ministry of Education (2008). *Pravilnik o dozvoli za rad nastavnika, vaspitača i stručnih saradnika* [Regulation on licence for work for teachers, preschool teachers and expert associates]. Serbia: Official gazette.

Ministry of Education (2012a). *Pravilnik o vrednovanju kvaliteta rada ustanova* [Regulation on evaluation of quality of institutions]. Serbia: Official gazette.

Ministry of Education. (2012b). *Quality standards of work of preschool institutions*. Serbia: Official gazette.

Ministry of Education. (2016). *Pravilnik o stalnom stručnom usavršavanju nastavnika, vaspitača i stručnih saradnika* [Regulation on continual professional development of teachers, preschool teachers and expert associates]. Serbia: Official gazette.

Miškeljin, L. (2014). Diversification – meanings and policies in practice of preschool education in Serbia. In *Models of pedagogic evaluation and strategies of quality development*. Belgrade: Faculty of Philosophy, Insitute for Pedagogy and Andragogy.

Miškeljin, L. (2015). The dimension of quality – access to preschool education. In *Research and education quality development in Serbia – state, challenges and perspectives*. University of Belgrade, Faculty of Philosophy, Institute for Pedagogy and Andragogy.

Moss, P. (2006). Structures, understandings and discourses: Possibilities for re-envisioning the early childhood worker. *Contemporary Issues in Early Childhood*, 7(1), 30–41.

Petrie, P., Boddy, J., Cameron, C., Heptinstall, E., McQuail, S., Simon, A., & Wigfall, V. (2009). *Pedagogy-a holistic, personal approach to work with children and young people, across services: European models for practice, training, education and qualification*. Unpublished briefing paper.

Statistical Office of the Republic of Serbia. (2017). *Pre-primary education in the Republic of Serbia, 2016/2017 school year*.

The Government of the Republic of Serbia. (2012). *Strategy for education development in Serbia 2020*. Belgrade: Cigoja.

Trebješanin, Ž. (2008). *Predstava o detetu u srpskoj kulturi* [Understanding of children in Serbian culture]. Belgrade: Sofos.

Trebješanin, Ž., & Jovanić, G. (2015). Promene u shvatanju deteta u srpskoj kulturi u poslednjih dvadeset pet godina [Change in the view of child in Serbian culture in the last twenty five years] *Primenjena psihologija*, 7(4), 549–563.

UNICEF. (1989). *The United Nations convention on the rights of the child*. Retrieved from www.unicef.org.uk/Documents/Publication-pdfs/UNCRC_PRESS200910 web.pdf

UNICEF. (2012). *Investing in early childhood education in Serbia*. Retrieved from Belgrade: www.unicef.org/serbia/WP_Preschool_education.pdf

UNICEF. (2017). Foreword. In P. D. Breneselović & Ž. Krnjaja (Eds.), *Kaleidoskop – osnove diversifikovanih programa predškolskog vaspitanja i obrazovanja* [Kaleidoscope – basis for development of diversified preschool programmes]. Belgrade: Institute for Pedagogy and Andragogy.

Woodhead, M. (2006). Changing perspectives on early childhood: Theory, research and policy. *International Journal of Equity and Innovation in Early Childhood*, 4(2), 1–43.

16 Early childhood education and care in Singapore

Aspiring for holistic early learning

Sivanes Phillipson, Eugenia Koh, Salwa Sujuddin and Sharmini Mohamed Sharif

Introduction

Early Childhood Education and Care (ECEC) in Singapore tends to be viewed with ambivalence, as its importance depended upon the directions of the government and to some extent, the need of the society, which fluctuated between child caring and formal education (Monk & Phillipson, 2017). Lacking natural resources such as tin and forestry that its neighbouring countries have, Singapore, with a population of 5.84 million as of 2017, is highly dependent on its human capital. As such, education is seen as the leading factor for the development of the nation's economics (Zhang, 2016). Accordingly, Singapore's educational system has been very much outcome-based, with less emphasis on children's holistic development. In line with this notion was the generally accepted norm that the nurseries and kindergartens in Singapore functioned as preparatory schools for compulsory education (Kamerman, 2007). Of course, in these preparatory schools early childhood teachers were expected to teach and prepare young children for formal schooling. However, recent changes in government legislation and provision have changed its focus to place an importance on children's development. This shift in paradigm, for what is considered as vital for early childhood development in Singapore, poses multiple challenges to the government for maintaining consistent application of rules and regulations around early childhood implementation. It is also a challenge to the early childhood educators to fulfil the expectations of the changes imposed by the government against parents' expectations for school readiness.

Hence, the aim of this chapter is to outline the historical overview of the early childhood environment, and recent reforms planned and enacted by the Singapore government in its aspirations to meet progressive trends in child development. The implications of these reforms against the backdrop of Singapore's competitive academic context are raised to show the challenges that ECEC faces, in embracing a holistic early education for children.

The changing landscape towards a more holistic development and education for Singapore children was first signalled in 1997, with Senior Prime Minister Goh Chok Tong introducing the nation's new directive in education policy as

"Thinking Schools, Learning Nation" (TSLN) (Goh, 1997). Subsequently, "Teach Less, Learn More" (TLLM) was raised by the nation's Prime Minister, Lee Hsien Loong, in his National Day Rally Speech in 2004,

> I think we should cut down on some of this syllabus. It would mean less pressure on the kids, a bit less rote learning, more space for them to explore and discover their talents and also more space for the teachers to think, to reflect, to find ways to bring out the best in their students and to deliver quality results. We've got to teach less to our students so that they will learn more.
>
> (Lee, 2004)

In that same year, Minister for Education Tharman Shanmugaratnam urged Singapore to place less emphasis on examinations and to enable students and teachers greater autonomy in learning through the TLLM directive. In 2015, he echoed similar views again on the importance of innovation and individuality, "That spirit of individuality, that free play of the mind, isn't best developed in a system that's highly competitive and focused on tests" (Ng, 2015, p. 100). Accordingly, the Ministry of Education in Singapore implemented a program of reforms that formed the creation of the Early Childhood Development Agency (ECDA), which is currently the cornerstone of ECEC in Singapore. To articulate the quality goals and regulations of Singapore's ECEC with these reforms, we begin this chapter with a historical overview of the early childhood environment for both kindergartens and childcare centres.

The beginnings of ECEC in Singapore

Provisions for ECEC in Singapore began as early as 1942, during the Second World War (Choo, 2010). During the war, most childcare centres were managed by the Child Welfare Society, while kindergartens were operated by religious bodies and private schools. They were initiated for very specific purposes – the childcare centres catered to custodial care, whereas the kindergartens focused on children's academic development. However, during the 1940s and 1950s, only those from middle- and upper-income families could afford to enrol their children in kindergartens (Choo, 2010). After the war had ended, the British administration formed the Social Welfare Department to help with the aftermath of the war, which later took over some of the childcare centres from the Welfare Society (Choo, 2010). This Department's childcare centres offered care to children from lower-income families to encourage mothers to return to the workforce, in order to help with their families' financial income. As more mothers joined the workforce in the effort to improve their families' economic status, the demand for childcare centres increased.

In 1977, the Singapore government handed over the operation of the childcare services to a non-public organisation and, in this case, the National Trades Union Congress (NTUC) (Choi, 2007). While making way for the NTUC to manage and operate the childcare services, the government provided the financial support as a cheaper option, rather than to run the childcare centres as a public establishment. Subsequently in 1992, the NTUC First Campus Co-operative Limited (NFC) was established and its main function was to oversee ECEC programmes and services (Yeo, 2013). To date, the NFC is a well-known and trustworthy preschool service provider that is affordable and accessible to all families in Singapore, with over 120 centres under its management (Yeo, 2013).

Whilst centres like the NFC catered for families that could afford childcare and kindergarten services, the government was also aware of education being the key to a better future for children from low-income families (People's Action Party (PAP) and Community Foundation, PCF, 2011). Incidentally, there was a notable gap in the academic achievement of children from low-income families. Thus, the Singapore government at the time saw the crucial need to educate its younger generation, particularly the disadvantaged children, in preparing them for primary school. By the early 1960s, the government began setting up low-cost kindergartens in disadvantaged communities with the help of the community leaders and volunteers (PCF, 2011).

As the nation's population grew, kindergartens became significantly popular among the parents who were keen on giving their children a head start in preparation for schooling. Additional kindergartens were set up island-wide and were made readily available and accessible to all the Singaporean children. The fees were kept low, to ensure that all Singapore families could afford to send their children to the kindergartens (PCF, 2011). Later, in 1986, the incumbent government, led by the People's Action Party (PAP) launched its charitable branch, the PAP Community Foundation (PCF), to manage its kindergartens. PAP Kindergartens were then renamed as PCF Kindergartens. With the new branding, PCF Kindergartens went through several refurbishments from its physical environment, in-house teachers' training to its curriculum. In meeting the needs of the communities, PCF's first childcare centre, SPARKLE*TOTS was launched in 1991. To date, PCF is the biggest anchor operator in the early childhood education sector, with over 300 kindergartens and 63 childcare centre island-wide (PCF, 2011).

Early childhood education and care as preschool education

Both the kindergartens and childcare services in Singapore are broadly known as preschool education. Although preschool education in Singapore is not mandatory, the majority of Singapore children attend preschool programmes (Zhang, 2016). The preschools cater to children under the age of 7 years old, which includes kindergartens (3 to 6 years old), childcare centres (18 months to 6 years old), infant and toddler care centres (2 months to 18 months) and playgroups (18 months to 2 years old). The childcare centres offer full day and half-day programmes, whilst kindergartens and playgroups offer 2–4 hour programmes (Zhang, 2016).

Based on the Singapore legislation, under the Education Act 1985, kindergartens are considered private schools and are required to be registered with the

Table 16.1 Types of preschools in Singapore

Childcare Centres		Kindergartens	Playgroups
492* Infant Care Centres	1,366* Childcare Centres	495*	Unknown
Ideal for children who require adult supervision outside regular school hours		3-year education structure	Follows a less formal curriculum, providimg opportunity to learn and socialise through structured and unstructured play
With half day (7am–1pm) and full day (7am–7pm) options		3–4 hours a day	Up to 3 hours a day
Located in void decks, bungalows, workplaces etc.		Located in void decks, bungalows, mosques churches etc.	-
May be private, non-profit, or government funded		May be private, non-profit, or government funded	Private
Varying programs		Varying programs	Varying programs
Varying fees		Varying fees	Varying fees
Government subsidy of S$150/$300 for working mothers (part-time/full-time)		No government subsidy for working mothers	No subsidy
Financial Assistance for low-income families available		Financial Assistance for low-income families available	Financial Assistance for low-income families not applicable

*Total no. of centres as of Q1 2017. Source: Early Childhood Development Agency (ECDA) accessed from https://skoolopedia.com/preschool-singapore-2015-infographic/ on 29 July 2017.

Ministry of Education (MOE) (Tan, 2007). Childcare centres, on the other hand, are under the purview of the Ministry of Social and Family (MSF), which was previously known as the Ministry of Community Development, Youth and Sports (MCYS). Childcare centres fall under the Childcare Centres Act, Chapter 37A, which provides the regulation and licensing for childcare centres (Tan, 2017). Currently, all Singapore preschools are managed by the government-funded service providers, community foundations, or privately owned organisations, including religious bodies, social and business organisations (Zhang, 2016). Table 16.1 provides a detailed overview of the types of preschools.

Tables 16.2 and 16.3 provide statistical information on childcare and infant care services, which are licensed by the Early Childhood Development Agency (ECDA), in terms of capacity, enrolment, fees and distribution, available as a quarterly report.

Table 16.4 further details teacher-student ratio in preschools. With the introduction of Para-Educators and Para-Educarers, MCYS refined the regulatory

Table 16.2 Statistics on childcare services as of Q2 2017

As at end of	2013	2014	2015	2016	2017 Q2
Total no. of childcare centres	1,083	1,143	1,256	1,342	1,382
Total no. of childcare centre places	101,597	109,694	123,327	137,278	143,468
Total enrolment*	73,852	83,928	95,414	103,221	108,351
Enrolment in full-day programme	65,650	75,518	86,898	95,357	100,640
Childcare programme fees					
Average full-day fees	$923	$953	$999	$1,014	$1,032
Median full-day fees	$830	$850	$900	$856	$867

*No. of children enrolled in full-day, half-day and flexi-care programmes.

Source: Early Childhood Development Agency (ECDA).

Table 16.3 Statistics on infant care services as of Q2 2017

As at end of	2013	2014	2015	2016	2017 Q2
Total no. of childcare centres offering infant care services	327	364	419	471	501
Total no. of infant care places	5,257	5,628	6,262	7,032	7,441
Total enrolment*	3,015	3,506	3,813	4,306	4,655
Enrolment in full-day programme	2,902	3,392	3,735	4,240	4,589
Childcare programme fees					
Average full-day fees	$1,376	$1,411	$1,452	$1,477	$1,495
Median full-day fees	$1,311	$1,311	$1,343	$1,357	$1,357

*No. of children enrolled in full-day, half-day and flexi-care programmes.

Source: Early Childhood Development Agency (ECDA).

Table 16.4 ECDA's recommended staff-student ratio for childcare centres

Age of children (group type)	Current staff to children ratio	Revised staff to children ratio (without para-educators/educarers)	Revised staff to children ratio (with para-educators/educarers)
18–30 mths (Playgroup)	1 : 8	1 : 8	1 + 1 : 12
30–36 mths (Nursery 1)	1 : 12	1 : 12	1 + 1 : 18
36–48 mths (Nursery 2)	1 : 15	1 : 15	1 + 1 : 20
48–84 mths (Kindergarten 1 & 2)	1 : 25	1 : 20* (K1) 1 : 25 (K2)	1 + 1 : 30

Source: www.ecda.gov.sg/PressReleases/Pages/Better-Support-for-Child-Care-Teachers-and-Better-Staff-Child-Interactions-Through-Para-Educators-and-Para-Educarers.aspx.

requirements of staff-student ratios in childcare centres to the following, with effect from 1 January 2013.

Since the beginning of preschool education in Singapore, the government has provided subsidies for childcare and kindergarten fees. Disadvantaged families who are eligible can apply for the Financial Assistance Schemes (FAS) for child and infant care, and the kindergarten subsidies from the government and non-government agencies (Tan, 2007). In 2001, the government introduced the Children Development Co-Savings (Baby Bonus) Scheme to encourage families to have more than one child. This scheme also assisted families with their children's childcare or kindergarten fees (Tan, 2007). In 2004, another financial scheme, the PCF Head Start Fund (HSF), was also introduced to help the low-income families to pay for their children's kindergarten or childcare fees. It also covered the purchases of books, uniforms, food and transportation expenses (PCF, 2011).

With these kinds of support for families to access preschool education, it is only apt that the government also turned their attention to the quality of educators working in the sector. In Singapore, the MOE leads the governance of teacher training and regulations and curriculum surrounding the workforce training in ECEC. The ministry's role and the impact of their implemented curriculum reforms on teacher education and curriculum in ECEC are discussed next.

Teacher education and curriculum of ECEC

In 1955, the MOE was established in Singapore (Ministry of Education is established – Singapore History, 2017). However, the MOE's predominant task then was to develop a new course of educational system for Singapore, as well as managing the pressing issues such as the unrest in the Singaporean Chinese schools (Sharpe, 1998). Given the imminent social and political issues during the early days of Singapore's independence, early childhood teacher training fell short under the Ministry's focus. It was only in 1969 that basic training provisions were offered for early childhood educators. Even so, the in-service training for preschool teachers was ad hoc and brief during its early days of implementation (Khoo, 2004). The Adult Education Board and the MOE provided basic training for teachers working with young children in a variety of educational settings (Sharpe, 1998). By 1981, this training provision was gradually managed by the Teachers' Training College (later renamed as the National Institute of Education). The teacher training began with a mere initial 60-hour training programme and later extended to 90 hours and eventually 120 hours (Khoo, 2004; Sharpe, 1998; Tan, 2017).

In 1985, the preschool teacher training underwent its first major development as a three-level training programme introduced by the Ministry of Community Development (MCD) (Lim, 1998). These were nationally accredited courses trained at the basic, intermediate and advanced levels, where both the childcare and the kindergarten staff were of differing levels of competence (childcare assistants, teachers and supervisors) (Lim, 1998; Sharpe, 1998). The basic course consisted of 120 hours of training; the intermediate course (Certificate in Preschool Teaching) consisted of 210 hours of training; and the advanced course (Certificate in Preschool Management and Administration) consisted of 120 hours in duration (Sharpe, 1998). These courses were provided by approved agencies by the MCD, which were a mix of both private and government agencies. These included the Kinderland Learning Centre, National Institute of Education (NIE), Regional Training Resource Center for Early Childhood Care and Education (RTRC) Asia, Singapore Institute of Management, PAP Community Foundation Early Childhood Institute and Association for Childcare Educators (ACCE) (Lim, 1998). In 1998, all the childcare centres were mandated under the Childcare Legislation to have fully trained teachers for licensing purposes (Sharpe, 1998). This legislative move prompted a surge in demand for the teacher training courses in terms of numbers, level of competency as well as the training facilities.

In 1990, a full-time pre-service course on Early Childhood Care and Education was introduced to attract more individuals to join the childcare sector, as a move towards alleviating trained teacher shortage in the childcare industry (Lim, 1998). With the aid of government funding programmes, such as the Skills Development Fund, both pre-service and in-service training courses enjoy subsidies as high as 70% of the course fees charged by the training providers (Lim, 1998). In 1991, the National Institute of Education (NIE) was established and these training courses were restructured to a two-tier certification programme: Level 1 (Certificate in Preschool Training), consisting of 210 hours of training, and Level 2 (Certificate in Preschool Management and Administration), of 120 hours of training (Lim, 1998). These two courses were equivalent to the previous intermediate and advanced courses respectively (Lim, 1998). While the NIE was the main training provider for most of these teaching training courses, there were other training providers, who complemented the need for these programmes, including the overseas universities such as Monash University since 2000.

In the continuous pursuit of improving the quality of preschool education in Singapore, the nation's policymakers constantly reviewed the professional standards for preschool teachers in terms of skill development and teacher training programmes (Ng, 2011). In 2000, an inter-Ministerial Taskforce between the MOE and the MCYS was established, with the aim of providing better consistency on preschool teacher training to raise the quality of preschool education (Ministry of Education & Ministry of Community Development and Sports, 2000). Other than the ministerial representatives, the taskforce also comprised of preschool professionals and practitioners from both, the childcare centres and kindergartens to better represent the training needs of all preschool settings in Singapore (Tan, 2017). In November 1999, a Preschool Education Steering Committee was established by the MOE (Ministry of Education & Ministry of Community Development and Sports, 2000). With representatives including the Senior Parliamentary Secretary, Ministry of Community Development and Sports (MCDS), and the representatives from MOE, MCDS, NIE, principals and professionals in early childhood education, the committee was formed with the mission to forge a training and accreditation framework. The focus was on areas such as defining desired outcomes, curriculum design and development, teacher training programmes, regulating the preschool education framework and conducting research (Ministry of Education & Ministry of Community Development and Sports, 2000; UNESCO International Bureau of Education, 2006).

In September 2011, MCYS announced the new early years' childcare and development initiatives (Ministry of Community Development, Youth and Sports, 2011). The first initiative was the Early Years Development Framework (EYDF), targeted at enhancing the quality of care and development of infants and toddlers aged three years and below (MCYS, 2011). The EYDF supported the Nurturing Early Learners (NEL) framework for a Kindergarten curriculum, which was developed earlier by the MOE in 2003 for children aged four to six years old (MCYS, 2011).

The NEL framework worked as a common guideline and standard for all preschools in Singapore when designing their individual curriculum (Nyland & Ng, 2015). This framework was considered one of the ministry's most drastic developments in preschool educational policy as yet, with the focus of the curriculum shifting to play-based learning and child-based teaching (Ng, 2011). In 2008, the MOE launched the Kindergarten curriculum guide, to translate the 2003 NEL framework into teaching that is more concrete and the learning principles (MOE, 2008). The framework embraced the core belief and principle that children learn best when given the space and freedom to explore and be actively engaged in their learning process (MOE, 2008). The framework focused on six main areas of a child's holistic development: aesthetics and creative expression, discovery of the world, language and literacy, motor skills development, numeracy and social and emotional development. The framework also stated six "learning dispositions" which a preschool teacher was expected to nurture: perseverance, reflectiveness, appreciation, inventiveness, sense of wonder and curiosity and engagement (PRAISE) (MOE, 2008). The guide proposed for teachers to undertake the role of a facilitator of the learning process, with a strong emphasis on child-directed learning and the teachers playing an observer role in assessing children's learning and development. In terms of teaching guidelines for preschool professionals, the guide proposed the iTEACH principles – integrated learning, Teachers as supporters of learning, Engaging children in learning through play, Ample opportunities for interaction, Children as active learners and Holistic development.

The framework was refreshed in 2012 and then revisited in 2013, with more detailed guidelines and recommendations on the implementation of practices in the preschool classrooms (MOE, 2012, 2013). However, the emphasis on the guidelines and principles that "children are curious, active and competent learners" still remained in the revised version of the framework (Ministry of Education, 2008, p. 25). It must be noted that, though the framework encouraged play as part of the early learning, this play-based learning was expected to be purposeful and not reflective of a Western concept of free play (Tan, 2017). Along these efforts, the Early Childhood Development Agency (ECDA) was launched in

April 2013 and served as the regulatory and developmental authority for the early childhood sector in Singapore. Until today, ECDA is an independent agency jointly overseen by the MOE and the Ministry of Social and Family Development (MSF), with governance shouldered by the MSF (Zhang, 2016).

The second initiative was a new training and certification pathway for early years professionals, better known in Singapore as educarers, who worked with children aged between 0–3 years old (MCYS, 2011). This initiative served to recognise the different competency levels – Infant/toddler Educarer, Beginning Educarer and Beginning Preschool Teacher, required of early childhood professionals working with children of different age groups. With this initiative, early years educarers could choose between the Workforce Skills Qualifications (WSQ) Certificate in Early Years (to work with infants and toddlers aged between two months to three years) and the WSQ Advanced Certificate in Early Childhood Care and Education (to work with older children aged 18 months to four years) (MCYS, 2011). This new training pathway was believed to cater to the developmental needs of potential educators to serve the surge in demand for educarers and early childhood professionals (MCYS, 2011).

The third initiative came in the form of multi-prong government subsidy programmes provided to pre-service educators, including the Early Childhood Capability Grant ($3,500 to $3,800 per student) and the ECDA Training Award ($16,000 to $40,000 per student) (Early Childhood Development Agency, 2017). For in-service centre leaders, teachers and educarers, a cash award of $12,000 was offered by the ECDA for teachers who pursued Professional Development Programmes. Hence, the next section describes how ECDA plays a role in catering for the children and community needs in ECE.

Regulation of ECEC delivery

As the current regulatory body of Singapore ECEC, the Early Childhood Development Agency's (ECDA) vision is based on the premise that every child in Singapore, no matter their background, deserves a head start in life through positive early childhood experience (Early Childhood Development Agency, 2017). This experience, they believe, comes from quality care and education, which supports children's holistic development and learning. ECDA focuses on three key indicators to promote quality ECEC – teacher quality, programme and curriculum quality and centre quality (Bautista, Ng, Munez, & Bull, 2016). Teacher quality is promoted through a continuous professional development programme master plan that ECDA have had since 2003. This programme caters for ECE teachers' professional development to develop and update their knowledge, skills and dispositions with customised pathways that meet their levels and specific needs. Currently, ECDA's professional development hours are structured at a minimum of 20 hours per year.

ECDA's other main function is to assess the early childhood providers for their operational licence as part of their work in ensuring the quality of early childhood care and education services in Singapore (ECDA, 2017). Through this work, they also ensure that centres have high quality programmes and curriculum quality following the principles of the Nurturing Early Learners (NEL) Framework. To maintain quality delivery of the ECEC service in preschools, the ECDA has various awards for centres to work with different initiatives such as the ECDA innovation guidance project and the ECDA innovation grant. ECDA supports the centres in the project implementation and the professional development for their projects. The aim of such initiatives is to allow centres to uplift their curriculum practice through action research and collaborative work with parents and wider community.

ECDA's quality assurance begins from the time a centre applies to be licenced to the time they are fully operational (ECDA, 2017). Using a pre-licensing checklist to evaluate a centre's premises, structures and suitability of the area where the premise is situated, ECDA officers are vigilant of building and operational defects that could pose a danger for the children and staff. For example, during these pre-licensing checks, the heights of play equipment for children in the centre would be measured, or the feasibility of the centre's evacuation plans would be assessed. During random licensing visits, ECDA officers also assess staff-child ratio, staff training, qualifications and requirements, first aid training, programme hours and operational staff. As a pre-requisite for any kinds of licensing, all the reported defects must be rectified in order to be issued a licence for the centre to operate. A newly opened centre will be given a year's licence and at the end of the first year, further audits and standards evaluation that requires compliance with ECDA rules will be carried out before any further licence is issued. If no deficiencies are sighted, the centres will be issued with a one- or two-year licence, depending on their meeting of the standards set by the ECDA's operational requirements. With these stringent regulations, ECDA ensures a consistency in the operational and quality standards of ECEC in Singapore (Bautista et al., 2016).

As the regulatory body in Singapore, ECDA's core business is to raise the quality of preschools in Singapore. This quality assurance and evaluation is articulated through an accreditation assessment system that preschools are encouraged to apply for. The accreditation is known as the Singapore Preschool Accreditation Framework (SPARK), in which preschools are evaluated using an instrument called the Quality Rating Scale (QRS) (ECDA, 2017). During the assessment, two ECDA evaluators, or more precisely known as validators, check through the centre's documents and observe lessons for appropriate practices and the children's reaction to the centre's environment. The main aim of the evaluation is to determine that a centre performs satisfactorily, according to the ECDA teaching and learning principles of catering for children's holistic development. Centres meeting all the requirements for relevant teaching and learning practices, as well as an appropriate learning environment, are endorsed as a SPARK preschool. With this accreditation system, preschools are guided by a set of quality and professional guidelines. The accreditation stamp provides parents with confidence in choosing the right preschool for their children (Bautista et al., 2016).

Besides being the watchdog for quality standards of preschool centres and their professionals, ECDA also oversees various aspects of early childhood centres' infrastructure, human resources and general operational support for the early childhood sector. Furthermore, ECDA also assists disadvantaged families by ensuring that their children's school fees are affordable, by, for example, providing subsidies and grants according to the household income or per-capita income. ECDA maintains all information regarding centre particulars such as the centre's capacity, school fee details, outbreak of diseases, licensee details and other personal information in a web portal called Childcare Link (www.childcarelink.gov.sg). Parents can also access Childcare Link to find information about the potential childcare centres, their fees, centre operating hours and additionally apply for children's enrolment in their chosen preschool.

ECDA's role in promoting quality ECEC also includes managing children's health and safety while attending preschools (Early Childhood Development Agency, 2017). The incidents that typically involve ECDA can be, for example, accidents in centre such as scalding caused by hot water or drink, suspicions of child abuse in the family or mishandling of children by the centre's staff. ECDA's role is to assist the centres to have a proper reporting channel in order to act in the best interest of children's welfare and development. Preschools are also required to notify ECDA for any communicable diseases, which are reported in the centre such as measles, rubella, hand-foot-and-mouth disease, chicken pox and stomach flu. ECDA officers subsequently conduct on-site checks at these centres to ensure standards of operating procedures are complied with, in order to prevent the diseases from further spreading. A centre may be issued a mandatory closure by the ECDA and the Ministry of Health, in the event that the number of cases is above the safe limit.

Overall, ECDA is the agency that has the responsibility in regulating the ECEC quality in Singapore, with the premise that children have a good start in their lives. The leaders in the early childhood sector leadership regard ECDA as an important agency in promoting holistic early education to children (Bautista et al., 2016). However, the question begets whether providing children with holistic early education and care is consistent with Singapore's cultural norm as a competitive society. This chapter thus concludes by discussing the implications of aspiring for holistic early education for Singapore children against the complexity of meeting societal needs.

Implications for holistic early education and care

In this chapter, we presented an overview of how Singapore embarked on a reformation of its ECEC curriculum and delivery. As discussed earlier, the aim of the NEL framework and ECDA's regulatory role was to ensure that the Singapore young children are provided with a holistic context of early education and care. The discussed government policies and norms urged a consistent message signalling the nation's reduced emphasis on rote learning and the direction towards training active and independent learners. There also seems a significant shift towards quality interactions between the teachers and the learners, with a view to foster a balance between both the academic and non-academic priorities of curriculum and learning (Ministry of Education, 2012). ECEC teachers or educarers in Singapore are seen to embrace these qualities more readily (Bautista et al., 2016) than Singapore parents. However, Singapore parents and society in general have a reason to be apprehensive about a less academic ECEC.

The competitiveness and the competency levels that primary school children face in their learning is not lessened as parents continue to push their children to do well academically. At the Primary Four level, students undergo "subject-based banding" based on the results of their school-based examinations (Ministry of Education, 2016). At Primary Six level, students are streamed into secondary schools, again based on their examinations result – this time from a state-wide Primary School Leaving Examination (PSLE) (Ministry of Education, 2015). With such high stakes placed on primary school education and examination results, it is of little wonder that Singapore parents are still nervous about the level of preparedness their children's preschool education is gearing them for the transition to primary school. After all, one of the main roles of preschools is to ensure a smooth transition for children to move from preschool to primary schooling (Tan, 2007; 2017).

The implications of this tension between a holistic early learning and formal schooling point to a gap, which is yet to be tackled by the Singapore government. To address this gap, the government may need to reduce its emphasis on high stakes testing at least at the primary school level or consider rolling back on its aspirations to achieve well-balanced children at an early age. Systematic research on the effectiveness of the reform, including effectiveness of preschool practice, teacher quality, and the parental perspectives of the curriculum outcomes for their children, may be a good way to inform the government's future decisions. Without doubt, the Singapore government will need to consider how to balance its priorities for holistic early learning against the Lion City's ferociously competitive society.

References

Bautista, A., Ng, S. C., Munez, D., & Bull, R. (2016). Learning areas for holistic education: Kindergarten teachers' curriculum priorities, professional development needs, and beliefs. *International Journal of Childcare and Education Policy, 10*(8), 1–18. doi:10.1186/s40723-016-0024-4

Choi, S.-H. (2007). Partnership with nonpublic actors: Singapore's early childhood policy. *UNESCO Policy Brief on Early Childhood*, 1–2. Retrieved from http://unesdoc.unesco.org/images/0014/001494/149486E.pdf

Choo, K. (2010). The shaping of childcare and preschool education in Singapore: From separatism to collaboration. *International Journal of Childcare and Education Policy, 4*(1), 23–34.

Early Childhood Development Agency. (2017). *A good start for every child*. Retrieved from www.ecda.gov.sg/pages/default.aspx

Goh, C. (1997). *Shaping our future: Thinking schools, learning nation*. Speech, The Opening of the 7th International Conference on Thinking at Suntec City

Convention Centre Ballroom. Retrieved from www.moe.gov.sg/media/speeches/1997/020697.htm

Kamerman, S. B. (2007). *A global history of early childhood education and care.* Background paper prepared for the Education for All Global Monitoring Report: Early Childhood Care and Education: UNESCO. Retrieved from http://unesdoc.unesco.org/images/0014/001474/147470e.pdf

Khoo, K. (2004). *Inter-ministerial collaboration in early childhood training in Singapore* (24th ed.). France: UNESCO Policy Brief on Early Childhood. Retrieved from http://unesdoc.unesco.org/images/0013/001374/137413e.pdf

Lee, H. (2004). Prime Minister Lee Hsien Loong's National Day Rally 2004 (English). *Prime Minister's Office Singapore.* Retrieved from www.pmo.gov.sg/newsroom/prime-minister-lee-hsien-loongs-national-day-rally-2004-english

Lim, S. (1998). Preschools in Singapore: A historical overview. *Early Child Development and Care, 144*(1), 5–12. http://dx.doi.org/10.1080/0300443981440102

People's Action Party Community Foundation. (2011). The PCF Story: Celebrating 25 Years of Growth. *PAP Community Foundation: News and Publications,* 1–44. Retrieved from www.pcf.org.sg/upload/item/News_Publications/PDFs/THE%20PCF%20STORY%20screen.pdf

Monk, H., & Phillipson, S. (2017). Early childhood educators' experiences and perceptions of professionalism and professionalisation in the Asian context. *Asia Pacific Journal of Teacher Education, 45*(1), 3–22. doi:10.1080/1359866X.2016.1147527

Ministry of Community Development, Youth and Sports. (2011). *Early years childcare and development receives a quality boost.* Retrieved from www.ecda.gov.sg/PressReleases/Pages/Early-Years-Child-Care-and-Development-Receives-a-Quality-Boost.aspx

Ministry of Education and Ministry of Community Development and Sports. (2000). *New framework for preschool teacher-training & accreditation.* Retrieved from www.moe.gov.sg/media/press/2000/pr18122000.htm

Ministry of Education. (2008). *Kindergarten curriculum guide* (1st ed., pp. 1–116). Republic of Singapore: Ministry of Education.

Ministry of Education. (2012). *Nurturing early learners: A curriculum framework for kindergartens in Singapore* (1st ed., pp. 11–110). Republic of Singapore: Ministry of Education.

Ministry of Education. (2013). *Nurturing early learners: A curriculum framework for kindergartens in Singapore* (1st ed., pp. 5–94). Republic of Singapore: Ministry of Education.

Ministry of Education. (2015). *From primary to secondary education.* Retrieved from www.moe.gov.sg/education/primary/from-primary-to-secondary-education

Ministry of Education. (2016). *Subject-based banding.* Retrieved from www.moe.gov.sg/education/primary/subject-based-banding

Ministry of Education is established – Singapore History. (2017). *E-resources. nlb.gov.sg.* Retrieved from http://eresources.nlb.gov.sg/history/events/c7cc9a2f-0cb2-44e8-bfe4-6220e3235c36#11

Ng, J. (2015). Education system "has to evolve" ' to spur creativity. *TODAY.* Retrieved from https://lkyspp.nus.edu.sg/ips/wp-content/uploads/sites/2/2015/04/TD_Education-system-has-to-evolve-to-spur-creativity_040715.pdf

Ng, J. (2011). Preschool curriculum and policy changes in Singapore. *Asia-Pacific Journal of Research in Early Childhood Education, 5*(1), 91–122.

Nyland, B., & Ng, J. (2015). International perspectives on early childhood curriculum changes in Singapore and Australia. *European Early Childhood Education Research Journal, 24*(3), 465–476. http://dx.doi.org/10.1080/1350293x.2015.1102416

Sharpe, P. (1998). Aspects of preschool education in Singapore. *Early Child Development and Care, 144*(1), 129–134. http://dx.doi.org/10.1080/0300443981440114

Tan, C. T. (2007). Policy developments in preschool education in Singapore: A focus on the key reforms of kindergarten education. *International Journal of Childcare and Education Policy, 1*(1), 35–43. http://dx.doi.org/10.1007/2288-6729-1-1-35

Tan, C. T. (2017). Enhancing the quality of kindergarten education in Singapore: Policies and strategies in the 21st century. *International Journal of Childcare and Education Policy, 11*(7). doi:10.1186/s40723–017–0033-y

UNESCO International Bureau of Education (IBE). (2006). *Singapore Early Childhood Care and Education (ECCE) programmes.* Geneva: UNESCO.

Yeo, N. (2013). *First campus celebrates 35-year journey to success.* Retrieved from Singapore Industrial & Services Employees' Union: www.ntuc.org.sg/wps/portal/up2/home/searchresultsdetails?WCM_GLOBAL_CONTEXT=/Content_Library/NTUC/Home/Working%20for%20U/aafd4e004e39828088d5aec7b9d67807

Zhang, K. (2016). Exploring options in early childhood care in Singapore: Programs and roles. *Childhood Educations, 92*(5), 377–382. doi:10.1080/00094056.2016.1226112

17 Early childhood education and care in Sweden

The context of Swedish preschool

*Pia Williams, Sonja Sheridan,
Susanne Garvis and Elisabeth Mellgren*

Introduction

The theoretical framework in this chapter is based on a sociocultural perspective on children's learning and development. From this viewpoint, communication and interaction become effective tools to learn new knowledge and skills, cultural values and create and develop social identity (Bruner, 1996; Vygotsky, 1978, 1986). Preschool is thus an important, collective context and a dynamic ground, where children encounter preschool staff, other adults and peers and learn through these relationships in a playful way (Siraj-Blatchford, 2007; Sommer, 2012; Williams, Sheridan & Sandberg, 2014). Collective processes constitute both the child and the social situation, where the child can experience its importance as a human being by being understood by others. This appears to be important part of children's lives, i.e. to be part of a socio-cultural practice (Svinth, 2013). To create such conditions for learning in educational environments, it is of vital importance for children to participate in programmes with engaged, experienced professional teachers, where interactions facilitate knowledge building and skills and attitudes (Siraj Blatchford, 2010; Williams, Sheridan & Pramling Samuelsson, 2016), and where children's cognitive, social and emotional learning are of equal importance. This approach is written in the Swedish preschool curriculum as well as it is deemed fundamental of practising and developing democratic understanding and democratic values (Swedish National Agency for Education, 1998/2011). In Sweden, preschool is a voluntary school form within the general education system (SFS 2010: 800). The municipality where the family lives is obliged to provide childcare for a lower fee, to children from one year of age to those parents who wish childcare.

As of the autumn of the year the child is three years old, the child is entitled to a free public preschool 15 hours a week, for the children already in preschool, the child remains in the same activities as before. Most children, 84% are in preschool and usually more hours than the 15 hours per week. It means that a child's formal education starts at this time in their life, regulated by curriculum goals (SFS, 2010, p. 800; Swedish National Agency for Education, 1998/2011). Most parents today also choose preschool for childcare and they are satisfied with it.

The National Agency parent survey (Swedish National Agency for Education, 2013), where the parents of 124,000 children participated, revealed that 90% felt that the staff did a good job, that children were safe and that preschool pedagogy met their expectations. However, there is dissatisfaction about large child groups and a concern about fewer trained preschool teachers in the preschool practice. In social media and daily press, parents and preschool staff post their concerns about preschool quality and especially in relation to group size (Pramling Samuelsson, Sheridan, Williams, & Nasiopoulou, 2014). Statistics from the Swedish National Agency for Education (2016) show a national average of 15.9 children per group with a ratio of 5.2 children per adult across all ages, a ratio that has not changed over the years. However, municipalities report that there is a large variation between preschools. The Swedish government has made some efforts to reduce the number of children in the preschool groups. The Swedish National Agency has formulated new benchmarks for group size in order to create better conditions for children and staff. For a toddler group (1–3 years-old), the benchmark is six to 12 children. For children in older age groups (3–5 years-old), the benchmark is nine to 15 children. The municipalities have major problems in structuring groups in order to comply with the benchmark. Partly because there are not enough trained preschool teachers, partly that there are not enough preschools to accommodate more or new, smaller groups. While waiting for the local municipalities to solve the problems with large child groups, preschool teachers tries to divide the children into smaller groups during part of the preschool day (Williams et al., 2016).

Present research in medicine, psychology, economics and social science clearly supports the view that not only the individual, but also the family and society benefit from spending resources on the youngest generation and has been found socio-economically profitable (Esping-Andersen, 2009; Heckman, 2011; Pramling Samuelsson & Wagner, 2012; Sylva, Melhuish, Sammons, Siraj-Blatchford & Taggart, 2010). Most effective for the individual, family and society are investments aimed at children between one to three years (Britto & Ulkuer, 2012). Children are entitled to a preschool of high quality where they can play, develop and learn in a healthy environment that provides care. Such a preschool contributes to give all children equal opportunities and lays the fundament for lifelong learning. The question of how preschool can create and maintain high quality therefore ought to be a top priority in society, as research suggests that high quality preschools with well-educated teachers also have the potential to improve equity and equality for children from diverse backgrounds (Sylva et al., 2010). But several studies show that the opposite has happened in Sweden today as preschools quality has declined (Sheridan & Pramling Samuelsson, 2009; Sheridan et al., manuscript). Inequality has increased and also the children's rights to a good and equal start in life have deteriorated (Malmö stad, 2014). Today, preschool receives children and families from many, different backgrounds and cultures. A complex task is to meet and integrate newly, arrived children from war-torn countries and support families in order to eliminate the segregation that exists in society. In this perspective, preschool can contribute and has impact on children's wellbeing and learning conditions, as well as their possibilities to be included in the Swedish society. Thus, preschool is not only part of the educational system but has gradually become a social project that legitimises the investment being made in early years (Heckman, 2006; Rubinstein Reich, Broman & Roth, 2017).

Internationally, decades of research on children's outcomes have taught societies that families engaged in preschool play a central role in positive learning experiences (Shonkoff & Phillips, 2000). For example, in the United States the Harvard Family Research Project promotes an integrated and comprehensive approach to engagement in early childhood settings (Centre on the Developing Child at Harvard University, 2007). In Australia, the E4 Kids longitudinal study also documents involvement of children and families in early childhood programs (Tayler et al., 2013). Findings from Australia also show the impact of family beliefs on the quality of early childhood (Garvis, Pendergast & Kanasa, 2012; Garvis, Lemon, Pendergast & Yim, 2013). While in the United Kingdom, the Effective Provision of Preschool Education project found that the family had a greater impact on children's outcomes than the preschool (Sylva et al., 2010). In Sweden, collaboration with families is regulated in the curriculum and is seen as fundamental for the work in preschool (Swedish National Agency for Education, 1998/2011).

The organisation of children in preschool

From an international perspective, an increasing proportion of children are in preschool from an early age (Organisation for Economic Cooperation and Development [OECD], 2012). During these first years of life, children develop cognitive, social, emotional, communicative and physical competences together with other children and adults. It is therefore of importance that preschool provides equal learning and developmental conditions for all children in society (Sheridan & Pramling Samuelsson, 2009; Sylva et al., 2010; Williams & Sheridan, 2016) and offer opportunities for children to form attachments with both adults and peers (Broberg, Hagström & Broberg, 2012; Williams, 2001; Williams & Sheridan, 2006). In Sweden, preschool is a key factor in the development of society and has been a part of strengthening the political agenda (Hägglund & Pramling Samuelsson, 2009). Thus, preschool appear not only to be shaped by society but also to shape society. Preschool provides parents opportunities for professional work and study and contributes to greater democratisation and equality between women and men, as well as parents' and children's rights to participation and influence (Broman, Rubinstein-Reich & Hägerström, 2002).

Swedish preschools rank high in international comparisons, although these measurements are more generally about what society does for children and families (Williams, Sheridan & Pramling Samuelsson, 2016). Other countries seem to be interested in the quality of Swedish preschools (Australian Conversation, 2015) as Sweden appears to be a useful example, as children from an early age are part of a coherent educational system, and the same ministry is responsible for both preschool and school. Indicators that are compared between countries are parental insurance length, accessible places for all children in preschool, funding support from the government, subsidised fees for parents, scope of trained personnel in preschool (at least one adult per 15 children), at least 1% of GDP transferred to childcare and that child poverty is lower than 10% (UNICEF, 2008).

The Swedish government spends 1.3% of GDP a year on preschool (European Commission, 2014). Approximately 84% of all children aged between one and five are enrolled (Swedish National Agency for Education, 2016). Sweden has a unique system for social reforms with a well-developed welfare system, preschools that are open to all children, high staff to child ratios, well-educated teachers, and in comparisons to other countries, small group sizes (OECD, 2012). In order to provide equity of access to children and families, the Swedish government subsidises preschool. There is a maximum fee of around 3% of the total family income for the first child, and then a decreasing sum for each additional child under 12 years of age in the family. Families do not pay for more than three children. In order to meet and support families' needs for care, preschool is usually open from 6:00 a.m. to 6:00 p.m. and the children spend on average 31 hours per week. The children can be organised in toddler groups (1–3 years-old), sibling groups (1–5 years-old) and older groups (3–5 years-old), but also alternative age-constellations.

Research shows that preschool teachers' competence and the quality of their communication and interaction creates different conditions for children's learning of content in preschool (Pramling Samuelsson & Sheridan, 2009). The teachers working in Swedish preschools are qualified, with about half of them having a 3.5-year long university degree and the other half having a nursery nurse certificate gained after two years at upper secondary/senior high school. The Swedish Education Act (SFS, 2010, p. 800) stipulates that preschool should be of high and equal quality, where equivalency can be defined, based on three, fundamental aspects: equal access to education, equal quality of education and that education should be compensating in order to give children an equal and good start in life. Swedish preschool has been highly ranked for many years in international comparisons, but a recent OECD report reveals that Sweden's international ranking has dropped from a previous first place. Fewer trained preschool teachers working in preschool and more children participating in preschool, leading to a larger amount of child groups, are some factors contributing to a lowering of the quality (Williams et al., 2016; Williams et al., manuscript). Studies also show that the quality of preschools both within and between municipalities varies significantly (Sheridan et al., manuscript). It gives children unequal conditions for wellbeing, learning, and an equal start in life.

Since 1996, preschool has been part of the Swedish educational system and in the most recent Education Act (SFS, 2010, p. 800) preschool became a school form in its own right within the overall educational system. Over the past decade, several changes have thus ensued. Preschool has received a revised national curriculum and a new preschool teacher education program has come into effect. Most children who attend preschool begin in their earliest years, leading to that about half of the children in preschool are between the ages of 1 to 3.

In 2013, the Swedish National Agency for Education removed their recommendation of a maximum of 15 children per group, for the reason that municipalities did not follow these guidelines. It was also claimed that compared with countries, such as Britain, the United States, China, Chile and Brazil, there were fewer children per adult in Swedish preschool. The removal of the recommendation led to intense debate about group size in Swedish preschools at various levels of society (Williams, Sheridan & Pramling Samuelsson, 2016) and as mentioned earlier, the Swedish National Agency for Education (2016) proposed a benchmark for group size in preschool. An emerging trend is to organise the children into age-homogenous groups, which is one-year olds, two-year olds etc. Another trend in Sweden as well as in Norway is to combine two traditional child groups into a large child-group of approximately 40 children and eight adults, here referred to as extended child groups and extended working-teams (Sheridan, Williams & Pramling Samuelsson, 2014; Seland, 2015). The rationale behind this organisation has pedagogical, organisational as well as economical aspects, and is based on an idea of a flexible organization for both children and teachers. For example, the schedule can be changed and adapted to the needs of the child group and the number of children, and the children can move between different activities. From an adult perspective, extended child groups can be seen as less vulnerable, giving greater opportunities for collegial learning and broadening the competences of the team. A team with more adults should also give more opportunities to interact and communicate with children. Considered from a child perspective, it can provide more peers of different ages and a flexibility to move and attend in several contexts. However, it also entails more for children to communicate through relationships, although it can be especially difficult for the youngest children to handle.

The Swedish preschool curriculum

In 1998, the first national curriculum for preschools was established (Swedish National Agency for Education, 1998/2011). It embraces the fundamental values, tasks and objectives of preschool and provides guidelines for preschool activities. It is linked to the curriculum for compulsory education (Swedish National Agency for Education, 2011/2016). Together, these curricula adopt a common view of knowledge, development and learning that leads to the overall goals of ensuring and enhancing quality throughout the education system. Within this curriculum, the preschool is referred to as an agent for change, listed as an individual actor. The main aim of preschool is to promote children's learning. The curriculum for the preschool (2011, p. 3) stipulates, "an important task of the preschool is to impact and establish respect for human rights and the fundamental democratic values on which Swedish society is based".

During 2011, a new preschool teacher education plan was implemented. The focus of both the revised curriculum and the new teacher education programme is clearly to strengthen content areas such as language, mathematics, technology and science, as well as documentation, evaluation and didactical issues. The ambition is to make preschool more pedagogical, in the sense that it will be more learning-oriented and of higher quality for all children (Swedish National Agency for Education, 1998/2011). Currently in Sweden, there is a discussion about more teaching needed in preschools. One might say that this is a way to raise expectations of preschools and to see the child as competent with great potential (Sommer, Pramling Samuelsson & Hundeide, 2010). Research shows, however, that specific structural conditions are no guarantee of high quality and that low-quality preschools are more vulnerable to decreases in resources (Sheridan et al., 2009).

When the curriculum was revised in 2016, increased requirements for transitions to preschool (for children aged 6 years) were one of the purposes as well as to enhancing the status of the pedagogical work carried out. The new content and objectives for preschool education place greater emphasis on literacy, mathematics, science and technology, with a greater focus on the implementation of these learning areas. Rooted in the Nordic perspective on preschool didactics (Pramling & Pramling Samuelsson, 2011), it is required that these content areas are integrated with goals relating to fundamental values, the development of social abilities, and play. These goals are formulated, as something the preschool should strive to ensure that every child learns and develops. In the curriculum, a new area of evaluation and development for quality in preschool was also introduced, known as systematic quality work. To enhance preschool quality, preschool teachers need to understand how the quality is constituted, can be discerned, evaluated, documented and improved through a systematic quality development work in everyday preschool practice. In Sweden, all preschools are required to work systematically with quality issues. This involves several interdependent steps that follow each other in a specific order. Although the concept of systematic quality work might be novel, the practice of following up, documenting and evaluating preschool activities has a long tradition as a means of discovering whether and in what ways preschool has contributed to children's learning and what children have learnt by being there (Sheridan, Williams & Sandberg, 2013).

Pramling Samulesson, Sheridan and Williams state (2006) that one characteristic of the Swedish preschool curricula is the description of the active child, who initiates communication and who is interested in the surrounding world. This child perspective can be traced back to Rousseau and differs from the child perspective often held in school. The active child is visible in the goals formulated as Development and learning with a responsibility of preschool to create conditions for children to develop in the formulated direction. Preschool shall form a unity in which the education is built on care, fostering and learning. The activities should stimulate play and creativity and use children's interest in learning and mastering new experiences, knowledge and skills. The flow of ideas and the diversity of views should be explored. Preschool should strive to ensure that children develop their identity and feel secure in this, develop their ability to listen, narrate, reflect and express their own views, develop their vocabulary and concepts as well as their communicative functions. Interrelated with the development and learning goals are "every-day-life-skills". These are corresponding to a number of qualities (in terms of properties and skills) like cooperative skills, responsibility, initiative, flexibility, reflectivity, active attitudes, communicative skills, problem-solving skills, critical stance, creativity, as well as an ability to learn to learn. These different qualities are seen as general and part of all preschool and school subjects, and form a central dimension in preparing the children of today for society of tomorrow (Pramling Samuelsson, Sheridan & Williams, 2006).

The role of communication and interaction is also as a key factor in the Swedish preschool curriculum, emphasised that through communication children makes meaning. The paradigm of learning is described as an internal relation between the child and the surrounding world and that development and learning are two aspects of the same phenomenon. Parents' cooperation is another important issue in the curricula. Historically, preschool was based on a philanthropic approach where fostering parents as well as children were part of the agenda. Today, the notion of collaboration between parents and preschool as equal partners are seen as vital for children's upbringing and an important contributor to children's learning and development. Information from parents collected in the form of regular surveys is used to change daily routines and content. Another goal to strive towards in Swedish curricula is to ensure that each child develops their ability to discover, reflect on and work on different ethical dilemmas and fundamental questions of life and daily reality.

To summarise, the Swedish preschool curriculum is both value- and learning-oriented. It embraces a societal strive for democracy and a spectrum of goals to be characterised as content and action in preschool practice.

Teaching and children's learning in Swedish preschool

Preschool helps children to become participants in wider cultural worlds and to learn to learn (Sylva et al., 2010). Preschool education and teaching are to be understood as didactical and learning-oriented processes, based on teacher-child communication and how children's playfulness and interests are integrated in more directed teaching efforts. Children's learning and development also need to be understood in light of contemporary challenges, posed by the information society. Many experiences that children gain today are mediated by different media, such as literature, movies, television, tech and games (Buckingham, Bragg, & Kehily, 2014; Findahl, 2014). Experiences gained through engaging in such media will be important to children's knowledge development and will contribute to our understanding of children's agency as well as their participation in, and promotion of, a sustainable future.

Studies have shown how the child's perspective and communicative strategies become critical in developing high-quality caring practices (Sheridan & Pramling Samuelsson, 2009) that aid children in their agency of handling challenging situations and conditions that threaten their wellbeing (Garvis & Lemon, 2014). This question touches upon how different professions can work together in institutions or between institutions (Bronstein & Abramson, 2003; Nilsson, Ferholt & Alnervik, 2015).

Conclusions

To conclude this chapter, we would like to return to the question of 'what conditions for wellbeing, learning and development that the Swedish preschool context provide for young children'? In the text, we have outlined the context for
Swedish preschool, by referring to research and policy documents as the Swedish preschool curriculum. Based on sociocultural perspectives the text underpins
that preschool as an important arena for children's wellbeing, early learning and
development. Studies show that confirmatory interaction between children contributes to the wellbeing among children. It may be about having a common
focus in play and doing things together, to experience body contact and the joy
of communication and shared activities (Seland, 2009; Vassenden, Tygesemb,
Brosvik, Alvestad & Abrahamsen, 2012; Vygotsky, 1978).

The conditions for children's wellbeing, learning and development are however
closely linked to preschool quality and the preschool teacher's competences to create playful, learning situations. Preschool teachers need continuous educational
training to maintain high quality in preschool practice. It involves competences
to direct children's attention to different contents in order to extend and deepen
their understanding and interests, to introduce new knowledge and didactical
skills (Williams, Larsson, & Veraksa, manuscript). It is also linked to a preschool
curriculum that encounters changes in society and maintains the fundamental of
practising and developing democratic understanding and democratic values from
a child perspective. In Sweden, the preschool curriculum is continuously revised
in order to meet these changes and prepare children to live in contemporary and
future society. Conditions for learning in preschool are influenced by ideologies
and theories that are developed in global ecosystems inextricably linking time,
culture and society to one another. Thus, the meaning of preschool quality and
preschool teacher competence is tied to both the influence of culture, context and
societal intentions relating to the child and childhood (Moss, 2004), as well as to
the political and educational intentions of preschool (Sylva et al., 2010).

Society is under constant change and development, and what goes on in preschool and conditions for children's learning and development are related to
these changes in society. Over the past decades, dynamic changes related to preschools and society has occurred in Sweden and also within early childhood education and care in Europe (Oberhuemer, 2013). One important issue is group
size. In Sweden, the government has taken some measures, through a benchmark
for group size. Nevertheless, there is still much to do in order to facilitate for
municipalities to implement these benchmarks and to meet the need of families and children. Research is needed of how to organise suitable group sizes in
municipalities to achieve positive outcomes for children and within the given
constraints of finance.

With the goal of maintaining high quality in early childhood education and giving children a good, safe and learning-oriented preschool, new preschool teachers
need to be trained. In international surveys and comparisons, Sweden has given
a high number of educated preschool teachers. New statistics show, however,
that only 39% of preschool teachers (Swedish National Agency for Education,

2016) have a university degree, and the others are mainly nursery nurses with a certificate gained after two years at upper secondary/senior high school. This has a significant impact on preschool quality and, in the long run, affects whether all children are getting an equal start in life. The benchmark on group size will mean even greater demand for educated preschool teachers. Preschool quality is dependent on the fact that there are university educated preschool teachers who can contribute both to the development and quality of teacher education and preschool practice.

Given the state of change, new ideas on the lives of children and their parents within early childhood will demand a significant cultural shift in the way research, policy and practice interact in the fields of child health and learning (Shonkoff & Fisher, 2013). The challenge for policy-makers and the early childhood profession is to move beyond the simple coordination of separate child and adult focused programs and to combine the best of both domains within a fully integrated strategy that is grounded in theories of learning, developmental science (research), and aligned with the preschool, community and policy levels (Shonkoff & Fisher, 2013).

As preschool and society (families, policy, profession and research) shape one another, conceptualisations about children are developed. All of these changes influence preschool practices, working conditions for preschool teachers, and conditions for children's learning and wellbeing, as well as policy on a societal level. In this way, children are often positioned as "central political agents" (Fleer, Hedegaard, & Tudge, 2009) as societal changes can take place within preschools. In Iceland for example, philosophical and pedagogical tensions in preschools appear to "mirror emerging questions in society as a whole about children, their upbringing and their early education" (Einarsdottir & Wagner, 2006, p. 178). As Bruner (1996) has suggested, cultural beliefs find their ways into all social institutions, including preschools.

While Swedish preschools are generally reported as having good conditions for children, problems still emerge from the profession's voice on difficulties implementing the curriculum's intentions. Nevertheless, the goal should always be to create a preschool practice and activities that are optimal for children with regard to wellbeing, play, learning and development.

References

Australian Conversation.(2015). *Why Swedish early learning is so much better than Australia's*. Retrieved from http://theconversation.com/why-swedish-early-learning-is-so-much-better-than-australias-35033

Britto, P., & Ulkuer, U. (2012). Child development in developing countries: Child rights and policy implications. *Child Development, 83*(1), 92–103.

Broberg, M., Hagström, B., & Broberg, A. (2012). *Anknytning i förskolan: vikten av trygghet för lek och lärande* [Affiliation in preschool: The importance of security for play and learning]. Stockholm: Natur & Kultur.

Bronstein, L. R., & Abramson, J. S. (2003). Understanding socialization of teachers and social workers: Groundwork for collaboration in the schools. *Families in Society, 84*(3), 323–330.

Bruner, J. (1996). *The culture of education*. Cambridge, MA: Harvard University Press.

Buckingham, D., Bragg, S., & Kehily, M. J. (Eds.). (2014). *Youth cultures in the age of global media*. Basingstoke: Palgrave Macmillan.Center on the Developing Child at Harvard University. (2007). *A science based framework for early childhood policy: Using evidence to improve outcomes in learning, behaviour, and health for vulnerable children*. Cambridge, MA: Harvard University Press.

Einarsdottir, J., & Wagner, J. T. (Eds.). (2006). *Nordic childhoods and early education. Philosophy, research, policy, and practice in Denmark, Finland, Iceland, Norway and Sweden*. Greenwich, CT: Information Age.

Esping-Andersen, G. (2009). *Incomplete revolution: Adapting welfare states to women's new roles*. Cambridge: Polity Press.

European Commission. (2014). *Key data on early childhood education and care in Europe 2014. Eurydice and Eurostat report*. Luxemburg: Publications Office at European Union.

Findahl, O. (2014). *Svenskarna och Internet 2014* [The Swedes and internet]. http://en.soi2014.se/01-the-spread-of-the-internet-has-not-let-up-completely/sweden-in-the-world-2014/

Fleer, M., Hedegaard, M., & Tudge, J. (Eds.). (2009). *Childhood studies and the impact of globalisation: policies and practices at global and local levels*. World Yearbook of Education 2009. London: Routledge.

Garvis, S., & Lemon, N. (2014). Enhancing the Australian early childhood teacher education curriculum about very young children. *Early Child Development and Care, 185*(4), 547–561. doi:10.1080/03004430.2014.939652

Garvis, S., Lemon, N., Pendergast, D., & Yim, B. (2013). A content analysis of early childhood teachers' theoretical and practical experiences with infants and toddlers in Australian teacher education programs. *Australian Journal of Teacher Education, 38*(9).

Garvis, S., Pendergast, D., & Kanasa, H. (2012). "Get real – we can't afford kindergarten": A study of parental perceptions of early years services. *International Journal of Early Years Education, 20*(2), 202–211.

Göteborgs Stad. (2014). *Skillnader i livsvillkor och hälsa i Göteborg. Hela staden socialt hållbar* [Differences in living conditions and health in Gothenburg. The whole city is socially sustainable]. Retrieved from http://socialhallbarhet.se/wp-content/uploads/2015/01/Skillnader-i-livsvillkor-och-h%C3%A4lsa-2014-Huvudrapport1.pdf

Hägglund, S., & Pramling Samuelsson, I. (2009). Early childhood education and learning for sustainable development and citizenship. *International Journal of Early Childhood, 41*(2), 49–63.

Heckman, J. (2006). Skill formation and the economics of investing in disadvantaged children. *Science, 312*(5782), 1900–1902.

Heckman, J. (2011, Spring). The economics of inequality. The value of early childhood education. *American Educator*. Retrieved from www.aft.org/pdfs/americaneducator/spring2011/Heckman.pdf

Malmö stad. (2014). *Malmös väg mot en hållbar framtid. Hälsa, välfärd och rättvisa* [Malmö road towards a sustainable future. Health, welfare and justice]. Malmö: Kommissionen för ett socialt hållbart Malmö.

Moss, P. (2004). Setting the scene: A vision of universal children's spaces. In Daycare Trust (Ed.), *A new era for universal childcare?* (pp. 19–28). London: Daycare Trust.

Nilsson, M., Ferholt, B., & Alnervik, K. (2015). Why Swedish early learning is so much better than Australia's. *Australian Conversation March 5 2015*. Retrieved from http://theconversation.com/why-swedish-early-learning-is-so-much-better-than-australias-35033

Oberhuemer, P. (2013). Early childhood workforce profiles in changing European ECEC Systems. In L. Miller, C. Dalli, & M. Urban (Eds.) *Radical reconstructions? Early childhood workforce profiles in changing European Early Childhood Education and Care Systems* (pp. 119–130). London: Springer.

Organisation for Economic Cooperation and Development. (2012). *Starting strong III: A quality tool box for early childhood education*. Paris: OECD.

Pramling Samuelsson, I., & Wagner, J. (2012). Open appeal to local, national, regional, and global leaders to secure the world's future. Prioritize early childhood development, education, and care. *International Journal of Early Childhood*, *44*(3), 341–346. doi:10.1007/s13158-012-0071-0

Pramling Samuelsson, I., Sheridan, S., & Williams, P. (2006). Five preschool curricula – in a comparative perspective. *International Journal of Early Childhood*, *38*(1), 11–30.

Pramling Samuelsson, I., Sheridan, S., Williams, P., & Nasiopoulou, P. (2014). Stora barngrupper i förskolan – ett medieperspektiv. In J. Balldin, J. Dahlbeck, A. Harju, & P. Lilja (Eds.), *Om förskolan och de yngre barnen: historiska och nutida nedslag* [Preschool and the youngest children: historical and contemporary decline]. Lund: Studentlitteratur.

Pramling, N., & Pramling Samuelsson, I. (Eds.). (2011). *Educational encounters: Nordic studies in early childhood didactics*. Dortrecht, Holland: Springer.

Rubinstein Reich, L., Tallberg Broman, I., & Vallberg Roth, A.-C. (2017). *Professionell yrkesutövning i förskolan* [Professional training in preschool]. Lund: Studentlitteratur.

Seland, M. (2009). *Det moderne barn og den fleksible barnehagen. En etnografisk studie av barnehagens hverdagsliv i lys av nyere diskurser og kommunal verkelighet* [The modern child and the flexible preschool. An ethnographic study of everyday life in preschool in light of recent discourses and municipal reality]. Trondheim: Norges teknisk naturvitenskapelige universitet. Norsk senter for barneforskning (NOSEB).

Seland, M. (2015). *Livet i den fleksible barnehagen* [Life in a flexible preschool]. Oslo: Universitetsforlaget.

SFS. (2010). *Skollag* [Swedish Education Act]. Stockholm: Utbildningsdepartementet.

Sheridan, S., & Pramling Samuelsson, I. (2009). *Barns lärande – fokus i kvalitetsarbetet* [Children's learning – focus on quality work]. Stockholm: Liber.

Sheridan, S., Williams, P., & Pramling Samuelsson, I. (2014). Group size and organisational conditions for children's learning in preschool: a teacher perspective. *Educational Research*, *56*(4), 379–397.

Sheridan, S., Williams, P., & Sandberg, A. (2013). Systematic quality-work in preschool. *International Journal of Early Childhood*, *45*(1), 123–150.

Shonkoff, J., & Phillips, D. (Eds.). (2000). *From neurons to neighbourhoods: The science of early childhood development*. Washington, DC: National Academy Press.

Shonkoff, J., & Fisher, P. (2013). Rethinking evidence-based practice and two-generation programs to create the future of early childhood policy. *Development and Psychopathology*, *25*(4.2), 1635–1653.

Siraj-Blatchford, I. (2007). Creativity, communication and collaboration: The identification of pedagogic progression in sustained shared thinking. *Asia-Pacific Journal of Research in Early Childhood Education*, *2*, 3–23.

Siraj-Blatchford, I. (2010). A focus on pedagogy: Case studies of effective practice. In K. Sylva, E. Melhuish, P. Sammons, I. Siraj-Blatchford, & B. Taggart (Eds.), *Early childhood matters: Evidence from the effective pre-school and primary education project* (pp. 149–165). London: Routledge.

Sommer, D. (2012). *A childhood psychology: Young children in changing times.* Basingstoke: Palgrave Macmillan.

Sommer, D., Pramling Samuelsson, I., & Hundeide, K. (2010). *Child perspectives and children's perspectives in theory and practice.* Milton Keynes: Springer.

Svinth, L. (2013). Pædagogers åbenhed for børnenes perspektiver og børns deltagelsesmuligheder i pædagogisk tilrettelagte aktiviteter [Teacher's openness to children's perspectives and children's opportunities for participation in educational planned activities]. *Psyke & Logos, 34,* 83–105.

Swedish National Agency for Education. (1998/2011). *Curriculum for preschool, Lpfö98.* Revised in 2010. Stockholm: Skolverket.

Swedish National Agency for Education. (2011/2016). *Curriculum for compulsory school, preschool class and the recreation centre.* Revised in 2011. Stockholm: Skolverket.

Swedish National Agency for Education. (2013). *Beskrivande data 2013.* Förskola, skola och vuxenutbildning [Descriptive data 2013. Preschool, school and adult education]. Skolverkets rapport nr. 399. Stockholm: Skolverket.

Swedish National Agency for Education. (2016). *Curriculum for the preschool, Lpfö-98.* Revised 2016. Stockholm: Fritzes.

Sylva, K., Melhuish, E., Sammons, P., Siraj-Blatchford, I., & Taggart, B. (2010). *Early childhood matters. Evidence from the effective pre-school and primary education project.* London: Routledge.

Tallberg Broman, I., Rubinstein Reich, L., & Hägerström, J. (2002). *Likvärdighet i en skola för alla – historisk bakgrund och kritisk granskning* [Equivalence in a school for all – historical background and critical review]. Stockholm: Skolverket.

Tayler, C., Ishimine, K., & Cloney, D. (2013). The quality of early childhood education and care services in Australia. *Australasian Journal of Early Childhood, 38*(2), 13–21.

UNICEF. (2008). *The childcare transition: A league table of early childhood education and care in economically advanced countries.* Florence: UNICEF Innocenti Research Centre.

Vassenden, A., Tygesemb, J., Brosvik, B. S., Alvestad, M., & Abrahamsen, G. (2012). *Barnehagens organisering og strukturelle faktorers betydning for kvalitet* [The organization of the kindergarten and the importance of structural factors for quality]. IRIS rapport 2011/029.

Vygotsky, L. S. (1986 [1934]). *Thought and language.* Cambridge, MA: MIT Press.

Vygotsky, L. S. (1978). *Mind in society. The development of higher psychological processes* (M. Cole, V. John-Steiner, S. Scribner, and E. Souberman, Eds.). Cambridge, MA: Harvard University Press.

Williams, P. (2001). *Barn lär av varandra. Samlärande i förskola och skola* [Children learn from each other, in preschool and school]. Göteborg: Acta Universitatis Gothoburgensis

Williams, P., & Sheridan, S. (2006). Collaboration as one aspect of quality: A perspective of collaboration and pedagogical quality in educational settings. *Scandinavian Journal of Educational Research, 50*(1), 83–93.

Williams, P., & Sheridan, S. (2016). *Barngruppers storlek i förskolan. En kartläggning av aktuell pedagogisk, utvecklingspsykologisk och socialpsykologisk forskning* [Group size in preschool. A survey of current pedagogical, developmental psychological and social psychological research]. Rapport 433. Stockholm: Skolverket.

Williams, P., Larsson, J., & Veraksa, A. (manuscript). Preschool children's collaboration and learning together. In N. Veraksa & S. Sheridan (Eds.), *Vygotsky in preschool education*.

Williams, P., Sheridan, S., & Pramling Samuelsson, I. (2016). *Barngruppens storlek i förskolan. Konsekvenser för utveckling och kvalitet* [Group size in preschool. Consequences for development and quality]. Stockholm: Natur och Kultur.

Williams, P., Sheridan, S., & Sandberg, A. (2014). Preschool – an arena for children's learning of social and cognitive knowledge. *Early Years, 34*(3), 226–240.

18 Early childhood education and care in Taiwan

The path to achieving high quality

Yvonne Yu-Feng Liu

Introduction

Reforms play a crucial role in educational development. While pursuing high-quality early childhood education is the international trend, there are significant changes that have occurred in the past decade in Taiwan. The root of ECEC in Taiwan was mainland China (1911–1947) and influenced by Japan during the colonisation period (1897–1941). After the retrocession of Taiwan, ECEC began to walk its own path by developing legislation and curriculum for young children. Between 1949 and 1981, as the number of young children increased, people paid more attention to children's education. Curriculum standards and teacher training of ECEC w developed. However, ECEC was not viewed as important as other educational stages because it was not within compulsory education and most preschool institutions were private (Duan, 2011; Hong, 2002).

In 1981, (Preschool Education Act) was announced and set an official position for early childhood education in Taiwan. With legislation underpinning the development of ECEC, important policies and further regulations started to form the picture of modern ECEC in Taiwan. Meanwhile, as the Taiwan total fertility rate was considered as the lowest in the world from 2009 (Liberty Times Net, 2010; The World Factbook, 2017), the government started to realise it was becoming a serious issue for national development. Former president Ma mentioned that the low birth rate was a problem of national security (Political Center of Now News, 2011). The reasons behind the low birth rate were, firstly, women's entry into higher education, causing late pregnancy and care cost for young children and, secondly, unfriendly natural, economic and social environments for the raising of children in Taiwan (Peng, 2009). This has become, and remains, a severe problem in Taiwanese society.

To present the developmental path to achieving high-quality ECEC along with the contextual and consistent changes in Taiwan, the purpose of this study is to review major policies and background from 2000 to 2016. This research focuses on: 1. What is the developed background and important legislation of ECEC? 2. What are the related policies and strategies to support ECEC's development? 3. What are the challenges in the path of achieving high ECEC quality? A literature review was conducted for this research. Government regulations, publications and related documents about ECEC in Taiwan were gathered and analysed for this study. International and local research as it relates to ECEC development in Taiwan is also considered as a reference in this study.

Background and foundation legislations of ECEC development in Taiwan

Regulations and policies from the 90s underpinned the process of change that stressed availability, equity and quality. Strategies from government match the criteria of high-quality ECEC in the world (The Economist Intelligence Unit, 2012).

In order to expand the availability of ECEC, the Ministry of Education used the setting of public preschools as an important policy in Ten-Year Plan of Early Childhood Education in Taiwan (Duan, 2011). From 2010, the Ministry of Education and the Ministry of Interior (2010) released the plan of Free Education for 5-year-old children. This free education plan began from outer-island and indigenous areas in 2010 and was extended to all 5-year-old children in Taiwan. Equity is another issue to which the government paid close attention. In 2004, the plan of supporting education for underprivileged 5-year-old children was implemented from outer-island and indigenous areas and then spread to children from low-income families in Taiwan (Sun, Lu, & Chang, 2014; Ministry of Education, 2008). Preschools were established from these underprivileged areas first, then expanded nationwide because the government viewed preschool education as an important phase before compulsory education (Duan, 2011).

Along with the strategies on availability and equality in ECEC, in order to unify ECEC quality and offer higher-quality preschool education, one important policy, the integration of early childhood education and care, was proposed. The purposes of this integration were unified authorities, regulations, teacher qualifications and curriculum between kindergartens and childcare centres (Chen, 2012). The discussion of the integration between kindergartens and childcare centres started in 1997, and enacted in 2011, based on the Early Childhood Education and Care Act (Ministry of Justice, 2015).

Looking back in history, ECEC in Taiwan was rooted in multiple sources and, gradually formed its own path by legislation in the 90s. The policies from 1990 to 2010 showed that government's focus on ECEC was care for basic issues, while the scope was nationwide. Those policies played as the overture to the developing direction of ECEC in Taiwan. Meanwhile, the implementation result of policies above was also viewed as an important reference in the preparation of the Early Childhood Education and Care Act.

Foundation of legislation

The foundation of modern ECEC development in Taiwan is the Early Childhood Education and Care Act. There are three reasons behind the legislation. Firstly, there were education and care systems for young children in Taiwan, which were based on different regulations and offered differing quality of education and care services. Secondly, it is important to strengthen the public's role and offer better environments for the upbringing of young children during the low birth rate situation (Duan, 2007). Thirdly, according to reports from international organizations, governments should play positive roles in integrating different authorities to promote better quality of ECEC (Taguma, Litjens, & Makowiecki, 2013).

The Early Childhood Education and Care Act is a crucial fundamental legislation for ECEC development in Taiwan. After 59 official meetings, four public hearings and a legislative process lasting 14 years, kindergartens and day cares in Taiwan were finally integrated as preschools supervised by the Ministry of Education (Ministry of Education, 2016b). The Act was announced officially in 2011, and promulgated from 2012. At that time, Taiwan was the first country in Asia that integrated education and care systems into one educare system (Shen, 2016; Duan & Hsiao, 2013).

As Article 1 in the Early Childhood Education and Care Act mentions, *the Act is enacted to ensure young children's right to appropriate education and care, establish guidelines of education and care, enhance the system of early childhood education and care, and safeguard their right to sound physical and psychological development* (Ministry of Justice, 2015a). There are seven chapters in the Early Childhood Education and Care Act, which includes establishment of preschools and educare service, personnel qualifications, protection of young children's rights, rights and obligations of the parents, and guidance towards preschools (Ministry of Justice, 2015a).

The Early Childhood Education and Care Act could be viewed as the page to open a new era of ECEC in Taiwan. The preparation process was rather long and included many dimensions. Policies of offering benefits and public services were usually implemented from rural areas and, then, spread to the whole nation. After the announcement of the Early Childhood Education and Care Act, there is finally a child-centred legislation, which takes care of children's needs in one act. This Act is also a solid foundation for all children's education and service institutions to follow and reference. Most important of all, the act unified education and care systems into one. There has been only one educare standard for all children in Taiwan ever since. The implementation of this new Act set the path to achieving quality ECEC in Taiwan. The supporting measures, which followed the Early Childhood Education and Care Act, elaborate upon critical concepts of the Act in order to enrich the process of implementation.

The implementation of the Early Childhood Education and Care Act

Regulations and strategies based on Early Childhood Education and Care Act played important roles in the process of achieving excellence in ECEC. There are 22 central and 8 local regulations that follow the main idea of Early Childhood Education and Care Act which were announced in 2011. Regulations included five categories, which are preschool institutions, curriculum and supporting service in ECEC, teacher qualifications, support for disadvantaged families, and preschool evaluation (Ministry of Justice, 2015a). Despite the new era of ECEC in Taiwan steered by Early Childhood Education and Care Act followed regulations, there are issues and challenges that remain since beginning the new phase.

Currently in Taiwan, the most discussed issue is teacher qualification. To unify and set a standard of preschool teacher quality in Taiwan, a new preschool teacher qualification was announced. Before 2011, teachers in kindergartens and childcare centres were cultivated from different paths. Kindergarten teachers were educated and trained in comprehensive universities that followed curriculum regulations from the department of higher education and the department of teacher education. While childcare centre teachers were taught at universities of technology that followed the plans from the department of technical and vocational education. Despite the names or authorities being different within these two paths, the content of each training program was similar. After the enforcement of the Early Childhood Education and Care Act, teachers who trained in universities of technology were qualified only as "educare givers[1]" but not "teachers" in preschools (Ministry of Justice, 2014; Ministry of Education, 2015a; Duan & Hsiao, 2013). According to the Act, there should be at least one teacher and one educare giver in a 6-year-old group. Care givers who worked as teachers are now unqualified for this 6-year-old group. About 26,000 educare givers lost their teaching positions in preschools, which aroused intense discussions and protests for their rights (Chang, 2014). To solve the issues and achieve unified teacher quality, the Standards of Pre-Service Professional Development Program for ECEC was announced in 2012. There are 32 credits for the ECEC professional program, which outlines the core training content for all preschool educators. The standards apply to departments from comprehensive universities and technology universities that cultivate ECEC educators (teachers and educare givers) (Ministry of Education, 2014). Moreover, the Act was amended on July 1, 2015. Preschool educare givers who previously worked as teachers in childcare centres before the enforcement of the Early Childhood Education and Care Act could keep their positions in preschool after 16 credits of professional training in teacher education (Ministry of Justice, 2015a; Chen, 2015).

In addition, there are challenges that needed to be considered. Preschool teachers and educare givers were employed based on two regulations[2] that refer to two different salaries and benefits. As there are no clear definitions of job responsibilities between teachers and educare givers, it is difficult for preschool directors to manage two types of preschool educators (Hu & Wu, 2013).

Teachers' quality is viewed as a key element in education development (Taguma, Litjens, & Makowiecki, 2013; The Economist Intelligence Unit, 2012). In the process of unifying teacher quality, teacher training content is now integrated into one standard. Preschool teachers should have bachelor's degree with 32 credits of ECEC professional program and 16 credits of professional training in teacher education (Ministry of Justice, 2014). The solo standard of educators' training and qualification is no doubt a starting point in the benign circle, though it is difficult to mediate different groups. However, when the Act talks about the working responsibility of preschools teachers and educare givers, there are limited documents and information to clarify the differences between them. The definition of preschool teacher and educare givers could be more directly connected to the training processes and certifications between these two types of educators.

The preschool educare curriculum framework

The ECEC Curriculum Framework played a major role in triggering related strategies. The first Standards of Kindergarten Curriculum of Republic of China was announced in 1932, and further amended in 1953, 1975, and 1987 (Huang & Hsue, 2000). As the development of ECEC in Taiwan continued, the discussion of curriculum framework in modern society was aroused. The Preschool Educare Curriculum Framework was first announced as a temporary version in 2012. After follow up research, meetings and discussions, the framework was amended and officially announced in 2016, and will be enacted on August 1, 2017 (Ministry of Education, 2016a).

According to the Preschool Educare Curriculum Framework, the purposes of ECEC in Taiwan are to build up a system for the welbeing of children, cultivate children to have virtue from the Confusion world, and equip children with core competences of lifelong learning as future citizens. The goal of the curriculum framework in ECEC is to cultivate children holistically through physical development and health, cognition, language, and social and arts learning areas via integrated activities designed to build up children's competence (Ministry of Education, 2016a).

There are two main projects related to promoting the idea of Preschool Educare Curriculum Framework for preschool educators. First, series seminars based on the curriculum framework for spreading ideas, content and implementation for high quality ECEC in Taiwan. Take the 2017 seminars as examples, where local governments are obligated to organise at least 30 hours of training courses and 36 hours of optional advanced courses for preschool educators (Ministry of Education, 2017a). There are also handbooks, online tutorial courses and online tools for curriculum design, which are organised by the government to support preschool educators, in order for educators to be fully aware of the Preschool Educare Curriculum Framework (Ministry of Education, 2015).

Second, on-site mentoring and guidance for quality improvement was started in 2006. This was a supportive project along with the integration of early childhood education and care policy. Research showed the results of individual consultations benefit both mentors and preschool educators (Duan & Ma, 2013). As the legislation and curriculum framework were officially announced, the goal of these consultations is to assist preschool teachers in professional development (Ministry of Education, 2016b; 2017b).

The implementation of policies and curriculum framework are like two leading powers in the path to achieving higher-quality ECEC in Taiwan. Regulations, plans and strategies from the Early Childhood Education and Care Act played a changing 'outside-in' force from context to educare system.

Institutions, educators and service standards were changed to obey the Act. The Early Childhood Educare Curriculum Framework, on the other hand, acted as an 'inside-out' mechanism from the core of the educare system to the whole context.

Current situation and challenges

There are three types of preschools in Taiwan, public, private and non-profit. The actual numbers of these three types of preschool are unbalanced. According to statistics by Ministry of Education (2017c), there are 2,002 public, 4,258 private, and 50 non-profit preschools in Taiwan (branch institutions were not included). The percentage of public, private and non-profit is 31.7%, 67.4%, and 0.7%, respectively. As to the number of children attending each institution, there are 129,199 in public, 342,095 in private, and 5,195 in non-profit preschools with the percentages as 27%, 71%, and 1%, respectively.

Operation, service hours and tuition in these three types of preschool institutions are different as well. Most of the public preschools are attached to public primary schools, which are operated and financed by the local government. Schools open from 8am to 4pm but not during summer and winter vacation (July, August and January). The tuition is approximately USD$100 per month (Taipei City Government, 2015). Private preschools are run by private cooperations, which are built independently. Educare service hours in private preschools are longer than public and open all working days throughout the year. The tuition is about USD$300 per month but varies from institution to institution (Central News Agency, 2016). The Regulations for Implementing Non-Profit Preschools was announced in 2012, and triggered the third and newer type of preschool in Taiwan. Non-profit preschools operate by not-profit groups or public-interested judicial individuals and are usually attached with public schools but some are independent (Ministry of Justice, 2015b). Educare service hours in non-profit preschools are similar to private preschools. Tuition in non-profit preschools is roughly USD$200, which is shared 70% by parents and 30% by local government (Department of General Affairs, 2016).

As for curriculum, public preschools follow the Preschool Educare Curriculum Framework. Learning in public preschools is integrated and developmentally appropriate for young children (Chen, 2015). Curricula in private preschools vary by the objective of each institution. In order to provide for parental aspirations of their children to be "ahead" of others, many private preschools offer drill activities in daily instruction. Subject teaching such as music, English and math are taught separately as specialised courses from different subject teachers. Hobby courses such as ballet, chess, karate and skating are also common in private preschools (Lee, 2014). There are also some private preschools that offer integrated learning through Montessori or Steiner approach (Lee, 2011; Cheng, 2011). Some of the characteristics in non-profit preschools are child-centred and developmentally appropriate instruction (Ministry of Education, 2016a).

From legislations to preschools, there seems a gap between policy and reality. According to the ECEC monthly tuition, the number of affordable preschools is far lower than parental need. The average salary in Taiwan is about USD$1600 per month (Directorate-General of Budget, Accounting and Statistics [DGBAS], 2017). Seventy percent of parents who send their children to preschools must pay at least USD$300 for a single tuition. Considering other daily expenses, this is a heavy burden for parents to bring up their children before age 6. The percentage of public or the developing non-profit preschool service, are reacting too slowly to remedy the urgency of this problem. As to service hours, these too are not enough to meet parental needs. However, working hours in Taiwan are much longer than the Organisation for Economic Co-operation and Development (OECD) average (DGBAS, 2016; OECD, 2017). The proper number of ECEC service hours should not only consider working hours but also focus on children's needs. Thus, the foundation of ECEC legislation and policies might be organised and implemented as a top-down route. In reality, more links outside ECEC policies and curricula are needed to form a web to be an effective ECEC system.

Despite governmental legislations and policies, there are still two challenges from the Taiwanese context in the developing path. First, there are learning myths from parents such as "win at the starting point" or "the earlier you learn, the more you can learn" which strongly influence the ECEC curriculum in preschools. In reviewing the ECEC development in Taiwan, there is continued progress in public investment, legislation, teacher qualification and curriculum. Learning myths, however, still in existence from Japanese colonization has not changed much (Wong, 2012). This challenge still exists according to the Education Yearbook from the Ministry of Education (Duan, 2012; Duan & Hsiao, 2013).

In context with the unbalanced ratio of public preschools and private preschools, it is understandable that parental expectations are often higher than curriculum framework from the government, especially in private preschools. To clarify parent's education myths and achieve higher quality ECEC, videos and brochures related to proper learning for young children were produced and appear on the Early Childhood Educare website, which is the official information centre of ECEC in Taiwan (Ministry of Education, n.d.).

Another way to reverse this situation of parental belief, in asking for curriculum, which are inappropriate for children, is to offer more public preschool education. In fact, in context with the low birth rate, it is difficult for local governments to set up additional public preschools. Non-profit preschools are a means to solve this problem. In 2014, 10 non-profit preschools were set up in Taipei, Tainan, Kaohsiung and Hsinchu City. In the coming phase, there will be 90 more preschools set up from 2015 to 2018 (Ministry of Education, 2015).

From the news and studies from non-profit preschools, there are at least three positive reactions from the field. First, the affordable price for parents. Parents who consider preschool education too costly now have more choices. Non-profit preschools are very popular so many have a waiting list (Hong, 2016). Second, curriculum in non-profit preschools is child-centred, developmentally appropriate, and supports preschool educators' professional development (Jian, 2016). Third, parents and community are involved in the developing or organizing process. Parents are invited to join meetings frequently and provide support and feedback to preschools. Non-profit preschools are one of the mechanisms in the development of the local community (KH Style, 2016).

According to the current situation of ECEC in Taiwan, the nature of preschool is one the biggest challenges in the process to achieve better quality. Over 60% of preschools are private and have to follow parents' needs and wishes on educare. Sometimes it is very difficult for preschool educators to present their professionalism in guiding children. It is easier for educators to find a better salary or professional position in public preschools, but these positions are very limited. Hence, private preschool educators change their working institutions or careers, which causes a high turnover rate in preschools which further leads to a vicious circle within ECEC context (Shen, 2016). The unbalanced ratio of public and private preschools also makes it difficult to learn policies or strategies from other countries (Liu, 2012). Fortunately, the policy of non-profit preschools appeared and started a new way for more proper learning in ECEC and has led the curriculum back to professionalism rather than a learning myth. This policy might be the niche for ECEC in Taiwan to achieve a better future and higher quality.

Conclusion

In conclusion, the Early Childhood Education and Care Act has made a sound basis in the developing path to achieve high quality ECEC in Taiwan. Regulations and related strategies, primarily supporting projects from the curriculum framework, play a crucial role and help steer the development. Along with the clear policy and significant improvements in ECEC, there are still challenges from the context, which need further serious consideration. Learning myths and the unbalanced ratio of preschools remain the most difficult challenges in the developing path of ECEC in Taiwan. Review of the development of ECEC in Taiwan, was slow from the 90s but has seen rapid improvement since the 2000s. As the legislation, policies, curriculum and supporting strategies are all accomplished the framework of achieving high quality of ECEC in Taiwan seems accomplished. How this scaffold guides the development of ECEC framework to connect internal elements and form a smooth ECEC system still needs careful examination in the future.

Notes

1 According to Early Childhood Education and Care Act, educare givers is not allowed to solely lead 6-year-old groups without teacher assistance. There shall be a teacher in every 6-year-old group.
2 Teachers were recruited and managed by Teacher's Act while educare givers were recruited and managed by Labor Standards Act.

References

Central News Agency. (2016). *MOE promote public educare service.* Taipei, Taiwan. Retrieved from www.cna.com.tw/news/firstnews/201610200160-1.aspx

Chang, S. (2014). Educare givers' protest: No coordinated sets of measures for The Early Childhood Education and Care Act. *China Times.* Retrieved from www.chinatimes.com/newspapers/20140513000503-260107

Chen, J. M. (2012). *The research of the integration of early childhood education and care policy.* Retrieved from National Academy for Education Research: http://wd.naer.edu.twΩ/project/NAER-101-24-C-2-05-00-1-21.pdf

Chen, P. W. (2015). *5 Keywords you should know about public preschool.* Retrieved from Education, Parenting, Family & Lifestyle: www.parenting.com.tw/article/5065774-%E8%AE%80%E5%85%AC%E5%B9%BC%E8%A9%B2%E7%9F%A5%E9%81%93%E7%9A%84%E4%BA%94%E5%80%8B%E9%97%9C%E9%8D%B5%E5%AD%97

Department of General Affairs. (2016). Jian-Hua non-profit preschools in Hsinchu City. *Hsinchu City Government.* Retrieved from www.hccg.gov.tw/ch/home.jsp?id=48&parentpath=0,16&mcustomize=municipalnews_view.jsp&toolsflag=Y&dataserno=201609050004&t=MunicipalNews&mserno=201601300028

Directorate-General of Budget, Accounting and Statistics. (2017). *Employee salary report 2012–2017.* Directorate-General of Budget, Accounting and Statistics, Executive Yuan, R.O.C. Retrieved from www.dgbas.gov.tw/public/Data/752284855USM8S5UA.pdf

Duan, H. Y. (2007). *Education yearbook of the Republic of China 2006.* Taipei: Ministry of Education. Retrieved from www.naer.edu.tw/ezfiles/0/1000/attach/4/pta_5138_2990038_02658.pdf

Duan, H. Y. (2011). *The review of education in Taiwan: From 1911–2011.* Taipei: National Academy for Educational Research. Retrieved from http://data.naer.edu.tw/public/Data/191518565171.pdf

Duan, H. Y. (2012). *Education yearbook of the Republic of China 2011.* Taipei: Ministry of Education. Retrieved from www.naer.edu.tw/ezfiles/0/1000/attach/9/pta_5274_2561844_96244.pdf

Duan, H. Y., & Hsiao, T. C. (2013). *The Republic of China Education yearbook 2012.* Taipei: Ministry of Education. Retrieved from www.naer.edu.tw/ezfiles/0/1000/attach/10/pta_5378_2162240_00183.pdf

Duan, H. Y., & Ma, T. L. (2013). The development strategies for private preschools to adapt to the transition society of Taiwan. *Journal of Early Childhood Education and Care,* (10), 1–18.

The Economist Intelligence Unit. (2012). *Starting well: Benchmarking early education across the world.* Retrieved from www.fitchburgstate.edu/uploads/files/CMRC/resources/StartingWell_LIEN_FoundationReport.pdf

Hong, D. H. (2016). 6th non-profit preschool in Kaohsiung. *Liberty Times Net.* Retrieved from http://news.ltn.com.tw/news/life/breakingnews/1853850

Hong, F. C. (2002). *History of early childhood education in Taiwan.* Taipei: Wunan.

Hu, J. P., & Wu, S. P. (2013). The influences of integrated preschool policy on the management of the education protection officer in the nursery affiliated with elementary schools: The experience and implication in Hsinchu City. *Journal of Civil Service,* 5(4), 87–138.

Huang, Y. S., & Hsue, H. (2000). *National academy of educational research.* Retrieved from Education Vocabulary: The Standards of Kindergarten Curriculum: http://terms.naer.edu.tw/detail/1303946/?index=1

Jian, R. L. (2016). The ideal and implementation of non-profit preschool. *The Educator Monthly, 587,* 24–32. Retrieved from http://sc.ttbf.org.tw/assets/uploads/monthly/monthly5848d07931bdd.pdf

KH Style. (2016). Non-profit preschools in Kaohsiung: For happier childhood. *China Times.* Retrieved from http://magazine.chinatimes.com/khstyle/20160111003410-300611

Lee, Y. H. (2014). *Subject teaching in private preschool.* Taipei, Taiwan. Retrieved from https://anntw.com/articles/20141021-8xLw

Lee, Y. J. (2011). To know preschools: Montessori approach. *Education, Parenting, Family Lifestyle.* Retrieved from www.parenting.com.tw/article/5026418-%E9%81%B8%E5%B9%BC%E5%85%92%E5%9C%92%EF%BC%8F%E8%AA%8D%E8%AD%98%E8%92%99%E7%89%B9%E6%A2%AD%E5%88%A9/

Liberty Times Net. (2010). Taiwan total fertility rate 2009: Lowest in the world. Retrieved from http://news.ltn.com.tw/news/life/breakingnews/317824

Liu, Y. (2012). The practice of equality: Early childhood education and care in Finland. *Bulletin of Educational Resources and Research,* 101–126.

Ministry of Education. (2008). Retrieved from www.kids.hc.edu.tw/uploadfile/%E6%89%B6%E6%8C%81%E4%BA%94%E6%AD%B2%E5%B9%BC%E5%85%92%E6%95%99%E8%82%B2%E8%A8%88%E7%95%AB.pdf

Ministry of Education. (2014). *The regulations of pre-service professional development program for ECEC.* Retrieved from Laws and Regulations Retrieving System: http://edu.law.moe.gov.tw/LawContent.aspx?id=GL000682&KeyWord=1010134732C

Ministry of Education. (2015). The project of non-profit preschool. *Early Childhood Educare.* Retrieved from www.ece.moe.edu.tw/wp-content/uploads/2016/06/%E6%8E%A8%E5%8B%95%E9%9D%9E%E7%87%9F%E5%88%A9%E5%B9%BC%E5%85%92%E5%9C%92%E5%AF%A6%E6%96%BD%E6%96%B9%E6%A1%881040119.pdf

Ministry of Education. (2016a). *Educational system: Early childhood education in Taiwan. Ministry of Education.* Retrieved from http://ws.moe.edu.tw/001/Upload/3/relfile/0/1146/eb6fe3e0-9cfc-4080-88c7-7123ebf8a267.pdf

Ministry of Education. (2016b). Preschool educare curriculum framework. *Early Childhood Educare.* Retrieved from www.ece.moe.edu.tw/?p=7545

Ministry of Education. (2017a). 2017 Seminars of preschool educare curriculum framework. *Early Childhood Educare.* Retrieved from www.ece.moe.edu.tw/wp-content/uploads/2017/02/106%E5%B9%B4%E5%BA%A6%E8%AA%B2%E7%A8%8B%E5%A4%A7%E7%B6%B1%E7%A0%94%E7%BF%92%E8%AA%B2%E7%A8%8B%E8%AA%AA%E6%98%8E.pdf

Ministry of Education. (2017b). *Numbers of preschools 1991–2017.* Retrieved from Statistical Summaries: http://depart.moe.edu.tw/ED4500/cp.aspx?n=1B58E0B736635285&

Ministry of Education. (2017c). Preschool consultation. *Early Childhood Educare.* Retrieved from www.ece.moe.edu.tw/wp-content/uploads/2017/02/106%E5%AD%B8%E5%B9%B4%E5%BA%A6%E5%B0%88%E6%A5%AD%E7%99%BC%E5%B1%95%E8%BC%94%E5%B0%8E%E7%94%B3%E8%AB%8B%E8%AA%AA%E6%98%8E%E6%9C%83.pdf

Ministry of Education. (n.d.). Proper learning in early age. *Early Childhood Educare.* Retrieved from www.ece.moe.edu.tw/?page_id=4930

Ministry of Education; Ministry of Interior. (2010). Free education for 5-year-old children. *Early Childhood Educare.* Retrieved from www.ece.moe.edu.tw/wp-content/uploads/2011/12/5-7.pdf

Ministry of Justice. (2014). Preschool Education Act. *Laws and Regulations Database of The Republic of China.* Retrieved from http://law.moj.gov.tw/LawClass/Law Content.aspx?PCODE=H0070007

Ministry of Justice. (2015a). Early Childhood Education and Care Act. *Laws and Regulations Database of The Republic of China.* Retrieved from http://law.moj. gov.tw/Eng/LawClass/LawContent.aspx?PCODE=H0070031

Ministry of Justice. (2015b). Regulations for implementing non-profit preschools. *Laws and Regulations Database of The Republic of China.* Retrieved from http://law.moj.gov.tw/Law/LawSearchResult.aspx?p=A&t=A1A2E1F1&k1=%E9%9D%9E%E7%87%9F%E5%88%A9%E5%B9%BC%E5%85%92%E5%9C%92%E5%AF%A6%E6%96%BD%E8%BE%A6%E6%B3%95

Organisation for Economic Co-operation and Development. (2017). *Average annual hours actually worked per worker.* Retrieved from https://stats.oecd.org/Index. aspx?DataSetCode=ANHRS#

Peng, X. Z. (2009). 8 Reasons cause the lowest birth rate in Taiwan. *Global Views Monthly.* Retrieved from www.gvm.com.tw/Boardcontent_15560.html

Political Centre of Now News. (2011). President Ma: Couldn't sleep because of the low birth rate problem. *Now News.* Retrieved from www.nownews.com/n/2011/11/19/456557

Shen, L. A. (2016). The Early Childhood Education and Care Act and implementation of the policy of integrating kindergartens and nursery schools. *Journal of School Administration*, 101, 185–200.

Sun, L. C., Lu, M. K., & Chang, H. Y. (2014). Study of implementation of early childhood education policy According to the equity in education: An example of the supportive education programes for five-years-old children. *Journal of National Taichung University: Education*, 28(2), 93–116.

Taguma, M., Litjens, I., & Makowiecki, K. (2013). *Quality matters in early childhood education and care.* Paris: OECD. doi:10.1787/9789264192829-en

Taipei City Government. (2015). Fees for public preschools in Taipei City. *Department of Education, Taipei City.* Retrieved from www.doe.gov.taipei/ct.asp?xItem=41589110&ctNode=33557&mp=104001

Wong, L. F. (2012). The development of early childhood education in Taiwan: A historical perspective. *Educational Resources and Research*, 104, 1–26.

The World Factbook. (2017). Country comparasion: Total fertility rate. *Central Intelligence Agency.* Retrieved from www.cia.gov/library/publications/the-world-factbook/rankorder/2127rank.html

19 Early childhood education and care in the Netherlands

A shift towards an integrated system aimed at enhancing children's development and learning

Pauline Slot

Introduction

The number of children enrolled in Early Childhood Education and Care (ECEC) has grown dramatically in the past two decades, and, by now, the vast majority of children attend some kind of centre-based ECEC. The Netherlands has a fragmented and split ECEC system. Historically two types of centre-based ECEC for children below four years of age exist, each with its own tradition and function: *day-care* centres for children from birth until age four years and centres originally referred to as *playgroups* for two-to-four year olds. From four years of age, children attend kindergarten, which is part of the primary school, with an enrolment rate of about 98%.

Day care falls under the responsibility of the Ministry of Social Affairs and Employment and, as such, has traditionally reflected a strong labour market perspective. With the increase of maternal employment to about 56% in 2004, the number of children enrolled in day care more than doubled between 1995 and 2005 resulting in an enrolment rate of about 20% of children below four years of age, which is still low in an absolute sense. The main reasons for not using day care were the lack of places, long waiting lists, and the high costs (Akgündüz & Plantenga, 2014). The Childcare Act of 2005 marked a major change by privatising the sector, introducing a subsidy system for parents, and introducing a statutory quality framework. The quality framework specified mostly structural preconditions concerning teacher's educational qualifications, group size and ratio. Further, the Act formulated that day care should be aimed at four broad goals, namely providing emotional security; fostering children's personal competences; fostering children's social competences; and transferring basic cultural values and norms. The OKE (Promoting Development through Quality and Education) Act of 2010 provided a strong impetus for the sector to develop beyond fulfilling a predominately care function, enabling parents to reconcile work and family life, to a stronger educational function supporting the broad development of children in its own right.

Playgroups, as part of the local welfare policies, first emerged in the 1960s with a strong social-cultural function allowing children to play with peers. These playgroups operate on a half-day basis in which children are enrolled for two half days a week. Playgroups are viewed as a gradual preparation for kindergarten illustrating a traditionally stronger educational function. This stronger educational focus is aligned with the targeted approach of combating early disadvantages in children that are related to low parental education levels or cultural minority background of the children that are typically enrolled in these provisions. This gradually resulted in the transformation into educationally oriented *preschools.* Since 2000, the implementation and monitoring of these targeted education programs carried out in the preschools fall under the Ministry of Education, Culture and Sciences.

Kindergarten has been integrated into primary schools following the Primary School Act of 1985. Although primary school is not compulsory until age five years, virtually all children enter primary school at their fourth birthday. Although kindergarten is part of the primary school, the practices differ greatly from the grades three to eight that are focused on formal instruction in typical school subjects.

The current state of affairs

Currently, more than 80% of all two- and three-year olds and about half of the children below two years of age participate in centre-based ECEC, which is above the Organisation for Economic Co-operation and Development (OECD) average, but only on a part-time basis (OECD, 2016a). Moreover, the enrolment shows social selection effects, which are related to the split system in the Netherlands. Although, on average only 20% of the children below four years of age do not attend any form of centre-based ECEC, this number is twice as high for children from the lowest income families (Centraal Bureau voor de Statistiek [CBS], 2015). In addition, the type of provision that is used depends on parent and home characteristics showing segregation tendencies already in an early stage of children's lives. It is common to use multiple care arrangements, such as combining centre-based care with home-based care or using centre-based day care together with informal care (often by grandparents).

Day-care provisions for 0–4 year olds

Currently about half of the children below four years of age attend a day-care centre for on average two full days a week (CBS, 2015). Day care is used only by dual-earning parents, which can be explained by the fact that subsidies via tax reduction are provided only if both parents are working or pursuing further (tertiary) education. Although the female employment rate in the Netherlands is about 77% and among the highest in Europe, this usually concerns part-time employment of, on average, 25 hours a week (OECD, 2016a). In addition, parental or family care in the home environment is highly valued for children, hence care by grandparents for one or two days a week is very common. Another explanation for the part-time usage of day care could be related to the costs for parents, which is among the highest in Europe and twice the OECD average (OECD, 2016a).

With the privatisation of the childcare sector in 2005, the number of available places has expanded dramatically and parents were given subsidies from the central government. From 2005–2008, these subsidies for parents were substantial and parents only paid half of the fee (Bettendorfer, Jongen, & Muller, 2015). However, with the financial crisis and related budget cuts from 2012 the costs for parents have increased, resulting in a decrease in the enrolment rate in an absolute sense (in the number of children enrolled) and in a relative sense (in the number of hours children were enrolled) (Akgündüz & Plantenga, 2014). The situation appears to have stabilised since 2015/2016. Overall, children in day-care centres are usually from middle- to higher educated parents belonging to middle- to higher income groups in the Netherlands. The centres operate from early in the morning until early in the evening, usually between 7am and 7pm for five days a week and all-year round, which is attuned to their working hours for most parents.

A small proportion of the children (approximately 9%) are enrolled in formal home-based care provided by child-minders (OECD, 2016a). Until 2005, this type of care was unregulated and informal. However, from 2005 home-based care became eligible for parents to receive subsidies via tax reduction if the child-minder complied with basic regulations in line with the regulations for centre-based care.

Preschool provisions for 2–4 year olds

Currently, about 30% of children attend a preschool before entering kindergarten at age four years. The first preschools, at that time called playgroups, had a social-cultural orientation with strong roots in the community and were part of the local welfare policy (Leseman & de Winter, 2013). These playgroups provided children with (better) play opportunities and promotion of social development. Nowadays, Dutch preschools mainly attract children from lower-educated parents and children with an immigrant, including second or third generation, background. This is a reflection of the current educational policy that is aimed at combating disadvantages at an early age by providing compensation programs in preschools.

In 1995, the first educational curricula or education programs for 3–6 year old disadvantaged children were implemented by a joint initiative of the Ministries of Welfare and Education. The first two programs concerned a Dutch adaptation of the High/Scope Curriculum (Schweinhart & Weikart, 1997; called *Kaleidoscoop* in the Netherlands) and the other, called *Piramide*, was an adaptation of the Success for All approach developed by Slavin and Madden (1999). Both programs were implemented in preschools and kindergarten departments of primary schools that collaborated to provide a continuous educational trajectory from age

3 up to age 6, before transition to Dutch third grade. Since 2000, the number of targeted centre-based compensation programs steadily increased to a nation-wide system. All programs have in common that they employ a play-based and holistic approach with an emphasis on four core domains: (Dutch as a second) language, math, motor and social emotional development. In order to receive municipal funding, only programs accredited by the national Accreditation Committee for Child and Youth Interventions of the Netherlands' Youth Institute can be used (www.nji.nl).

Preschools operate during the same hours as schools, usually between 9 and 12am in the morning and between 1 and 3pm in the afternoon. Preschools are open for 40 weeks a year and have regular vacations, aligned with primary schools. Disadvantaged children, eligible for the education programs based on low parental education levels or immigrant background, receive a minimum of 10 hours of ECEC, usually four half-days a week, of which parents pay a very limited income-based fee. Non-eligible children, whose parents also pay an income-based fee, are enrolled in the same centres, but for only two half days a week (usually 5 hours).

Kindergarten for 4–6 year olds

Kindergarten, as part of primary schools, is publicly funded and concerns children aged four-to-six years. Although not compulsory before age five years, parents are entitled to free kindergarten from age four years and almost 100% of the children are enrolled on their fourth birthday. Children attend kindergarten for about 20 hours a week. Traditionally, the attendance was divided among three full days from 8.30–3.00 pm with a lunch break in between on Monday, Tuesday and Thursday and two shorter days from 8.30–12.30pm on Wednesday and Fridays. In this model, children used to go home for lunch, as mothers did not work outside of the house (or adapted their working hours according to the school schedule). Still, Wednesdays and Fridays are the most common days for mothers to be at home, which is also apparent in less usage of other types of care such as day care on these days. As female labour market participation grew, more children used in-between-school care during lunch, which was usually provided by volunteers at schools. Since 2006, this in-between-school care has been professionalised. Every school is now obliged by law to provide this type of care, although they usually invite an external childcare organisation to organise this service (Inspectorate of Education, 2008). At the same time, a new movement advocated the five-equal-days model in which children go to school for the same amount of time for all five days, resulting in days from approximately 8.30am – 2pm.

Collaboration between the different provisions

Currently there are different ways in which the teachers of the three different provisions collaborate, particularly in view of addressing the education gap among disadvantaged children. As a part of the educational policy in combating early disparities, preschools (and increasingly day-care centres) and kindergartens work with the targeted education programs. The main idea of these programs is to provide children with a continuous curriculum across the 2–6-age range. Hence, there is some collaboration between preschools and kindergartens in the program they use and the implementation of these programs. Also, as children's development is monitored as part of working with these programs, this information is handed over to the kindergarten teachers (with the consent of parents) when children transition from preschool to kindergarten, so children can be supported in their development based on their individual needs. Sometimes this information is discussed during a meeting between the preschool and kindergarten teachers, but most times, it is in the form of a short report. Another way for collaboration between the different sectors concerns meetings, often at the municipal level, to discuss the developments and new policy directions than can be implemented at the organisational level. These meetings mostly occur in view of local (educational) policy and involve the directors of the organisations.

Structural and process quality

According to a comparative review by the OECD (2006), the structural characteristics of Dutch ECEC are in the mid-range of quality. For teachers working in day care or preschool the minimum educational requirement is a three-year vocational training in a relevant area. The average group size is dependent on children's age and ranges from 12 for babies until 16 for three-year-olds. Relatedly the children-to-staff ratio also varies depending on the age of children and ranges from 4 for babies until 8 for three-year-olds. As age-heterogeneous groups are very common, there are rules set to calculate the maximum group size and ratio depending on the particular age composition in the group. The same requirements apply to preschools, although the variation in group size and ratio is more limited as these provisions have more age-homogeneous groups with only two- and three-year olds. For kindergarten, the structural conditions are a little different. Teachers in kindergartens are required to have a four-year Bachelor degree in teaching. Although, there are no strict regulations concerning group size, this usually is between 20–30 children. Sometimes there is an assistant, particularly in schools with a high proportion of disadvantaged children, but usually there is only one teacher per classroom. As schools receive extra funding from the municipality when they have a higher proportion of disadvantaged children (related to low parental education levels or cultural minority background), this money is mostly used to appoint another (assistant) teacher or to lower the group size.

Concerning the process quality, or the quality of teacher-child interactions, several studies have shown that Dutch ECEC teachers, in all types of provisions across the 0–6 age range reveal moderate to high levels of emotional support in showing positive and affectionate relations, responsiveness and child-centredness in their interactions. By providing clear classroom routines and rules, teachers aid in developing children's self-regulation skills (Helmerhorst, Riksen-Walraven, Vermeer, Fukkink, & Tavecchio, 2014; Slot, Leseman, Verhagen, & Mulder,

2015; Slot, Boom, Verhagen, & Leseman, 2017; pre-COOL Consortium, 2015). However, the facilitation and support of children's cognitive and language development is considered, on average, to be low to moderate. This pattern of results reflects the state of affairs in most western countries.

Curriculum

In the Netherlands, there is a common understanding of what is considered to be of importance in ECEC (Sylva, Ereky-Stevens, & Aricescu, 2015; Slot, 2016). A large survey among 285 parents and 300 teachers revealed a strong emphasis on supporting the development of children's social-emotional and interpersonal skills or 'soft skills', which appeared important for children below and above three years of age (Broekhuizen, Leseman, Moser, & van Trijp, 2015). Learning-related skills and pre-academic skills are viewed as increasingly more important as children get older and particularly parents attach more value to these so-called 'hard skills' compared to teachers.

Although there is no legislated national or local curriculum, the basis for everyday pedagogy and practice is laid out in the Childcare Act of 2005 that stipulated the focus on the four core goals of providing emotional security, enhancing children's personal and social competence, and transferring cultural values and norms. Based on this act researchers and stakeholders jointly developed a Pedagogical Framework for day-care provisions (Singer & Kleerekoper, 2009). This framework reflects the holistic view on children's development as it takes a broad approach to children's development and learning. In this framework all developmental domains, cognitive, language, creative, moral and physical, are theoretically underpinned and further elaborated with ample examples for implementation in practice. It is unknown to what extent this framework is used in actual practice.

There is a shared and common view across all types of provisions that ECEC should incorporate a holistic view on children's development, which is reflected in a strongly play-oriented pedagogical approach. An observational study in 376 day care and preschool classrooms revealed that free play was the predominant activity children were involved in during a regular morning (Slot et al., 2015). This reflects the typical Dutch pattern of practices in ECEC that are strongly child-centred and provide ample opportunities for play, with some activities initiated by the teachers such as creative (e.g. arts-and-crafts or music) and educational activities (e.g. book reading and making puzzles) (Slot et al., 2015).

At the same time, there is evidence of a gap in children's skills as young as two years of age, based on family background characteristics such as parental education level and home language (Leseman & Veen, 2016), that requires a stronger educational approach to maximally support and foster their development in order to (partly) close this gap (Socioeconomic Advisory Council, 2016). This is the main aim of the targeted education programs that are now widespread in Dutch preschools and are increasingly also being used in day-care provisions. However, a stronger integration of social-emotional or interpersonal skills (i.e.

self-regulation, learning to learn, curiosity or creativity) and pre-academic learning related skills (i.e. general learning skills and domain-specific skills, such as pre-literacy and numeracy), in the curriculum deserves more attention to prepare children adequately for life in the 21st century (Socioeconomic Advisory Council, 2016; Slot, 2016). Striking a good balance between play, especially exploratory and enriching play with an active and supporting role of the teacher, and the provision of educational activities aimed at children's broad development and learning related skills remains important. A large cohort study among two-year olds indeed illustrated the benefits of play-enriching activities and high-quality educational interactions in narrowing the education gap in disadvantaged children three years later (Leseman et al., 2017).

The kindergarten curriculum is characterised by a lot of time for free play, a child-centred approach and the use of specially designed play-work materials (Leseman, 2002). Classrooms are usually age-heterogeneous combination classes with first and second graders (4–5 and 5–6 year old children) in one group in the majority of primary schools (80%). Classrooms are organised by several 'activity centres' or play areas (e.g. construction centre, play-work centre, creativity centre, house centre for pretend play). The average curriculum reflects a certain eclecticism and consists of the following elements: circle time intended to enhance language development and communication skills, book-reading, play-work lessons in which children work with special materials in small groups under guidance of the teacher (for instance, paper, glue and scissors, folding paper, textile, string beads, clay, paint or colour-pencils, sorting games). There are also work lessons involving special developmental materials (e.g. puzzles, sorting games, memory games) and worksheets for the older kindergarteners, to prepare them for formal instruction (focusing on pre-literacy and numeracy).

Governance and quality monitoring

Two different ministries are responsible for ECEC in the Netherlands: the Ministry of Social Affairs and Employment and the Ministry of Education, Culture, and Sciences. Basic quality monitoring in day care and preschools, falling under the Ministry of Social Affairs and Employment, is done by the municipal public health authority and is focused on basic safety and health (hygiene), structural characteristics (e.g. group size, ratio and teacher's qualifications) and the presence of a pedagogical work plan. In addition, there is a periodic evaluation of the process quality of representative samples of day care and preschool provisions conducted by a national research consortium (e.g. Fukkink et al., 2013; de Kruif et al., 2009; Vermeer et al., 2005). In addition, the Inspectorate of Primary Education monitors additional aspects in centres working with targeted education programs that are part of the national priority policy for disadvantaged children (i.e. of low educated or cultural minority parents). These aspects concern, for instance, whether the centre works with an accredited education program and with teachers, who are trained and certified to work with this program. Evaluation also focuses on aspects of implementation of the program, such as the availability of a year-plan for the themes and activities, presence of an extra teacher, and the use of an observation- or test-based child development monitoring system regarding the four core domains of language, math, motor skills and social emotional development.

Kindergartens, as part of primary schools, fall under the Ministry of Education, Culture, and Sciences, although in the Dutch primary school system the actual governance is decentralised to local or regional school boards which are organised according to the confessional pillars (e.g. protestant, roman catholic, Islamic schools or neutral public schools). School boards are responsible for several primary schools in a city or region and have a high degree of autonomy, but should conform to national statutory rules regarding teachers' educational qualifications, and lesson hours per week, on the one hand, and to the learning goals and achievement standards specified in the Primary School Act, on the other hand. Within these boundaries, schools and school boards are free to select education programs, curricula, instruction methods and child achievement monitoring systems. Quality monitoring is done by the Inspectorate of Primary Education and is based on children's test-based performance on standard norm-referenced tests and checklists (language, math, literacy, social-emotional competence and citizenship), the use of a monitoring system, and the teaching process related to the key goals formulated in the broad domains of language, math, social studies, creativity and movement.

Moving towards an integrated ECEC system

The current ECEC system in the Netherlands is fragmented as children from disadvantaged backgrounds attend preschools using targeted education programs, whereas children from more affluent families tend to be enrolled in day-care provisions. This segregation effect is a result of the targeted educational policy in the Netherlands that has focused on the implementation of education programs in preschools only. Preschools are provided with municipal subsidies to ensure availability for eligible children and maintain or enhance quality of the provided program. Dutch research has shown that children from disadvantaged families already lag behind in their social-emotional, language and cognitive development as early as two years of age (Mulder, Hoofs, Verhagen, Van der Veen, & Leseman, 2014). There is evidence that the quality of interactions, particularly support for children's learning and development, in preschools is higher than in day-care centres (Slot et al., 2017), which can be partly explained by the use of the targeted education programs (Slot et al., 2015). This higher quality and relatedly the use of the education programs, in turn, have shown to narrow the education gap at age five years (Leseman & Veen, 2016; Leseman et al., 2017). At the same time, recent results from the OECD not only showed an average decline in students' basic academic skills compared to 2006, but also highlighted increasing disparities at age 15 years as the differences between low and high performing children were caused by social background factors (OECD, 2016b).

There are several recent developments that are focused on promoting equal opportunities for all children. Broadly speaking, these developments are along two lines. First, there are several initiatives to enhance quality in ECEC for children below four years of age. Second, there are developments taking place in aligning ECEC and primary school in terms of a continuous curriculum across all developmental domains and ages and concerning active collaboration between professionals working in the two sectors.

With the implementation of the OKE Act in 2010 both day care and pre-school provisions fall under the same statutory quality framework meaning that both types have to adhere to the same structural and process quality standards. Moreover, this act characterises a shift in the function of ECEC moving from a care oriented approach as a right for *parents* in order to reconcile work with a family life to a stronger educational approach as a right for *children* to develop to their full potential. In 2013, a new policy initiative was launched in order to re-evaluate the statutory quality framework based on the Childcare Act of 2005. Policymakers had several discussions with renowned researchers, practitioners from the field, local policymakers and other stakeholders, such as from the municipal health authority, to revise the quality framework. The newly proposed framework, still to be approved by the parliament, shows a shift from focusing on strict (structural) regulations involving a lot of paper work that was not always considered useful towards a more process-oriented approach of monitoring interactional quality and aspects known to contribute to this, such as professional development (Ministry of Social Affairs and Employment, 2017). The four basic goals set out in the Childcare Act of 2005 have been further elaborated and now show more explicit continuity across ages (e.g. between day care and primary school) and across settings (e.g. between primary school and after-school care).

At the same time there is a joint initiative by several important stakeholders (including an organisation of municipality representatives, the council for primary education and organisations representing the childcare sector) to establish a legal entitlement to 16 hours of ECEC for all children from age two-to-four years (Sociaal Werk Nederland, 2017). The basis for this initiative is to establish a universal provision for all children as a means to promote broad development and provide all children with a good start at school. An important prerequisite for this is a close collaboration between day-care provisions, preschools and schools, thus maximizing continuity of the provided education and care between 0–12 years. An initiative building on these principles is the so-called *integrated child centre* for 0–12 years where day care, preschool, primary school and after-school programs are integrated into one centre. A first step for these integrated child centres is to provide all these services on the same location so children have the opportunity to be involved in a range of different activities that foster their broad development and learning. The next step concerns collaboration between the different organisations and the professionals of these organisations, resulting in *one* team of professionals based on a shared pedagogical vision and mission and central leadership (Landelijk Steunpunt Brede Scholen, 2014).

Conclusion

Kindergarten for four- to six-year-old children has a long history and is well established in the primary school system, whereas the Dutch ECEC system for children below age four years showed major changes in the past two decades. The day-care sector expanded rapidly in the past years and the enrolment rate has increased from about 10% to over 80% of children below age four years. The majority of children attend day care or preschool on a part-time basis for, on average, two days a week. The two main types of centre-based care, cay care and preschool, target a different population (children from dual-earner families and mostly disadvantaged children respectively), but the traditional differences in orientation and function have largely disappeared. The day-care sector has shifted from a merely care or job market orientation to a strong developmental and educational function with specific attention to addressing inequalities in an early stage, which is in line with the goals of the preschools using the targeted education programs.

The structural characteristics of the Dutch ECEC system can be considered of mid-range quality compared to other European countries. The group size and children-to-staff ratio are relatively favourable, but teachers working with children below age four years tend to have lower educational qualifications than other European countries. However, the findings concerning process quality show a highly comparable picture with mid- to high levels of social-emotional quality and lower levels of interactions fostering children's learning and development. This pattern of findings applies to the full range of 0–6 provisions.

Although there is no legislated curriculum for children below age four years and kindergarten, there is consensus about what is important for children, which is apparent from the practices in ECEC. Adopting a child-centred approach children are allowed ample time for free play with the provision of some group activities focused at enhancing children's learning and development, such as shared book-reading, circle time or arts-and-crafts activities. There is increasing attention for fostering children's school readiness, particularly in view of addressing early inequalities, but this is mostly based on a play-based approach. In the second year of kindergarten there is a stronger focus on children's pre-academic skills and more formal ways of learning, such as with worksheets, are used in preparation of the transition to first grade.

Current developments in ECEC focus on integrating and more strongly aligning different ECEC provisions to better support children's broad development and enhance their chances in life. The importance of collaboration between the different sectors is growing rapidly, despite challenges at the legal and administrative level. The collaboration and alignment of ECEC is taking place along different lines. At the policy level, the new proposal for an overarching quality framework for provision for 0–4 year olds further integrates the two types of centre-based provision for this age range. This alignment concerns the structural preconditions as well as the curricular focus in everyday practices and quality of interactions. The further improvement of process quality is highly valued and having professional development opportunities and coaching on the job are now part of the newly proposed quality framework as important prerequisites of process quality. The proposal also notes the importance of collaboration both within the same sector (e.g. 0–4 year olds) and between different sectors (e.g. day care and preschool with kindergarten). Along the same lines, there are also developments in the field characterised by a strong investment of different stakeholders, such as the integrated child centres for 0–12 years.

References

Akgündüz, Y. E., & Plantenga, J. (2014). Childcare in the Netherlands: Lessons in privatisation. *European Early Childhood Education Research Journal, 22*(3), 379–385.

Bettendorf, L. J., Jongen, E. L., & Muller, P. (2015). Childcare subsidies and labour supply – Evidence from a large Dutch reform. *Labour Economics, 36,* 112–123.

Broekhuizen, M. L., Leseman, P. P. M., Moser, T., & van Trijp, K. (2015). *Stakeholder study. Values beliefs and concerns of parents, staff, and policy representatives regarding ECEC services in nine European countries.* CARE: Curriculum & Quality Analysis and Impact Review of European Early Childhood Education and Care, Utrecht University

Centraal Bureau voor de Statistiek. (2015). Retrieved from www.cbs.nl/nl-nl/nieuws/2015/39/peuters-lage-inkomensgroepen-blijven-vaker-thuis

de Kruif, R. E. L, Riksen-Walraven, J. M. A., Gevers Deynoot-Schaub, M. J. J. M., Helmerhorst, K. O. W., Tavecchio, L. W. C., & Fukkink, R. G. (2009). *Pedagogische kwaliteit van de opvang voor 0- tot 4-jarigen in Nederlandse kinderdagverblijven in 2008.* Amsterdam: NCKO.

Fukkink, R. G., Deynoot-Schaub, G., Helmerhorst, K., Bollen, I., & Riksen-Walraven, M. (2013). *Pedagogische kwaliteit van de kinderopvang voor 0- tot 4-jarigen in Nederlandse kinderdagverblijven in 2012.* Amsterdam: NCKO.

Helmerhorst, K. O., Riksen-Walraven, J. M., Vermeer, H. J., Fukkink, R. G., & Tavecchio, L. W. (2014). Measuring the interactive skills of caregivers in childcare centres: Development and validation of the caregiver interaction profile scales. *Early Education and Development, 25*(5), 770–790.

Inspectorate of Education. (2008). *Van overblijven naar tussenschoolse opvang. Wat is er veranderd in de informatievoorziening voor ouders en leerlingen?* Retrieved May 1, from www.rijksoverheid.nl/ . . . van-overblijven-naar-tussenschoolse-opvang/38963c.pdf

Landelijk Steunpunt Brede Scholen. (2014). *Op weg naar een IKC* [On our way to an integrated child centre]. Retrieved from www.poraad.nl/files/themas/school_kind_omgeving/brochure_op_weg_naar_een_ikc.pdf

Leseman, P. P. M. (2002). Early childhood services in The Netherlands: Structure, tensions, and changes. In L. Chan & E. J. Mellor (Eds.), *International developments in early childhood services* (pp. 134–152). New York/Bern: Peter Lang.

Leseman, P. P. M., & de Winter, M. (2013). 1.2. Early childhood services and family support in the Netherlands. In *Improving the lives of children and young people: case*

studies from Europe (pp. 15–32). World Health Organisation. Online at http://
www.euro.who.int/en/publications/abstracts/improving-the-lives-of-children-
and-young-people-case-studies-from-europe.-volume-1.-early-years

Leseman, P. P. M., Mulder, H., Verhagen, J., Broekhuizen, M., van Schaik, S., &
Slot, P. (2017). Effectiveness of Dutch targeted preschool education policy for
disadvantaged children: Evidence from the pre-COOL study. In H.-P. Blossfeld,
N. Kulic, J. Skopek, & M. Triventi (Eds.), *Childcare, early education and social
inequality: An international perspective* (pp. 173–193). Cheltenham, UK: Edward
Elgar Publishing.

Leseman, P. P. M., & Veen, A. (2016). *Pre-COOL cohortonderzoek. Effecten van
kwaliteit van voorschoolse instellingen* (Report 947). Amsterdam: Kohnstamm
Instituut.

Ministry of Social Affairs and Employment. (2017). *Ontwerpbesluit kwaliteit kinderopvang en peuterspeelzaalwerk*. Retrieved from www.rijksoverheid.nl/documenten/
besluiten/2017/03/10/ontwerpbesluit-kwaliteit-kinderopvang-en-peuter
speelzaalwerk

Mulder, H., Hoofs, H., Verhagen, J., Van der Veen, I., & Leseman, P. P. M. (2014).
Psychometric properties and convergent and predictive validity of an executive
function test battery for two-year-olds. *Frontiers in Psychology, 5*(733), 1–17. doi:
10.3389/fpsyg.2014.00733

OECD. (2006). *Starting strong II: Early childhood education and care*. Paris, France:
OECD Publishing.

OECD. (2016a). *Netherlands 2016. Foundations for the future. Reviews of national
policies for education*. Paris, France: OECD Publishing.

OECD. (2016b). *PISA 2015 results (Volume I): Excellence and equity in education*.
Paris, France: OECD Publishing.

Pre-COOL Consortium. (2015). *Pre-COOL cohortonderzoek. Technisch rapport
tweejarigencohort derde meting 2012–2013* (Rapport nr. 937). Amsterdam: Kohnstamm Instituut.

Schweinhart, L. J., & Weikart, D. P. (1997). The high/scope preschool curriculum
study through age 23. *Early Childhood Research Quarterly, 12*(2), 117–143.

Singer, E., & Kleerekoper, L. (2009). *Pedagogisch kader kindercentra 0–4 jaar*. Netherlands: Elsevier gezondheidszorg.

Slavin, R. E., & Madden, N. A. (1999). Success for all: Effects of prevention and
early intervention on elementary students' reading. In L. Eldering & P. Leseman
(Eds.), *Effective early education. Cross-cultural perspectives* (pp. 305–332). New
York: Falmer Press.

Slot, P. L. (2016). *Curriculum voor het jonge kind*. Uitgave Kennisdossier kinderopvang BKK Oktober 2016.

Slot, P. L., Boom, J., Verhagen, J., & Leseman, P. P. M. (2017). Measurement properties of the CLASS Toddler in ECEC in the Netherlands. *Journal of Applied Developmental Psychology, 48*, 79–91. doi:10.1016/j.appdev.2016.11.008

Slot, P. L., Leseman, P. P. M., Verhagen, J., & Mulder, H. (2015). Associations
between structural quality aspects and process quality in Dutch early childhood
education and care settings. *Early Childhood Research Quarterly, 33*, 64–76.
doi:10.1016/j.ecresq.2015.06.001

Sociaal Werk Nederland. (2017). Retrieved from www.sociaalwerknederland.nl/?file=
14404&m=1491233011&action=file.download

Socioeconomic Advisory Council [SER]. (2016). *Gelijk goed van start. Visie op het toekomstige stelsel van voorzieningen voor jonge kinderen.* Den Haag: SER.

Sylva, K., Ereky-Stevens, K., & Aricescu, A.-M. (2015). *Overview of European ECEC curricula and curriculum template.* WP2.1 Curriculum and quality analysis impact review, CARE. Report.

Vermeer, H. J., van IJzendoorn, M. H., de Kruif, R. E. L., Fukkink, R. G., Tavecchio, L. W. C., Riksen-Walraven, J. M. A., & van Zeijl, J. (2005). *Kwaliteit van Nederlandse kinderdagverblijven: Trends in kwaliteit in de jaren 1995–2005.* Leiden, Amsterdam, Nijmegen: NCKO.

20 Early childhood education and care in Turkey

Şenil Ünlü Çetin

History of Turkish early childhood education (ECE)

The history of ECE dates back to the Ottoman Empire period. During the Ottoman Empire, the first legal ECE practices were seen in the period of Fatih Sultan Mehmet, in the form of schools where children aged 5–6 learned how to write, how to read the Koran and how to pray. Then in 1913 with the Code of Temporary Elementary Education, preschools were identified as the first step for primary schools and it was decided to open these schools in every part of the country (Akyüz, 1996; Ural, 1986, as cited in Taner-Derman& Başal, 2010). In the first years of the Turkish Republic, there were 80 preschools in 38 cities catering to a total of 5,880 children (Başal, 1998). ECE was discussed in the seventh National Education Council in 1962 and, after that, the first Preschool Regulations were published. In 1977, the Early Childhood Education Bureau was established under the head of the General Directorate of Elementary Education. In 1992, the General Directorate of Early Childhood Education was established under the auspices of the Ministry of National Education (MEB) (Bilir ve Ark, Arı, Gönen, Üstün, & Pekçağlayan, 1998). In 1994, the first National Early Childhood National Curriculum was published and it was revised in 2002, 2006 and lastly 2013. In the present times, ECE is regulated by the Ministry of National Education and the Ministry of Family and Social Policy (ASPB).

Turkish education system and early childhood education

Overall structure of the Turkish education system

The Turkish national education system is composed of formal and informal education systems. The formal education system includes 12 years of compulsory education that covers the period from primary education to high-school education. The second system, informal education, aims to reach citizens who have not been enroled in or who stayed out of formal education (MEB, 1973).

The Turkish formal education system is divided into three levels. The first level is primary education and it consists of four years. Since 2012, children aged 66 months have to begin primary education. The second level is four-year middle school education and the third level is four-year high school education. Early childhood education is a part of the formal education in Turkey. However, it is not included in the compulsory education period, which means that enrolment in ECE is optional.

In Turkey, early childhood education was initially defined at the 14th National Education Council in 1993 as follows:

> Pre-primary education is an integral part of a fundamental educational process that is appropriate for the development of children aged 0–72 months. It takes into account individual differences and provides a rich and stimulated environment. It supports children's physical, intellectual, emotional and social development, guides them according to the cultural values and prepares them for primary education.
>
> (Ministery of Education (MEB), 1993)

The same definition is still used.

Early childhood education and preschool education are terms that are used interchangeably in Turkey. Preschool education refers to the education of children who are too young for compulsory education. Public preschools, which are run by the MEB, are either established in independent buildings and called "anaokulu (mother-school/kindergarten/infant school)" or in primary school buildings (anasınıfı) and in girls' vocational high schools and other educational institutions in the form of practical classrooms. The MEB provides ECE for children aged 37–66 months.

In addition to the MEB, the Ministry for Families and Social Policies (ASPB) Department of Children Services is responsible for early childhood education and the care system in Turkey. Crèches, centres providing education and care to 0–36-month-old children, and day-care centres that provide education and care for children aged 37–66 months old, are under the responsibility of the ASPB.

ECEC registered to the Ministry of Family and Social Policy

Program: Crèches, that provide education and care services for 0–36-month-old children, should follow the MEB's National ECE Curriculum for children aged 0–36 months (ASPB, 2015). Day-care centres, in which education and care services are provided for children aged 37–66 months, should follow the MEB's National Early Childhood Education Curriculum for children aged 36–66 months (ASPB, 2015).

Physical conditions: There are some strict rules governing the physical requirements. For instance, both crèches and day-care centres should have a garden which has at least 1.5 m² for each child; they should be located far away from base stations; they should be at least 100 m away from any places such as coffee houses, gaming arcades, bars etc., and they should have fire escape systems. Moreover, crèches should have an independent sleeping room with stable sleeping beds. In addition to this room, there should be play and crawling rooms. The capacity of the centre, i.e the maximum number of children who can enrol in a crèche, is decided according to the total area of the sleeping room. In addition to these rooms, there should be an independent diaper changing area that includes special cabinets for each baby.

For day-care centres, all regulations are the same except for the independent sleeping room. In these centres, bed chairs are allowed to be used and an independent sleeping room is not required. There should be one toilet for every 20 children (ASPB, 2015).

Staff qualifications: The founder, the owner of the ECE centre, is responsible for providing the correct atmosphere for education and care in the centre, for providing needed materials, meeting the building requirements, hiring the staff, paying their salaries etc. There are no requirements regarding the educational level of the founder.

The director of the centre is responsible for the registration of children, taking all the action with regard to meeting the children's educational, physical and safety needs, establishing contact with families, organizing parent meetings, delegating the duties among the staff and supervising them, planning in-service education for the staff, etc. To be a director, one should have at least a two-year university diploma from the departments of child development or social services and two years' experience in ECEC centres. Other than this, individuals are accepted who have a four-year university degree from the departments of social services, psychological counseling and guidance, psychology, child development and education, early childhood education and child development.

Teachers in these centres are known as group supervisors. Educators who have two- or four-year university degree from the departments of child development and education, child development or early childhood education are primarily preferred as group supervisors. However, individuals who have graduated from the child development programs at girls' vocational high schools can be a group supervisor as well. Group supervisors are responsible for conducting activities that support children's entire development; preparing care and educational activities; filling the forms that are required for each child; adapting the educational program to cater for special-needs children and preparing the needed material for the education process. One individual can be responsible for only one group (ASPB, 2015).

Child adult ratio: For children aged 0–36 months there should be at least one group supervisor and at least one caregiver for every ten children. For children aged 37–66 months there should be one group supervisor for every 20 children. For each group, there should be at least one caregiver in the group (ASPB, 2015).

Price: The fee of the ECEC service is determined by the centre. There are no regulations regarding the lowest or upper limits of the prices (ASPB, 2015).

ECEC centres registered with the Ministry of Education

In parallel with the purpose of National Turkish Education System, the purpose of the Turkish early childhood education system is to ensure the physical, mental and emotional development of the children, and the acquisition of good habits; to prepare children for primary education; to ensure equal opportunities for those living in difficult conditions, and to ensure that the Turkish language is spoken correctly and well (MEB, 2013).

The MEB is responsible for preschools. Preschool education in Turkey covers the voluntary education of children aged 37–66 months. Preschools are named "anaokulu", "anasınıfı" and "uygulama okulu".

Anaokulu refers to ECE centres that are established as independent buildings for children aged 37–66 months; *anasınıfı* refers to ECE classrooms that are for children aged 48–66 months and established in the buildings of elementary, secondary and religious schools as classrooms and *uygulama sınıfı* refers to ECE classrooms that are established in vocational high schools for children aged 37–66 months (MEB, 2015).

Daily schedule: ECEC centres managed by the Ministry of Family and Social Policy and by the MEB have to follow the National Early Childhood Education Curriculum.

As of 2014, all public preschools run by the MEB switched to half-day programs to make more children benefit from early childhood education. However, in some cases (if there are not enough enrolments) education is given for a whole day. In preschools, in which dual (morning and afternoon sessions) early childhood education is provided, club classes can be opened in case of need.

Physical conditions: For public ECECs, there are no specific regulations regarding physical conditions. As mentioned before, these centres are established either as independent preschool buildings or as classrooms in elementary, secondary schools, religious schools or vocational high schools.

However, for private ECECs registered with the MEB there are some requirements. According to the Regulations Governing Standards for Private Education Centres, in private ECE centres there should be a manager room, a sleeping room (optional, at least 10 m³ air volume and 3m² space per child), a play activity room (at least 15 m²), a playground (at least 1,5 m² space per child), a dining hall (optional), and toilets (one for every 30 children) (MEB, 2012)

Staff qualifications and child adult ratio: In public ECECs, teachers should have at least a four-year university degree from the department of early childhood education. In public preschools managers should have at least a bachelor degree from the departments of early childhood education or child development. Additionally, in order to be a manager or assistant manager in public preschools individuals should have previous management experience.

The regulations governing child-adult ratio require one teacher for at least ten and at most 20 children. Since it is not allowed to open a new class for less than ten children, in some cases class size can be increased to 25 (Ministry of National Education, 2004).

National Early Childhood Education Curriculum

Up until the 1900s, ECE in Turkey had been run through a framework program and principles rather than a specific ECE curriculum. The first draft curriculum was accepted in 1989 and went into practice in 1994 (Pökön, 2003). This program was revised in 2002, 2006 and lastly in 2013. The first program was developed around target behaviors in eight competency areas: development of self-awareness, development of self-care skills, emotional development, social development, cognitive development, language development, development of aesthetic and creativity (Kandır, 2002, p. 9; Kandır, Özbey & İnal, 2010, p. 78 as cited in Gelişli & Yazıcı, 2012, p. 88). Following this, two curriculums were developed around target behaviors in four main areas: cognitive and language development, social and emotional development, psychomotor development and self-care skills. The latest version of the national curriculum separates cognitive and language development and is developed around five main areas. The terms used have also changed from 1994 to 2013. For example the term "target and target behaviors" in the 1994 curriculum changed to "target and expected behaviors" in 2002, "goals and objectives" in 2006 changed to "objectives and indicators" in the 2013 curriculum (see Table 20.1 for examples). Whatever the names, behaviors that are expected to be gained by the children are in parallel with the goals of the national elementary education and general education system, as well.

The National Early Childhood Education Curriculum (National ECEC) is a child-centred, developmental curriculum which has a helicoid structure and an eclectic model. The National ECE Curriculum aims to support all developmental areas spontaneously. Through its helicoid structure it provides teachers with flexibility and the opportunity to use objectives and indicators more than once in a year based on the needs of the children. It expects teachers to use subjects as a means to help children reach objectives and indicators.

Play is accepted as the work of children and it is placed at the centre of all the learning process in the curriculum. Similarly, creativity and the education of values are expected to be integrated into all learning activities instead of treated separately from other developmental areas.

Teachers in the National ECE Curriculum: Children are perceived by National ECE Curriculum as active learners who build their own knowledge. It is the teachers' responsibility to provide opportunities for children to learn, explore and investigate. Teachers are expected to do this by observing children and identifying their developmental needs, by organizing the learning environment and preparing monthly and activity plans in order to meet those needs.

Child observations: Teachers are expected to conduct continuous observations for each child using special observation forms provided in the National ECE Curriculum (look at assessment part for detail information).

Organizing the learning environment: Teachers are responsible for organizing the environment to support children's active learning and exploring processes. The curriculum suggests that the classroom be divided into "learning centres". The curriculum calls for various different centres in the classroom including centres for science and nature, music, language, books, blocks, water and sand. In the event that the classroom is too small, it is suggested that two related centres be combined. Teachers are expected to update each centre based on the objectives and indicators of the month. Also, teachers are free to create a learning centre that fits the objectives and indicators or special days in the year as needed.

Table 20.1 Examples of objectives and indicators for each developmental area

---

Cognitive Development

Objective 1: Pay attention to object/event/case.
Indicators: S/he focuses on the object/event/case that should be paid attention to. S/he asks questions about the object/event/case that arouse his/her attention. S/he explains object/event/case that arouses his/her attention in detail.

Objective 7: Group objects or entities based on their features.
Indicators: S/he groups objects or entities according to their colors, length, size, shape, texture, voice, taste, smell, amount and its intended use.

Language Development

Objective 1: Differentiate sounds.
Indicators: S/he says the direction of the sound; says the source of sound; says the feature of the sound; says the similarities and differences between sounds; makes sounds similar to given sounds.

Objective 10: Read visual material.
Indicators: S/he examines visual materials; explains visual materials; asks questions about visual materials; answers questions related to visual materials. By using visual materials s/he creates compositions such as events, stories.

Socio-emotional Development

Objective 1: Introduce him/herself.
Indicators: s/he introduces his /her name, surname, age, physical and emotional features.

Objective 8: Respect differences.
Indicators: S/he says s/he has different features; says people have different features; engage each activity with different peers.

Psychomotor Development

Objective 1: Make displacement movements.
Indicators (exp): Walk according to given directions. Run according to given directions. Jump to a specific distance on both feet. Jump with one foot, etc.

Objective 5: Move accompanied by music and rhythm.
Indicators: S/he makes rhythms by using his/her body, objects and traps; simple dance steps. S/he dances accompanied by music and rhythm. S/he makes different movements in succession accompanied by music and rhythm).

Self-care Skills

Objective 1: Apply basic self-care to his/her body.
Indicators: S/he combs his/her hair; brushes teeth; wash hands and face; goes to the toilet.

Objective 4: Eat adequately and healthily.
Indicators: S/he eats and drinks adequately, tries to eat at the main meal time, avoids unhealthy foods and drinks, takes care of dining etiquette.

Monthly plan: It is a working plan drawn up by the teacher that includes the objectives, indicators and concepts of the month, planned field trips and parent involvement activities and the assessment process (National ECEC, p. 50). At the end of each month, depending on the observations they have made, teachers identify the objects and indicators for the next month and organise activities around them. Teachers are able to prepare their own flexible teaching programs according to the children's needs.

Activity plans: Teachers are expected to plan activities according to the objectives and indicators of the month. The program prefers integrated activities. The goal of an activity is to help children to reach indicators rather than teaching a subject. In any activity plan there should be detailed information about the concepts that will be covered in the learning process, the materials, the learning process, ways to involve parents (optional), ways to assess children, the activity itself and the adaptation process (if there is a special needs child).

Assessment in the National ECE Curriculum: The curriculum expects teachers to assess their educational programs, the children and their own teaching processes for each activity at the end of each month. Child Assessment is done through following observations process;

Child observations: Teachers are expected to conduct continuous observations for each child using a "Child Observation Form" provided in the National ECE Curriculum. This form asks teacher to observe the child's physical, cognitive, social-emotional and language development and self-care skills. These observations are collected at the end of the semester and used to fill out a "Child Development Report". This report is prepared twice a year by the teacher and shared with parents.

Program Assessment gives information about the consistency of planned and achieved outcomes for each activity, for each month, each semester and the year. In order to assess a program, National Curriculum provides two checklists for teachers in addition to daily evaluations done at the end of each day and activity evaluations done at the end of each activity. These checklists are called "Checklist for Objectives and Indicators" and "Checklist for Concepts". The former includes all objectives and indicators as rows and the names of the months as columns. Teachers are expected to put a tick next to each objective and indicator that is used in the monthly plan. At the end of one semester, for instance, by examining the checklist, teachers are able to see to what extend they focused on each developmental area, on which objectives and indicators they worked less or more, which objectives and indicators they have not worked on in that semester and should focus on for the next semester, etc. The latter has a similar form, but in this form instead of objectives and indicators there are concepts (the curriculum suggests that teachers address some concepts about time (for instance day and night), directions (left-right), colors, shapes, feelings (happy-sad), contrasts (beautiful-ugly; living-nonliving), numbers (from 1–20), etc.).

Teacher Assessment involves self-assessment through which teachers are expected to understand their own strengths, dispositions and weaknesses and update their own skills.

Inclusion in the National ECE Curriculum: The Special Education Decree-Law (No. 573) of 1997 emphasises the inclusion of special needs children into the regular educational system with their peers. Also with the same law, the inclusion of special needs children into the ECE system is made compulsory and free of charge for 3–5 years old. Also, in the Regulations for Early Childhood Education, it is said that there should be at least one special needs child for a class of ten and two for a class of 20 children.

Inclusion is given importance by the National ECE Curriculum, as well. Teachers are expected to adapt their program according to the needs of the special needs child. This adaptation process aims to include special needs children into the learning process in the same way as with normally developed children. Teachers are also expected to provide individualised education program for children with special needs.

In order to increase teachers' ability to include children with special needs in their educational program, National ECE Curriculum provides a special chapter on "how to support children with special needs". This chapter provides information on visual disabilities, hearing disabilities, autism, orthopedic disabilities, ADHD and mental disabilities. In the chapter, initially the type of special need is explained with its symptoms. Then some suggestions are presented to support special needs children in terms of self-care skills, motor, socio-emotional, language and cognitive development.

Although written documents seem to support inclusion, national statistics indicate that inclusion is not successfully implemented. According to MEB Statistics for 2015/2016, 1,174,409 special needs children were enroled in formal education and only 191,670 of them were enroled in ECE. The quality of inclusion in ECE is arguable, as well. The majority of studies have indicated that, although Turkish ECE teachers believe in the importance of inclusion, they lack the qualifications needed to provide appropriate inclusion of special needs children (Altun & Gülben, 2009; Gök & Erbaş, 2011; Özaydın & Çolak, 2011; Varlıer & Vuran, 2006).

Parental involvement in National ECE Curriculum: Parental involvement has been an important part of the National ECE Curriculum. In their studies Köyceğiz, Ağaçdan, Akaydın, Yorgun and Tezel-Şahin (2016) investigated the 1994, 2002, 2006 and 2013 ECE programs used in Turkey with respect to parental involvement and concluded that more importance is given to parental involvement than in the past.

In 2013, the MEB prepared a guidebook called "Guidebook for Family Support and Education Integrated with the ECE Program (OBADER)" to help teachers establish and run effective school-parent communication. This guidebook provides information on how to involve parents in the early childhood education process and what teachers can do to increase their parenting abilities.

Studies on parental involvement in Turkey indicated that both pre-service (Ahioğlu-Linberg, 2014; Cevher-Kalburan, 2014, Uludağ, 2008) and in-service ECE teachers (Akkaya, 2007; Demircan,2012; Erdoğan & Demirkasımoğlu,2010; İnal,2006; Kaya, 2007) believe in the importance of parental involvement. Unfortunately, parent involvement activities conducted by ECE teachers are limited to parent meetings and in most cases teachers contact parents only when there are problems (İnal, 2006). Similarly, Erdoğan and Demirkasımoğlu (2010) stated that parental involvement is limited to meetings and school visits to learn about their children's progress and that neither in-service teachers nor administrators make enough effort to increase parental involvement.

Another problem in parental involvement is low involvement rates of fathers. In Turkey, as in many countries, parental involvement mostly refers to mother involvement. This situation is clearer in early childhood education. Ünlü-Çetin (2016a) found that mothers get involved in parental involvement activities more than fathers and that the main reasons are the fathers' working obligations, the organization of parental involvement activities during the day, female domination in ECE centres and widely accepted traditional gender role perceptions in society. Unfortunately, not enough effort is being made to eliminate these barriers for father involvement. For instance, OBADER does not stress the importance of father involvement specifically (Ünlü-Çetin, 2016b).

National statistics about the Turkish ECEC system

Schooling ratio: In the 2015–16 education year, the net schooling ratio was 33.26% among children aged 3–5 months, 42.96% among children aged 4–5 and 55.48% among children aged 5. When birth dates are considered, statistics indicate a similar trend, i.e. that the schooling ratio increased with the age. For children born in 2012 (3 years old) the schooling ratio is 11.74, while it is 33.56 for children born in 2011 and 67.17 for children born in 2010 (MEB, 2016). This indicates that children in Turkey are enroled in the ECE system one year before compulsory education. This also reflects the views held by parents regarding ECE. Rather than being perceived as a systematic educational process ECE is widely perceived as preparation for school environment and formal school life.

Number of ECE centres: By 2016, there were a total of 27,793 ECE centres in Turkey. These included 6,788 are kindergartens and 21,005 preschool classes. Of these ECE centres 23,135 are public, while the remaining 4,658 are private ECE centres. Preschool classes constitute the majority of public ECE centres. There are only 1,386 ECE centres, which are registered by the Ministry for Families and Social Policies (MEB, 2016).

Number of children enroled in ECE: A total of 1,209,106 children undergo ECE in these schools. The majority of children (1,017,436) are enroled in public ECE programs. There is a total of 531,176 male and 486,260 female children in public ECE centres and 102,173 male children and 89,497 female children in private ECE centres. Although the number of male children who undergo ECE is higher in almost all kinds of ECE centres, the difference between male and female children's engagement to ECE is not so large.

Number of early childhood educators: In total there are 72,228 early childhood educators working in the Turkish ECE system. The majority of these educators work in public ECEC (n=54,145) and mainly in preschool classes (n=52,443). The remaining 18,083 early childhood educators work in private ECECs. The majority of these teachers work in ECECs that are registered with the MEB (n=11,688), while only 6,395 early childhood educators work in ECECs that are registered to ASPB.

Statistics indicates that ECE in Turkey is dominated by female teachers. In total, there are 72,228 early childhood educators in Turkey of whom only 3,871 of them are male. The majority of these male teachers work in public preschool classes (n=2,096). Unfortunately, there are no male early childhood educators in public ECECs as the centres are not registered with the MEB, community-based institutions, minority preschools and private ECECs that are registered with the ASPB.

Early childhood teacher education system

With the establishment of the Higher Education Council in 1982, teacher education institutions in Turkey have been transformed into 4-year programs run by university education faculties (Deniz & Şahin, 2006).Teacher education programs belong to the Education Faculties at public and private universities. After completing eight semesters successfully an individual gains the right to get an undergraduate degree. The content and length of the courses and the required competencies of graduates are defined and governed by the Higher Education Council (HEC).

The early childhood teacher education programs consist of major area courses, professional teaching knowledge and general knowledge courses. There are also elective courses that are determined by the faculties (HEC, 2007). The aim of the Turkish early childhood teacher education program has been built around the teacher competencies proposed by the MEB (2008) and NAEYC (2009). These have been developed using the relevant literature about early childhood teacher qualities such as possessing pedagogical content knowledge, guiding parental involvement, assessing the ECE program and children's development, having effective communication skills, cooperation between the school and the community and seeking life-long professional development (MEB, 2008, p. 2–14).

Challenges within the ECEC system in Turkey

On paper, the picture related to ECE in the Turkish education system is in keeping with international standards and indicates an improvement both in quality and quantity when compared to the past. Unfortunately, in practice the situation is different. Here, some important problems regarding the Turkish ECEC system will be mentioned.

The first and one of the most important problems is the policies regarding ECEC is based according to the report by AÇEV (2016), stating that there are confusing policies regarding target-schooling ratios for ECE in the following year. For instance, in the 10th Development Plan the goal was to reach 70% gross schooling ratio for children aged 4–5 by the end of 2018. However, this rate falls below the target set by the MEB for children aged 4–5 years at the end of 2014. That is, the government does not intend to increase the schooling ratio in the period up to 2018. In addition, this situation indicates the disconnection between the different governmental departments regarding ECE.

The second problem that should be mentioned is the place of ECE in the National Education System. In 2012, the Turkish education system was changed to a 4+4+4 system (which used to be 5+3+3) and the age for compulsory education was lowered from 72 months to 60–66 months of age. Unfortunately, still ECE is not compulsory and this caused the majority of children (4/10 in the age group of 5) to begin formal education without having ECE (AÇEV, 2016).

Since ECE is neither compulsory nor free of charge, enrolments rates are lower in disadvantaged socioeconomic status. For instance, in a study conducted by TNS Global in February 2015 (cited in AÇEV, 2016), 50% of the parents who have children in the early childhood age bracket reported that they did not send their children to ECEC mainly because there were no ECE centres around (48%) and because of the higher prices of ECE centres (23%). A huge difference between low and high SES was also found. The percentage of the parents who reported that their children were not enroled in ECE was 56% for low and 44% for high SES.

Another problem is related to the supervision of the ECE system for both MEB- and ASPB-registered ECEs. Supervision in the MEB is conducted by inspectors who are not from the field of ECE. Since they do not have enough knowledge of ECE, their supervision relies on structural issues and numbers rather than quality and these individuals are not able to provide beneficial guidance to ECE teachers (AÇEV, 2016; Uyanık, 2007).

Conclusion

In this chapter, the Turkish ECE system was described with almost all its components, based on the written documents provided by the MEB, MFSP and research. In conclusion, it can be said that the Turkish ECE system is one that is still developing, which is not where it should be. Based on the challenges experienced in the ECEC system, solutions should be provided by government. Firstly, ECE should be compulsory and free of charge at least for one year before primary education. There should be a strong supervision process that provides guidance to ECE teachers. The MEB should take charge of ECE centres that are for children aged 0–36 months and should provide strong supervision and in-service training for the staff of these schools. Differences between low and high SES with respect to availability for ECE should be eliminated or at least minimised. The early childhood teacher education process should be strengthened by increasing the quality of staff in the field and improving the teacher education curriculum by providing more opportunity for prospective teachers to gain field experience.

References

AÇEV (Anne-Çocuk Vakfı) & ERG (Eğitim Reformu Girişimi). (2016). *Her çocuğa eşit fırsat: Türkiye'de Erken Çocukluk Eğitiminin Durumu ve Öneriler*. İstanbul,

Anne Çocuk Vakfı. Retrieved from www.egitimreformugirisimi.org/wp con tent/uploads/2017/03/ERG_HERKES-%C4%B0C%C4%B0N-ESIT-FIRSAT TURKIYEDE-ERKEN-COCUKLUK-EGITIMININ-DURUMU-VE-ONER-ILER.web_.pdf

Ahioğlu-Linberg, E. H. (2014). Final year faculty of education students' views concerning parent involvement. *Educational Sciences: Theory & Practice*, *14*(4), 1352–1361.

Aile ve Sosyal Politikalar Bakanlığı (ASPB) (2015) *Özel Kreş ve Gündüz Bakımevleri ile Özel Çocuk Kulüplerinin Kuruluş ve İşleyiş Esasları Hakkında Yönetmelik*, Available Online at http://www.resmigazete.gov.tr/eskiler/2015/04/20150430-4.htm

Akkaya, M. (2007). *Öğretmenlerin ve velilerin okul öncesi eğitim kurumlarında uygulanan aile katılım çalışmalarına ilişkin görüşleri*. Unpublished Master Thesis, Anadolu University, Eskişehir.

Akyüz, Y. (1996). Anaokullarının Türkiyede Kuruluş ve Gelişim Tarihçesi. *Milli Eğitim*, *132*, 11–18.

Altun, T., & Gülben, A. (2009). Okul öncesinde özel gereksinim duyan çocukların eğitimindeki uygulamalar ve karşılaşılan sorunların öğretmen görüşleri açısından değerlendirilmesi [Çevrimiçi sürüm]. *Ahmet Keleşoğlu Eğitim Fakültesi Dergisi, 28*, 253–272.

Başal, H. A. (1998). *Okul Öncesi Eğitime Giriş*, Bursa: Uludağ Üniversitesi Basımevi.

Bilir, Ş., Arı, M., Gönen, M., Üstün, E., & Pekçağlayan, N. (1998). *Okul Öncesi Eğitimcisinin Rehber Kitabı*. Ankara: Aşama Ltd. Şti.

Cevher-Kalburan, N. (2014). Early childhood pre-service teachers' concerns and solutions to overcome them (the case of Pamukkale University). *South African Journal of Education, 34*(1), 1–18.

Demircan, H. Ö. (2012). *Developmentally appropriate practice and parental involvement in preschools: Parent and teacher perspectives*. Unpublished PhD Thesis, Middle East Technical University, Ankara.

Deniz, S., & Şahin, N. (2006). The restructuring process of teacher training systemin Turkey: A model of teacher training based on post-graduate education (PGCE). *Journal of Social Sciences, 2*(1), 21–26.

Erdoğan, Ç., & Demirkasımoğlu, N. (2010). Ailelerin eğitim sürecine katılımına ilişkin öğretmen ve yönetici görüşleri. *Educational Administration: Theory and Practice, 16*(3), 399–431.

Gelişli, Y., & Yazıcı, E. (2012). Türkiye'de uygulanan okul öncesi eğitim programlarının tarihsel süreç içerisinde değerlendirilmesi, *Gazi Üniversitesi Endüstriyel Sanatlar Eğitim Fakültesi Dergisi, 29*, 85–93.

Gök, G., & Erbaş, D. (2011). Okul öncesi eğitimi öğretmenlerinin kaynaştırma eğitimine ilişkin görüşleri ve önerileri. *International Journal of Early Childhood Special Education, 3*(1), 66–87.

Higher Education Council. (2007). Türkiye'nin Yükseköğretim Stratejisi. *Yüksek Öğretim Kurulu Başkanlığı, Ankara*, 1–236.

İnal, G. (2006). *Öğretmenlerin Anaokulları ile Anasınıflarındaki Programlara Ailelerin Katılımı Konusundaki Görüşlerinin Değerlendirilmesi*. Unpublished Master Thesis, Hacettepe University, Ankara.

Kaya, R. (2007). *The attitudes of preschool teachers towards parent involvement*. Unpublished Master Thesis, Middle East Technical University, Ankara.

Köyceğiz, M., Ağaçdan, M., Akaydın, D., Yorgun, E., & Tezel-Şahin, F. (2016). Milli Eğitim Bakanlığı okul öncesi eğitim programlarında aile katılımının dünü ve bugünü, *Journal of International Social Research, 9*(45), 619–625.

Ministry of National Education. (1973). *Basic code of national education.* Retrieved from http://mevzuat.meb.gov.tr/html/temkanun_0/temelkanun_0.html

Ministery of National Education. (1993). *14. National Education Council.* Istanbul: Ministery of Education Publishing.

Ministry of National Education. (2004). *Okul Öncesi Eğitim Kurumları Yönetmeliği.* Available Online at http://mevzuat.meb.gov.tr/html/25486.html

Ministry of National Education. (2008). *Okul Öncesi Öğretmenliği Özel Alan Yeterlikleri.* Ankara: Millî Eğitim Basımevi.

Ministry of National Education. (2012). *Instruction of private education centre standards.* Retrieved from http://mevzuat.meb.gov.tr/html/ozelogrkurstd_0/ozelogrkurstd_0.html

Ministry of National Education. (2013). *Early childhood education curriculum.* Retrieved from http://tegm.meb.gov.tr/meb_iys_dosyalar/2013_04/04124340_programkitabi.pdf

Ministry of National Education. (2015). *Milli Eğitim Bakanlığı Eğitim Kurumları Yöneticilerinin Görevlendirilmelerine Dair Yönetmelik.* Retrieved from http://mevzuat.meb.gov.tr/html/egitimkurumyon/egitkuryon.html

Ministry of National Education. (2016). *National education statistics: Formal education 2015/16.* Retrieved from http://sgb.meb.gov.tr/meb_iys_dosyalar/2016_03/18024009_meb_istatistikleri_orgun_egit m_20152016.pdf

National Association for the Education of Young Children. (2009). *NAEYC standards for early childhood professional preparation programs. A position statement of the National Association for the Education of Young Children.* Washington, DC: NAEYC.

Özaydın, L., & Çolak, A. (2011). The views of preschool education teachers over mainstreaming education and over in-service education program of mainstreaming education at preschool education. *Kalem Eğitim ve İnsan Bilimleri Dergisi, 1*(1), 189–226.

Pökön, A. (2003). *Fransa ve Türkiye Okul Öncesi Eğitim Sistemlerinin Karşılaştırmalı İncelenmesi.* Unpublished Master Thesis, Marmara University.

Taner-Derman, M., & Başal, H. A. (2010). Qualitative and quantitative developments and evaluations in preschool between the foundation of the republic and today. *The Journal of International Social Research, 3*(11), 560–569.

Uludağ, A. (2008). Elementary pre-service teachers' opinions about parental involvement in elementary children's education. *Teaching and Teacher Education, 24,* 807–817.

Uyanık, M. (2007). *Ders Teftişinde Müfettiş Uzmanlaşmasının Önemi (Muğla İli Örneği). Yayınlanmamış Yüksek Lisans Tezi.* Muğla: Muğla Üniversitesi.

Ünlü-Çetin, Ş. (2016a). *Anne ve Babaların Gözünden Okul Öncesi Eğitimde Baba Katılımı: Mevcut Durum, Sorunlar ve Beklentiler,* Sözel bildiri, 3. Uluslararası Avrasya Eğitim Araştırmaları Kongresi, 31 Mayıs-03 Haziran 2016, Muğla, Türkiye.

Ünlü-Çetin, Ş. (2016b). Okul Öncesi Eğitim Programı ile Bütünleştirilmiş Aile Destek Eğitim Rehberi'nde (OBADER) toplumsal cinsiyet eşitliği vurgusunun baba katılımı özelinde incelenmesi, *Current Research in Education, 2*(2), 61–83.

Varlıer, G., & Vuran, S. (2006). Okul öncesi eğitimi öğretmenlerinin kaynaştırmaya ilişkin görüşleri, *Educational Sciences: Theory & Practice, 6,* 578–585.

21 Early childhood education and care in the 21st century

A unique global overview

Sivanes Phillipson, Heidi Harju-Luukkainen and Susanne Garvis

Introduction

This book set out to highlight the early childhood education and care of 19 different nations across the globe with the view that each nation has its own different cultural, social and political contexts. The rationale behind such a view has to do with the contention that the political and social attention on Early Childhood Education and Care (ECEC) has increased over the past decade, with many countries undertaking educational reforms that are still ongoing. Children's access to preschool provision has been broadened because policymakers have recognised the benefits of good quality early childhood education and care on children's learning and development (OECD, 2012). International studies conducted in OECD participating countries, including those represented in this book, found that children attending ECEC are usually better prepared for primary school with the potential to achieve higher education outcomes (OECD, 2017). Good quality early education and care helps with school readiness by ensuring that the transition to school is a seamless experience. This seamless experience exists, only if quality early education and care are implemented by achieving targets around quality goals and regulations of delivering early education and care (OECD, 2015). Along with these quality goals and regulations sits the need to have curriculum that are both guiding and binding to ensure consistent implementation of ECEC within the cultural contexts of each country. Governments globally are therefore increasingly recognising that ECEC plays a crucial role in developing their country's social and economical potential in the future. Despite increased knowledge and significant progress in many of the countries, several challenges remain.

One challenge across the world, especially evident for readers of this book and noted by the OECD repeatedly in their reports (OECD, 2012, 2015, 2017), is that the ECEC systems internationally are very diverse. As the Canadian authors in this book aptly propose, the diversity screams of "consistently inconsistent" implementations and deliveries of ECEC to children, not only in Canada but also across many countries included in this book. Obviously, the observed difference is reflected in the way each chapter responds to the three main themes of ECEC in this book:

1) What are quality goals and regulations in the country's early childhood education and care?

2) Design and implementation of curriculum and standards in the country specific to early childhood education and care.

3) Cultural constraints and gains surrounding early childhood education and care.

Close reading of the chapters showed that there are various national systems with considerable diversity in policies, practices, qualifications, aims, access and other indicators, giving children different possibilities and future prospects. It is apparent from the authors' discussions that the ECEC in each country are based on each country's political agendas and cultural needs that have evolved from local histories and priorities.

Despite the diversity, the contributions in this book provide a unique overview of the ECEC policies and practices across the world. The overview highlights the latest research and information on the governance, curriculum and pedagogy of 19 different countries. The overview most importantly serves as a baseline in articulating the complexities of delivering quality ECEC across these countries, hence, demanding a critical reflection of one's own current context. As a conclusion for this book, we thus critically reflect on key variables of the ECEC, which are found in the policies and practices of the 19 countries presented in this book. These key variables are namely, terminology, governance of ECEC, qualifications and wages of ECEC practitioners and universal access or children's rights to education.

Terminology

Terminology used for early childhood education and care services in each country obviously reflects the social and cultural context of the country. Therefore, there are a variety of terms that are used to describe the early childhood provision in the countries. Table 21.1 shows the overview of the terminologies used for the ECEC services in each country and the ages of children associated with those deliveries.

The terminologies used in each country distinguish between care services and prior-to-school services. Often, terms like nursery, crèche, day care, childcare or infant and toddler care centres include the youngest children who are under the age of two, as can be seen in countries like Turkey and Singapore. These kind of centres are concerned mainly with the care of infants and toddlers, and this concept of care is highlighted more in some countries by calling the practitioners as care workers. Interestingly, in Korea, childcare is offered for care of children up to five years of age, signifying the importance of care for young children prior to school. In Singapore, the concept of care seems to marry the concept of education more explicitly in line with the societal expectation for early education. The carers in that country are called educarers.

Preschool and kindergarten are terms often used to describe the settings where there is more emphasis on education rather than care for older children, usually

Table 21.1 Overview of terminologies used for ECEC deliveries

Countries	Terminology	Ages
Australia	Childcare, nurseries, day care, preschool, kindergarten	0–5 years
Canada	Childcare, nurseries, preschool, kindergarten	1–6 years
Chile	Nursery, preschool,	0–4 years
Denmark	Day care, preschool, kindergarten	1–6 years
Estonia	Preschool	18 months to 7 years
Finland	Preschool	1–5 years
Germany	Kinderkrippe, kindergarten, day care, preschool, hort	0–6 years
Greece	Childcare, kindergarten	
Iceland	Playschool, preschool	1–6 years
Korea	Childcare, kindergarten	0–5 years
New Zealand	Playcentre, extended family-led centres, kindergarten	0–5 years
Norway	Kindergarten	1–5 years
Russia	Preschool	3–7 years
Serbia	Preschool kindergarten	6 months–6 years
Singapore	Childcare services, infant and toddler care centres, Preschool, kindergarten	2 months–6 year olds
Sweden	Preschool	1–5 years
The Netherlands	Day care, playgroups in preparation for formal schooling and kindergarten integrated into primary school	0–6 years
Taiwan	Preschool, kindergarten, childcare	2–6 years
Turkey	Crèche, day care, preschool	0–6 years

between the age of three to five years in some countries and up to six years of age in others. Russia is an exception with having children up to seven years of age in their preschool. Whereas Chile has their preschool age defined only until four years of age. Worthy of note is that all countries in this book present education and care as an integrated concept within the preschool or kindergarten – indicating that both education and care are a part of their services. This is not surprising since historically the articulation of kindergarten personified both learning and care for children (Prochner, 2009).

One important factor to consider, however, is that the terminology for many countries has been translated into English using suitable English words. Often in translation, words can have a unique cultural understanding embedded that may not be the same in different contexts. This is evident in countries like New Zealand, which has centres that are translated as being led by extended family known as whānau-led.

Governance of ECEC

National laws on ECEC are usually focused towards general regulations of the ECEC sector and this can be in the form of legislated acts. The legislated acts or in some countries such as Korea, historical practices prescribe systems of the ECEC deliveries. The most common system seen in many countries in this book is known as the integrated system. For example, Australia, Estonia, Finland, Germany, New Zealand, Russia, Norway and Sweden seem to fall within this category. The integrated system is usually monitored and administered by a government ministry or agency, with the aim to provide a seamless and better quality ECEC in relation to access, staffing and preparation for school. Alternatively, the Netherlands chapter outlines a split system of ECEC delivery, which basically means that several agencies or ministries are responsible for the regulation and standards of services. A similar system seems to exist strongly in Greece and to a lesser extent in Singapore, as in recent years in Singapore a single agency, ECDA, seems to play a more dominant role. This fragmentation of responsibility can stem more from traditional divisions of government organisational roles than from the real needs of young children and their families (OECD, 2017).

Governance of practices can also be seen through national policy documents that are in the format of frameworks. These curriculum frameworks work as operational plans, which are developed to guide the implementation of regulations and practices within the ECEC settings. What is distinctive in the ECEC sector is that the policies guiding the work are often multi-sectoral. They involve, among others, education, social and health care sectors, depending on the country in question. In some countries, like Finland and Sweden, all of these sectors provide their own laws and regulations for the ECEC setting, which makes working in the ECEC setting challenging for practitioners. In Canada and Australia, policies are province or state based respectively. For Canadian and Australian practitioners, their biggest challenge is the need to have a good understanding of different policy requirements in order to be efficient in their role as educators or carers (Prochner, 2009).

However, what is apparent from all the countries in this book is that they do have a form of curriculum or framework for ECEC that guides the practical implementation of caring and education that young children need for overall growth and development. In all of the countries represented in this book, there is at least one curriculum or a framework for the older children attending ECEC. However, this is not necessarily the case for the younger children. For example, in Taiwan and Germany there is no guiding document for the work with younger children. In some countries like Singapore, there are different curriculums for different age groups with Early Years Development Framework for children three years and below and the Nurturing Early Learners. In the Nordic countries like Iceland, Finland, Sweden, Denmark and Norway there is only one curriculum or framework for all children under the age of six or seven. The same is apparent in Korea with the Nuri Curriculum. To make the situation even more complex, some of the countries such as Australia and Canada have several curriculums, each for every state or jurisdictions. However, in Australia the Early Years Learning Framework seems to be the dominant point of reference for most practitioners. In addition, the status of the curriculum or framework in the country can vary. For example, in the Netherlands, the curriculum is more informal, while in many other countries it is an official document.

Furthermore, the kinds of curricula in each country show the preferred pedagogical approaches that are implemented in each ECEC context. The Finnish, Swedish, Norwegian, Icelandic and Danish early childhood education systems, for example, can be characterised in terms of a holistic approach. This approach encourages play, relationship as well as children's curiosity. The approach builds on children's own interest and resists something that could be called as school preparatory approach (Kamerman, 2007). A more school preparatory approach that has a systematic approach to learning with embedded assessments can be seen in Asian countries such as Singapore, Taiwan and Korea. However, as the Singapore authors have discussed, this formal educational approach is now being viewed less favourably by the ruling government. This changing perception, of course, leads to paradoxical situations for educational contexts that are competitive in nature (Ng, 2017).

Qualifications and wages of the ECEC practitioners

With the changing perception of the importance of ECEC in children's development, the scrutiny on early childhood teacher and care workers' quality and status comes into full consideration. The chapters in this book clearly delineate a variety of teacher qualifications and evolution of professional development and learning for the ECEC practitioners. Since OECD has emphasised that the quality of services is dependent upon staff quality as well (OECD, 2015), it is not surprising that governments internationally increase their investments in teacher education and training. The purpose of this investment is to deliver high-quality outcomes that further reflect in enhanced cognitive and social outcome for young children. In other words, the ECEC practitioners are well trained, preferably to have skills in engaging with the children and the families in activities that are beneficial for children's overall development.

A few countries in this book, for example, Singapore, South Korea, Estonia and Australia, are imposing minimum qualifications for the ECEC educators. In many countries, especially the Nordic countries including Germany require up to postgraduate level qualifications for their ECEC teachers. Basically, the ECEC sector across all these countries demand sets of specific skills, knowledge and competencies that contribute positive child development. However, as Seo in the South Korean chapter laments, "It is paradoxical that there is often unnecessary regulation of what is considered reasonable professional behaviour in the context of the lack of support for professional standards that could ensure higher-quality educational services for young children" (Fromberg, 2003). Seo's lament signals the mismatch between what is expected of ECEC professionals and the training and preparation support provided for them in many countries internationally.

Further, the policy documents of these countries are connected to teacher training and education, which makes teacher training an important governmental policy agenda. However, in this book, there seems to be a diversity even in terms of the qualifications of ECEC practitioners. The qualification requirements vary from certificate or diploma attained at vocational level to postgraduate degree at a master's level. For example, in Singapore and Australia, it has been a long-standing practice that certificate level qualifications are accepted for ECEC workers. In recent years, both countries have started promoting tertiary qualification at the bachelors (undergraduate) level to ensure that most ECEC centres have at least one bachelor-qualified staff in the premises. A similar situation is observed in Canada and Serbia. Most of the other countries in this book stress tertiary qualification as the requirement for their ECEC educators. Iceland takes the standard further, where a postgraduate level master's degree in early education is mandated for all new preschool teachers.

The trend in this book shows that the qualification of practitioners is somehow dependent upon the ECEC system of the country. In some countries such as The Netherlands and Singapore, there is a split system approach to providing care for younger children and preschool for children aged 3–5. Apart from multiple governing organisations, as mentioned before, this split approach means that often the qualifications of practitioners are different in the younger and the older age groups. However, many countries presented in this book, in their country's Governance discussion, practice an integrated system where all children under primary school age, attend the same centres. Within this system, the ECEC practitioners have to meet the same requirements of qualifications regardless of child's age.

Of note, the wages of the ECEC practitioners are amongst the lowest in the teaching profession across the countries in this book. Richardson and Langford in chapter three suggest that "The only consistent feature of the childcare workforce in Canada is that it is predominantly female, undervalued, and marginalised." This remark is not far from the truth across the globe. In Australia, for example, ECEC workers, who are mainly women, are paid an average of 23 Australian dollars per hour. Similarly, crossing to Estonia, the wages for ECEC workers are also low. Accordingly, research has shown that teachers generally perceive teaching as a career which is demanding but has low returns in terms of wages (Richardson & Watt, 2006). Such low salary packages may have negative impact on teachers' professional development as there is research evidence that points to positive relationship between low teachers' salary and lower motivation, job dissatisfaction and high attrition rates (Davidson, 2007; Webb et al., 2004). Hence, the equalisation of the salary of preschool educators to teachers in primary and secondary schools is a priority in some nations like Estonia and Germany.

Universal access – children's right to education and care

Along with the raising awareness around the ECEC staff quality, comes the question of universal access for all children to ECEC services. The debate around universal access has always encompassed the children's right to education and care, which culminated through the ground-braking publication of the United Nations Convention on the Rights of the Child in 1989. According to this convention, children have the right to have a say on issues affecting their lives and they essentially have the right to education as a part of their development. In line with this sentiment, all of the countries represented in this book seem to have realised this goal with a few truly providing universal access. While many providing access more to those children coming from a low income and migrant background. Serbia, on the other hand, is currently developing a mechanism to provide children in their country with the universal or subjective right to ECEC. Significant government funding has been given to increase participation rates.

In the Nordic countries (including Estonia) children have the right to attend ECEC after parental leave. In some other countries like Germany, Turkey, South Korea, The Netherlands, New Zealand, Australia, Chile, Serbia and Singapore, children can attend from an earlier age. While children can participate in the ECEC services in different countries however, this does not mean that universal access is available for all participating children. Some countries have universal access agreements based on age. For example in Australia, while children can attend the ECEC services from six weeks of age, universal access is only available for children in the year before the first year of schooling (usually children aged 3.5 years). While it is important that countries have universal access policies, they should be available to all children participating in ECEC services. By having policies aimed at certain age groups (such as three years onwards) or their family background, the true definition of 'children's rights to education' as stipulated in the United Nations convention is only partially fulfilled. It is important that community groups, the research community and non-government organisations continue to lobby government policy makers to allow universal access for all children, not just some.

Many of the universal access policies also have time stipulations. The most common was access to 15 hours a week. Again, the question raised is about time limits for universal access. Are time limits appropriate? Should all children have access to 15 hours or only some children? In many countries in this book, there are no time limits for universal access to primary or secondary school. This perhaps reflects the emergence of ECEC as a recent education institution in many countries and an institution that is not firmly established within the government policy. Furthermore, ECEC systems in different countries may still be fragmented from government education portfolios (where primary and secondary school may be administered) and instead located in government portfolios of social services or community affairs where service provision is often dictated by economic discourse. Yet again, this raises questions about the actual purpose of ECEC in each of the countries and if the focus is on care or education. Nevertheless, nearly all the countries in this book require a stronger focus on allowing all children access to the ECEC services.

Concluding thoughts

ECEC across the world is diverse. This book has provided a global understanding of how children have access to education and cared for, across many different countries. While there has been a global increase in ECEC and the implementation of various curricula and policy support, this book also highlights that more is still needed to support all children. Understanding that ECEC provision is different across the world also helps us to question and reflect upon what is done well and what needs to be improved in our own respective countries. We also begin to realise that even though we may be using the same terminology (such as universal access), the actual meaning is context dependent and culturally bound.

This book also shows that the global flow of ideas around ECEC is important. More discussion and open dialogue is needed across countries. This book has only managed to provide a snapshot of some, but not all of the countries in the world. Understanding the ECEC provision in different contexts not only allows the sharing of ideas but also provides a set of principles that all governments should implement. Here research has an important role to disseminate important findings about ECEC policy and provision by sharing different models and approaches. ECEC research also has the potential in making boundaries visible and allows the questioning of evidence and current policy within and across countries. If we want all children to potentially have equal access to ECEC, it must start with adults, who have the power to make the change, who see the possibilities and understand the importance of early learning and care. Perhaps the real question should be "How are we, as adults, supporting the next generation to make the world a better place?"

References

Davidson, E. (2007). The pivotal role of teacher motivation in Tanzanian education. *The Educational Forum, 71*(2), 157–166. doi:10.1080/00131720708984928

Fromberg, D. P. (2003). The professional and social status of the early childhood educator. In J. P. Isenberg & M. R. Jalongo (Eds.), *Major trends and issues in early childhood education: Challenges, controversies, and insights* (2nd ed., pp. 177–192). New York: Teachers College Press.

Kamerman, S. B. (2007). *A global history of early childhood education and care*. Background paper prepared for the Education for All Global Monitoring Report: Early Childhood Care and Education, UNESCO.

Ng, P. T. (2017). *Learning from Singapore: The power of paradoxes*. London: Routledge.

OECD. (2012). *Starting strong III: A quality toolbox for early childhood education and care*. Paris: OECD Publishing. http://dx.doi.org/10.1787/9789264123564-en

OECD. (2015). *Starting strong IV: Monitoring quality in early childhood education and care*. Paris: OECD Publishing. http://dx.doi.org/10.1787/9789264233515-en

OECD. (2017). *Starting strong 2017: Key OECD indicators on early childhood education and care*. Paris: OECD Publishing. http://dx.doi.org/10.1787/9789264 276116-en

Prochner, L. (2009). *History of early childhood education in Canada, Australia and New Zealand*. Toronto, ON: UBC Press.

Richardson, P. W., & Watt, H. M. G. (2006). Who chooses teaching and why? Profiling characteristics and motivations across three Australian universities. *Asia-Pacific Journal of Teacher Education, 34*(1), 27–56. doi:10.1080/13598660500480290

Webb, R., Vulliamy, G., Hämäläinen, S., Sarja, A., Kimonen, E., & Nevalainen, R. (2004). Pressures, rewards and teacher retention: A comparative study of primary teaching in England and Finland. *Scandinavian Journal of Educational Research, 48*(2), 169–188. doi:10.1080/0031383042000198530

Index

Made in the USA
Monee, IL
04 September 2023

42131000R00155